TRADITIONS IN WORLD CINEMA

TRADITIONS IN WORLD CINEMA
General Editors
Linda Badley (Middle Tennessee State University)
R. Barton Palmer (Clemson University)

Founding Editor
Steven Jay Schneider (New York University)

Titles in the series include:
Traditions in World Cinema
by Linda Badley, R. Barton Palmer and Steven Jay Schneider (eds)
0 7486 1862 7 (hardback)
0 7486 1863 5 (paperback)

Japanese Horror Cinema
by Jay McRoy (ed.)
0 7486 1994 1 (hardback)
0 7486 1995 X (paperback)

New Punk Cinema
by Nicholas Rombes (ed.)
0 7486 2034 6 (hardback)
0 7486 2035 4 (paperback)

Forthcoming titles include:

African Filmmaking: North and South of the Sahara
by Roy Armes
0 7486 2123 7 (hardback)
0 7486 2124 5 (paperback)

American Commercial-Independent Cinema
by Linda Badley and R. Barton Palmer
0 7486 2459 7 (hardback)
0 7486 2460 0 (paperback)

Italian Neorealist Cinema
by Peter Bondanella
0 7486 1978 X (hardback)
0 7486 1979 8 (paperback)

The Italian Sword-and-Sandal Film
by Frank Burke
0 7486 1983 6 (hardback)
0 7486 1984 4 (paperback)

Czech and Slovak Cinema: Theme and Tradition
by Peter Hames
0 7486 2081 8 (hardback)
0 7486 2082 6 (paperback)

TRADITIONS IN WORLD CINEMA

Edited by

Linda Badley, R. Barton Palmer and
Steven Jay Schneider

EDINBURGH UNIVERSITY PRESS

© in this edition Edinburgh University Press, 2006
© in the individual contributions is retained by the authors

Transferred to Digital Print 2010

Edinburgh University Press Ltd
22 George Square, Edinburgh

Typeset in 10/12.5 Adobe Sabon
by Servis Filmsetting Ltd, Manchester, and
Printed and bound in Great Britain by
CPI Antony Rowe, Chippenham and Eastbourne

A CIP record for this book is available from the British Library

ISBN 0 7486 1862 7 (hardback)
ISBN 0 7486 1863 5 (paperback)

CONTENTS

Traditions in World Cinema is a series of books devoted to the analysis of currently popular and previously underexamined or undervalued film movements from around the globe. The volumes in this series have three primary aims: (1) to offer undergraduate- and graduate-level film students accessible and comprehensive introductions to diverse and fascinating traditions in world cinema; (2) to represent these both textually and contextually through attention to industrial, cultural and socio-historical conditions of production and reception; and (3) to open up for academic study and general interest a number of previously underappreciated films.

The flagship volume for the series offers chapters by noted scholars on traditions of acknowledged importance (the French New Wave, German expressionism), recent and emergent traditions (New Iranian, post-Cinema Novo), and those whose rightful claim to recognition has yet to be established (the Israeli persecution film, global found footage cinema). Other volumes concentrate on individual national, regional or global cinema traditions. As the introductory chapter to each volume makes clear, the films under discussion form a coherent group on the basis of substantive and relatively transparent, if not always obvious, commonalities. These commonalities may be formal, stylistic or thematic, and the groupings may, although they need not, be popularly identified as genres, cycles or movements (Japanese horror, Chinese *wenyi pian* melodrama, Dogma). Indeed, in cases in which a group of films is not already commonly identified as a tradition, one purpose of the volume may be to establish its claim to importance and make it visible.

Each volume in the series includes:

- an introduction that clarifies the rationale for the grouping of films under examination;
- concise history of the regional, national or transnational cinema in question;
- summary of previous published work on the tradition;
- contextual analysis of industrial, cultural and socio-historical conditions of production and reception;
- textual analysis of specific and notable films, with clear and judicious application of relevant film theoretical approaches.

For Bill and Carla

ACKNOWLEDGEMENTS

Steven Jay Schneider conceived and founded the Traditions in World Cinema series, and his knowledge of international film genres and passion for the cinema are reflected in this volume's scope and shape. Without his groundwork and energetic leadership in the project's initial stages, neither the book nor the series would exist. We regret that he has had to withdraw from the final stages of the project, but we hope he finds that the resulting volume reflects in some way the vision he had for it.

A huge debt of gratitude is owed to Sarah Edwards at Edinburgh University Press, whose encouragement and support have been unfailing. For her assistance, efficiency and especially for her patience, we are profoundly grateful. Working on a collaborative book of this kind is always both an adventure and an education. The experience of editing this volume has been especially gratifying because of the prodigious range, expertise and talents of the contributors. For the privilege of learning from and working with them, and for their generosity and patience, we extend our heartfelt thanks.

We are indebted to Middle Tennessee State University for providing Linda Badley with a Summer Salary Grant and to the Calhoun Lemon Endowment at Clemson University for supporting Barton Palmer's released time from teaching and research expenses. Special thanks are owed to Karine Gavand, our tireless graduate research assistant at Middle Tennessee State University who, during the project's final stages, read and responded to drafts and checked facts and titles. Her proficiency in several languages and first-hand knowledge of international cultures have proven to be especially valuable assets. She performed many of the difficult tasks that fall to an editor with far more sophistication and efficiency than we had any right to expect.

Finally, we thank Bill Badley and Carla Palmer for their generous tolerance of their respective spouses' preoccupation with this work and for support and companionship throughout what has proven to be a long haul. The dedication of the volume only inadequately expresses all that is owed to them.

PREFACE

Toby Miller

Perhaps the most important thing to do when thinking about 'world cinema' is to destabilise the term, to question the logic of each word. Clearly, the concept is designed to go beyond two central rubrics for film followers, critics and historians: national cinema and Hollywood. In this sense it is to be welcomed. But it also buys into the semantic field of 'world music', a tidy agglomeration that suits the marketing and governing principles of major multinational industrial concerns but deracinates the cultural histories and conflicts that make possible its very components. 'World' is not so much a sign of a cosmopolitan relativism, where diverse cultures are permitted promiscuous interplay, as it is a sign that massive changes in population, and the emergence of a New International Division of Cultural Labor,[1] have generated affluent audiences equipped to enjoy a *mélange* of difference under the jurisdiction of a small number of corporate conglomerates. 'Cinema' is equally problematic, given that most 'films' are viewed on television sets via broadcast, cable, satellite, tape or disk, while the future of 'film' creation and reception seems likely to be digital. China provides the first major data on the appeal of movies in 'digital' versus 'film' theatres, and the difference is clear (see table overleaf).

But the idea of long-form recorded drama available via audiovisual technology, sometimes for collective, anonymous consumption and sometimes for domestic, familiar consumption, remains. While we must be careful not to lump together distinctly different producing and viewing formats and experiences, the term 'cinema' may well continue to describe something that makes sense to audiences, gaffers, censors, culturecrats, newspaper editors and critics.

Percentage difference of digital versus conventional releases

Title	Star Wars 2	Harry Potter – Chamber	Finding Nemo
Screen #	1.7	4	8.4
Box office	11.6	14.25	22
Admissions	248.8	290	151.02
Ticket Price	171.8	138	155.84
Revenue per screening	426.3	247	234.7

Source: Adapted from Zhou (2004).[2]

And just because 'world cinema' and 'world music' exist as signs of commodification and governmentality, dominated by the First World and subject to technological change, this does not characterise their totality, as Ana María Ochoa (2003)[3] has convincingly demonstrated. And using these concepts does not militate against further subdivision and problematisation. For example, Edward Buscombe's magisterial *Cinema Today* (2003)[4] is a coffee-table volume in its pictorial splendour and format, but an innovatively subversive one in its intellectual design. For Buscombe includes the usual suspects, but also such chapter headings as 'Gay and Lesbian Cinema' and 'X-Rated', thereby extending and querying the ideas of space and connoisseurship that superintend the normal science of film history and criticism.

And despite claims that cinema is dying because of the Internet and television, films are still important cultural phenomena, as these 2002 expenditure figures indicate:

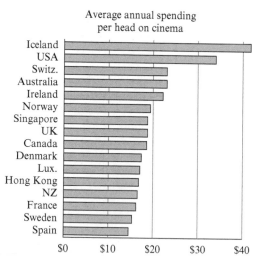

Average annual spending per head on cinema

Source: *Screen Digest* (2002).[5]

Over 4,000 movies are made each year, evidence enough of a thriving production culture. But once we examine which films are actually seen, the numbers are not indicative of a Panglossian pluralism. US companies own between 40 and 90 per cent of the movies shown in most parts of the world. This is not to deny the importance of other screen cultures: non-US-based people of colour are the majority global filmmakers, with much more diverse ideological projects and patterns of distribution than Hollywood. For example, the various language groups in India produce about a thousand films a year, and employ two and a half million people across the industry.

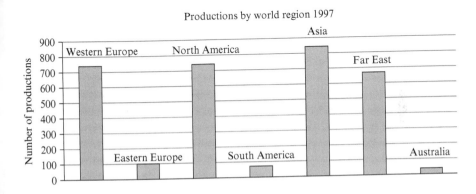

Productions by world region 1997

Source: Hancock (1998).[6]

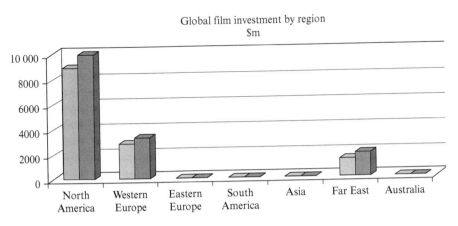

Global film investment by region
$m

Key: light shading = 1996; dark shading = 1997
Source: Hancock (1998).[7]

But where does this filmmaking end up? Arthur Andersen predicted in 2000 that Indian cinema would earn US$3.4 billion in overseas sales by 2005[8] – but given that firm's probity, we must wait to find out! For even with its vast production, strong export trade and extraordinary filmmaking tradition, China's total overseas sales of films between 1996 and 2000 amounted to just US$13.86 million.[9] In 2001 and 2002, the top twenty films in the world were from the US, if one controls for such co-production conceits as that *Scooby-Doo* (Raja Gosnell, 2002) is Australian, *Bridget Jones's Diary* (Sharon Maguire, 2001) British and the *Lord of the Rings* trilogy (Peter Jackson, 2001–03) New Zealand. Between 1996 and 2002, of the most remunerative twenty films released in Europe, each one was from the US, with the exception of *Notting Hill* (Roger Michell, 1999) and some co-productions that used British studios, such as the James Bond franchise.[10]

In that context, volumes such as this one and the series that it seeks to represent are of great importance. The editors and contributors record alternatives to this domination. They transcend the categories of nations to consider regions, genres and histories as classificatory mechanisms for understanding film. They give us critical tools and an infrastructure of memory for contextualising the past, present and future of audiovisual production. In a time when the extraordinary global hegemony of the United States is so dominant across commercial, military and cultural sectors, any and every sophisticated source that chronicles alternatives is more than necessary. For what if, as per the global dreams of so many, today's US domination, seemingly so violent and so overwhelming, actually signals the blazing end to an epoch? What if foreign investors suddenly declined to buy the stocks and bonds needed to sustain the gigantic US current account deficit and the nation's bizarre consumption rituals, or the Euro displaced the dollar as the world's unit of exchange?[11] Then alternative possibilities, visions from elsewhere, would become crucial. As the most prominent sign of the old order of US domination, film will be one of the first places we look for those new visions, drawing on the heritages and the struggles so ably outlined in this collection.

NOTES

1. Toby Miller, Geoffrey Lawrence, Jim McKay and David Rowe, *Globalisation and Sport: Playing the World* (London: Sage, 2001); Toby Miller, Nitin Govil, John McMurria and Richard Maxwell, *Global Hollywood* (London: British Film Institute, 2001).
2. Tiedong Zhou, 'China: The Operation and Development of Digital Cinemas', *European Cinema Journal*, 6, 1 (2004), p. 3. As the table indicates, digital releases are considerably more profitable than conventional ones in terms of percentage of box-office revenues, admissions, ticket price and revenues per screening. This is often the case even though digital releases constitute only a small percentage of total screenings. For example, *Finding Nemo* was released on thirty digital and 690

regular screens, but the digital releases accounted for 22 per cent of the box office (Zhou, 'China', p. 3).

3. Ana María Ochoa, *Músicas Locales en Tiempos de Globalización* (Buenos Aires: Grupo Norma, 2003).

4. Edward Buscombe, *Cinema Today* (London: Phaidon Press, 2003).

5. 'Average Annual Spending Per Head on Cinema', *Screen Digest* (2002), http://www.screendigest.com/ (accessed 5 February 2005).

6. David Hancock, 'Global Film Production'. Paper prepared for EURO-MEI Venice Conference, 29–30 August 1998, European Audiovisual Observatory, http://www.obs.coe.int/oea_publ/eurocine/global_filmproduction.pdf.en (accessed 5 February 2005).

7. Ibid.

8. 'Andersen Report on Indian Cinema', *Reuters*, 2000. *diehardindian.com* <http://www.diehardindian.com/ntertain/morenter/cinema.htm> (accessed 7 July 2005).

9. 'Chinese Film Industry to go Global', *China Daily*, 29 March 2001, http://www.chinadaily.com.cn/english/home/index.html (accessed 5 February 2005).

10. European Audiovisual Observatory, *Focus 2003: World Film Market Trends/ Tendances du marché mondial du film*, 9 (2003), p. 25, http://www.obs.coe.int/online_publications/reports/focus2003.pdf (accessed 5 February 2005); Peter Calder, 'The Hoard of the Rings', *New Zealand Herald*, 29 November 2003.

11. World Trade Organization, *World Trade Developments in 2001 and Prospects for 2002*, Geneva, 2 (2003), http://www.wto.org/english/res_e/statis_e/its2002_e/its02_general_overview_e.htm (accessed 5 February 2005).

NOTES ON CONTRIBUTORS

Roy Armes is Emeritus Professor at Middlesex University in London. He has written widely about cinema over the past forty years, concerned initially with European cinema and subsequently with third-world filmmaking. For the past decade he has specialised in African cinemas. His most recent book is *Post-Colonial Images: Studies in North African Film* (Indiana University Press, 2005).

Linda Badley is Professor of English and film studies at Middle Tennessee State University. She has published widely on topics in contemporary literature, television and film studies and is the author of *Film, Horror, and the Body Fantastic* (Greenwood) and *Writing Horror and the Body: The Fiction of Stephen King, Clive Barker, and Anne Rice* (Greenwood). Current projects include *Lars von Trier* (Illinois) and (with Barton Palmer) *American Commercial-Independent Cinema* (Edinburgh).

Nitzan Ben-Shaul received his PhD in Cinema Studies from New York University. He is Senior Lecturer and former acting chair of the Film and Television Department, Tel-Aviv University. He is the author of *Mythical Expressions of Siege in Israeli Films* (Edwin Mellen Press), *Introduction to Film Theories* (Tel Aviv University Press) and *A Violent World: Competing Images of Terror* (forthcoming from Rowman & Littlefield). He has published several articles on film, television and new media theory (e.g. *Third Text*, *New Cinemas Journal*), and on Israeli cinema (e.g. *Zmanim*).

Peter Bondanella is Distinguished Professor of Comparative Literature and Italian at the University of Indiana-Bloomington, and past President of the American Association for Italian Studies. He is the author of such books as *Italian Cinema: From Neorealism to the Present* (third revised edition, Continuum), *The Films of Federico Fellini* (Cambridge University Press), *The Cinema of Federico Fellini* (Princeton University Press) and *The Films of Roberto Rossellini* (Cambridge University Press). His latest book is *Hollywood's Italians: Dagos, Palookas, Romeos, Wiseguys, and Sopranos* (Continuum, 2004).

Corey Creekmur is an Associate Professor in the Department of English and the Department of Cinema and Comparative Literature at the University of Iowa, where he also directs the Institute for Cinema and Culture. He is the co-editor of *Out in Culture* (Duke University Press) and the author of a forthcoming book on gender and sexuality in the Western; he is also editing a critical edition of *The Adventures of Sherlock Holmes* and has published a number of essays on popular Hindi cinema.

Adrian Danks is Head of Cinema Studies in the School of Applied Communication, Royal Melbourne Institute of Technology (University). He is President and co-curator of the Melbourne Cinémathèque, co-curator of the Australian Cinémathèque and editor of the journal supplement *Cteq: Annotations on Film* (published in the e-journal *Senses of Cinema*). He has published widely on the cinematic representation of place, the relationship of domestic photography to cinema, film culture, film restoration, Australian cinema and cinematic authorship. His writing has appeared in a range of books and journals including: *Senses of Cinema, Metro, Screening the Past, Real-Time, Screen Education, 1001 Movies You Must See Before You Die* and *Twin Peeks: Australian and New Zealand Feature Films*. He is currently co-editing a book on overseas-financed films made in Australia (*Australian International Pictures*).

Peter Hames is Honorary Research Associate and former Subject Leader in Film and Media Studies at Staffordshire University and is programme advisor on Eastern Europe to the London Film Festival. His books include *The Czechoslovak New Wave* (second edition, Wallflower Press, 2005) and, as contributing editor, *The Cinema of Central Europe* (Wallflower Press, 2004) and *Dark Alchemy: The Films of Jan Švankmajer* (Flicks Books, Greenwood Press, 1995). He is currently co-editing *Cinema in Transition* (Temple University Press) with Catherine Portuges. He has also contributed to *Post New Wave Cinema in the Soviet Union and Eastern Europe, Five Filmmakers: Tarkovsky, Forman, Polański, Szabó, Makavejev, The BFI Companion to Eastern European and*

Russian Cinema, National Cinemas in Post-war East-Central Europe, 100 Years of European Cinema: Entertainment or Ideology?, Censorship: An International Encyclopedia and *East European Cinemas in New Perspectives.*

Randal Johnson is Professor of Brazilian Literature and Cinema at the University of California, Los Angeles. He is author or editor of *Brazilian Cinema* (with Robert Stam; Columbia University Press), *Cinema Novo x 5: Masters of Brazilian Cinema* (University of Texas Press), *The Film Industry in Brazil: Culture and the State* (University of Pittsburgh Press), *Tropical Paths: Essays on Modern Brazilian Literature* (Garland Publishing), *Antônio das Mortes* (Flicks Books), *Black Brazil: Culture, Identity and Social Mobilization* (with Larry Crook; UCLA Latin American Center Publications) and Pierre Bourdieu's *The Field of Cultural Production* (Columbia University Press). He is currently writing a book on Portugal's Manoel de Oliveira.

Robert Kolker is Visiting Professor of Media Studies at the University of Virginia and Emeritus Professor of English at the University of Maryland. He is author of a number of books on film, including *A Cinema of Loneliness* (Oxford University Press); the textbook and CD-ROM, *Film, Form, and Culture* (McGraw-Hill); and editor of *Alfred Hitchcock's Psycho: A Casebook* (Oxford University Press).

Myrto Konstantarakos is Senior Lecturer in Film Studies at Middlesex University. She has founded *New Cinemas: Journal of Contemporary Film*, is the editor of *Spaces in European Cinema* (Intellect Books, 2000) and *Contemporary Italian Cinema* (Wallflower Press, 2005), and the author of *Cinema on the Urban Margins: Visions from Europe and Latin America* (Intellect, 2003).

Jay McRoy is an Assistant Professor of English and Film Studies at the University of Wisconsin – Parkside. He is the editor of *Japanese Horror Cinema* (Edinburgh University Press, 2005) and the author of *Nightmare Japan: Contemporary Japanese Horror Cinema* (forthcoming from Rodopi University Press). His writings on horror literature and film have appeared in numerous books and journals, including *Horror Film: Creating and Marketing Fear* (University Press of Mississippi, 2004), *New Punk Cinema* (Edinburgh University Press, 2005), *Paradoxa: Studies in World Literary Genres, Scope: The Online Journal of Film Studies, Science Fiction Studies*, and *The Journal of the Fantastic in the Arts.*

Toby Miller is Professor of English, Sociology, and Women's Studies and Director of the Program in Film & Visual Culture at the University of

California, Riverside. His teaching and research cover the media, sport, labour, gender, race, citizenship, politics and cultural policy. Toby is the author and editor of over 20 books, and has published essays in more than thirty journals and fifty volumes. His current research covers the success of Hollywood overseas, the links between culture and citizenship, and anti-Americanism.

Negar Mottahedeh is Assistant Professor of Film and Literature at Duke University. Her doctoral thesis from the Department of Cultural Studies and Comparative Literature at the University of Minnesota traces the history of visual productions in nineteenth-century Iran. Her work has been published in *Camera Obscura, Signs, Iranian Studies* and *Comparative Studies of South Asia, Africa and the Middle East.* Her book on national variations in cinematic language and the new Iranian cinema is forthcoming from Duke University Press.

Richard Neupert is professor of Film Studies at the University of Georgia. His books include *A History of the French New Wave* (University of Wisconsin Press) and *The End: Narration and Closure in the Cinema* (Wayne State University Press). He has also translated two books: Michel Marie, *The French New Wave: An Artistic School* (Blackwell) and Jacques Aumont et al., *Aesthetics of Film* (University of Texas Press).

R. Barton Palmer is Calhoun Lemon Professor of Literature at Clemson University. Among his many books on film are *Hollywood's Dark Cinema: The American Film Noir* (second revised and expanded edition, University of Illinois Press), *Joel and Ethan Coen* (University of Illinois Press), *Twentieth-Century American Fiction on Screen* (Cambridge University Press), *Nineteenth-Century American Fiction on Screen* (Cambridge University Press) and (with David Boyd) *After Hitchcock: Imitation/Influence/Intertextuality* (University of Texas Press).

Steven Jay Schneider is a PhD candidate in Philosophy at Harvard University and in Cinema Studies at New York University's Tisch School of the Arts. He is the author of *Designing Fear: An Aesthetics of Cinematic Horror* (Routledge), editor of *Freud's Worst Nightmares: Psychoanalysis and the Horror Film* (Cambridge University Press), *1001 Movies You Must See Before You Die* (Barrons), *Fear without Frontiers: Horror Cinema across the Globe* (Fab Press) and *New Hollywood Violence* (Manchester University Press) and co-editor of *Underground U.S.A.* (Wallflower) and *Horror International* (Wayne State University Press).

Christina Stojanova is an academic, curator and writer focusing on cultural semiotics and historical representation in Central and Eastern European cinema, interwar German cinema and the cinema of Quebec. She teaches at McMaster University, Ontario, Canada. She has contributed to *Cinema 2000* (2000); *European Cinema in the Age of Globalization* (2002), *Cinema and Globalization* (2003), *Alternative Europe: Eurotrash and Exploitation Cinema Since 1945* (2004), *Horror International* (2005) and *The Cinema of Central Europe* (2005), and is currently preparing her book *Dual Vision: The Eastern European Cinema and the Totalitarian State 1948–1989*.

J. P. Telotte is a Professor and Undergraduate Director in Georgia Tech's School of Literature, Communication, and Culture. Co-editor of the journal *Post Script*, he has published on a wide range of film and literary topics. His most recent books are *Disney TV* (Wayne State University Press), *The Science Fiction Film* (Cambridge University Press) and *A Distant Technology: Science Fiction Film and the Machine Age* (Wesleyan University Press).

Stephen Teo is the author of *Hong Kong Cinema: The Extra Dimensions* (British Film Institute) and *Wong Kar-wai* (British Film Institute). His writings have focused on Hong Kong and Asian films, and he is currently completing his next book *Johnnie Gets His Gun: The Action Films of Johnnie To* for Hong Kong University Press. He was recently awarded his PhD at the RMIT University, Melbourne.

INTRODUCTION

Linda Badley and R. Barton Palmer

Global Hollywood, no matter how one defines the precise financial and institutional terms of its supranational and national character, has beyond any doubt dominated the history of the cinema as a popular art form since the 1920s. Indeed, the control of the world marketplace in entertainment film that the American industry currently enjoys (and the textual forms by which that control is maintained) can be seen as the end product of a manifest destiny whose general characteristics were established well before the Second World War. This is surely true in spite of the break from the classic, studio-era Hollywood that the so-called 'New' Hollywood has effected over the last three decades. A good, long look at the hard numbers of current film production and exhibition, however, as Toby Miller demonstrates in his preface, reveals a different and surprisingly little known story that disputes Hollywood's claim to control the world market in film. In fact, the current reality of cinema broadly considered, and the more than one hundred years of its history as a cultural form, are by no means reducible to the monolithic (or perhaps better Taylorised) flow that emanates from Hollywood. There are alternatives to be noted and chronicled that belong to what, for lack of an adequate term, might be called 'world cinema', or traditions of filmmaking that flourish beyond the 'global' Hollywood orbit. There are forms of difference, astonishing in their multiversity and claims to uniqueness, that demand and repay critical attention. These must be recognised not only in and for themselves and understood on their own terms, but also as they have 'dialogised' the particular shape that the American commercial film has assumed, prompting it to evolve in often unpredictable directions.

Film scholars have of course for some decades paid attention to difference as manifested especially in the oeuvres of valued auteurs, in genres broadly conceived (the musical, the *film noir*, the horror film), and in national cinemas, which are customarily read as expressing, as well as establishing, cultural alternatives to Hollywood, challenging the Americentric perspective of global cinema history. This book, and the series of volumes it introduces, proposes a different, more inclusive and perhaps more flexible analytical tool, one that locates and promotes the significance of other forms of difference. We hope that a focus on what we call 'traditions' will prompt renewed attention to important aspects of cinema history and bring to proper notice those that until now have been underappreciated and never fully understood. Traditions, as we use the concept, are bodies of films whose commonalities (usually the result, at least in large part, of the particular conditions of their production) make them worthy of collective study. Most often, cinematic traditions are 'national' in the sense that they include only texts that constitute a form of difference within a larger, more diffuse and varied body of national films, and yet there are often indispensable transnational connections that foreclose any understanding of the tradition solely within the terms of its 'native' culture. Thus the tradition of the British new wave, as its name suggests, is profitably understood as similar in some important respects to French New Wave filmmaking and to the more general phenomenon of 'new waves' and 'new cinemas' that emerged as such a prominent feature of post-1950s cinema in Europe, Latin America and even Hollywood itself in the early post-studio era.

Sometimes traditions are generic as well as national developments, inviting, as in the case of Japanese horror film, the tracing of formal and thematic affinities to both a transnational body of conventions and also to particular developments within a national cinema. The traditions whose histories and characteristics are analysed in this volume sometimes can be understood as movements, as forms of self-conscious group practice that reveals itself not only in filmmaking but also in the formulation of critical-theoretical dogma and the issuing of manifestos. Sometimes, as in the case of films made from found footage, the tradition is defined by the nature of the material practice involved, regardless of any national, institutional or aesthetic connection among its practitioners, who may be unknown to one another. To put this another way, some traditions are self-defining and self-promoting, others the result of a critical decision to treat disparate films as a body. The chapters collected here often adopt familiar perspectives to identify a number of cinematic traditions, calling attention to how 'nationality', 'genre' and 'materiality', sometimes operating in concert, have produced important forms of difference. This volume thus limns the outlines of a world cinema distinct from (though influenced by and influencing) the standard Hollywood product.

The chapters are organised into six geographic subdivisions and also in more or less chronological order, so as to trace lines of influence (where they exist).

The volume moves from long-celebrated and now 'canonical' European movements to what is often known as 'world' cinema proper: the traditions of Latin America, Africa and the Middle East, and Asia. We begin with the European avant-garde and 'new wave' cinemas that by the mid-1960s were identified as an international art cinema. These traditions provided an alternative or 'counter-cinema' to the 'classical' Hollywood film, even as they influenced many subsequent movements and practices across the globe. The four chapters that open *Traditions in World Cinema* thus lay the groundwork for the rest of the volume. At the same time, these chapters on German expressionism, Italian neorealism, French *nouvelle vague* and the British new wave respectively reopen debates about the precise nature and value of traditions in need of re-evaluation despite their apparent canonical status.

In his examination of German expressionism, J. P. Telotte moves beyond the largely socio-cultural concerns of the critical tradition best exemplified by Siegfried Kracauer's *From Caligari to Hitler* (1947) to focus on that tradition's aesthetic as an 'oppositional strategy', whose dissonance, artifice and inherent self-reflexivity challenged the authority of standard representations in the 1920s and later. Rejecting the naturalist assumptions that supported wartime norms, and applying defamiliarisation techniques adapted from theatre, painting and the graphic arts, German expressionist cinema evoked a dreamlike realm of 'troubled' perceptions and replications. Telotte finds that films such as *The Cabinet of Dr. Caligari* (*Das Kabinett des Doktor Caligari*, 1919) depict sinister, deceit-filled relationships between show and audience. As he points out, the showman's construction of replications is the key to such otherwise dissimilar texts as *The Golem* (*Der Golem*, 1914, 1920) and *Metropolis* (1926). In its subversion of certainty, including its interrogation of the 'trusting' relationship between medium and audience, German expressionism has exerted a widespread and continuing influence on European and American art film traditions, including, most recently, global postmodernist cinema.

It was with diametrically opposed principles – a return, following the disastrous impact of the Second World War, to a realistic cinema of documentary photography, on-location shooting and non-professional actors – that Italian neorealism is customarily thought to have changed cinematic history. Rejecting the studio-bound conventions and entertainment ideology of films made in the Hollywood tradition, Italian neorealism provided a model for, even as it stimulated the emergence of, the overtly politicised 'new waves' that took shape in the 1950s. In a departure from this essentialising view, however, and offering a preview of his forthcoming volume, *Italian Neorealist Cinema*, Peter Bondanella demystifies the notion of neorealism as a self-conscious movement with 'universally agreed-upon . . . principles'. What is called 'neorealist' cinema he reveals to be a 'hybrid' of conventional and experimental techniques with an ancestry in Fascist and pre-Fascist industrial and documentary film practices.

Where influential postwar critics, most of them Marxist, had political reasons for stipulating that neorealism effected a dramatic break with tradition, Bondanella emphasises the many continuities between prewar and postwar Italian cinema. Focusing on key directors Roberto Rossellini, Vittorio De Sica, Luchino Visconti and Federico Fellini and their signature films, he redefines the concept 'realism' in relation to their individual styles, noting interconnections with the neorealist fiction of Italo Calvino. Neorealism's integrity thus derives less from any agreement on a single cinematic style, Bondanella argues, than from 'a common aspiration to view Italy without preconceptions and to employ a more honest, ethical, but no less poetic cinematic language'.

The chapters on the French, British and Czech new waves, respectively, cover three of a succession of innovative film movements that, born out of the global cultural revolution of the 1960s, erupted throughout Europe and in parts of Latin America. Led by a vigorous young generation of film-school educated director-writers, these 'new waves', as they were called after the French *nouvelle vague* (a term first employed to describe an energetic youth culture that manifested itself in many different ways), were characterised not only by a profound *cinéphilie* (an intense fascination with films and the culture that could be built around them), but also by reformatory, often iconoclastic political concerns. As Richard Neupert shows, it was the French New Wave that, more than any other movement, renewed first a national and then an international cinema at every level – 'from modes of production to narrative innovations to film theory and criticism', eventually prompting the academic study of film, which now began to be understood as an art form as well as an institution of mass culture. Neupert provides a vivid overview of conditions that contributed to the movement: a young, sensitised audience, a social setting centred around ciné-clubs, a critical renaissance brought about by journals such as *Cahiers du Cinéma*, friendly government institutions and new technologies, especially portable, lightweight camera and sound recording equipment. After positioning the central figures and films – Claude Chabrol, François Truffaut, Eric Rohmer and Jean-Luc Godard – he surveys the entire field of the *jeune cinéma* (youthful cinema), zooming in to examine (and sometimes reposition) film artists whom he views as key members of the Left Bank Group, but whose work is often seen as peripheral to the movement. Neupert's essay establishes the importance of the work of directors such as Agnès Varda, Jacques Demy and Jaques Rozier, even as he provides glimpses into the work of this wildly diverse spectrum of filmmakers, demonstrating 'the vast and rich array of talent' that made the *nouvelle vague* so important to the subsequent development of world cinema.

In 'The British New Wave: A Modernist Cinema', R. Barton Palmer reassesses a movement that, acclaimed in the 1960s for its break with tradition and for its realistic treatments of northern provincial lower-middle-class life, subsequently lost critical favour on two counts. On the one hand, unlike the Italian neorealist classics, these British films were long thought to have failed to offer a serious analysis of class relations. On the other hand, unlike the *nouvelle vague*, they were derived from the celebrated theatrical productions and novels of a generation of 'angry young men' and were thus considered to be less 'personal' and original, cinematically speaking. Bringing to light a complex of industrial and aesthetic threads and intersections (including the 'Free Cinema' movement initiated by Lindsay Anderson and Karel Reisz), Palmer shows how the British wave is best understood as a modernist cinema – as part of the culture of European modernism that by 1965 included (in addition to literature) an art film tradition that itself had been imprinted by the Italian neorealists. What was distinctive in films such as Tony Richardson's *Look Back in Anger* (1958) and Shelagh Delaney's *A Taste of Honey* (1961), the chapter's showpiece, is the bringing of a poetic, modernist sensibility to realist narrative and drama.

Launching Part II, which introduces Central, Eastern and Northern European traditions, and providing a preview of his forthcoming volume on *Czech and Slovak Cinemas*, Peter Hames goes beyond the customary depiction of the Czech new wave as simply an unpolitical directors' cinema – in contrast to Jean-Luc Godard's counter-cinema or the committed Latin American 'Third' cinemas. Hames examines in depth one of the Czech wave's paradoxes – that it preceded even as it paralleled the nation's move towards 'democratic socialism'. The film movement began in 1963, five years before the Prague Spring break from traditional Eastern bloc communism, prompting a Russian invasion that summer to 'restore order'. Hames focuses on connections between the film industry and the movements that advocated political change, demonstrating how the 'new wave' films, though subsidised by the state, nevertheless reflected and contributed to the reform movement within Communism. In a society that politicised everything, the faithful documentation of common life as found in the films of Miloš Forman and Ivan Passer (much like the novels they were often based on) constituted a political statement as did formal dissent from the stylistic prescriptions of socialist realism, as found in the work of Věra Chytilová, became political. Czech new wave films provided alternative images to the conventions preferred by the state and thus must be counted as interventions in the political process.

The next two chapters in this part, like those in Parts III and IV, explore a wide spectrum of (mostly) recent and contemporary cinemas in Central, Eastern and Northern Europe, Latin America, Africa and the Middle East. In some instances, the evolution of these traditions has been heavily influenced by the avant-gardism of German expressionism and the modernism of Western European 'new waves'. But, manifesting a strong, often nationalistic desire to create alternative forms of cinema, these movements have been marked as well by resistance to western formal and thematic conventions (including those of Hollywood).

Perhaps the newest of European waves, the unlikely, 'punk', late-1990s Danish movement known as 'Dogma' was not 'born' in any authentic sense but fabricated. On one level, the manifesto of the movement is a pastiched send-up of the revered theoretical texts of the 1960s new waves. On another level, this 'theorising' is little more than an ingenious publicity stunt. As Linda Badley points out, Dogma constitutes a reinterpretation and reassertion of new wave agendas. Though some have sought to minimise the movement's importance, she argues that this tradition has had a global, political impact through its well-publicised renunciation of the unstated 'rules' of hegemonic Hollywood style and its rapid production of a small group of technically, thematically and emotionally provocative films. Reinforcing a radical anti-aesthetic with their own Scandinavian and more broadly European art film heritage of austerity and angst, the Dogma 'brothers' (led by Lars von Trier) have forced international cinema to watch. Dogma has released filmmaking from an aesthetic backed by technology and the market and returned cinema to its roots in theatrical performance, inspiring a parallel movement in the theatre. Dogma filmmakers have utilised digital video in groundbreaking ways, arming independent filmmakers around the world, while provoking a plethora of experimental ventures throughout the media.

The product of a tiny Scandinavian country known for its stability, progressive social programmes and reserve, Dogma could scarcely be more different from the cinemas of the post-Communist regimes of Eastern and Central Europe that Christina Stojanova investigates. Contemporary post-Communist cinemas are distinctive in their reaction against the European art film, and modernism or avant-gardism in general. These traditions have responded instead to a commercial demand for popular entertainment, especially genre film. Examining a vast number of films produced in formerly Communist Eastern European countries over the past ten years (1992–2002), Stojanova scrutinises this revival (or reconstitution) of a popular genre cinema, understanding this development as an attempt to palliate the vast political and economic changes that have torn apart post-Communist societies. She finds that the post-Communist melodrama reflects social change only in private, emotional terms, while the Mafiosi thriller offers catharsis through its attractive fantasy of masculine agency. In contrast, the recently revived nationalist epic attempts to resolve individual and collective anxieties through a celebratory exploration of the past. With its emphasis on genre and changing gender roles, this timely chapter analyses the collective fantasies and desires that current films from Poland, Hungary, Slovenia, the Czech Republic and Russia reflect in the service of a popular entertainment cinema.

Part III takes up the recent developments in Latin American filmmaking that respond to drastic regime shifts as well as to changes in industrial and social conditions. Randal Johnson and Myrto Konstantarakos focus on the newest Latin

American traditions that, having emerged in Brazil and Argentina beginning in the mid-1990s, both sustain and depart from the 'Third Cinema' of the revolutionary past.[1] In the process, the authors demonstrate how, through culturally dislocating decades of dictatorships and cycles of economic crisis, Latin American cinemas continue to develop and flourish. The spectacular re-emergence of Brazilian cinema both at home and internationally owes much to a new generation of filmmakers who have continued the legacy of 1970s *Cinema Novo* of Glauber Rocha and Carlos Diegues, even as this post-*Cinema Novo* tradition distances itself aesthetically and politically from the earlier movement's experimental style. Displaying an astonishing diversity, post-*Cinema Novo* encompasses comedy, intense drama, period films, biographies and documentaries, while many filmmakers collaborate with production companies such as Globo or with American distributors. New Argentine cinema since 1995, by way of contrast, has emerged in much more desperate political and economic circumstances, which are reflected in its low-budget, *cinéma vérité* style. If post-crisis Brazilian film is reclaiming its domestic and international markets and becoming cautiously 'commercial' – with the award-winning *City of God* (*Cidade de Deus*, 2002) and *Motorcycle Diaries* (2004) as recent evidence of international success – the new generation of Argentine filmmakers, the product of some twenty film schools established by the late 1980s, openly rebel against the existing industry, rallying around the theme of 'independence' and creating a boom in festivals and events, as Myrto Konstantarakos demonstrates. Like post-*Cinema Novo*, however, new Argentine filmmakers, including the acclaimed Pablo Trapero and Lucrecia Martel, are less interested in politics than in developing a diverse and vital film industry; they too prefer a traditional, conservative aesthetic. These directors share an interest in utilising gritty urban locations, developing a collective filmmaking style, emphasising the diversity of regions and voices, and disregarding party politics. Made literally out of the misery of urban marginalisation, these Argentine films reflect, even if they do not reflect upon, the conditions of their production.

In Chapter 10, a preview of his forthcoming *African Cinema: North and South of the Sahara*, Roy Armes provides a touchstone for Part IV, which covers African and Middle Eastern traditions, in which filmmaking is shaped less by regional or national identity than by ideology. Armes's chapter uncovers the determinative influence of 'beliefs about morality, social responsibilities and gender relations, on the one hand . . . and assumptions about race, on the other'. Indeed, few other generalisations suffice in accounting for cinema in Africa, a region in which vastness and multiracial and multilingual diversity has often promoted, even as it has been shaped by, resistance to colonial regimes. Returning to the origin of these traditions in pre-independence filmmaking, Armes accounts for five distinct early models on the African continent: the French colonial model; the pioneer work of Tunisian independent Albert

Samama Chikly in the 1920s; apartheid era South African cinema (1910–96); Egyptian cinema of the 1930s; and Algerian revolutionary cinema. Egyptian cinema, the first truly African film industry, was dominated by Misr Studios, which exported forty films a year and specialised in melodramas that, in contrast to the colonial or Hollywood forms of the genre, presumed a collective and unchallengeable fatality. French Communist documentary filmmaker René Vautier produced the final and best-known model of African pre-independence filmmaking. Accompanying Algerian resistance fighters during that country's war of independence (1954–62), Vautier made *Algeria in Flames* (*Algérie en flammes*, 1959), founded a film school and subsequently organised collectives for making pro-liberation films that, enjoying broadcasting on both Eastern and Western television, managed to reach a diverse, international audience. Sadly, the dictatorships that developed subsequently throughout Africa made the collectivist Vautier model – which anticipated revolutionary Third Cinema – inconceivable for post-independence filmmakers. Lacking the industrial resources developed in Egypt and South Africa, even renowned filmmakers like Ousmane Sembene are now forced to work alone, yet within rigid state-defined limits.

Chapters 11 and 12, by Nitzan Ben-Shaul and Negar Mottahedeh respectively, bring us to the present with their focus on Israeli and New Iranian cinemas. While their differences may seem obvious, both cinemas are distinguished by their creative responses to the ideological purposes thrust upon them, aimed at fostering the cultural and political life of their newly created states. Israeli cinema is distinguished from that of its Arab neighbours and aligned with the West, from which it has imported filmmakers and styles since its first feature in 1956, *Hill 24 Doesn't Answer* (*Giv'a 24 Eina Ona*), directed by the British Thorold Dickinson. Ben-Shaul locates a tradition of 'persecution films' within the larger context of the national cinema. These give voice to the theme, central to Jewish culture, of 'a persecuted people living in a besieged state and facing a threatening world', making distinctive uses of narrative structure, visual and aural composition, and characterisation.[2] But by far the major development in Middle Eastern cinema, however, as Negar Mottahedeh demonstrates, is New Iranian film, whose unchecked brilliance and vitality have garnered international acclaim for more than two decades at a time when, paradoxically, heavy censorship had been imposed on the industry following the Islamic revolution of 1979. Seeking to mould a post-revolutionary culture detached from both East and West that would be 'purely' Islamic and national, the regime mandated a desexualised cinematic language. Forbidding western-style visual cues for narrative continuity, the new 'modesty laws' have affected Iranian filmmaking style in fundamental ways. Most notably, they have problematised western cinema's systems for creating cohesion and meaning. As Mottahedeh shows, these limiting conditions of production have given rise to a number of remarkable films by a gallery of directors, including the internationally acclaimed Abbas Kiarostami and Moshen Makmalbaf. No doubt, the New Iranian tradition of filmmaking has affected world cinema's ways of seeing.

In dramatic contrast to most of the traditions explored in Parts I to IV, Asian cinemas, the subject of Part V, have developed and flourished more or less independently until fairly recently, when through global video and DVD distribution in particular they have been able to exert a profound international impact. Asian industries now routinely produce more films than their North American and Western European counterparts combined, with India alone releasing a thousand films a year. Such productivity, as Miller notes in the preface, certainly challenges accepted notions of global Hollywood's supposed dominance. Hindi cinema, or 'Bollywood', as it is popularly (and condescendingly) known in the West, an ethnic tradition that has dominated popular Indian filmmaking since independence (1947), further undermines the authority of terms like 'genre', 'national' and even 'film' by dissolving distinctions between cinema and musical entertainment, as Corey Creekmur demonstrates in Chapter 13. These films defy assumptions based on limited western models of film narrative, dispensing not only with realism and causality but also to a large degree with storytelling. In contrast to the Hollywood musical, whose narrative is 'interrupted' by musical numbers, commercial Hindi cinema is a medium for presenting songs that are occasionally disrupted by narrative. The film song itself is the primary formal and thematic element of this tradition, one whose impact has at last begun to register in the West, for example, in the Bollywood/Hollywood hybrids of Mira Nair and Baz Lurman's *Moulin Rouge* (2001).

In contrast to Creekmur, Stephen Teo chooses genre as a reference point from which to distinguish a tradition of Chinese *wenyi pian* or melodrama, which has achieved international popularity. The 'civil'/sentimental romance film developed from postwar Chinese and Hong Kong melodrama, traditions that it has interrogated and modified. Descended from the theatrical tradition of *wenming xi* (literally, 'civilised dramas') and the 'progressive' melodramas of the 1930s, which dealt with modern social problems instead of drawing on traditional myths, the *wenyi pian* is a love story in a contemporary setting. Popular with female audiences, films in this tradition (as in the Hollywood 'woman's picture') feature a romantic triangle, a sensitive hero and a noble, self-sacrificing heroine. As Teo demonstrates, the *wenyi pian* depicts wistful, would-be lovers suffering from the conservative familial and social restraints and rituals that they scrupulously observe. Beginning with Fei Mu's *Spring in a Small Town* (*Xiao cheng zhi chun*, 1948), these films are characterised by *qing*, sentimental or 'civil' emotion produced through tension with the dictum that desire must be constrained by Confucian family ethics. Exploring the *wenyi* film's adversarial relationship with the ascendant martial arts genre since the late 1960s, Teo demonstrates how it has prospered even to infiltrate the latter in Ang Lee's 2000 hit *Crouching Tiger, Hidden Dragon* (*Wo hu cang long*) and to experience a postmodern revival epitomised in Wong Kar-wai's *In the Mood for Love* (*Huayang nianhua*, 2000) and, even more recently, western off-shoots such as Sofia Coppola's *Lost in Translation* (2002).

Although horror film has had international attention as a distinctive compo-nent of the Japanese film industry since the 1950s and 1960s, its currently unprecedented popularity has been confirmed by the phenomenal success of the Nakata Hideo's *Ringu* (1998) and its various, internationally made, sequels and remakes. In Chapter 15, a provocative introduction to his edited volume *Japanese Horror Cinema* (2005), Jay McRoy accounts for the current national and global appeal of the genre's newest wave. He explains that haunting power and intensity of these films in terms of their focus on the body and the mon-strous as allegorical motifs formed in reaction to western cultural imperialism and by the struggle to maintain a coherent national identity. Concentrating on the productions of visionary directors such as Kurosawa Kiyoshi, Miike Takeshi, Tsukamoto Shinya and Nakata, McRoy surveys Japanese horror cinema's most important subgenres including the *Kaidan* or avenging spirit film, the *daikaiju eiga* or giant monster film, the apocalyptic film, the techno-body horror film, and the torture film. The popular *kaidan*, for example (*Kwaidan* (*Kaidan*, 1964); *Ringu*; *Audition* (*Ōdishon*, 1999)), is the traditional tale of a 'wronged', usually female, spirit who returns in characteristic bodily form (long black hair, single inverted eye) to avenge an injustice and whose ter-rifying corporeality, especially evident in recent films, reflects the paradoxical and changing familial and economic role of women in Japanese culture.

The sixth and final part of *Traditions in World Cinema* calls attention to two traditions that are often excluded from 'world' cinema: American movements both within and outside of Hollywood that have challenged classic studio prac-tice even as they have reinvigorated American cinema; and transnational or global traditions, movements, trends or genres. In Chapter 15, Robert Kolker discusses the work of the 'New' (post-studio era, mostly film-school educated) American directors of the 1970s including Martin Scorsese, Francis Ford Coppola, Steven Spielberg, Stanley Kubrick and Robert Altman. Inspired by the auteurist art cinema of the European new waves, several of these young direc-tors entered the industry by way of the exploitation productions of Roger Corman and, artfully deploying sex and violence, showed Hollywood that allowing directors creative control was profitable, creating a window of oppor-tunity. Kolker focuses on Coppola's *The Godfather* (1972), Scorsese's *Taxi Driver* (1977) and *GoodFellas* (1990) and Altman's *McCabe and Mrs. Miller* (1972), films that are creatively indebted to the European art film even as they revisit Hollywood techniques, motifs, and genres. Undermining the 'rules' of genres thought to be intrinsically American, such as the gangster film and the Western, these directors infused counter-cultural values and their own personal visions into their films, subverting all things stereotypically American and reinventing classical Hollywood forms. Although this 'Hollywood renaissance' is over, its spirit continues in the revival of American independent film, as exemplified in the work of current auteurs such as Todd Haynes, Todd Solondz and Jim Jarmusch and in flourishing underground, exploitation and alternative cinemas on the contemporary American scene.

In addition to new American traditions, Part VI seeks to exemplify transnational or global traditions, movements, trends or genres that counter hegemonic practice. These might include, for example, feminist independent film, international horror cinema or post-punk film, a tradition that is explored for the first time in *New Punk Cinema* (2005), edited by Nick Rombes.[3] In Chapter 16, Adrian Danks explores the transnational practice of found footage or compilation cinema, a tradition whose concern is the ephemeral and overwhelmingly material culture of cinema itself. A 'hybridised and impure tradition' whose 'junk' aesthetic and technique of recycling and recontextualising the detritus of previous films and technologies – travelogues, home movies, archival footage, advertising – found footage cinema both exemplifies and protests audio-visual culture. Using seminal works by Joseph Cornell (*Rose Hobart*, 1936) and Bruce Conner (*A Movie*, 1958) as touchstones, Danks covers a historical and ideological range of contemporary practitioners and links the tradition to cultural and aesthetic movements from Cubism to Surrealism and early European politicised collage. Exemplified in Soviet montage, Cuban agit-prop documentary, postwar American avant-garde, post-1970s feminist and queer filmmaking in Canada and Australia, compilation cinema has lately reclaimed its status as an 'alternative' (subcultural, environmentalist, even anti-capitalist) cinema. Ultimately, however, compilation cinema resists categorisation, much less any unified or progressive history. Danks disputes, for example, critic William C. Wees's distinction between collage (as critique) and appropriation (as accommodation). Indeed, the temptation to differentiate belies and runs counter to the breakdown of demarcations, the movement of images and sounds across recognised borders that epitomises this tradition's dispersive spirit.

It is our hope that in a similar spirit the Traditions in World Cinema series volumes (including this one) will dispute and usefully break down for further analysis established demarcations in the field of film studies – not only the sweeping generalisation carried in the term 'global Hollywood' but also what is customarily and very reductively known as 'world cinema', which signifies those limited forms of difference that can easily be marketed to an international audience. Like the chapters collected here, forthcoming volumes seek to identify and promote those cinemas that exist across different worlds – that is, across national, industrial, cultural and economic borders that conventional accounts of 'current cinema' too often ignore.

NOTES

1. Influenced by the politically engaged cinema of the Italian neorealists, the collectivist cinema of protest that came to be known as 'Third Cinema' emerged in late 1950s Latin America to produce films that surfaced on the first-world festival scene, winning acclaim and prizes. Brazilian *Cinema Novo* was followed in 1967 by Cuban post-revolutionary 'Imperfect Cinema', developed by filmmakers Julio García Espinosa, Sara Gómez, Santiago Álvarez and Tomás Gutiérrez Alea, and by Argentina's *Grupo Cine Liberación*, centred around Fernando Pino Solanas and Octavio Getino.
2. In another way, Israeli cinema perhaps resembles that of its Arab neighbours as viewed by Armes – in its presentation of individual crises in terms of the collective, and in its cyclical, even fatalistic narrative patterns.
3. Post-punk cinema combines the punk spirit of experimentation, the current revival of American independent film, the Dogma 95 movement and the do-it-yourself and digital revolutions, and includes films such as *The Blair Witch Project*, *Memento*, *Run, Lola Run*, *Time Code* and *Requiem for a Dream*.

PART I

EUROPEAN TRADITIONS

1. GERMAN EXPRESSIONISM

A cinematic/cultural problem

J. P. Telotte

EXPRESSIONIST ORIGINS

While expressionism was already an active movement in German art and theatre prior to the First World War, it gained widespread attention and even a kind of cultural embrace in what Siegfried Kracauer has described as 'the intellectual excitement surging through Germany after the war'.[1] This 'Aufbruch' or upwelling of intellectual and cultural activity was prompted by a variety of social conditions: the establishment of a liberal government headquartered at Weimar, the abolition of state censorship, the new popularity of Marxism and a general rejection of the past that had precipitated the horrors of the First World War. More generally, this atmosphere encouraged an openness to various new political ideas – on both the left and the right – while opening the door for a variety of avant-garde art movements of the day, foremost among them expressionism, to participate in an ongoing critique of postwar German society.

That 'excitement' to which Kracauer refers had an invigorating influence on most of the arts in Germany, but with expressionism and its highly visual nature, it would find particularly fertile ground in the cinema and give birth to a film tradition that would have a lasting impact on other national cinemas. This flowering of expressionism involved a rejection not only of much that was associated with the wartime status quo, but also of an aesthetic that supported the familiar world, the naturalist assumption that the 'real' could be conventionally depicted. As a result, expressionist art in practically every way seemed to suggest a protest against the norm: the extremes of language in the plays and manifestos, the alienating and menacing cityscapes of the graphic art, the grotesque and caricatured figures of paintings, the sinister shadows and unbalanced images of the films, and the recurring themes of madness, duplicity and alienation. For these reasons, Richard Murphy suggests that we read expressionist art primarily as a kind of aesthetic 'oppositional strategy', one that aimed 'to defamiliarise vision and to unlock conventionalised constructions'.[2]

That defamiliarisation proceeded by a number of techniques drawn from the different expressionist-influenced arts, all converging in the creation of what Murphy terms 'a variety of oppositional discourses' that strike at 'the very structure of the representational system'.[3] Thus, in a concerted effort to show how, as R. S. Furness offers, 'an essential, inner reality may be made more accessible by deliberate distortion and *unreality*',[4] the emerging expressionist cinema drew on methods found in the theatre, painting and graphic arts, such as stylised sets, exaggerated acting, distortions of space, heavy use of shadows, irregular compositions that emphasise oblique lines, as well as specifically filmic techniques like low-key lighting, dutch angles and composition in depth, to create a vision that pointedly challenges the authority of classical representation. Those techniques served to trouble the audience's customary perceptions and prodded them to recognise how much their sense of the world was carefully constructed by various cultural conventions.

One more specific effect would become especially symptomatic of a German expressionist cinema, as we shall see. For consistent with that troubling of perception came a recurrent emphasis on the very nature of the film experience, as a form that had, in much of its early years, been largely associated with realistic representation came to be seen as embedded in that pattern of cultural constructions, and thus as potentially participating in the sort of inurement that expressionism challenged. This theatrical or reflexive element surfaces in a variety of ways in expressionist and expressionist-influenced films. The film that has historically been seen as the most important early entry in the movement, *The Cabinet of Dr. Caligari* (*Das Kabinett des Doktor Caligari*, 1919), focuses on a travelling carnival, a show, as it explores the relationship between that show and its audiences – a relationship that proves both duplicitous and dangerous. Similarly, the show and its performers or exhibits form the narrative hub of such films as *Waxworks* (*Das Wachsfigurenkabinett*, 1924), *Variety* (*Varieté*, 1925) and *The Blue Angel* (*Der Blaue Engel*, 1930). The ability to create precise or convincing reproductions of the human form proves a key motif in works like *Homunculus* (1916), *The Golem* (*Der Golem*, 1914, 1920), *The Student of Prague* (*Der Student von Prague*, 1913, 1926), and *Metropolis* (1926). And the nature of the audience, particularly as they are easily seduced by their perceptions, recurs in *Caligari, Metropolis, Dr. Mabuse, the Gambler* (*Dr. Mabuse, der Spieler – Ein Bild der Zeit*, 1922) and *Pandora's Box* (*Die Büchse der Pandora*, 1929). Lotte Eisner in her seminal study of German expressionist cinema, *The Haunted Screen*, notes how expressionist cinema constantly seems to depict a 'world of shadows and mirrors'.[5] It is a particularly telling observation about these films since it strikes to the core of what might be termed their filmic self-consciousness, their ready evocation of a realm of troubled perceptions and constant reproductions.

THE EXPRESSIONIST 'PROBLEM'

Metropolis, one of the most widely seen and discussed works in German film history, climaxes on a troublingly stylish note that speaks to this issue of troubled perception. The rioting workers, whose revolt against the city's masters has destroyed their underground city and nearly killed their children, form a wedge-like group and march – rhythmically, uniformly, even mechanically – up the Cathedral steps to meet with Joh Fredersen, the city's ruler. After near tragedy, they seem broken, already returned to the repressed, herd-like state in which they were seen at the film's start, when they were similarly shown marching in geometric groups to and from their numbing, slave-like labours. Reduced to a uniform group, the workers for all their efforts seem to have accomplished nothing and the narrative trajectory to have brought us back to the social circumstance, as well as the stylised note, on which the film began. While this transformation of the revolting workers into a nearly decorative mass is visually striking, producing an effective composition, it is troubling because of the way it seems to undermine the spirit of the expressionist aesthetic that has given *Metropolis* much of its visual allure and that seemed central to the revolutionary spirit of this and other German expressionist films.

For expressionism, when first brought to the screen in the post-First World War era, seemed to bear a clearly subversive visual potential, like that associated with such other avant-garde movements as constructivism and surrealism when they too migrated to the cinema. As Murphy explains, its effort at creating 'an alternative reality' through its exaggerations and stylisations represented 'a powerful revolutionary drive', suggesting that the 'previous reality' of bourgeois life had 'lost its legitimacy'. [6] If the expressionist actor – on the stage and in such films as *The Cabinet of Dr. Caligari*, *Nosferatu* (*Nosferatu, eine Symphonie des Grauens*, 1922) and *Waxworks* – moved in a stilted and eerily unnatural fashion, 'externalizing himself completely' with no effort 'to feign reality', as drama critic Paul Kornfeld offered,[7] it was supposedly to help audiences see both human nature and the human condition in a new and revealing light. And if expressionist narratives, with their sense of a nearly alien environment – typified by such films as *The Golem* and *Metropolis* – seemed ruled by playwright Yvon Goll's dictum that 'pure realism was the worst error of all literature', [8] it was to foster precisely the sort of critical estrangement that later distinguished the socially conscious drama of Bertolt Brecht. In fact, Kracauer notes that while expressionism had attained an advanced development in painting and literature prior to The First World War, it only truly 'acquired a public' after the war precisely because it seemingly spoke 'to a revolutionized people', combining 'the denial of bourgeois traditions with faith in man's power freely to shape society and nature'.[9]

In retrospect, though, that notion of a 'revolutionized' audience perhaps puts the case too strongly, or at least the case for why a seemingly subversive aesthetic would have found such a level of acceptance, both in Germany and elsewhere. For as Metropolis's climactic scene suggests, with its stark – and dark – visualisation of a repression lingering to undermine any sense of liberation or enlightened consciousness, the expressionist aesthetic could work almost independently of any social thrust, as if it were drained of any but a formal function. This possibility is one that Eisner allows, as she notes how a vague sense of 'mysticism and magic', reminders of 'the ghosts which had haunted the German romantics' of the previous century, had become widespread in the chaotic postwar era, not only reflecting a general sense of anxiety in Germany, but also underscoring a cultural emphasis on 'abstraction' over the 'absolute' or 'objective'.[10] Consequently, any announced anti-bourgeois social or political thrust, she holds, was often qualified by the almost 'intentionally obscure' nature of most expressionist art,[11] a nature that repeatedly 'sidetracked' its adherents 'into the snares of abstraction'.[12]

And yet expressionism, particularly as it flourished in the German cinema at this time, certainly seemed to reach for more. In its best examples, we find, even in those instances of stylistically 'sidetracked' films that Eisner criticised, a persistent effort to strike a bargain between style and narrative, between aesthetic concerns and political ones, between the abstract and the all-too-concrete and objective world of Weimar Germany with its constant reminders of the difficult conditions of existence in that country – the scarred veterans in the streets, hyperinflation, the often-violent political rallies, etc. To examine this effort at striking a narrative bargain, I want to consider a range of key expressionist films: the movement's earliest touchstone The Cabinet of Dr. Caligari; the middle-period Waxworks, directed by Paul Leni who was himself an expressionist painter and setdesigner; and the later Metropolis, notable as the most elaborate and costly film to employ an expressionist aesthetic, while also for many marking the end point for that movement in Germany, even though it would continue to impact other national cinemas.

THE CABINET OF DR. CALIGARI

Discussions of expressionist film almost invariably start with The Cabinet of Dr. Caligari, although certain stylistic and thematic elements that would become identified with this tradition already appear in such films as the prewar

Student of Prague and *Das Haus ohne Tür* ('The House Without a Door', 1914). Yet *Caligari* is usually singled out partly because the film is credited with making cinematic expressionism popular, but also because its use of that style had, almost from the start, raised the question of how an avant-garde aesthetic might fit within conventional – and largely realist – cinematic practice. In his study of German film, *From Caligari to Hitler*, Siegfried Kracauer explains how Hans Janowitz and Carl Mayer, co-authors of the *Caligari* script, created a story that attacked the 'absolute authority' that had produced the horrors of the recent World War. Their tale of a somnambulist, Cesare, who commits murders under the guidance of a psychiatrist, Dr Caligari, metaphorised the situation of 'the common man who, under the pressure of compulsory military service, is drilled to kill and to be killed', with the tale's 'revolutionary meaning' appearing clearly in its conclusion 'with the disclosure of the psychiatrist as Caligari: reason overpowers unreasonable power, insane authority is symbolically abolished'.[13] Janowitz's suggestion of using a visual style that supported this subversive narrative met with the approval of director Robert Wiene, who agreed on employing as set designers three artists, Herrmann Warm, Walter Rohrig and Walter Reimann, all affiliated with the Berlin *Sturm* group which promoted expressionism in all the arts.[14] Yet as finally deployed, that style did not seem entirely consistent with Janowitz and Mayer's intentions. For Fritz Lang, who was originally assigned to direct, suggested using a framing device to structure the narrative as a flashback account, told by the character Francis to a fellow inmate in an insane asylum. The effect was to turn the expressionist-styled main story, placed within this frame, into the apparent vision of a madman, leaving Janowitz and Mayer to protest that this approach 'perverted, if not reversed, their intrinsic intentions', transforming 'a revolutionary film' – in both plot and visual style – into 'a conformist one'.[15] As the writers saw it, their story of a menace at work within society and in its leaders had become one in which the real menace is simply a problem of the individual human psyche, a problem that, as the psychiatrist offers at the film's conclusion, can easily be 'cured'.

Certainly, the frame device Lang suggested does have some of this 'taming' effect since the murders it depicts are distanced both temporally and spatially from the narration. And the notion that the expressionist style's impact was largely undermined seems consistent with Eisner's view of the German film establishment of the time, which she sees as only being interested in the avant-garde for economic reasons; as she opines, it 'latched on to anything of an artistic kind in the belief that it was bound to bring in money in the long run'.[16] And yet it seems clear that *Caligari*'s expressionist look extends even into the narrative's framing elements, and that, partly as a result of the visual scheme's extensiveness, the narrative retains an unsettling, even subversive effect. For it simply bulks beyond any conventionally realist cinema and, in both style and subject, allies itself with the fantastic – an alliance that for many would come to seem natural to expressionism. As Tzvetan Todorov has suggested, the fantastic narrative always 'represents an experience of limits';[17] it plays at – and with – the margins of the normal world and of typical experience. With this fantastic kinship, in their combination of the everyday and the unexpected, expressionist narratives like *Caligari* or Arthur Robison's *Warning Shadows* (1923) draw explicit attention to the process of representation, including that of the cinema.

While the framing scenes lack much of the painted shadows and jagged lines that characterise the flashback narrative, that of the town of Holstenwall during its annual fair, the stark white wall that serves as a backdrop to Francis's account, the layered images, spider-like trees and chiaroscuro lighting clearly link to the visual style of the rest of the film, as does the use of parallel irises to emphasise the characters and locale in both the frame and the flashback. Moreover, the angularly painted yard of the asylum, seen in the final sequence, looks little different from the twisted and distorted streets of Holstenwall, and the strangely-shaped cell into which the 'insane' Francis is thrust at the film's end simply echoes the similarly nightmarish cells within the frame-tale in which are cast both the supposed Holstenwall murderer and the captured Dr Caligari. The visual style, in short, seems largely consistent, as if the vision of a dangerous, even insane, society could simply not be contained or bracketed within the narrative 'trick' of the flashback.

We might trace one reason for that lack of containment back to what Murphy describes as 'a particular "logic" of perception' at work in the film, one that at every turn 'cloaks identities and phenomena in ambiguity'.[18] Throughout the narrative, for example, we remain unsure of the location or circumstances in which Francis recounts his fantastic tale, of the real identity of the 'mountebank' Dr Caligari, and of the status of the Cesare character (manipulated victim or monster?). The result is that the film takes on a kind of dream-like quality, one marked by what Murphy terms a 'representational instability'[19] that produces a constant potential for duplicity and double-dealing – in both frame and flashback – as the narrative sets up the potential that everyone and everything may be other than it initially seems, and that our very ability to see or comprehend the world around us is constantly open to compromise. This subtle sense of instability not only strikes at the realistic nature of the cinema, but also opens onto the plastic and thus imaginary space of film itself – or what Anthony Vidler has termed a 'totalizing plasticity'[20] – as it projects the sense of a world that is simply sprung from a mind and that obeys the laws of that mind, rather than those of time and space that bind the real world.

Moreover, *Caligari* implicates the audience – and thus their world – in that 'plasticity' through its emphasis on the act of seeing. Most obviously, the film's setting at the fair, as S. S. Prawer reminds, recalls, especially for that early audience, that the travelling fair or carnival was a typical 'home of the earliest cinema-shows', with its often-lurid enticements evoking the very 'promises . . . which lure us into the cinema'.[21] The images of Francis and Alan, along with the many other rapt spectators, at Caligari's 'show' of Cesare further suggests the power of such spectacles within what has been termed 'the society of the spectacle',[22] and that power is underscored as the film provides viewers with a kind of metonymic image of their own situation. For in order to determine if the mountebank Caligari and his somnambulist Cesare are involved in the mysterious murders, Francis keeps watch one night outside their caravan. Looking through a window – which recalls the movie screen itself – he sees Caligari with Cesare asleep in his box. Yet when Cesare is captured while trying to kidnap Jane, Francis learns that this innocent scene had been carefully constructed to fool any observers, that the box contained a dummy crudely fashioned to look like Cesare, and that Caligari had often resorted to this ruse, this acting, to throw off suspicions. Thanks to this contrived seeing and Caligari's own 'special effects', he had easily fooled him and the authorities about the real nature of his activities.

What *Cabinet of Dr. Caligari* thus offers is a most effective use of an avant-garde technique, certainly one that proved visually striking and that affirmed a connection between film and other art forms. If it was not quite the overt strike at bourgeois society that Janowitz and Mayer in their original story had intended, it did manage another level of interrogation, compelling viewers to reconsider how their world was 'framed' for them and their level of responsibility as spectators of that world. In this way *Caligari* managed to strike a deal between a style that many saw as simply sensationalistic and a variety of social concerns that are fundamentally embedded in the constructed world of the cinema.

WAXWORKS

For Leon Barsacq, the essential expressionist element of Paul Leni's *Waxworks* is architectural. That architecture, especially of the film's first two episodes, which focus on the Baghdad of the Arabian Nights and the Moscow of Ivan the Terrible, largely 'determines the behaviour and attitudes of the characters by preventing them from moving about normally' and forcing their bodies 'to bend, to double up, to move jerkily, and to make abrupt gestures'.[23] This effect follows largely from the sort of *interior* world that the film describes, as events occur largely within a wax museum (the frame for the narrative and its final episode), within the palace of the Caliph of Baghdad or the small apartment of Assad the baker, and within the cellar/dungeon of the Kremlin or a wedding hall. Characters are constantly bound by their surroundings, and that bondage is replicated throughout the film, as when the Caliph, a self-described 'fat man', hides himself inside Assad's oven, when Ivan the Terrible relegates himself to his cellar prison, and when the writer dreams he and the museum proprietor's daughter are being pursued throughout the museum and the surrounding maze-like streets by the killer Spring-Heeled Jack. Low-ceilings, oblique lines and constant shadows create the sense that the world is closing in on these characters and make their mannered, unnatural postures seem appropriate to this topography that closely recalls in style that of *Caligari*.

And yet that effective matching of topography and character is hardly unproblematic and represents only a portion of the expressionist thrust of *Waxworks*. While it effectively alludes to ways in which people are bound by their cultural conditions – of the Caliph's court and his unbridled appetites, of Ivan's sadistic and paranoid nature – it also suggests that these conditions are largely the stuff of ancient history, of *other* cultures and ultimately of the imagination. For they are, after all, conjured up from the mind of a young writer who has answered an advertisement asking for someone to 'write startling tales about these wax figures'. The episodes are thus visualisations of his efforts at creating narratives to fit with the lurid circumstances of the displays. And the last menacing sequence, in which Spring-Heeled Jack stalks the writer and the young girl, is finally revealed to be just a dream, a problem that, as in *Caligari*, has emerged from the individual's imagination as he fantasises more 'startling' possibilities for these wax figures. For all of its wildly carnivalesque trappings, dark images and repressive topography, then, *Waxworks* too seems ready to draw back from any subversive implications, to treat its narrative forebodings as little more than dark humour, a joke on both the writer who has drifted off to sleep and the filmgoers who have similarly drifted into this dream of a movie.[24]

Yet also like *Caligari*, it consistently frames these fantasies within a context we might term reflexive, and thus one that in some ways poses a more universal challenge to representation and the world to which its exaggerated stylings allude. It is, after all, set at a fair and, more particularly, within a wax museum dubbed 'Panopticum', that is, a kind of transparent world, devoted to the pleasures of seeing. Within this realm, the fairgoers are not only invited to view some of the more fantastic elements of their world, but to project themselves into that world – to perceive it as if these monstrous wax figures are alive and capable of menacing them. Thus when the writer accepts the task of fashioning a startling tale about how Haroun-Al-Raschid lost his arm, he quickly imagines himself as Assad, a baker in ancient Baghdad, who is married to Zarah, a figure he visualises, as a dissolve indicates, from the museum's daughter for whom he has taken a fancy. Troubling that relationship, though, are the easy visual seductions of this world, as the Caliph glimpses Zarah and determines to have her, while Assad, in turn, fixes upon stealing the Caliph's wishing ring as a way of assuring Zarah's affection. And as each approaches his goal, he finds himself cast into a spectator's position, each spying upon the other in an effort to obtain his desires – a spying that is rendered difficult by the expressionist context of shadowy lighting and confining structures, and one that invariably points toward the situation of the moviegoers in their dark confines. The mutual frustrations at fulfilling those desires further implicate both the cinematic and social situations by underscoring the elusiveness of those images.

The following Ivan the Terrible sequence further examines that spectatorial role by identifying it with the predations and, ultimately, the insanity of Czar Ivan. For the narrative begins by describing Ivan's delight in stealing into the Kremlin's dungeons to watch 'the dying agonies of his poisoned victims', measuring out their final agonies against an hour glass on which he has their names inscribed, thereby furthering their agony – and his pleasure – by making them view their lives metaphorically draining away. That spectatorial delight, though, produces a kind of self-consciousness in Ivan, who fears his official poisoner might poison him, inscribe his name on an hourglass, and so turn him into a spectator at his own demise, and who fears that assassins might be watching him as he travels to the wedding of a noble's daughter. The result is a series of repositionings, as the Czar dons the noble's robes so that the noble is assassinated in his place, and, at the subsequent wedding, glimpses the bride and desires to replace the bridegroom. Yet these efforts at controlling the spectator position – at maintaining his status as a kind of ideal voyeur/movie viewer – only turn Ivan into the subject of everyone's gaze, transforming him from the privileged viewer to the object of all eyes, the horrified looks of all the wedding guests. His eventual madness, as he comes to believe he has been poisoned and so compulsively watches an hourglass bearing his name, constantly reversing it before its sands can run out, only underscores the dangers of that privileged spectator's position Ivan has tried to reserve for himself. He who has sought to control all seeing, to project whatever image he desires while remaining the unseen spectator, finds he cannot escape from being positioned as both subject and spectator.

Lotte Eisner's description of the concluding Spring-Heeled Jack sequence further comments on this issue of the spectator. She terms this sequence the 'most Expressionist' element of the film, thanks to 'its sliding corners, its continually shifting surfaces, its walls yielding without revealing what they conceal. It is a chaos of forms' set against 'an infernal darkness'.[25] That sense of visual fluidity, of a plastic spectacle, speaks precisely to the film experience, particularly to the way in which film places its audience in a world bound by its own *cinematic* rules – of time, space and even logic. It thereby reminds them, even if in its own joking way – and indeed, the film ends with the characters laughing, in a fashion most fitting for its carnival setting – of the manipulated representations that are the norm in both the cinematic realm and that seemingly festive world they inhabit. Its appropriateness here, though, is also due to the way in which this sequence, like the Ivan episode, turns the spectatorial tables on its characters, as the writer and the girl, both workers within the Panopticum, suddenly and inexplicably – through the logic of a dream – find themselves thrust into the dark world of Spring-Heeled Jack: watched, stalked and transformed into his potential victims. While the sequence can end with a laugh of relief as the writer awakens from his dream, it serves as an effective coda for the film, a reminder of how easily the viewer can become the viewed, and how very fluid and unstable this world remains.

METROPOLIS

That sense of instability, as the opening of this chapter suggests, is built into the very fabric of a film that many would see as the final major expressionist production, Fritz Lang's *Metropolis*. Its tale of a futuristic city uses expressionist visual styling to address one of the constant difficulties facing every cinematic anticipation of the future: how to extrapolate a suitably futuristic or 'other' look. Through its canted camera angles, obscuring shadows, and oblique lines of composition, all familiar expressionist hallmarks, the film effectively distances its dystopian city from the urban present to suggest the sort of strangeness and dynamism audiences might associate with the future. At the same time, the tale's revolutionary element, as the city's leaders plot to replace the workers with robots and the workers eventually rebel against their slave-like treatment, evokes a world that, despite all of its magnificent structures, was every bit as unstable as Weimar Germany and linked to the more personal stories of obsession and murder of *Caligari* and *Waxworks*. In this respect especially *Metropolis*, as the largest and most expensive project of Germany's Ufa studio, bears testimony to Klaus Kreimeier's notion that, at this time, 'Ufa's studios were . . . a "melting pot" for Weimar and for both its progressive and regressive elements'.[26]

While the film's effort to bring together these different elements, to find a kind of narrative accommodation of these conflicting cultural tendencies, seems somewhat forced and unconvincing, as the film's conclusion suggests, it consistently develops its own logic of perception in a way that makes its 'bargain' more satisfying. The film depicts a society that has moved to such extremes that the workers – the 'hands' of society, as the film styles them – and the administrators – the 'head' – have lost all meaningful contact, with the former becoming little more than slaves of the latter. Instead of issuing in a revolutionary action, this schism has produced a kind of religious hope, preached by the girl Maria, in the imminent appearance of a saviour, a 'heart' that might restore these elements of society to their natural union. But as Lang himself would offer years later, 'You cannot make a social-consciousness picture in which you say that the intermediary between the hand and the brain is the heart – I mean that's a fairy tale – definitely',[27] and he blames that bit of unreality on his wife Thea von Harbou's script. Because of that problematic scheme, though, the film's deeper logic only emerges as it explores how easily all people are seduced by appearances – by the very stuff of silent cinema.

Certainly, audiences even today are immediately taken by the look of Lang's city of the future: its monumental buildings, pleasure gardens and massive machines. Drawn in by those images, we only gradually learn, like young Freder, Joh Fredersen's son, that they disguise a subjugated populace, a culture ultimately at odds with itself. And the key emblem of that conflict becomes the robot that Fredersen and the scientist Rotwang create to manipulate the workers and maintain their hold on power. A sign simultaneously of the ideal worker – obedient to orders, tireless, inhuman – and of the ruling class – able to lead the workers as they see fit – the robot is first tested on the wealthy young men of the city. Dancing at a nightclub, it draws all eyes, as a montage of staring faces underscores, excites their passion and easily induces them to believe it is a real woman, not a cold metal creation. Following that debut, the robot, in the guise of Maria, similarly rouses the workers, turning a kind of sexual excitement into a revolutionary mania, one in which they destroy the machines supporting the city while forgetting about their homes and children that depend on those same machines. It seems that no one here is quite safe from those visual seductions that the film pointedly lodges in modern technological life, and which it extends to various subplots: the worker Georgi, who changes places with Freder and becomes enchanted by the world of the privileged; the ancient inhabitants of Babylon, who, as a flashback recounts, became obsessed with the image of a tower as a monument to their own greatness; Rotwang, who fantasises that Maria is a reincarnation of his lost love Hel; and even Fredersen, who, gazing through the panoramic windows of his rooftop office, often seems mesmerised by the city as if it were a giant cinematic spectacle.

In illustrating and thus laying bare these various sorts of visual seductions, *Metropolis* offers far more than the simple formulaic accommodation of 'head', 'hands' and 'heart' articulated in its final scene and later repudiated by Lang. Certainly, it strikes at authority in much the way that *Caligari* sought to do, even as it also criticises the workers, suggesting in that final wedge-like image how easily they become little more than a leaderless mass. But authority and the workers ultimately find common cause in that sense of seduction, in the recognition that all are too easily swayed from a common path – diverted from a utopian to a dystopian future – by the images of their world, by the enticements of modern technological culture, which, of course, include that pre-eminent technological art, the movies themselves.

CONCLUSION

As Richard Murphy reminds, the expressionist movement is finally 'a notoriously difficult phenomenon to pin down to any clear ideological line', both in its own time and today. Thus its subjects range from the highly fantastic – as in *The Golem* or Lang's *Destiny* (1921) – to the historical and naturalistic – as with *Danton* (1921) and *Asphalt* (1928). Yet its very position as an oppositional mode served an important 'decentring function'.[28] Certainly, it opened the way, at least for a brief moment in film history, for an alternative, non-realistic approach to film narrative, as well as for a newly stylised inflection in established film genres. Because of various economic and political imperatives in the 1920s and early 1930s, many of those involved in the expressionist movement – notably figures like Fritz Lang, Karl Freund, F. W. Murnau and Paul Leni – would leave the German cinema and help spread an expressionist tradition, particularly in America. And there expressionism would pay special dividends in the development of fantasy-oriented genres for which it would furnish a sustaining style, and from which American fantasy films of the 1930s, especially works like *The Man Who Laughs* (1928), *Frankenstein* (1931), *The Mummy* (1932) and *Mad Love* (1935), would draw so profitably.

In that notion of 'decentring', though, we need to see more than just a generic function, more than simply the opening up a new vein of fantasy. It speaks as well of expressionism's insistently subversive nature. For what the expressionist film tradition ultimately decentred, as this discussion has suggested, was point of view itself, a normally stable and unexamined – because it conventionally was rendered as invisible – component of film narrative. Images of how we see, images of the spectator, images of the careful construction of perspective abound in expressionist films, as well as in those which draw on this tradition. Thus, in trying to link Lang's German films with his later American ones, Raymond Bellour would note how they are similarly 'disjunctive, provoking the eye'.[29] Through that sort of provocative attitude, the expressionist tradition has repeatedly forced viewers to confront the extent to which conventional narratives and, indeed, conventional society carefully constructs their everyday experience.

Paul Virilio has noted how in the modern technologised world we all risk becoming 'victims of the set', thanks to the 'industrialization of perception, the ultimate coup d'état' that has become the very condition of modern life.[30] What expressionist cinema did was, often through its own stylised and rather strange sets, to struggle against that victimisation by reminding viewers of the extent to which they were all, in a sense, being Potemkin-ised by the status quo, by the 'set' constructed for them by the same culture that had produced the slaughter of the First World War. It is a struggle that we see repeated today, in the various works of Tim Burton, David Cronenberg and David Lynch, and in such expressionist-influenced films as *Dark City* (1998), *The Matrix* (1999) and the Japanese *anime* version of *Metropolis* (2000). These and other works underscore the widespread, truly international impact of the expressionist tradition, and its continuing influence on a postmodern cinema. As R. S. Furness declares, the expressionist artist seemed to respond to a 'need to point beyond', to suggest that 'the ultimate meaning of the world might lie beyond its purely external appearance'.[31] By calling into question the very manner in which we see – and are allowed to see by a variety of cultural restrictions – almost ironically by distorting the common images of our world, expressionism challenged the normal order of representation both within the cinema and outside of its confines. While certainly a mode characterised by shadows, distortions and darkness, it thereby helped to shed a new light on the everyday world and, in this way, effected its own sort of revolutionary consciousness, one that remains a vital legacy today.

NOTES

1. Siegfried Kracauer, *From Caligari to Hitler: A Psychological History of the German Film* (Princeton, NJ: Princeton University Press, 1947), p. 38.
2. Richard Murphy, *Theorizing the Avant-Garde: Modernism, Expressionism, and the Problem of Postmodernity* (Cambridge: Cambridge University Press, 1999), p. 59.
3. Ibid., p. 202.
4. Richard S. Furness, *Expressionism* (London: Methuen, 1973), p. 88.
5. Lotte Eisner, *The Haunted Screen*, trans. Roger Greaves (Berkeley, CA: University of California Press, 1973), p. 129.
6. Murphy, *Theorizing the Avant-Garde*, 57.
7. Paul Kornfield, 'Epilogue to the Actor', in Walter H. Sokel (ed.), *German Expressionist Drama: A Prelude to the Absurd* (Garden City, NY: Doubleday, 1963), p. 7.
8. Yvon Goll, 'Two Superdramas', in Walter H. Sokel (ed.), *German Expressionist Drama: A Prelude to the Absurd* (Garden City, NY: Doubleday, 1963), p. 10.
9. Kracauer, *From Caligari to Hitler*, p. 68.
10. Eisner, *The Haunted Screen*, pp. 9, 13.
11. Ibid., p. 10.
12. Ibid., p. 18.
13. Kracauer, *From Caligari to Hitler*, pp. 64, 65.
14. For background on the decision to employ an expressionist style in *Caligari*, see Kracauer, pp. 67–9, and Eisner, pp. 18–20.
15. Kracauer, *From Caligari to Hitler*, pp. 66–7.
16. Eisner, *The Haunted Screen*, p. 19.
17. Tzvetan Todorov, *The Fantastic: A Structural Approach to a Literary Genre*, trans. Richard Howard (Ithaca, NY: Cornell University Press, 1975), p. 93.
18. Murphy, *Theorizing the Avant-Garde*, p. 205.
19. Ibid., p. 207.
20. Anthony Vidler, *Warped Space: Art, Architecture, and Anxiety in Modern Culture* (Cambridge, MA: MIT Press, 2000), p. 106.
21. Prawer, S. S., *Caligari's Children: The Film as Tale of Terror* (Oxford: Oxford University Press, 1980), pp. 191–2.
22. Guy Debord's *The Society of the Spectacle*, trans. Donald Nicholson-Smith (New York: Zone Books, 1995) describes the development of postmodern culture in terms of its dependence on visual spectacle.
23. Leon Barsacq, *Caligari's Cabinet and Other Grand Illusions: A History of Film Design*, rev. Elliott Stein (New York: New American Library, 1976), p. 34.
24. Given this element of almost macabre humour in *Waxworks*, it seems most appropriate that director Paul Leni would, as his first effort after coming to America, do the comic mystery *The Cat and the Canary* (1927). Shortly after he would again

explore this curious mixture of tones with the aptly titled horror tale *He Who Laughs* (1928).

25. Eisner, *The Haunted Screen*, p. 122.
26. Klaus Kreimeier, *The Ufa Story: A History of Germany's Greatest Film Company, 1918–1945*, trans. Robert and Rita Kimber (New York: Hill & Wang, 1996), p. 110.
27. Peter Bogdanovich, *Fritz Lang in America* (New York: Praeger, 1967), p. 124.
28. Murphy, *Theorizing the Avant-Garde*, pp. 49, 73.
29. Raymond Bellour, 'On Fritz Lang', in Stephen Jenkins (ed.), *Fritz Lang: The Image and the Look* (London: British Film Institute, 1981), p. 34.
30. Paul Virilio, *The Art of the Motor*, trans. Julie Rose (Minneapolis, MN: University of Minnesota Press, 1995), p. 79.
31. Richard S. Furness, *Expressionism*, p. 20.

RECOMMENDED FILMS

The Cabinet of Dr. Caligari (*Das Kabinett des Doktor Caligari*, Robert Wiene, 1919)
Dr. Mabuse, the Gambler (*Dr. Mabuse, der Spieler – Ein Bild der Zeit*, Fritz Lang, 1922)
The Golem (*Der Golem*, Paul Wegener, 1920)
The Joyless Street (*Die Freudlose Gasse*, G. W. Pabst, 1925)
Metropolis (Fritz Lang, 1926)
Nosferatu (*Nosferatu, eine Symphonie des Grauens*, F. W. Murnau, 1922)
The Student of Prague (*Der Student von Prague*, Henrik Galeen, 1926)
Variety (*Varieté*, E. A. Dupont, 1925)
Warning Shadows (*Schatten – Eine nächtliche Halluzination*, Arthur Robison, 1923)
Waxworks (*Das Wachsfigurenkabinet*, Paul Leni, 1924)

RECOMMENDED READINGS

Budd, Michael (ed.) (1990) *'The Cabinet of Dr. Caligari': Texts, Contexts, Histories.* New Brunswick, NJ: Rutgers University Press.
Coates, Paul (1991) *The Gorgon's Gaze: German Cinema, Expressionism, and the Image of Horror.* Cambridge: Cambridge University Press.
Eisner, Lotte (1973) *The Haunted Screen*, trans. Roger Greaves. Berkeley, CA: University of California Press.
Furness, Richard S. (1973) *Expressionism*. London: Methuen.
Kracauer, Siegfried (1947) *From Caligari to Hitler: A Psychological History of the German Film.* Princeton, NJ: Princeton University Press.
Kreimeier, Klaus (1996) *The Ufa Story: A History of Germany's Greatest Film Company, 1918–1945*, trans. Robert and Rita Kimber. New York: Hill & Wang.
Murphy, Richard (1999) *Theorizing the Avant-Garde: Modernism, Expressionism, and the Problem of Postmodernity.* Cambridge: Cambridge University Press.
Murray, Bruce A. (1990) *Film and the German Left in the Weimar Republic.* Austin, TX: University of Texas Press.
Petro, Patrice (1989) *Joyless Streets: Women and Melodramatic Representation in Weimar Germany.* Princeton, NJ: Princeton University Press.
Scheunemann, Dietrich (ed.) (2003) *Expressionist Film: New Perspectives.* New York: Camden House.

2. ITALIAN NEOREALISM

The postwar renaissance of Italian cinema

Peter Bondanella

Peter Bondanella

From Fascism to neorealism

Until recently, film historians saw an abrupt break between Italian cinema under Fascism (1922–43) and the neorealist brand of cinema that became famous all over the world in the decade immediately following the end of the Second World War. In fact, the Italian neorealist cinema relied upon directors, scriptwriters, directors of photography, actors, set and costume designers, and producers who were all active in the industry during the period of fascist government in Italy. All too many ideological, political and personal interests were served in Italy by pretending that neorealism marked a sharp break with the fascist past. In recent years, the question of the origins of neorealist cinema has become more of an aesthetic and historical issue than a question arousing political passions. As a result, film historians have corrected the view that the development of Italian cinema during the neorealist period was a sharp break with the past, acknowledging the many elements of continuity that connect prewar and postwar Italian cinema. Most importantly, an interest in film realism in both the prewar and postwar Italian cinema provides such continuity.

Unlike Hitler or Stalin, who were his contemporaries, Mussolini did not aim at total control over the content or style of the Italian commercial cinema. For propaganda purposes, Mussolini relied on documentary films and newsreels produced by LUCE, an acronym for L'unione cinematografica educativa. The fascist regime actually viewed Hollywood as its model and saw cinema more as entertainment than as propaganda. Consequently, under Fascism, the industry remained relatively free to pursue filmmaking without encountering overwhelming difficulties with official censorship. Of the over 700 films made during the regime's lifetime, only a handful can be said truly to embody fascist ideology. The fascist regime also carried out a number of projects that would assist the rebirth of Italian cinema in the neorealist period. In 1934, cinema was added to the prestigious arts festival in Venice: the Biennale. The regime founded a major film school, the Centro Sperimentale di Cinematografia in 1935, and shortly thereafter, in 1937, Benito Mussolini inaugurated one of the world's great film complexes, Cinecittà. Both institutions are still in operation and provide some of the backbone of the present industry. Several film journals, such as the official organ of the Centro, *Bianco e nero*, and *Cinema* (edited by Mussolini's son Vittorio) helped to spread information about foreign theories and techniques through translations and reviews. Most of the great directors, actors, technicians and scriptwriters of the neorealist period received their training under Fascism, and some of them, such as Roberto Rossellini (1906–77), made their first important films in the service of Mussolini's government.

Even before the outbreak of the Second World War, Alessandro Blasetti (1900–87), one of the dominant figures of the fascist era, employed non-professional actors, on-location shooting and a realistic style – features later to be identified with neorealism – in his film *1860* (1934). This patriotic, nationalistic movie celebrating Italy's independence in the previous century linked Garibaldi's Redshirts to Mussolini's Blackshirts by connecting the struggle to unify Italy in the nineteenth century with the rise of the fascist regime, whose avowed goal was revitalising Italian political life in the twentieth century. During the partisan struggle against the Fascists and the Nazis (1943–45), Communist partisans from the Communist Party wore red kerchiefs, asserting that this struggle continued Garibaldi's political mission to achieve Italian liberty. Another of Blasetti's films – *The Old Guard* (*Vecchia guardia*, 1935) – employs a documentary style to depict Mussolini's March on Rome to seize power.

The search for a cinema of realism before the outbreak of the Second World War did not end with Blasetti, and a number of directors enjoying the support of Mussolini's regime all worked toward that goal. Many of the characteristics film historians too quickly identify with postwar Italian neorealism – in particular, the use of non-professional actors, a preference for authentic locations as opposed to studio sets, an interest in current events and a documentary-style photography – were actually pioneered in the late fascist period by a number of talented directors. For example, *The Siege of the Alcazar* (*L'assedio dell'Alcazar*, 1940), directed by Augusto Genina (1892–1957), celebrates the defence of the fortress in Toledo during the Spanish Civil War by Franco's fascists. It is an excellent example of what was defined in the late fascist period as a *documentario romanzato* or 'fictional documentary', a combination of historical facts and events with elements of romanticised fiction. In practice, this usually meant adding a love story to adventure stories or tales of military heroism, and this kind of hybrid plot would be typical not only of prewar cinema, but also postwar neorealism. The most significant documentaries shot for the Italian armed forces by Francesco De Robertis (1902–59) – *Men on the Bottom* (*Uomini sul fondo*, 1940) or *Alfa Tau!* (1942) – as well as by De Robertis's young protégé, Roberto Rossellini, were 'fictional documentaries'.

In Rossellini's case, a trilogy he made for the fascist regime shortly before Mussolini's downfall – *The White Ship* (*La nave bianca*, 1941), *A Pilot Returns* (*Un pilota ritorna*, 1942) and *The Man with a Cross* (*L'uomo dalla croce*, 1943) – anticipates the better-known neorealist trilogy that made his fortune: *Open City* (*Roma, città aperta*, 1945), *Paisan* (*Paisà*, 1946) and *Germany Year Zero* (*Germania, anno zero*, 1947). In all six of Rossellini's films both before and after the war, the director employed a realistic style that he had first learned while making government documentaries. His film signature reflects not only the lessons learned from Russian theories of editing (popular at the Centro Sperimentale as well as among the intellectuals who contributed to the journal *Cinema*), but also the use of authentic locations rather than studios, non-profesional actors, grainy photography typical of newsreels and the fictional-ised storylines of the 'fictional documentary' variety.

Thus, even before the postwar appeals by Cesare Zavattini (1902–89) for a revolutionary neorealist cinema shot in the streets of war-torn Italy with minimal scripts, non-professional actors and authentic locations, these very goals were anticipated and praised by an important manifesto written in 1933 by Leo Longanesi, a staunch supporter of Mussolini and the journalist who was said to have invented the motto, 'Mussolini is always right!' Longanesi, like Zavattini, advocated extremely simple and sparse films without artificial sets, with realism as the cinema's ultimate goal. The leftist fascist intellectuals who collaborated with Vittorio Mussolini on the film review *Cinema* and who would later, for the most part, become leftist Marxists after the fall of the regime, all called for an authentically 'Italian' realism and even suggested as a model the literary production of realist writer Giovanni Verga (1840–1922). These 'Young Turks' included future neorealist directors Luchino Visconti (1906–76), Michelangelo Antonioni (1912–) and Giuseppe De Santis (1917–97).

With the fall of Mussolini and the end of the war, international audiences were suddenly introduced to Italian films through a few great works by Rossellini, De Sica and Visconti. With the end of fascist censorship, Italian directors were now free to merge the desire for cinematic realism (a tendency already present in the fascist period) with social, political or economic themes that would never have been tolerated by the regime. Italian neorealist films often took a highly critical view of Italian society and focused attention upon glaring social problems, such as the effects of the Resistance and the war, poverty or chronic unemployment. Like the films made by a number of directors seeking to create a realistic school of Italian cinema before war broke out, these new directors – now dubbed neorealists by critics who praised the 'new' realism they believed such directors sought to create – rejected, in some instances, traditional dramatic and cinematic conventions associated with the commercial cinema in both Rome and Hollywood. Some (though very few) even wanted to abandon literary screen-plays altogether to focus upon improvisation, while most preferred to chronicle the average, undramatic daily events in the lives of common people with the assis-tance of a literate script. But almost all neorealists agreed that the 'happy ending' associated with many Hollywood films was to be avoided at all costs.

Neorealism privileged on-location shooting rather than studio work, as well as the grainy kind of photography associated with documentary newsreels. While it is true that for a while, the film studios were unavailable after the war, neorealist directors shunned them primarily because they wanted to show people what was going on in the streets and piazzas of Italy immediately after the war. Contrary to the legend that explains on-location shooting by its sup-posed lower cost, such filming often cost a great deal more than work in the more easily controlled studios; in the streets it was never possible to predict lighting, weather and the unforeseen occurrence of money-wasting disturbances. Economic factors do, however, explain another characteristic of neorealist cinema – its almost universal practice of dubbing the soundtrack in post-production rather than recording sounds on supposedly 'authentic' locations. That was, indeed, a money-saving technique. Perhaps the most original charac-teristic of the new Italian realism was the brilliant use made of non-professional actors, especially by Rossellini, De Sica and Visconti. Yet many films considered neorealist depend upon excellent performances by seasoned professionals.

Film historians have unfortunately tended to speak of neorealism as if it were an authentic movement with universally agreed-upon stylistic or thematic prin-ciples. The truth is that Italian neorealism cinema represents a hybrid of trad-itional and more experimental techniques. Moreover, political expediency often forced discussions of postwar neorealism to ignore the important elements of continuity between realist films made during the fascist era and the realist films made by neorealists. After 1945, no one in the film industry wanted to be asso-ciated with Mussolini and his discredited dictatorship, and most Italian film critics were Marxists so they could not be expected to deal dispassionately with neorealism's ancestry. While the controlling fiction of the best neorealist works was that they dealt with universal human problems, contemporary stories and believable characters from everyday life, the best neorealist films never com-pletely denied cinematic conventions, nor did they always totally reject Hollywood codes. The basis for the fundamental change in cinematic history marked by Italian neorealism was less an agreement on a single, unified cine-matic style than a common aspiration to view Italy without preconceptions and to employ a more honest, ethical but no less poetic cinematic language in the process.

The most influential critical appraisals of Italian neorealism – those by André Bazin or Roy Armes, for example – constantly emphasise the fact that Italian neorealist cinema rested upon artifice as much as realism and established, in effect, its own particular realist conventions. But generally, all too many critics (especially those with little knowledge of prewar Italian cinema) have focused lazily upon the formulaic statement that Italian neorealism equalled no scripts, no actors, no studios and no happy endings. In a look back at Italian neorealism in 1964 occasioned by a new edition of his first and perhaps best novel, *The Path to the Nest of Spiders* (*Il sentiero dei nidi di ragno*, 1947), Calvino reminds his readers that Italian neorealism was never a school with widely shared theoretical principles. Rather, it arose from a number of closely associated discoveries of an Italy characterised by a popular culture that had traditionally been ignored by 'high' Italian culture. Neorealist film and literature replaced an official cinema or literature characterised by pompous rhetoric and a lack of interest in the quotidian and the commonplace.

NEOREALIST CLASSICS

The masterpieces of Italian neorealism are represented by Roberto Rossellini's *Open City* and *Paisan* – both of which were scripted with Federico Fellini (1920–94); Vittorio De Sica's *Shoeshine* (*Sciuscià*, 1946), *The Bicycle Thief* (*Ladri di biciclette*, 1948) and *Miracle in Milan* (*Miracolo a Milano*, 1951) – all scripted with Zavattini; and Luchino Visconti's *Obsession* (*Ossessione*, 1942) and *The Earth Trembles* (*La terra trema*, 1948) – respectively loose adaptations of James Cain's *The Postman Always Rings Twice* (1934) and Verga's *The House by the Medlar Tree* (1881).

In retrospect, it was clear that something original was brewing within the Italian cinema with the appearance of Visconti's *Obsession*. Assisted by a number of the young Italian intellectuals associated with the review *Cinema*, Visconti took James Cain's 'hard-boiled' novel (without, incidentally, paying for the rights) and turned the crisp, first-person narrative voice of the American writer's work into a more omniscient, objective camera style, as obsessed with highly formal compositions as Visconti's protagonists are by their violent passions. Visconti shows an Italy that includes not only the picturesque and the beautiful but also the tawdry, the ordinary and the insignificant. Simple gestures, glances and the absence of any dramatic action characterise the most famous sequence in the film: world-weary Giovanna (Clara Calamai) enters her squalid kitchen, takes a bowl of pasta and tries to eat it reading the newspaper but falls asleep because of her exhaustion. Postwar critics praised neorealist cinema for respecting the duration of real time in such scenes. Equally original in the film is Visconti's deflation of the 'new' man Italian Fascism promised to produce. Even though the film's protagonist Gino is played by Fascist Italy's matinee idol, Massimo Girotti (1918–2003), his role in the film is resolutely not heroic and even has implicitly homosexual leanings. Even Visconti's patron and friend Vittorio Mussolini rejected such a portrayal of Italian life. Interestingly enough, Benito Mussolini screened the film and did not object to its distribution.

Obsession announced a new era in Italian filmmaking, but at the time very few people saw the film or realised that the aristocratic young director would go on to have such a stellar career. It was the international success of Rossellini's *Open City*, reflecting perfectly the moral and psychological atmosphere of the immediate postwar period, that alerted the world to the advent of Italian neorealism. With a daring combination of styles and moods, Rossellini captured the tension and the tragedy of Italian life under German occupation and the partisan struggle out of which the new Italian republic was subsequently born. *Open City*, however, is far from a programmatic attempt at cinematic realism. Rossellini relied on dramatic actors, not non-professionals. He constructed a number of studio sets (particularly the Gestapo Headquarters where the most dramatic scenes in the film take place) and thus did not slavishly follow the neorealist cry to shoot films in the streets of Rome. Moreover, his plot was a melodrama in which good and evil were so clear-cut that few viewers today can identify it with realism. Even its lighting in key sequences (such as the famous torture scene) follows expressionist or American *film noir* conventions. Rossellini aims to move our emotions rather than our intellects with a melodramatic account of Italian Resistance to Nazi oppression. In particular, the children present at the end of the film to witness the execution of partisan priest Don Pietro (Aldo Fabrizi) point to renewed hope for what Rossellini's protagonists call a new springtime of democracy and freedom in Italy.

Paisan reflects to a far greater extent the conventions of the newsreel documentary, tracing in six separate episodes the allied invasion of Italy and its slow process up through the boot of the peninsula. Far more than *Open City*, *Paisan* seemed to offer an entirely novel approach to film realism. Its grainy film, the awkward acting of its non-professional protagonists, its authoritative voice-over narration and the immediacy of its subject matter – all features we associate with newsreels – do not completely explain the aesthetic quality of the work. Rossellini aims not at a merely realistic documentary of the Allied invasion and Italian suffering. The film develops a philosophical theme, employing a bare minimum of aesthetic resources to follow the encounter of two alien cultures that results in an initial incomprehension, but eventual kinship and brotherhood.

Compared to the daring experimentalism and use of non-professionals in *Paisan*, De Sica's neorealist works seem more traditional and closer to Hollywood narratives. Yet De Sica uses non-professionals – particularly children – in both *Shoeshine* and *The Bicycle Thief* even more brilliantly than Rossellini. In contrast to Rossellini's dramatic editing techniques, which owe something to the lessons he learned from making documentaries and studying the Russian masters during the fascist period, De Sica's camera style favoured the kind of deep-focus photography normally associated with Jean Renoir and Orson Welles. *Shoeshine* offers an ironic commentary on the hopeful ending of *Open City*, for its children (unlike Rossellini's) dramatise the tragedy of youthful innocence corrupted by the world of adults – a theme De Sica continues from one of his best films produced before the end of the war, *The Children Are Watching Us* (*I bambini ci guardano*, 1942). The moving performances De Sica obtains from his non-professional child actors in *Shoeshine* arise from what the director called being 'faithful to the character': he believed that ordinary people could do a better job of portraying ordinary people than actors ever could.

De Sica's faith in non-professional actors was more than justified in his masterpiece, *The Bicycle Thief*, which also employs on-location shooting and the social themes of unemployment and the effects of the war on the postwar economy that so many critics see as the norm in neorealism. The performances of Ricci (Lamberto Maggiorani), the unemployed father who needs a bicycle in order to make a living for his son hanging posters on city walls, and Bruno (Enzo Staiola), his faithful son, rest upon a plot with a mythic structure: a quest. Their search for a stolen bicycle – its brand is ironically *Fides* ('Faith') – suggests that this is not merely a political film denouncing a particular socio-economic system. Social reform may change a world in which the loss of a mere bicycle spells economic disaster, but no amount of social engineering or even revolution will alter the basic facts of life – solitude, loneliness and individual alienation.

De Sica's *Miracle in Milan* abandons any attempt at a pseudo-documentary realism and narrates a fable or fairytale. Even though Zavattini, De Sica's scriptwriter, made the well-known pronouncement about neorealist cinema that 'the true function of the cinema is not to tell fables', that is exactly what he and De Sica did. *Miracle in Milan* is a comic parable about the rich and the poor, a parody of Marxist concepts of class struggle. De Sica and Zavattini show us poor people who are just as selfish, egotistical and uncaring as some wealthy members of society once the poor gain power, money and influence. In this wonderful film, De Sica abandons many of the conventions of neorealist 'realism'. Not only does he rely upon veterans of the serious theatre for his cast, but he also employs many tricks of the trade: superimposed images for magical effects, process shots, reverse action, surrealistic sets, the abandonment of normal notions of chronological time and the rejection of the usual cause-and-effect relationships typical of the 'real' world. At the conclusion of the film, the poor mount their broomsticks and fly off over the Cathedral of Milan in search of a place where justice prevails and common humanity is a way of life. *Miracle in Milan* stretches the notion of what constitutes a neorealist film to the very limits.

Visconti's *The Earth Trembles* is one of the most ambitious of all neorealist works. An adaptation of Verga's 1881 naturalist novel, *The House by the Medlar Tree*, it is coloured by the Marxist theories of Antonio Gramsci. In many ways, this film fits the traditional definition of Italian neorealism better than other equally famous works of the period. No studio sets or sound stages were used, and the cast was selected from the Sicilian fishing village of Aci Trezza, the novel's setting. Visconti even refused to dub the film in standard Italian, preferring the more realistic effects of the Sicilian dialect and synchronised sound. It is thus one of the few neorealist classics that do not employ post-synchronisation of the soundtrack. The film's visuals underline the cyclical, timeless quality of life in Aci Trezza. Visconti's signature slow panning shots with a stationary camera, and his long, static shots of motionless objects and actors, result in a formalism that bestows dignity and beauty on humble, ordinary people.

These masterpieces by Rossellini, De Sica and Visconti are indisputably major works of art that anticipate or capture a new spirit in postwar Italian culture and remain original contributions to film language. But with the exception of *Open City*, they were relatively unpopular within Italy and achieved a critical success primarily among intellectuals and foreign critics. One of the paradoxes of the neorealist era is that the ordinary Italians such films set out to portray were relatively uninterested in their screen self-image. In fact, of the approximately 800 produced between 1945 and 1953 in Italy, only a relatively small number (about 10 per cent) could be classified as neorealist, and most of these works were box-office failures. The Italian public was more interested in Italian films that employed, however obliquely, the cinematic codes of Hollywood or in the vast numbers of films imported from Hollywood itself.

ITALIAN NEOREALISM AND HOLLYWOOD GENRES

A number of less important but very interesting neorealist films were able to achieve greater popular success by incorporating traditional Hollywood genres within their narratives. Luigi Zampa's *To Live in Peace* (*Vivere in pace*, 1946) turns the tragedy of Rossellini's war movies into comedy, prefiguring the many important Italian films in the *commedia all'italiana* tradition of the 1960s that dealt with serious social problems. Alberto Lattuada's *Without Pity* (*Senza pietà*, 1948), scripted in part by Fellini, depicts an interracial love affair between a black American soldier and an Italian prostitute, a theme few Hollywood directors would dare to develop at the time. It also reflects the conventions of the American *film noir* and gangster film. Giuseppe De Santis's *Bitter Rice* (*Riso amaro*, 1948) employs American popular culture in an entirely different way: as a Marxist, he portrays the Italian fads of boogie woogie music, chewing gum and beauty contests as corruptive American capitalist elements threatening a pure proletarian Italian popular culture.

Bitter Rice was the neorealist exception: a box-office hit. It has also been called a neorealist colossus because its shooting involved a large production budget and extensive time on real locations (the rice fields of northern Italy) that were anything but inexpensive. For the first time in a neorealist film, De Santis introduced sex appeal in the form of Silvana Mangano, whose tight sweaters and ample cleavage begin the tradition of the Italian *maggiorata* or 'sweater girl'. Finally, Pietro Germi's *The Path of Hope* (*Il cammino della speranza*, 1950) imitated the Hollywood Westerns of John Ford to chronicle the immigration of Italian miners from impoverished Sicily to new lives in France. Films such as these continued the shift away from the war themes of Rossellini to the interest in postwar reconstruction typical of De Sica's best efforts, but they are even more important as an indication of how Italian cinema moved gradually closer to conventional American themes and film genres. Neorealist style in these films becomes more and more of a hybrid, incorporating elements taken from the commercial cinemas of Hollywood or Rome.

BEYOND NEOREALISM: NEW DIRECTIONS IN THE 1950S

Although Italian intellectuals and social critics preferred the implicitly political and sometimes even revolutionary messages of the neorealist classics, it soon became evident that the public preferred either Hollywood works or Italian films made in the Hollywood spirit. And even the great neorealist directors soon became uncomfortable with the restrictive boundaries imposed upon their subject matter or style by such well-meaning critics. In Italian cinema history, this transitional phase of development is often called the 'crisis' of neorealism. In retrospect, the 1950s witness a natural evolution of Italian film language toward a cinema concerned with psychological problems and a search for a new style no longer defined solely by the use of non-professionals, on-location shooting and a documentary style.

Crucial to this historic transition are a number of early films by Antonioni, Rossellini and Fellini. In *Story of a Love Affair* (*Cronaca di un amore*, 1950), Antonioni's first feature film, the director employs a plot indebted to Cain's novel *The Postman Always Rings Twice* and to American *film noir*. But his distinctive photographic signature is already evident: characteristically long shots, tracks and pans following the actors; modernist editing techniques that attempt to reflect the rhythm of daily life; and philosophical concerns with obvious links to European existentialism.

Fellini's early works continue this evolution from neorealist preoccupation with social problems. In *The Vitelloni* (*I vitelloni*, 1953), Fellini provides a portrait of six provincial characters which another neorealist director might have employed as an indictment of small-town Italian society. But here, as in his later works, Fellini is more interested in creating a private poetic universe of his own than in social criticism. Moreover, the main thrust of his work concerns the clash of illusion and reality in the dreary lives of his flawed characters. This implicit symbolism looms even larger in two masterful films he made in this period that established his international reputation as an auteur: *La Strada* (*La strada*, 1954) and *The Nights of Cabiria* (*Le notti di Cabiria*, 1956). In both pictures, each of which was awarded an Oscar for Best Foreign Film, Fellini moves beyond mere portrayal of provincial life to reveal a new dimension, one motivated by a personal poetic vision and a particular Fellinian mythology concerned with spiritual poverty and the necessity for grace or salvation (defined in a strictly secular sense).

Finally, in a series of films made as vehicles for his mistress Ingrid Bergman, and particularly in *Viaggio in Italia* (*Voyage in Italy*, 1953), Rossellini aims to move beyond what he called the 'cinema of reconstruction' to films that explored psychological problems, employed middle-class protagonists rather than the workers, partisans and peasants of the neorealist classics, and experimented with very different camera styles, avoiding the kinds of pseudo-documentaries that were so popular earlier.

The Heritage of Italian Neorealism

Neorealism's legacy was to be profound. The French New Wave (Jean-Luc Godard, François Truffaut, Jacques Rivette, Eric Rohmer et al.) embraced neorealism as proof that filmmaking could be possible without a huge industrial structure behind it and that filmmakers could be as creative as novelists. In particular, they appreciated the psychological move beyond neorealism in Antonioni and Rossellini. In non-western countries (notably India and Brazil), the classics of neorealism inspired filmmakers to shoot simple stories about ordinary people. Even in the Hollywood of the immediate postwar period, such important works as Jules Dassin's *The Naked City* (1948) and Edward Dmytryk's *Christ in Concrete* (1949) show the direct influence of neorealism's preference for authentic locations within the American tradition of *film noir*.

Most importantly, however, a second generation of Italian directors reacted directly to the model of neorealist cinema. The early films of Pier Paolo Pasolini (1922–75), Bernardo Bertolucci (1941–), Marco Bellocchio (1939–), Paolo (1931–) and Vittorio (1929–) Taviani and Ermanno Olmi (1931–), particularly those shot in black and white, returned in some measure to the conventions of documentary photography, non-professional actors, authentic locations and social themes. But this second generation also combined lessons from their neorealist predecessors with very different ideas taken from the French New Wave, and they were far more committed (except for Olmi) to an aggressively

Marxist world-view. Olmi continued to be true to the neorealist preference for non-professional actors in such important works as *The Sound of Trumpets* (*Il posto*, 1961), *The Fiancées* (*I fidanzati*, 1963) or his best film, *The Tree of the Wooden Clogs* (*L'albero degli zoccoli*, 1978). The neorealist heritage may still be detected, always with a postmodern twist, in the films of Nanni Moretti (1954–) such as *Dear Diary* (*Caro diario*, 1993) or *The Son's Room* (*La stanza del figlio*, 2002). In its quest for narrative simplicity, true-to-life stories, real locations, everyday language in dialogue, important social and political issues in its content as well as its frequent use of non-professional actors, Italian neorealism established a benchmark for authenticity in the cinema that continues to offer an alternative model to lavishly financed productions, studio work, the star system and cinema conceived of as merely entertainment rather than a 'slice of life'. While Italian neorealism always sought to develop stories that reflected the burning social questions of the immediate postwar period, it also maintained extremely high artistic standards. Its greatest practitioners were all authentic auteurs and eventually became identified with the European art cinema of the 1960s after their cinematic styles had transcended their neo-realist origins.

RECOMMENDED FILMS

Bitter Rice (*Riso amaro*, Giuseppe De Santis, 1948)
The Bicycle Thief (*Ladri di biciclette*, Vittorio De Sica, 1948)
The Earth Trembles (*La terra trema*, Luchino Visconti, 1948)
Miracle in Milan (*Miracolo a Milano*, Vittorio De Sica, 1951)
Obsession (*Ossessione*, Luchino Visconti, 1942)
Open City (*Roma, città aperta*, Roberto Rossellini, 1945)
Paisan (*Paisà*, Roberto Rossellini, 1946)
Shoeshine (*Sciuscià*, Vittorio De Sica, 1946)
Umberto D. (*Umberto D.*, Vittorio De Sica, 1952)
Voyage in Italy (*Viaggio in Italia*, Roberto Rossellini, 1953)

RECOMMENDED READINGS

Armes, Roy (1971) *Patterns of Realism: A Study of Italian Neo-Realist Cinema.* London: Tantivy Press.
Bacon, Henry (1998) *Visconti: Explorations of Beauty and Decay.* Cambridge: Cambridge University Press.
Bazin, André (1971) *What is Cinema? Part II*, trans. Hugh Grant. Berkeley, CA: University of California Press.
Bondanella, Peter (1993) *The Films of Roberto Rossellini.* New York: Cambridge University Press.
Bondanella, Peter (2001) *Italian Cinema: From Neorealism to the Present*, 3rd rev. edn. New York: Continuum.
Marcus, Millicent (1986) *Italian Cinema in the Light of Neorealism.* Princeton, NJ: Princeton University Press.
Overbey, David (ed.) (1978) *Springtime in Italy: A Reader in Neorealism.* Hamden, CT: Archon Books.

Re, Lucia (1990) *Calvino and the Age of Neorealism: Fables of Estrangement*. Stanford, CA: Stanford University Press.

Rocchio, Vincent F. (1999) *Cinema of Anxiety: A Psychoanalysis of Italian Neorealism*. Austin, TX: University of Texas Press.

Sitney, P. Adams (1995) *Vital Crises in Italian Cinema: Iconography, Stylistics, Politics*. Austin, TX: University of Texas Press.

3. THE FRENCH NEW WAVE

New stories, styles and auteurs

Richard Neupert

The New Wave was above all an aesthetic adventure and the emergence of new talents . . . But to produce these talented people, adventurous producers were needed with money and a good eye.[1]

Between 1958 and 1964, scores of young film directors managed to write and direct hundreds of films in France. They were quickly labelled the French New Wave. Never before had so many new filmmakers entered the industry without having first worked their way slowly and faithfully up the studio production ranks. Moreover, these young directors were determined to shake up the film world by presenting a stunning array of unconventional stories told in bold new styles. Most of the stories were aimed at a young audience, so they featured very contemporary issues, including sexy themes about seduction and betrayal. These films also helped launch a new generation of stars. New Wave movies were produced quickly with very low budgets that made them look spontaneous, especially in contrast to 'professional' main-stream cinema. Actors, without make-up, wandered along city streets while hand-held cameras captured their movements. The French New Wave changed for ever the whole notion of how movies could be made. But this film movement did not fall announced from the sky. The New Wave was truly a social phenomenon, arising thanks to a wide range of influences and causes. The result is perhaps the richest and most exciting period in world film history.

FILM CRITICISM AND FRANCE'S NEW WAVE SOCIETY

One of the most important mechanisms behind the New Wave's rise was France's post-Second World War cultural context, especially the writings, teaching and mentoring provided by film critic André Bazin. 'André Bazin, the tireless organiser of the cultural terrain, as well as film critic and theorist, was at the very heart of Parisian cinephilia', or intense love of the cinema, writes Antoine de Baecque.[2] Thanks to Bazin, his friends and his colleagues, Paris of the 1950s was like no place on earth: this was where people sought out films from the past, debated their relative values, evaluated their directors and wrote lively articles on films past and present. The New Wave owes more to the study of film history than does any other film movement, and its films reflect a unique fascination, respect and understanding for their place in world cinema. This is also why the New Wave became such an exemplary movement for cinema studies: it valorises a detailed knowledge of film history as well as film technique and storytelling.

André Bazin not only wrote film criticism, he was also in charge of the film division of the Work and Culture bureau, so he organised ciné-clubs and led debates on movies anywhere people would gather. By the early 1950s, the two most vital proving grounds for the passionate investigation of film history and practice were the film journal *Cahiers du Cinéma*, co-edited by Bazin and Jacques Doniol-Valcroze, and the French Cinémathèque, where director Henri Langlois programmed screenings. The many ciné-clubs and art cinemas in Paris, and around France, were virtually an extension of the work by Bazin and Langlois. Film critic and New Wave director François Truffaut liked to quip that André Bazin was his true father, while Henri Langlois's Cinémathèque provided his only formal education.[3] Truffaut's comrade Claude Chabrol also notes that, thanks to Bazin and Langlois, an atmosphere privileging the serious evaluation of film existed in the 1950s: 'We began truly to reflect upon the way the story was constructed, the details of mise-en-scène, the clever dialogue and acting'.[4] While other directors certainly knew many films from the past, this generation prided itself on watching hundreds of movies, good and bad. The ciné-clubs and Cinémathèque ran everything from silent Valentino epics to classics by F. W. Murnau and Howard Hawks genre films. This apprenticeship helped the eventual New Wave filmmakers see movies in a new light, and that experience marked their subsequent experiments in film practice. But many larger cultural factors besides this passionate cinephilia helped generate a New Wave cinema.

Importantly, the label *nouvelle vague* was a trendy journalistic expression already in vogue in 1950s France before it was ever applied to the cinema. The 'New Wave' was initially a phrase applied to the post-Second World War generation in France, identified as somewhat rebellious toward established French institutions. This was a generation with an unusual sense of unity, while it also identified with international culture and even consumerism. They considered themselves closer to James Dean and American jazz than to Jean Gabin and Jean-Paul Sartre. In 1957, *L'Express* magazine even held a national survey to assess the values and concerns of the 'new wave' French population between fifteen and thirty years of age. Thus there was already a sort of fascination with French youth culture and its interests when a stream of new movies with younger, less conventional stars, writers and directors came along. Critics and spectators alike were anxiously waiting to be able to identify a 'new wave in cinema' and pounced eagerly on the first signs of its existence. A sudden increase in the number of films by younger, first-time directors in 1957 and 1958 allowed critics to qualify them as part of this New Wave: 'The label "nouvelle vague" was quickly applied to everything that was considered anti-conformist, such as Pierre Kast's *Le bel âge* (1960) and *On n'enterre pas le dimanche* (*They Don't Bury on Sundays*, 1959) by Michel Drach. But it was François Truffaut, the angry young man, who incarnated this new French cinema in all its ambition, richness, and complexity'.[5]

But how would the audience really know a New Wave movie when they saw one, much less decide that Truffaut's *The 400 Blows* (1959) might be 'more' New Wave than someone else's movie? New Wave films were initially recognised for how their innovative stories, styles and production practices broke the rules of commercial French cinema. Significantly, there was a widely held perception in France during the 1950s that French cinema was losing its vitality. Not only were young critics (and future directors) Truffaut, Chabrol, Eric Rohmer, Jean-Luc Godard and Jacques Rivette churning out impassioned reviews and articles at *Arts* and *Cahiers du Cinéma*, but even the director for the society of French ciné-clubs, Pierre Billard, complained in early 1958 that mainstream films had become sterile and stagnant.[6] Some of the most commercially successful French films were being dismissed as an outdated 'Tradition of Quality' by critics such as Truffaut, whose 1954 article, 'A Certain Tendency of the French Cinema', initiated bitter attacks against the themes and styles of popular French films. By 1958, French cinema was bogged down by dated dramaturgy inherited from theatre, predictable aesthetic choices and story structures, and a closed shop production system built around seniority rather than creativity.[7] The new cinema would have to be created by talented young people not tainted by their association with this 'papa's cinema', so the first films made on the margins of the French industry that seemed to offer new themes and styles were quickly welcomed by anxious critics. This frustration with mainstream cinema and anticipation of a New Wave help explain why Claude Chabrol's *Le beau Serge* (1958) and *The Cousins* (*Les cousins*, 1959), François Truffaut's *The 400 Blows* and Alain Resnais' *Hiroshima, mon amour* (1959) were thrust so suddenly into the spotlight. Truffaut's and Resnais' first features won awards at the 1959 Cannes Film Festival, while a group of young directors, including Godard, announced future projects, generating real hope and excitement for a radical renewal in French cinema.

Already in 1959, Noël Burch noted that a defining New Wave trait was that these directors had not begun as assistant directors and were, on average, just 32 years old. This was already quite surprising. That most of these directors came directly from film criticism or other arts rather than professional film-making schools or studios made them even more unusual.[8] Their relatively young age and lack of a practical background were embraced as advantages rather than drawbacks and appealed to the fans of new French culture. But, the New Wave was more than young directors, it was also a group of young actors, performing with more spontaneous, 'honest' styles in stories written by young people and aimed at young people. Brigitte Bardot became an important pre-cursor, thanks to *And God Created Woman* (1956), directed by her 28-year-old husband, Roger Vadim. Her bold performance was heralded as a revolution in acting. By 1960, scores of actors, including Jeanne Moreau, Jean-Paul Belmondo and Jean-Pierre Léaud, were turning out even more vibrant and casual performances. With the arrival of a cluster of films by Louis Malle, Claude Chabrol, Alain Resnais and François Truffaut, cultural critics could confidently announce that a New Wave cinema had begun by 1959. Importantly, these films brought new faces and perspectives at every level of production. As Michel Marie explains, 'The New Wave brought a new gener-ation of technicians, creative collaborators, camera operators, and writers into a profession that had been very closed and isolated'.[9]

This cluster of highly talented young people entering the industry was just one small symptom of important shifts underway in 1950s French society. Film culture was spurred on by an aesthetically engaged young audience as well as directors. It was an audience with a better education and more disposable income, seeking out its own literature, music and cinema. Antoine de Baecque argues that France's post-Second World War audience is distinguished by its unusual *cinéphilie*, the deep fascination with the cinema, which went beyond movie-going to reading journal articles and interviews with directors rather than short reviews, attending ciné-clubs to debate the merits of various directors, and entering a sort of film cult world of dedicated ciné-worship: 'Cinephilia is a system of cultural practice privileging the rites of seeing, speaking, and writing' about movies.[10] Moreover, he argues that the New Wave, with so many of its filmmakers coming from criticism or at least frequenting ciné-clubs, provided a rich apprenticeship in how to watch films and see them in historical context. For instance, reading Jean-Luc Godard's rave review of Ingmar Bergman's repre-sentation of the title character in *Monika* (1954) was essential background information for 1960s audiences to appreciate fully Patricia (Jean Seberg) in Godard's first feature, *Breathless* (*A bout de souffle*, 1960).[11] Knowing Seberg's amazing role in *Bonjour Tristesse* (Otto Preminger, 1958), as well as Godard's earlier short films and his film criticism, also added to the audience's interpretation of Patricia. Thanks to the general cinephilia of the times, audiences looked at movies quite differently in 1960. Viewers were thus much more open to challenging films such as Alain Resnais' *Hiroshima mon amour* and *Last Year at Marienbad* (*L'année dernière à Marienbad*, 1960). For de Baecque, the New Wave is inseparable from that rare cultural atmosphere in France, which was quickly spreading abroad, where movies like *Breathless* and *Hiroshima mon amour* found huge audiences in New York, London, Berlin and elsewhere.

Further fueling the New Wave were new government financial aid rules, with the Minister of Culture, André Malraux, encouraging experimentation by writers, directors and producers. Alternative filmmaking practices were also made possible by new technologies, including lightweight, less expensive cameras and new portable magnetic tape recorders that revolutionised the conditions of production. Most of these new directors shot quickly and cheaply with unusually small crews. While they could not afford colour film or long rehearsal times, their stories nonetheless appeared very contemporary because they used the same portable, hand-held cameras as television documentary crews of the day. It has been argued that the New Wave was the first film movement to have stylised life in the present tense, offering glimpses of contemporary fashions and behaviours to its own participants in their own movies filled with their gestures, words and lifestyles.[12] Thus the New Wave was made possible by an audience, a social setting, a critical renaissance, government institutions and new production options that all motivated a new generation of film technicians, artists and even producers to forge an alternative cinema. The first successful directors to manipulate and excel in these conditions during 1957 and 1958 included Louis Malle (*L'ascenseur pour l'échaufaud* (*Lift to the Scaffold; Elevator to the Gallows*), 1957; *The Lovers* (*Les amants*), 1958), Chabrol (*Le beau Serge, The Cousins*), Alain Resnais (*Hiroshima, mon amour*), Marcel Camus (*Black Orpheus* (*L'Orphée noir*), 1959) and Truffaut (*The 400 Blows*), but they were hardly alone.

THE *CAHIERS* DIRECTORS

Among this initial group, Chabrol and Truffaut, followed closely by Godard with *Breathless*, became the core of the so-called *Cahiers* directors, which would soon include Pierre Kast (*Le bel âge*, 1958), Jacques Doniol-Valcroze (*L'eau à la bouche* (*A Game for Six Lovers*), 1959), Jacques Rivette (*Paris nous appartient* (*Paris Is Ours*), 1961) and Eric Rohmer (*Le signe de lion* (*The Sign of Leo*), 1962). This was a group of young men strongly formed by their roles as colleagues writing for *Cahiers du Cinéma*. Known as the 'Young Turks' for their youthful audacity, they were bold critics adhering for the most part to a strong belief in auteur criticism, the notion that directors were the creative equivalents of novelists and should be evaluated for how their own morality and mise-en-scène shape their films. Since *Cahiers du Cinéma*, and much of film criticism by the early 1960s, celebrated distinctive auteurs, the New Wave fit right in with the critical perspective of the moment. Significantly, these young critics-turned-directors were unabashedly determined to become distinctive auteurs in their own right. In interviews, the young *Cahiers* filmmakers discussed other directors and film history, but rarely granted much credit to their crews, producers or actors. Their allegiance was initially to each other as they strove to dominate the film festivals, magazine covers and Parisian screens. For many international critics, these several young men 'were' the New Wave, and they certainly took full advantage of the attention.

Chabrol and Truffaut were celebrated as important New Wave figures in part because they followed Louis Malle's lead and formed their own production companies to make low-budget feature films. Both men offered new models for combining financial independence with personal filmmaking, and both were fortunate enough to gain initial funding thanks to their young wives. Chabrol's wife Agnès inherited enough money to allow him to establish his company, AJYM, and produce first *Le beau Serge*, and immediately afterward, *The Cousins*, as well as movies by several of his friends. Chabrol's first pictures featured the talented young actors Jean-Claude Brialy and Gérard Blain, both of whom had already acted in short films by Godard and Truffaut. Chabrol's stories were set in contemporary France, with *beau Serge* shot on location in the countryside using a reduced crew and local people whenever possible as extras and minor characters. *The Cousins* was filmed in Paris, much of it in the streets and even sports cars of 1958 France. Many aspects of Chabrol's first two features were taken from his life: like Brialy's character in *Le beau Serge*, Chabrol had once been sent to the country to recuperate from an illness and, like Blain's character, the Chabrols had lost a first child.

Truffaut married Madeleine Morgenstern, the daughter of a film distributor, which helped him launch his short *Les mistons* (*The Kids/The Brats*, 1957) and then *The 400 Blows*. The latter film evocatively presented the elegant yet simple tale of a young boy, Antoine Doinel (Jean-Pierre Léaud), growing up in an unhappy family in Paris. This tale too was highly autobiographical, and included many details from Truffaut's own childhood, with Antoine's sidekick René (Patrick Auffray) as a virtual stand-in for Truffaut's real-life buddy Robert Lachenay. Truffaut even cast some parts with actors who resembled the people of his own life, and many, including Truffaut's parents, saw the movie as a direct and even pathetic attack on his family. It too was shot on location in Parisian neighbourhoods Truffaut knew well. Much like Malle just before them, Chabrol and Truffaut's first features were very successful with critics, at film festivals and at the box office.

The sudden success of such films was a shock to established French produc-ers, many of whom quickly became believers in the positive power of the concept of the young auteur: 'It assumed, in effect, a totality of creation, from the script through to the final cut'.[13] New Wave auteurism also allowed a new marketing angle, as interviews with the passionate, young writer-directors became a key part of the publicity campaigns. Statements by Truffaut, Chabrol and Godard in particular made constant reference to film history and their own informed mise-en-scène choices, emphasising that their unusual use of direct sound, discontinuity editing or hand-held cameras to follow their characters through the streets were not mistakes or acts of desperation, but rather vibrant syntheses of lessons from film history – lessons learned in the Cinémathèque rather than on the sets of commercial French pictures. They, and their New Wave films, were clearly the results of France's own, radical cinephilia. Unfortunately, Bazin died in 1958 during the first days of Truffaut's production and never saw the amazing results of his Young Turks' films, but Truffaut dedicated *The 400 Blows* to Bazin. Every film of the era owed to his influence.

Michel Marie explains that the New Wave cinema became equivalent to an artistic school. His list of New Wave traits is very functional. Exemplary films had an auteur-director responsible for reworking the scenario, retaining control through the final cut. Small budgets safeguarded creative freedom and allowed for a more personal cinema, with producers only helping with financing, dis-tribution contracts and publicity. Along with the use of location shooting, small crews, freer acting styles and flexible production conditions, many of the con-ventional cinematic constraints automatically fell by the wayside, 'erasing the borders between professional and amateur cinema and those between fiction films and documentary'.[14] For most film critics in the early 1960s, and for Marie, Truffaut was the New Wave's central figure, thanks both to his key role in 1950s film criticism and the immense success of his first feature. *Cahiers du Cinéma* remained the New Wave's house publication, spelling out its critical ideals and continuing to print reviews by and about its own critic-filmmakers.

INDIVIDUAL STYLISTS AND THE LEFT BANK GROUP

Beyond the *Cahiers du Cinéma* directors, however, scores of young French directors were also exploring these new cinematic options. One in particular, Jacques Rozier, was celebrated by the *Cahiers* directors as a perfect example of the production and aesthetic practices of the new French cinema. Rozier's *Adieu Philippine* was featured on the cover of the famous special issue of *Cahiers du Cinéma* dedicated to the *nouvelle vague*. It is also considered one of the purest examples of New Wave style by Marie, who labels it 'a naturalist masterpiece' for its loose script, casual visual style, modern themes and fresh acting style that add up to deliver a 'spontaneity of everyday experience'.[15] Produced by

Georges de Beauregard, who also funded Godard's *Breathless*, Demy's *Lola* and Varda's *Cléo from 5 to 7*, among many others, *Adieu Philippine* captures every trait identified with the freewheeling New Wave aesthetic.

The story is very loosely organised and rather simple: two young women meet a brash young television employee who has just been called up for military service in Algeria. Both women fall for him, and they decide to accompany him across France on his leisurely trip to meet his ship. Working under the improvisational influence of both Jean Renoir and ethnographer Jean Rouch, Rozier shot his film with direct sound, but unfortunately the volume was too uneven, so later the actors had to re-dub their own voices. It was a movie truly 'written' with camera and microphone; a rigorous shooting script never existed, and the loose style fits the aimlessness and loose morality of the characters. *Adieu Philippine* was championed by Godard ('The best French film in recent years'), Alain Resnais ('A masterpiece worthy of Jean Vigo') and others at *Cahiers*. Several years later, film theorist Christian Metz selected it as a test case for semiotic analysis since it offered a catalogue of editing devices to help illustrate his 'Grand Syntagmatic' for film studies. Metz wanted to prove that rigorous analysis of shot-to-shot and scene-to-scene transitions within individual films was necessary to understand how films generated meaning, or signified. *Adieu Philippine*'s unconventional structure thus strengthened the connections between New Wave filmmaking practices and new methods in film criticism.[16] Rozier continued to make short films, but, like his protagonist, he went into television, and has been rather minimised by auteurist historians since he made only the one feature film during the New Wave era. But Rozier, along with other individual stylists of the New Wave such as Michel Drach, Marcel Hanoun, Philippe de Broca and Jean-Pierre Mocky, helps prove the vast and rich array of talent that distinguishes the French New Wave from other eras in cinema.

Another significant facet of the New Wave involves Alain Resnais, Chris Marker, Agnès Varda, novelist Alain Robbe-Grillet and Jacques Demy, who have often been placed in their own subset known as the Left Bank Group. These were directors who shared some personal and cinematic traits that often seemed to distinguish them a bit from the *Cahiers* critics-turned-directors. These directors operated with more connections to other art references, including photography and the new novel, and they systematically explored film form as well as the boundaries between documentary and narrative. Their relation to the New Wave varies from historian to historian, in part because it could be argued that these devoted filmmakers would have managed to make feature films without the presence of the *Cahiers* directors or the furore over a New Wave. In some respects this is true. Resnais, Varda and Demy had already managed to shoot short documentaries and narratives during the 1950s. Agnès Varda formed her own tiny company, Ciné-Tamaris (which still functions today), to create *La Pointe Courte* (1954–55). Yet she did not make her first widely distributed feature, *Cléo from 5 to 7*, until 1962, at the height of the New Wave. While Varda does not like being considered a 'precursor' to the New Wave, she admits that it was thanks to the successes of Truffaut, Chabrol, Godard and others that she could interest Georges de Beauregard in helping produce *Cléo from 5 to 7*.[17] That Varda, as well as Resnais, Demy and Robbe-Grillet, each managed to write and direct some of their greatest and most experimental features during this short period of time is proof in the value of including them within the New Wave. Their films, as much as those by Chabrol, Truffaut or Godard, challenged the existing production norms and presented challenging new characters, themes and techniques. Moreover, they all participated in the same cinephilia as the *Cahiers* directors, even if they did not write film criticism.

In fact, Alain Resnais and Chris Marker had been part of post-Second World War film culture from the start. They first met Bazin during the late 1940s and helped organise ciné-clubs. Later, Resnais, who had become a friend of the *Cahiers* team, introduced Agnès Varda to the young critics. Thus, by the mid-1950s, most of the figures for the 'young French cinema' and future New Wave were already actively involved in French film culture and were sharing ideas, debating preferred directors and eventually showing one another how to operate cameras and editing machines. It was Resnais, with his experience on documentaries, who helped Chabrol, Truffaut and Varda, among others, learn some of the more practical aspects of filmmaking. When Varda's *La pointe courte* was shown without a commercial distributor, Bazin was at the screening and labelled her a new, young auteur, which gave her film – and Resnais' editing work on it – new attention from the other future directors. The New Wave is unified in part by the shared influences and effects these writer-directors had on one another, and the eventual Left Bank Group is just as central to the New Wave's traits and existence as any other participants.

The New Wave and Its Legacy

Significantly, the eventual surge of films came to dominate the New Wave social phenomenon so that rather than the phrase referring to a generation or collective mentality, by the 1960s 'New Wave' meant movies. While these films were born during the era of auteur criticism, they progressed along with changes in narrative theory. The context and influence of André Bazin was followed by new French cultural theories. Gradually, theoretical arguments on myth and structuralism by Claude Lévi-Strauss and Roland Barthes became just as influential for the New Wave as Bazin and the new novel had been in the 1950s. Films by Resnais, Godard, Varda and Rivette in particular were beginning to require that critics become versed in new methodologies, including cultural signs and ideological theories. The New Wave challenged critical models as well as film vocabulary, at the very moment when universities around the world were beginning to offer film courses. Thus New Wave films worked hand in hand with other traditions of modern European cinema to jump-start the academic acceptance of film studies.

In the end, these brash young filmmakers managed to renew every level of the cinema, from modes of production to narrative innovations to film theory and criticism. If the movement *per se* can be said to end around 1964, it is because market conditions made it tougher for so many new directors to get their films distributed, while many of the initial directors were now permanent fixtures of French cinema and could hardly be considered 'new' anymore. Beyond France, however, this youthful rebellion continued to inspire new generations to explore the possibilities of entering the cinema in their own lands. A final legacy has been the continued importance in France of 'first-time directors', who continue to receive special financial arrangements from the government and generate at least 25 per cent of all French films produced each year.[18] The world's cinema, as well as film studies itself, continues to owe a great debt to 1950s French cinephilia and the New Wave it inspired.

NOTES

1. Marc Ruscart, 'Les productions de la nouvelle vague: une aventure esthétique', *La Nouvelle vague et après* (Paris: Quimper and Cahiers du Cinéma, March, 1986), p. 34.
2. Antoine de Baecque, *La Cinéphilie: invention d'un regard, histoire d'une culture 1944–1968* (Paris: Fayard, 2003), p. 36.
3. From an interview in *Arts* (20 March 1968) reprinted in François Truffaut, *Truffaut by Truffaut*, ed. Dominque Raboudin (New York: Harry N. Abrams, 1987), p. 33.
4. Wilfrid Alexandre, *Claude Chabrol: La traversée des apparences: biographie* (Paris: Félin, 2003), p. 71.
5. Gérard Camy, 'Les Années rupture (1960–1979)', in Claude Beylie (ed.), *Une histoire du cinéma français* (Paris: Larousse, 2000), p. 101.
6. Pierre Billard, '40 moins de 40', *Cinéma 58* (February 1958), p. 5.
7. Claire Clouzot, *Le Cinéma français depuis la nouvelle vague* (Paris: Nathan, 1972), p. 3.
8. Noel Burch, 'Qu'est-ce que la Nouvelle Vague?' *Film Quarterly*, 13, 2 (Winter 1959), pp. 16–17.
9. Michel Marie, *The French New Wave: An Artistic School*, trans. Richard Neupert (Malden, MA: Blackwell, 2002), p. 71.
10. de Baecque, *La cinéphilie*, p. 4.
11. de Baecque, *La cinéphilie*, pp. 28, 31.
12. Antoine de Baecque, *La Nouvelle vague: Portrait d'une jeunesse* (Paris: Flammarion, 1998), pp. 15–6.
13. Camy, 'Les Années rupture (1960–1979)', p. 101.
14. Marie, *The French New Wave*, pp. 71–2.
15. Ibid., pp. 97, 120.
16. Christian Metz, *A Semiotics of Film Language*, trans. Michael Taylor (New York: Oxford University Press, 1974), pp. 177–82.
17. Personal conversation with Agnès Varda, October 2002, Madison, Wisconsin.
18. René Prédal, *Le jeune cinéma français* (Paris: Nathan, 2002), p. 1.

RECOMMENDED FILMS

Adieu Philippine (Jacques Rozier, 1963)
Le beau Serge (Claude Chabrol, 1959)
Breathless (*À bout de souffle*, Jean-Luc Godard, 1960)
Cléo from 5 to 7 (*Cléo de 5 à 7*, Agnès Varda, 1962)
The Cousins (*Les cousins*, Claude Chabrol, 1959)
Hiroshima mon amour (Alain Resnais, 1959)
Jules and Jim (*Jules et Jim*, François Truffaut, 1962)
Lola (Jacques Demy, 1961)
Shoot the Piano Player (*Tirez sur le pianiste*, François Truffaut, 1960)
Vivre sa vie (Jean-Luc Godard, 1962)

RECOMMENDED READINGS

Andrew, Dudley (1990) *André Bazin*. New York: Columbia University Press.
de Baecque, Antoine (2003) *La cinéphilie: Invention d'un regard, histoire d'une culture 1944–1968*. Paris: Fayard.
de Baecque, A. (1998) *La nouvelle vague: Portrait d'une jeunesse*. Paris: Flammarion.
Douchet, Jean (1999) *The French New Wave*, trans. Robert Bonnono. New York: Distributed Art Publishers.
Hayward, Susan (1993) *French National Cinema*. London: Routledge.
Lanzoni, Rémi Fournier (2002) *French Cinema: From Its Beginnings to the Present*. New York: Continuum.
Marie, Michel (2003) *The French New Wave: An Artistic School*, trans. Richard Neupert. Malden, MA: Blackwell.
Monaco, James (1976) *The New Wave*. New York: Oxford University Press.
Neupert, Richard (2003) *A History of the French New Wave*. Madison, WI: University of Wisconsin Press.
Williams, Alan (1992) *Republic of Images: A History of French Filmmaking*. Cambridge, MA: Harvard University Press.

4. THE BRITISH NEW WAVE

A modernist cinema

R. Barton Palmer

An Era of New Waves

The end of the 1950s witnessed the advent in Europe (and soon afterward in Latin America) of a succession of what came to be known within global film culture as 'new waves' (sometimes 'new cinemas'). These eruptions of powerfully innovative production, characterised by the emergence to prominence of youthful directors/writers, would endure into the 1970s, even longer, arguably, in some cases. Such movements were to leave indelible impressions on filmmaking of all kinds in the post-studio period, which became in some sense an era of new waves as older forms of textuality were radically transformed along with the institutions that had sustained them. The new waves occasionally assumed the more definitive and self-conscious shape of artistic movements properly speaking, with those involved issuing manifestos as they developed a sense of group identity and practice. Sometimes, however, they were less organised and coherent responses to changing conditions within the industry, film culture and the wider society – to be characterised as a group practice only by critics or journalists.

The new waves provided an alternative to the pre-eminence of the largely Taylorised American product, the so-called 'classical Hollywood film', whose dependence on compelling narrative, glamorous stars and popular genres was widely influential, if seldom closely or effectively imitated.[1] The new waves soon became an important (perhaps the most important) part of the international art cinema, which by 1965 had established itself as a powerful form of counter-Hollywood filmmaking.[2] The art cinema was strongly marked by modernist approaches to the medium that had little use for star glamour and repetitious genres. Modernist films tend to emphasise complex characters and intellectual themes, often in an episodic or loosely structured fashion. They do not depend upon the excitement generated by the plot-centred forms of narrative that Hollywood customarily offered.[3] The new waves redefined and renewed the national cinemas involved, providing them with a flow of financially successful and critically acclaimed productions that reflected native culture, utilised home-grown talent and frequently garnered favourable international notice, especially after successful distribution in the United States, where the international art cinema had been an important presence in exhibition since the early 1950s.

Unquestionably the most important of these movements, the French *nouvelle vague*, examined in detail in by Richard Neupert in Chapter 3 of this volume, flourished during the years 1959–63. Because of its subsequent influence on filmmaking around the world, the French New Wave constituted, in the words of film historian Michel Marie, 'one of the most famous cinematic moments in film history,' and this judgement has rarely been contested.[4] Here it is necessary to treat certain aspects of French New Wave filmmaking that are important for an understanding of the British new wave, a movement across the Channel that, as its customary name suggests, is often likened to this continental tradition and with which it shares much in common, most especially a critical engagement with realism.

The French New Wave was ushered in by the sudden pre-eminence of a relentlessly youth-oriented culture opposed to the values and tastes of the previous generation, which became ridiculed as old-fashioned or irrelevant. During a time of rapid cultural change, the French New Wave films quickly achieved popularity in spite of their minimal (from a Hollywood perspective) production values and often their deliberately home-made look. The customary hierarchy of values was stood on its head. What had been high (the tradition of literary excellence, technical 'expertise' and self-conscious seriousness epitomised by the popular and critically acclaimed commercial filmmaking of Jean Delannoy, René Clement and Yves Allégret) was now thought low, and vice versa. In the critical bombardment that preceded the New Wave assault on French commercial practice, such establishment directors found their work treated with disrespect. Most influential was the broadside fired by critic (later director) François Truffaut, who indicted his honoured elders for practising a pseudo-art of adaptation that depended too heavily on the cultural value of literary masterpieces.[5] The *Cahiers du Cinéma*, which published Truffaut's sally, eventually became the unofficial house organ of the *nouvelle vague* directors, providing a public forum in which their tastes in film and theories of the medium might find expression.

Dominated by directors like Truffaut and his circle (see Neupert, Chapter 3),[6] the French New Wave filmmakers were cinephiles in their twenties who desired to put something of their youth, energy and love for the medium into their films. *The 400 Blows (Les 400 coups)*, Truffaut's low-budget essay at autobiography, opened in the late spring of 1959 and soon achieved an amazing critical and popular success, not only winning its director the prize that year at Cannes but making more than triple its production costs in a matter of months. Early the next year, Godard, who (like Truffaut) had devoted much time to studying and writing about the cinema, enjoyed a comparable triumph with his first feature, *Breathless (A bout de souffle)*. With its insistent questioning of the rules of cinematic practice and its exploitation of a 'B' crime movie plot of crime and punishment, Godard's film offered a very different kind of viewing experience. These two releases thus established the stylistic and thematic extremes of the movement.[7]

They also, however, shared several important qualities in common. Both were heavily invested in a realism modelled obviously on the Italian neorealist films of the late 1940s and early 1950s for which New Wave directors, when writing criticism, expressed great admiration. This characteristically New Wave stylisation was achieved by, among other devices, relying on location shooting; 'natural', less prepared mise-en-scène; looser, even improvised forms of 'script'; and, often, amateur actors. Both films (and the directorial bodies of work they epitomise) also correspond to what theorist David Bordwell has identified as the principles of 'art-cinema narration', including 'a more tenuous linking of events', the building up of scenes around chance encounters and the abandonment of plot schemata or deadlines. In Bordwell's view, such departures from classical Hollywood practice find their source in the desire of the art cinema to 'exhibit character'.[8] And, to be sure, few characters in the history of the medium have proven more memorable than Truffaut's engaging youthful truant, Antoine Doinel (Jean-Pierre Léaud) and Godard's outlaw couple, Michel Poiccard (Jean-Paul Belmondo) and Patricia Franchini (Jean Seberg), whose love affair – if that is the proper term to describe their relationship – sizzles with sensuality even as it eludes full understanding and conventional closure.

A BRITISH NEW WAVE?

While Truffaut and Godard, along with others of their circle, were writing criticism for *Cahiers* but before they had broken into filmmaking themselves, a cinematic movement was taking shape in Britain, where, as in France, it was part of a larger cultural shift. There was, however, a crucial difference between the developments in the two film industries. The *nouvelle vague* certainly had its connections to literary innovations (particularly the emergence to prominence of the *nouveau roman* or 'new novel' form pioneered by Alain Robbe-Grillet, who would eventually experiment with filmmaking as well). In contrast, however, developments in the British industry had from the beginning much more substantial literary roots, broadly speaking. What came to be known as the British new wave can, in fact, be best understood, if only in part, as an extension of the changes in subject matter, style and theme that had first taken place during the 1950s in poetry, novels and on the commercial stage, which was then experiencing an amazing burst of creative energy similar to the revitalisation that transformed Broadway in the immediate postwar era. Only some *nouvelle vague* productions (particularly several later films by Truffaut) were literary adaptations, whereas *all* the principal productions of the British new wave were.

Because the change of direction in the British cinema was not defined by the emergence, in the manner of the *nouvelle vague*, of a coterie of critics turned director/writers who were able to make low-budget films on the margins of the commercial national cinema, some film historians have questioned the appropriateness of the label 'new wave' to describe this series. Peter Wollen typifies this position when he suggests that, contrary to French practice, the British series of films is not particularly marked by the leadership of a group of prominent auteurs or by a primacy of place accorded to purely cinematic rather than literary influences. Most tellingly perhaps, Wollen indicts the British directors and their films for their 'aesthetic preference' for realism over entertainment, while he praises Truffaut and company for holding to a third position that transcends 'this shallow antinomy': modernism.[9] Wollen is correct in that what he refers to as the 'young English cinema' is more literary than its French counterpart, and that the former is not a cinema of auteurs if by this term we mean, somewhat narrowly, director/writers. But the facts do not fit his view that these British films engage strictly with realism in a parochial and local sense rather than with the more general European modernism of the art cinema, which was profoundly affected by the Italian neorealist movement. We may grant that the various new waves differ from one another in substantial ways. We could hardly expect divergent national cultural, political and artistic traditions to exert no influence on cinematic developments. But if we understand the term 'new wave' to mean an emergent, youth-oriented national movement of the period that became a part of the international art cinema, then the 1950s and 1960s witnessed what is properly called a British new wave. And this was a movement that, contra Wollen, had its cinematic, as well as its literary, roots.

REALISM, TINSEL AND FREE CINEMA

The development of a 'young cinema' in Britain that affiliated itself with the international art film was surprising, to say the least. By the middle 1950s, the

British film industry had experienced three decades of continual crisis, relieved only intermittently by the fixing of quotas (1937), the imposition of high duties on competing films imported from Hollywood (1947) and the establishment (1949) of a government-funding agency (the National Film Finance Corporation) whose role was to provide 'end money' for native productions. However encouraged by favouring legislation, British filmmakers had achieved little sustained success either in the domestic market, where American movies were more sought after by exhibitors, or abroad, where the British product found it difficult to compete for screen time. Hollywood lured away home-grown talent, including Alfred Hitchcock and a huge gallery of star performers, writers and other craftsmen, while the major studios, all located in or around London and tied closely to the West End theatre, seemed able to conceive only dramas that reflected middle-class, southern values and sensibilities, often without much appeal for a broader national audience. Entertainment films, or 'tinsel' (to use a common expression of the time), were for the most part Hollywood productions, and many of the country's more sophisticated viewers disparaged the thematic insubstantiality and escapist rhetoric of the films that came from across the Atlantic.

Within British cinema culture, the valued 'other' of American tinsel was realism, a practice defined to some extent by its refusal of Hollywood fantasy (in its various forms) and even of fictionality itself. As it developed as a group movement during the 1930s, supported by government and private industry and under the leadership of a talented filmmaker and theorist John Grierson, British documentary filmmaking assumed a definite politics by the advent of the Second World War: left-wing, reformist (sometimes patronisingly), admiring of the 'authentic lives' led by the working class – such as fishermen (*North Sea*, 1938) and factory workers (*Industrial Britain*, 1933). During the Second World War, documentary techniques were utilised in making fiction films (such as the justly celebrated *Target for Tonight*, 1941) that supported the struggle against Germany and Japan, heroicising the 'ordinary' men and women who risked their lives for king and country.

Pseudo-documentary fictional films that eschewed the escapist glamour of Hollywood tinsel remained an important and profitable area of British production during the 1950s, with significant releases such as *The Cruel Sea* (1953) and *The Colditz Story* (1955) enjoying a certain international as well as domestic popularity. Such filmmaking was in large measure the legacy of Grierson and the other documentarians of the 1930s, and it constituted a tradition of quality that promoted national identity (albeit of a somewhat restricted sort) and thematic seriousness, with its enshrinement of the democratic resistance to totalitarianism. Earning equal acclaim was a related series, the social problem films that dealt with issues ranging from juvenile delinquency (*The Young and the Guilty*, 1958) to racism (*Sapphire*, 1959), prostitution (*Passport to*

Shame, 1958) and even homosexuality (*Victim*, 1961). Most of these realist fiction films were notable for their divergence, at least in significance part, from the international pattern for cinematic entertainment set by Hollywood, even though the American cinema of the period featured a similar genre. The appeal of the British social problem films of the 1950s depended more on an engagement (if sometimes rather superficial) with political and cultural concerns rather than on star appeal and conventions such as screen romance. Like the comparable Hollywood product, however, the British social realist films of the 1950s emphasised compelling narrative and socially conservative conclusions more than complex characters. Productions were usually built around established performers and did not feature self-conscious stylisation. These films were middle-class in their point of view, treating working-class characters and culture with either restrained distaste or affable condescension according to the 'moral' demands of the narrative.

British film culture of the time, however, saw the emergence of another form of realism that found its source in an offshoot of the Griersonian tradition, the poetic realism of Humphrey Jennings, a documentarian who, in the 1940s, offered consciously stylised and aestheticised versions of the everyday. Jennings had worked as a painter and poet and felt more fondness for surrealism than for the reformist politics that had animated Grierson's work.[10] In the late 1940s, a group of cinephiles at Oxford transformed the Film Society magazine into a platform from which they pled for an increased awareness of the cinema as an art form. Though generally hostile to British filmmaking, the talented editorial group at *Sequence* – notably Gavin Lambert, Lindsay Anderson and Karel Reisz – were *amateurs*, not only of the international art cinema and noted Hollywood productions, but also of Jennings's films, which they saw as exemplifying a 'poetic realism' that gave equal emphasis to the 'real' and the sensibility of the director who imposed his vision and hence style upon it. *Sequence* promised to provide, as did the *Cahiers du Cinéma* in France, an influential forum for a less traditionally-minded film culture (as opposed to the more mainstream *Sight and Sound*), but it ended publication in 1952 after only fourteen issues. Like Truffaut, Godard and others in France, however, Anderson and Reisz were eager to move into filmmaking, so that a national cinema they regarded as misdirected in its allegiance to establishment values and ignorant of the realities of a post-imperial Britain might be revitalised by a turn toward the 'poetry of everyday life'. They named the movement they founded 'Free Cinema', and it followed a call to arms penned by Anderson (published in 1956 in *Sight and Sound*, it bore the strident title 'Stand Up! Stand Up!').[11]

For three years (1956–59) Anderson, Reisz and others sponsored a series of six programmes at London's National Film Theatre. While some of the films exhibited were foreign (e.g. Roman Polanski's *Dwaj ludzie z szafa* (*Two Men and a Wardrobe*), 1958 and Truffaut's *Les mistons* (*The Brats*), 1957), the bulk of the features were documentaries made in the Jennings style that celebrated, in the appropriately poetic style, the working lives and recreations of the lower class. In *Momma Don't Allow* (1955), for example, Reisz (assisted by Tony Richardson) took his camera inside the Wood Green Jazz Club which catered to a youthful trade, while in *Every Day Except Christmas* (1957) Anderson paid cinematic homage to the workers at Covent Garden's fruit, vegetable and flower market. Perhaps the most interesting aspect of these films was their visual style. Taking advantage of newly available lightweight equipment, these Free Cinema productions offered a stylised, energetic realism reminiscent of the later neorealist films and of *nouvelle vague* productions such as *The 400 Blows*. This unglamourised, carefully 'unprepared' style would become a prominent feature of the new wave fictional films, especially those shot by the masterful director of photography Walter Lassally (often assisted by camera operator Desmond Davis).

Some of the prominent new wave directors, it might be pointed out, were not formally a part of the Free Cinema movement. But all were experienced in realist and documentary filmmaking. John Schlesinger (*A Kind of Loving*, 1962; *Billy Liar*, 1963; *Darling*, 1965) did early work in television and directed a number of short topical and arts features; he directed the British Academy Award winner *Terminus* (1961) for the prestigious British Transport Films series. Jack Clayton (*Room at the Top*, 1959; *The Pumpkin Eater*, 1964) served with the RAF film unit during the Second World War, directing several documentaries. Sidney J. Furie (*The Leather Boys*, 1964) got his start in Canadian television. Bryan Forbes (*The L-Shaped Room*, 1962) broke into directing with two social realist films, *The Angry Silence* (1960) and *The League of Gentlemen* (1959). All these directors saw themselves as realist filmmakers broadly speaking, constituting the latest development in that national tradition Samantha Lay has termed 'British social realism'; what they had in common was their 'fascination with the details and minute rituals of everyday life, the interest in ordinary people and their dialects, and their use of location shooting'.[12] Lay, however, offers an unbalanced account of the new wave. She does not discuss how these directors also shared an interest in literary adaptation.

ANGRY YOUNG MEN – AND WOMEN

In regard to the British new wave, changes in the literary environment of the era are equally significant, but they are more complex and difficult to summarise than purely cinematic ones.[13] As the 1950s began, the anti-modernism of writer/critics Angus Wilson, J. B. Priestley, C. P. Snow and others expressed itself in a preference for social relevance and provincialism (as opposed to the metropolitanism of Woolf and Joyce), and this new literary fashion for direct expression and entertaining writing in the realist tradition was given national exposure with the founding of a new literary series, *First Reading*, on the BBC Third Programme under the leadership of novelist John Wain. This series conferred substantial popularity on a number of new poets, including Donald Davie, Thom Gunn and Philip Larkin; this new wave of poetry and poets, also rejecting what they saw as the *préciosité* of modernists such as Eliot and Yeats, was soon given a label by journalist J. D. Scott, who christened it 'The Movement'.[14] Wain's influential bestseller, *Hurry On Down* (1953), along with Kingsley Amis's *Lucky Jim* (1954), both of which deal with dissatisfied young men from the provinces, showed that novel readers had a taste for what one reviewer called 'the picaresque eccentric', especially if such a character's iconoclasm, unconcern with traditional pieties and unabashed devotion to self-indulgence all had a distinctly northern flavour. Iris Murdoch's sensational first novel, *Under the Net* (1954), with its unabashed disrespect for traditional values, bore a strong resemblance to the works of Wain and Amis, but unlike them had a London setting.

The signal literary event of the period, however, was neither the appearance of the first novels by Wain, Amis and Murdoch nor the successful anthologising of the Movement poets in D. J. Enright's *Poets of the 1950s*. It was, instead, the opening night of John Osborne's *Look Back in Anger* at the Royal Court Theatre on 8 May 1956. The play features the dissatisfaction of protagonist Jimmy Porter with the state of post-imperial British society, with the upper-class wife for whom he feels a destructive passion and with his job operating a stall in the local market (a position for which his university education overqualifies him). At first ignored by critics and audiences, *Look Back in Anger* eventually became a sensational hit, especially after the play's publicist coined the phrase 'angry young man' to describe its protagonist. Osborne and the Royal Court followed with another hit in a similar vein, *The Entertainer*, while Stratford's Theatre Royal (under the talented direction of Joan Littlewood) in 1958 produced *Wunderkind* Shelagh Delaney's *A Taste of Honey*, loosely based on her Liverpool childhood. Anger at the failing institutions and social anomie of contemporary Britain, the 19-year-old Delaney showed, was not an exclusively male prerogative. The gritty, deglamourised dramatisation of working-class life in these plays led to their somewhat derogatory designation as promoting a 'kitchen sink' realism, though this theatrical tradition also made room for iconoclastic class warfare fantasy in David Mercer's *Morgan: A Suitable Case for Treatment* (Reisz directed the film adaptation in 1966).

Eschewing the comic sending-up of bourgeois respectability to be found in the fiction of Wain and Amis, a number of young realist novelists had by the end of the 1950s produced a series of bestsellers that, in the serious vein of Osborne and Delaney, gave vent to an anger with a pronounced Northern voice; the most notable were Stan Barstow's *A Kind of Loving*, Alan Sillitoe's *Saturday Night and Sunday Morning* and the novella-length *The Loneliness of the Long Distance Runner*, David Storey's *This Sporting Life*, John Braine's *Room at the Top*, Lynne Reid Banks's *The L-Shaped Room*, Elliot George's *The Leather Boys*, Penelope Mortimer's *The Pumpkin Eater* and Keith Waterhouse's *Billy Liar* (which had been brought to the stage by Willis Hall). Along with the theatrical hits by Osborne, Delaney and Mercer, these novels would provide the basis for the British new wave films, beginning with Jack Clayton's adaptation of *Room at the Top*, which appeared (with interesting coincidence) in 1959, the same year as the initial films released by Truffaut and Godard. The effective marriage of literary and cinematic traditions can be glimpsed in the most successful of the British new wave productions, including director Tony Richardson's mounting of Delaney's groundbreaking autobiographical drama.

A TASTE OF HONEY: FREE CINEMA'S THEATRICAL MODERNISM

In 'A Certain Tendency of the French Cinema', Truffaut lampoons the 'quality' productions of his elders for their lack of cinematic-ness, but, perhaps surprisingly, he neither condemns nor dismisses filmmaking based on literary sources. In fact, Truffaut defends what is essentially a conservative position about film/literature adaptation, pillorying well-known screenwriters for their decision to honour the spirit rather than the letter of their novelistic source text, an approach, so it seemed to the young critic, that results in excessive literariness. The novel turned into a film, Truffaut argues, should be reinterpreted by a 'man of the cinema'; only he can devise the properly filmic equivalents of literary form.

Tony Richardson was not only a man of the cinema. He was also a man of the theatre, and so perhaps especially qualified to undertake the adaptation of a play whose Broadway production he had himself directed. Richardson first made an impact on the British arts scene with his work for the Royal Court Theatre in the middle 1950s, especially his direction of the epoch-making *Look Back in Anger*. But he did not confine himself to stage work. Richardson also contributed sparkling, occasionally polemical film criticism to *Sight and Sound*, and he was the driving force behind *Momma Don't Allow*, securing financing from the BFI so that he and Reisz could direct and produce the documentary for Free Cinema exhibition. Having achieved phenomenal success at the Royal Court, Richardson decided to invest time and energy in commercial filmmaking, founding the Woodfall Production company with John Osborne and Harry Saltzman in 1958 with a view toward making the kind of alternative films soon labelled as 'new wave'. For Woodfall, Richardson oversaw the film adaptations of Osborne's two stage successes, *Look Back in Anger* (in 1958) and *The Entertainer* (in 1960), both of which were 'opened out' in the developing new wave style with an excellent use of real locations or their effective simulacra. Rejecting the most obvious device of the European naturalist tradition, the single, invariant domestic playspace, with its suggestions of claustrophobia and entrapment, Richardson for the film versions of the two plays displays, in Stephen Lacey's view, 'an almost documentary impulse . . . indicated in the way in which the camera frequently dwells on the environments before introducing the characters and picking up the narrative'. Thus Richardson, in 'professing a freedom from the limitations of stage naturalism . . . exercises the right of the cinema to show, as well as refer to, the contemporary world in which it is located'.[15] In *A Taste of Honey* (1961), Richardson's 'documentary impulse' is arguably more complex and effective, the product, it would seem in part, of his creative re-use of techniques and motifs gleaned from *The 400 Blows*, a film that similarly attempts to 'capture' reality in order to authenticate its fictional narrative.

The autobiographical tales from Delaney (with Richardson contributing substantially to the film script) and Truffaut are equally energetic and poignant, tracing the growth to problematic maturity of two rebellious, strong-minded adolescents, who share, in addition to an irrepressible drive toward independence, the misfortune of broken homes and dysfunctional parents. In a Midland port and industrial town, 17-year-old Jo (played by newcomer Rita Tushingham) is awkward and inattentive at school, where lessons and games seem equally pointless; as Richardson first shows her, she is earning the strong rebuke of her displeased teachers, in a sequence that seems closely modelled on the famous schoolroom opening of Truffaut's film. Unlike Antoine Doinel, however, Jo has nearly satisfied the government's requirement for schooling and can soon leave to begin her own life. Jo's mother, Helen (Dora Bryan), is a self-indulgent ne'er do well, who drags her daughter from one cheap bedsitter to the next, skipping out without paying rent to a succession of landladies. Much married, but never to Jo's father, Helen is planning to take yet another husband, a loud, often drunk urban sharpster with money, Peter (Robert Stephens), who is much younger than her and shows little tolerance for the sarcastic, unpleasant Jo. Reluctantly, Peter takes Jo along with Helen for a Blackpool outing, but the girl's ill humour and argumentativeness soon earn her a trip home. She enters into a casual relationship with a young sailor, Jimmy (Paul Danquah), who happens to be black, and they wind up having sex before he departs on a freighter, likely never to return. Much to Jo's displeasure, Helen and Peter do get married, and Jo is left to fend for herself, having now completed her mandatory schooling. She gets a job at a shoe store, but her wages barely pay for the flat she rents; this problem is solved when one of her customers, Geoff (Murray Melvin), a mild-mannered gay man who is just a bit older, persuades her to accept him as a roommate. After Jo discovers she is pregnant with Jimmy's child, the pair become a couple, enjoying romps in the countryside, a visit to a travelling carnival and making preparations for the baby (with Geoff sewing clothes and decorating the flat). Because Jo is shy, Geoff goes to the clinic for information about pregnancy and birth. Their domestic happiness is soon shattered when Helen, deserted by Peter, returns and forces Geoff to leave.

Like many of the New Wave films, *A Taste of Honey* betrays some connection to the social problem films of the era. It treats, so to speak, miscegenation, juvenile delinquency, unwed motherhood and family breakdown, exploring, more generally, the dynamics of social class and the decay of the inner city (Salford is used for the impressive location set-ups). But these aspects of contemporary British life are never thematised as problems to which, in the manner of the genre, the institutions of social welfare are called upon to address and resolve. Instead, the 'Free Cinema' aesthetic prevails. Walter Lassaly's camera finds haunting beauty in the slow passage of a freighter through the harbour, children at play in a wasteland, an Easter Sunday parade, the bare hills above the city and schoolgirls playing basketball, as the film's scenes of dramatic repartee, particularly between Jo and her mother, contrast with long sequences shot silent that carefully fill out the varied environment that the characters inhabit. In contrast to the play's presentation of Jo's entrapment by the room in which she has taken refuge from the uncertainties of life with her mother, the film catches the characters in energetic movement. At the end she emerges from the flat, once again seemingly stymied by her mother's domineering fecklessness, to watch the local children dancing around a Guy Fawkes bonfire. The film's last shot catches Jo lighting a sparkler to celebrate not only the holiday, but, at least presumably, her spirit, which cannot be extinguished. The sense of optimistic irresolution Richardson devises is purely visual, and it finds its source not in Delaney's playscript, but in the famous closing sequence of *The 400 Blows*, with Antoine Doinel caught in freeze-frame, having run as far as he can from the Borstal where he had been confined. As in the European modernist art film, Richardson and Delaney offer compelling, complex and deglamourised characters, who are caught up in an episodic narrative that owes nothing to genre or convention and who are carefully observed in the environment that shapes but does not contain them.

THE LEGACY

The British new wave had run its course by 1963 as principals of the movement, like Jack Clayton and Tony Richardson, turned to other kinds of projects. But both these directors, along with Reisz, Anderson, Schlesinger, Forbes and others, continued through the following decades to produce films that, like their new wave progenitors, interestingly engaged with the tradition of the European art film. Schlesinger's *Sunday, Bloody Sunday* (1971), Forbes's *The Whisperers* (1966), Clayton's *The Pumpkin Eater*, Reisz's *The French*

Lieutenant's Woman (1981) and Anderson's *If . . .* (1968), among many other similar entrants into the international market, testify to the enduring importance of the movement. A new generation of filmmakers coming to prominence in the 1980s has likewise kept the tradition of modernist social realism alive. These practitioners of so-called 'Brit Grit', particularly Mike Leigh and Ken Loach, like the new wavers of the 1960s, have committed themselves to realism rather than tinsel, eschewing the more extreme forms of cinematic modernism for films that speak directly, if with style and subtlety, to the contemporary world.

NOTES

1. David Bordwell, Janet Staiger and Kristin Thompson, *The Classical Hollywood Cinema: Film Style and Mode of Production to 1960* (London: Routledge, 1985).
2. See Steve Neale, 'Art Cinema as Institution', in Catherine Fowler (ed.), *The European Cinema Reader* (New York: Routledge, 2002), pp. 103–20.
3. For further discussion of this different aesthetic see David Bordwell, 'Art Cinema as a Mode of Practice', in Fowler, *The European Cinema Reader*, pp. 94–102.
4. Michel Marie, *The French New Wave: An Artistic School*, trans. Richard Neupert (Oxford: Blackwell, 2003), p. 1.
5. François Truffaut, 'A Certain Tendency of the French Cinema', in Joanne Hollows, Peter Hutchings and Mark Jancovich (eds), *The Film Studies Reader* (London: Arnold, 2000), pp. 58–62.
6. Richard Neupert calls Truffaut the 'ringleader' in *A History of the French New Wave Cinema* (Madison, WI: University of Wisconsin Press, 2002), pp. 161–206.
7. Neupert observes that of Truffaut and Godard that 'their films have the least in common of any two New-Wave era directors . . . [yet] taken together denote for many cinema students today the essence of the New Wave while also suggesting its broad spectrum of stories and styles' (*A History of the French New Wave Cinema*, p. 161).
8. David Bordwell, *Narration in the Fiction Film* (Madison, WI: University of Wisconsin Press, 1985), pp. 206, 207.
9. Peter Wollen, 'The Last New Wave: Modernism in the British Films of the Thatcher Era', in Lester Friedman (ed.), *Fires Were Started: British Cinema and Thatcherism* (Minneapolis, MN: University of Minnesota Press, 1993), p. 37.
10. For further discussion see *The Humphrey Jennings Film Reader*, ed. Kevin Jackson (London: Carcanet, 1993).
11. See Erik Hedling, *Lindsay Anderson: Maverick Film-Maker* (London: Cassell, 1998) for a full discussion of this manifesto and, more generally, of his career.
12. Samantha Lay, *British Social Realism* (London: Wallflower, 2002), p. 60.
13. A fully detailed literary history of the period is found in Harry Ritchie, *Success Stories: Literature and the Media in England, 1950–1959* (London: Faber & Faber, 1988).
14. The classic account of these developments is found in Blake Morrison's *The Movement: English Poetry and Fiction of the 1950s* (Oxford: Oxford University Press, 1980).
15. Stephen Lacey, 'Too Theatrical by Half?', in *British Cinema of the 1950s: A Celebration*, eds Ian MacKillop and Neil Sinyard (Manchester: Manchester University Press, 2003), p. 165.

Recommended films

The Entertainer (Tony Richardson, 1960)
A Kind of Loving (John Schlesinger, 1962)
The Leather Boys (Sidney J. Furie, 1963)
The Loneliness of the Long Distance Runner (Tony Richardson, 1962)
Look Back in Anger (Tony Richardson, 1959)
The L-Shaped Room (Bryan Forbes, 1962)
Room at the Top (Jack Clayton, 1959)
Saturday Night and Sunday Morning (Karel Reisz, 1960)
A Taste of Honey (Tony Richardson, 1961)
This Sporting Life (Karel Reisz, 1963)

Recommended readings

Geraghty, Christine (2000) *British Cinema in the Fifties: Gender, Genre and the New Look*. London: Routledge.

Hill, John (1986) *Sex, Class, and Realism: British Cinema 1956–63*. London: BFI.

Houston, Penelope (1963) *The Contemporary Cinema*. Harmondsworth: Penguin.

Lay, Samantha (2002) *British Social Realism: From Documentary to Brit Grit*. London: Wallflower.

MacKillop, Ian and Sinyard, Neil (2003) *British Cinema in the 1950s*. Manchester: Manchester University Press.

Murphy, Robert (1992) *Sixties British Cinema*. London: BFI.

Ritchie, Harry (1988) *Success Stories: Literature and the Media in England, 1950–1959*. London: Faber & Faber.

Shellard, Dominic (2000) *British Theatre in the 1950s*. Sheffield: Sheffield Academic Press.

Taylor, John Russell (1962) *Anger and After: A Guide to the New British Drama*. Harmondsworth: Penguin.

PART II

CENTRAL, EASTERN AND
NORTHERN EUROPEAN TRADITIONS

5. THE CZECHOSLOVAK NEW WAVE

A revolution denied

Peter Hames

The state of Czechoslovakia came into being in 1918 following the break-up of the Austro-Hungarian Empire after the First World War, and the borders of the new country were confirmed by the peace settlement of 1919. During the Austro-Hungarian period, the Czech lands of Bohemia and Moravia had been ruled from Vienna, while Slovakia had been a part of Hungary. Despite their close linguistic links, this was the first time that the two nations had been politically united for more than a thousand years. The union did not survive in the post-Soviet era, and the country divided into the Czech and Slovak republics in 1993.

While filmmaking in the Czech lands has a long history dating back to the 1890s productions of Jan Kříženecký, Czech cinema did not make a major international impact until the 1960s, with the advent of what, echoing the term used to describe developments in France in the late 1950s, came to be known as a 'new wave'. Despite regular and substantial production since the end of this period, Czech cinema has never recovered the international reputation it then enjoyed. Slovakia, where feature film production did not develop until after the Second World War, has never achieved the same international recognition, even though it is accurate to speak of a Slovak, as well as of a Czech, new wave. The two industries must nonetheless be considered together, as differing parts of a common culture.

Of course, international commercial and critical success are not the same; they arise from a range of factors, of which the quality of the films is only one.

Apart from the widely acclaimed releases of the 1960s new wave, films of international significance have been produced throughout the more than seven decades of modern Czechoslovak history. Gustav Machatý, the first Czech 'art film' director, made films in the 1920s and 1930s (*The Kreutzer Sonata* (*Kreutzerova sonáta*), *Erotikon*, *Ecstasy* (*Extase*)). The animated films of Jiří Trnka and Karel Zeman enjoyed a world reputation in the 1950s, while the subversive surrealist films of Jan Švankmajer were produced mainly in the 1970s and 1980s. Jan Svěrák's *Kolya* (*Kolja*) won an Oscar in the 1990s.

Given the predominant 'western' mindset that sees Central and Eastern European countries as waiting for 'enlightenment'[1] and economic/industrial development, and as reflectors or recipients of cultural benefits from the outside, many significant cultural developments have remained strictly internal, receiving little attention in the West. The Czech and Slovak films granted 'international' significance are therefore those that have been screened or have won awards at West European festivals and, more rarely, attracted the interest of the US Academy of Motion Picture Arts and Sciences. The selection processes involved in such forms of recognition are hardly weighted in favour of Central and Eastern European productions. And yet there have also been times, especially in the 1950s, 1970s and 1980s, when the communist authorities in Czechoslovakia were anxious that particular titles should not receive the oxygen of Western publicity, thus making it difficult for important films to become known outside the country.

This was not true during the 1930s, when the country enjoyed democratic rule. At the second international film festival at Venice in 1934, three Czech and Slovak films attracted attention: Machatý's 'scandalous' and lyrical *Ecstasy*, featuring Hedy Kiesler (later Lamarr), condemned by the Vatican, Josef Rovenský's equally lyrical *The River* (*Řeka*) and Karel Plicka's record of Slovak folk culture, *The Earth Sings* (*Zem spieva*), edited by Alexandr Hackenschmied (who later, in the USA, as Alexander Hammid, worked as photographer and co-director of several of Maya Deren's avant-garde films). All three of these productions are dominated by their pastoral settings, with Jan Stallich's photography on *Ecstasy* and *The River* forming the prototype of what came to be known as 'Czech lyricism'. Both *Ecstasy* and *The River* did substantial overseas business. Czechoslovak films achieved further successes at Venice in succeeding years.

THE BEGINNINGS OF THE NEW WAVE: THE REJECTION OF SOCIALIST REALISM

While the lyrical and poetic tradition continues to be an important element in Czech filmmaking, this aesthetic was not the primary ingredient in the movement that came to be known as the Czech new wave (1963–69). The term 'new wave', much like its French equivalent, referred to a group of directors who came to prominence in the early 1960s and produced an extremely varied group of films that not only won awards at international festivals (including two Oscars), but spearheaded the first significant inroad of Czech and Slovak films into international markets. Director Miloš Forman has often stated that his generation of filmmakers was less influenced by outside influences (including domestic ones) than by their own reaction against the 'bad' films they saw around them. They were determined to replace the propaganda images of Socialist Realism, the official aesthetic of the Soviet bloc countries, with those of real life.

The Czech new wave depended on the talents of a substantial group of young directors, almost all of whom produced debut features that achieved domestic and international recognition: Miloš Forman (*Black Peter/Peter and Pavla* (*Černý Petr*), 1963), Věra Chytilová (*Something Different* (*O něčem jiném*), 1963), Jaromil Jireš (*The Cry* (*Křik*), 1963), Jan Němec (*Diamonds of the Night* (*Démanty noci*), 1964), Pavel Juráček and Jan Schmidt (*Postava k podpírání* (*Josef Kilián*), 1964), Evald Schorm (*Everyday Courage* (*Každý den odvahu*), 1964), Ivan Passer (*Intimate Lighting* (*Intimní osvětlení*), 1965), Hynek Bočan (*No Laughing Matter* (*Nikdo se nebude smát*), 1965), Antonín Máša (*Wandering* (*Bloudění*), 1965) and Jiří Menzel (*Closely Observed Trains/Closely Watched Trains* (*Ostře sledované vlaky*), 1966). Other directors of the same generation included Juraj Herz (*The Sign of Cancer* (*Znamení Raka*), 1966), Karel Vachek (*Elective Affinities* (*Spříznění volbou*), 1968), Drahomíra Vihanová (*Deadly Sunday* (*Zabitá neděle*), 1969) and Zdenek Sirový, best known for his *Funeral Rites* (*Smuteční slavnost*, 1969).

Slovak cinema, though dependent on different institutional structures throughout the Communist period, interacted with these developments at various stages. Štefan Uher, who made his debut in 1958, made an important precursor of the wave with his *Sunshine in a Net* (*Slnko v sieti*, 1962), while the Slovak wave proper established itself in the late 1960s with the work of Juraj Jakubisko (*Crucial Years/Christ's Years* (*Kristove roky*), 1967), Dušan Hanák (*322*, 1969) and Elo Havetta (*Party in the Botanical Garden* (*Slávnosť v botanickej záhrade*), 1969). But defining the new wave solely as a movement of directors who made their debuts in the 1960s also poses problems. How should we classify the Slovak-Czech duo of Ján Kádar and Elmar Klos, who took co-directing credits on one of the most internationally acclaimed productions of the era, the Oscar-winning *A Shop on the High Street/The Shop on Main Street* (*Obchod na korze*, 1965); Vojtěch Jasný, whose *All My Good Countrymen* (*Všichni dobří rodáci*, 1968) won the Best Direction prize at Cannes in 1969; Karel Kachyňa, whose *The Ear* (*Ucho*, 1969) attracted much attention at Cannes in 1990 when it was released after a twenty-year ban; and František Vláčil, whose *Marketa Lazarová* (1967) was voted the best Czech film of all time in 1998? Technically, these were not members of the 'wave', having made their debuts in 1938 (Klos), 1945 (Kádar), and 1950 (Jasný, Kachyňa,Vláčil). The Czechoslovak new wave was not just a 'jeune cinéma', a youth movement in the French tradition reacting against an older generation. There was an interaction between generations in which different groups challenged the status quo and they employed a range of thematic and stylistic elements.

The film industry was nationalised in 1945, three years before the Communist takeover of 1948 on the basis of plans formulated during the war by a group centred on the Czechoslovak Film Society. The purpose of nationalisation was not to promote orthodoxy by producing official propaganda; it was to encourage a freedom of expression that was restricted in a system driven purely by profit. As Czech critics have pointed out, in a country limited by size and language (in that the Czech language has limited international usage), the notion of a subsidised culture was hardly new or original. State sponsorship was normal for museums and galleries, for theatrical and musical performance. If the cinema was seen as part of this wider culture, then nationalisation, which could protect it in some degree from foreign competition, was by no means a radical development. In fact, the Czech 'new wave' of the 1960s can be seen as a realisation of the hopes for and potential of a system based on the notion of public service.

Although the Communist leader, Klement Gottwald (President 1948–53), had promised that artistic orthodoxy would not be a characteristic of the 'Czechoslovak road to socialism', the Soviet model of Socialist Realism was rapidly and extensively applied, not least in the cinema. It is notable that film production (typically between thirty and forty features a year prior to 1989, when it dropped to fifteen to twenty) was reduced to some ten to twelve features a year at the height of Stalinist control in the early 1950s. Socialist Realism prescribed a standardised plot whose politically optimistic (i.e. pro-socialist) ending resulted from nominal conflicts between 'positive' and 'negative' characters. Such narratives represented society not as it was but as it ought to develop. While the chain of cause and effect followed the 'rules' of classical narrative, the ideological and class bases of the characters were often made verbally explicit. As Herbert Eagle has observed, 'characters represent their value systems clearly, and conflicts are seen in unambiguous terms . . . The official socialist realist system . . . encouraged the production of grossly distorted representations of actual life and actual history'.[2]

THE EARLY FILMS OF FORMAN, CHYTILOVÁ AND JIREŠ

The first films of Forman, Chytilová and Jireš (all 1963) offered striking contrasts to this sanitised and propagandistic view of reality. In Forman's *Black Peter*, the hero, Petr is an employee in a supermarket who is unsuccessful in both his work and in his love life. As 'store detective', he gazes in bewilderment as a woman fills her bag from the shelves. As well as presenting a character who does not conform at all to Socialist Realist guidelines, the film offered a portrait of everyday reality without the approved stereotypes.

In her debut feature, Chytilová followed the *cinéma vérité* inclinations of her short film *A Bagful of Fleas* (*Pytel blech*, 1962), set among factory girls. *Something Different* recounts the training of the gymnast, Eva Bosáková, concluding with the success she achieves in the world championships. Chytilová juxtaposes this real story with a fictional account of a married woman who, locked into a sterile marriage, conducts a secret affair. The film interrogates two different lifestyles, analysing female roles. The striking structural combination of fiction and documentary singles the director out as a pioneer in the development of women's cinema.

In Jireš's *The Cry*, the hero is a television repairman whose wife is expecting her first baby. Facing a future as a father, he answers a number of service calls that bring him into contact with a cross-section of society. These chance encounters touch on the threat of war, the promise of sexual infidelity, the cynicism of bureaucrats and the existence of racism. The film provides a portrait of the far from perfect world into which the child will be born. While *The Cry* hardly presents a positive view of reality, its complex deployment of flashbacks and flashforwards, combined with a lyrical style, give it an energy and poignancy that were to prove characteristic of much of Jireš's later work.

Despite their joint concern with rejecting 'official' reality, the three directors had different starting points, with both Chytilová and Jireš pursuing more formal interests in their later work, even as Forman (in his American films) made a place for himself within more mainstream commercial cinema. In fact, the training of the filmmakers at FAMU (the Prague Film School) had laid an emphasis on students developing their own individual styles. This emphasis on creativity rather than orthodoxy led to a sustained commitment to what is now termed 'auteur' cinema.

Nonetheless, it's also true that Forman's style was shared by his colleagues and collaborators, Ivan Passer and Jaroslav Papoušek (*The Best Age* (*Nejkrásnější věk*), 1968), both of whom developed variations on what can be regarded as a group style. Forman himself has always emphasised the collaborative nature of their shared endeavours (in fact this was something he missed when working on his first American films). In their use of themes from everyday life, non-actors and a style based on observation, they were clearly influenced by Italian neorealism. In fact, in his emphasis on ordinary people observed at work (*Black Peter*, *Loves of a Blonde/A Blonde in Love* (*Lásky jedné plavovlásky*), 1965), Forman was following in the path of that movement's latter-day exponent, Ermanno Olmi (*Il Posto*, 1961). Passer's *Intimate Lighting*, which deals with a visit to the country by a classical musician and his girlfriend, is arguably more 'middle class' in its orientation, but is an extraordinarily perceptive study of relationships. Forman's *The Firemen's Ball/It's Burning, My Love!* (*Hoří má panenko!*, 1967), the comic study of how a local fire brigade fails in its attempts to organise both a raffle and a beauty competition, was perceived, even before it was filmed, as something more, as an attack on the Communist Party itself. Forman's respect for ordinary people, often praised in his earlier work, here turned more satirical, striking into what one critic identified as 'the spiritual heart of Stalinism'. The film's deglamourised portrait of young beauty competitors was disapproved of by an unlikely – but perhaps predictable – alliance of Italian co-producer Carlo Ponti, Communist bureaucrats and US film distributors.

Chytilová's subsequent pictures showcase her interest in formal innovation and creating 'outside the rules' and her *Daisies* (*Sedmikrásky*, 1966) and *The Fruit of Paradise* (*Ovoce stromů rajských jíme*, 1969) are two of the few avant-garde films made anywhere under conditions of feature production. *Daisies* is a Dadaist farce in which, as Herbert Eagle[3] suggests, the principle of anarchy is balanced by one of structure. It tells of the adventures of two alienated teenagers who decide that, since the world is meaningless, everything is permitted. In fact, *Daisies* is an entirely non-narrative film based on the principles of the game (the game the girls play is called 'it matters – it doesn't matter'). The characters have no individuality, no psychology, and the film itself can best be described as a sequence of happenings unified by a concern with food. As her co-scriptwriter Ester Krumbachová put it, the filmmakers decided, apart from a few basic dialogues, to be bound by absolutely nothing. Chytilová's cinematographer (and husband) Jaroslav Kučera, observed that, in most films, images were always 'of something' and were fundamentally illustrative. In *Daisies*, he was interested in images that might create their own meaning, as in abstract art.

If possible, *The Fruit of Paradise* is even more opaque. Made in collaboration with a provincial theatre group, it treats the relationship between a man and his wife (based on the prototype of Adam and Eve) and her tempting by the somewhat more fascinating Robert (the devil). While drawing more on theatre and avoiding the montage style of *Daisies*, Kučera's cinematography produces some rich textural effects that are enhanced by a powerful music score by Zdeněk Liška.

Jireš's second feature was made in collaboration with the novelist, Milan Kundera, who was also a lecturer at FAMU. Though based on his *The Joke* (*Žert*), the screenplay was prepared before the novel's publication in 1967, and the film completed production in the months following the Soviet invasion of 1968. Ludvík, the film's hero, had been condemned in the 1950s to work in the 'black units' (penal battalions) after taunting his Stalinist girlfriend with the subversive phrase 'Long Live Trotsky!' on a postcard. Released during the

1960s, he determines to revenge himself on his former best friend who had chaired the student group that condemned him. His chosen method, the seduction and abuse of his friend's wife, proves revenge to be counter-productive. *The Joke*'s strength lies in the way in which it juxtaposes moments from the story's two time periods, provoking reflection on the connection between a past too subject to moral simplification and a supposedly 'reformist' present.

The film gives the lie to the frequent (western) charge that the Czech new wave, unlike Godard and Gorin's 'counter cinema' or Latin American 'Third Cinema', was unpolitical. The targets were different, of course – not capitalism, but rather state socialism. If there was no scope for a cinema outside of state subsidy, it was also quite apparent that the reform movement within Czechoslovak Communism was reflected widely within, and often spearheaded by, the films of the 'new wave'.

Of course, in a society were everything was politicised, deviating from the approved viewpoint became a political matter. Documenting everyday life as it was experienced, as did Forman and Passer, and dissenting from approved aesthetic principles, as did Chytilová, became a matter of politics since the authorities preferred society to be depicted in an idealised manner and in conventional forms. Given the mass media orthodoxies of globalised culture, it could be argued that such strategies also have their political role elsewhere.

Towards a Critical Cinema

In the mid-1960s, the most explicit criticism came from the works of Evald Schorm, in particular *Everyday Courage* and *Return of the Prodigal Son* (*Návrat ztraceného syna*, 1966). Written by Antonín Máša, *Everyday Courage*'s central character is a political activist; the film reflects critically on both his mission and also on wider social developments. Committed to the building of a socialist society, the protagonist finds his image of certainty collapsing all around him. Schorm's approach to this subject is sympathetic, but the film nonetheless suggests the existence of a social crisis and was blacklisted by President Novotný for a year. In *Return of the Prodigal Son*, Schorm examines the case of an intellectual who attempts suicide and is admitted to a mental hospital. The film demonstrates that the man's mental condition is linked to the problems of society as a whole, and in this way it explicitly addresses moral questions of principle and compromise.

Prior to 1968 and the advent of the political reforms of the Prague Spring, films often addressed political issues in an indirect, oblique or Kafkaesque manner. Jan Němec's *Diamonds of the Night* focuses on two Jewish boys escaping from a Nazi death train to create a film that addresses themes of youth and age, life and death, hunters and the hunted. Lifted out of the real world, the narrative offers neither socialist solutions nor a clear ending. Pavel Juráček's and Jan Schmidt's *Josef Kilián* explicitly refers to the Kafkaesque absurd in its comic story about a man led on a journey through an increasingly sinister and meaninglessly bureaucratic society.

In 1966, Němec made what was probably the most critical of all new wave films: *The Party and the Guests/A Report on the Party and the Guests* (*O slavnosti a hostech*). The story involves a group of people on a picnic who are 'invited' to an open-air birthday party for a political leader. Reminiscent of Václav Havel's plays, this absurdist story is constructed from largely 'meaningless' dialogue, comprising such incidents as an 'interrogation' by the secret police, attempts to impose order on disorderly guests, sycophantic speeches, visions of an idyllic future and the pursuit of a missing guest with hunting dogs. Intriguingly, director Evald Schorm plays the guest who flees the scene, refusing to participate in the overall conformity. Prominent members of the Prague intellectual community played many of the main roles. Juráček's *A Case for the New Hangman/A Case for a Rookie Hangman* (*Případ pro začínajího kata*, 1968), based on the third book of Jonathan Swift's *Gulliver's Travels*, similarly takes its protagonist on a journey through the structures of power. While the targets of these films would have been fairly clear to a Czech audience, it is equally true to say that the films apply to all structures of bureaucratised power, which of course were not (and are not) limited to Czechoslovakia in the 1960s.

Overt criticism of Communist policies only became possible during the Prague Spring of 1968, when attempts to renew the egalitarian and democratic traditions of socialism allowed for a critical review of policies that had been followed since the 1950s. *The Joke* has already been discussed, but Jasný's *All My Good Countrymen* presented a damning portrait of the collectivisation of agriculture and the divisions within the local community and party bureaucracy. The script had originally been written eleven years earlier.

The fact that the new wave played a political role cannot be denied, but the films offer much more than a coded attack on the government. As Milan Kundera once said, the importance of the art of Central and Eastern Europe lies in the way in which it offers new testimony about mankind. To reduce this art to nothing more than politics would be to murder it, in the worst tradition of Stalinist dogmatists.[4]

The Stalinist bureaucrats who consolidated their power after the Soviet-led suppression of the Prague Spring did, of course, resort to such simplifications when judging what kinds of art should be produced and distributed. From 1969 onwards, well over a hundred feature films were banned. The reasons included unacceptability of both theme and style and, of course, directors and writers, principally those who were among the many who went into exile or had been banned from the industry. But while this is evidence of a determination to suppress dissent in all its forms (in effect, the liquidation of a culture), such repression tells us little about the political significance of the films at the time that they were made.

The striking feature is that the wave began in 1963, five years before the Prague Spring, and therefore occurred in parallel with the 1960s move towards the 'democratic socialism' associated with the Communist Party's Action Programme of April 1968. The Marxist philosopher Karel Kosík has made some important observations regarding the role culture played in political change. Arguing about the rejection of what he called 'concrete totality', he wrote that culture, and in particular cinema, revealed the ways in which life in such a manipulated world had become impossible. Thus issues first raised within creative culture were subsequently addressed by philosophers and social scientists.[5]

LITERARY SOURCES: MENZEL AND HRABAL

As well as the fiction of Kundera (*No Laughing Matter* and *The Joke*) and Josef Škvorecký (Schorm's *End of a Priest* (*Farářův konec*), 1968, and Menzel's *Crime in the Nightclub* (*Zločin v šantánu*), 1968), the work of a wide range of novelists proved to be important as source material. Perhaps the most influential of these was Bohumil Hrabal, whose novella provided the basis for Menzel's Oscar-winning comedy *Closely Observed Trains*, probably the most internationally acclaimed film of the entire wave. Hrabal's work, which began to be published in the mid-1960s, was characterised by its ironic approach to the idiosyncrasies of everyday life. Hrabal drew directly on his experiences as a railway dispatcher, brewery assistant and wastepaper destroyer – a variety of jobs to which, despite a degree in law, he found himself condemned by the Nazi occupation, and subsequently, by Communist disapproval of his 'negative' writings.

His work often took a 'stream of consciousness' form, incorporating a variety of avant-garde and surrealist elements within an overall realist framework. The collection of short stories *Pearls of the Deep* (*Perličky na dně*) inspired the new wave tribute of the same name, made in 1965, to which Chytilová, Jireš, Schorm, Němec and Menzel all contributed episodes. Two additional stories, brought to the screen by Passer and Herz, were separately released. Hrabal collaborated on the scripts and had walk-on parts in all the episodes.

Closely Observed Trains, made the following year, focuses on the story of a young apprentice at a provincial railway station during the Nazi occupation. At first, he is preoccupied with losing his virginity, a pursuit beside which the Nazis seem an unnecessary distraction. But he ends up losing his life planting a bomb on a Nazi munitions train. A film whose humour in many ways recalls the subversive model of Jaroslav Hašek's novel *The Good Soldier Švejk*

(*Dobrý voják Švejk*, 1921–23), Hrabal's vision is softened by Menzel's cele-bration of a range of stubbornly individualistic characters. The film is uncon-ventional (the protagonist dies), but the authorities were more disturbed by its casual attitude to the wartime resistance movement and the depiction of a hero whose 'martyrdom' is almost independent of his own actions.

Menzel's and Hrabal's next comedy, *Skylarks on a String/Larks on a String* (*Skřivánci na niti*, 1969), was not released until 1990, when it won the Golden Bear at the Berlin Film Festival. It deals with life at a steel mill in the 1950s, where members of the middle classes are undergoing re-education through forced labour. A film more explicitly focused on the group than *Closely Observed Trains*, it also examined the human individual in adversity. Its refer-ence to one of the most shameful aspects of the political history of the 1950s was enough to ensure that it joined other 'subversive' films in the safe of the Barrandov studios.

THE SLOVAK WAVE

The Slovak wave, which boasted some of the most original 'art' movies of the 1960s, was scarcely given a chance to take off. Jakubisko's *Crucial Years* met criticism when it was completed, but *The Deserter and the Nomads* (*Zbehovia a pútnici*, 1968) was only allowed to be screened at foreign festivals, *Birds, Orphans, and Fools* (*Vtáčkovia, siroty a blázni*, 1969) was not released until 1990 and *See You in Hell, Friends!* (*Dovidenia v pekle, priatelia!*, 1970), despite circulating earlier in an unauthorised version made available by its Italian co-producer, was not completed until 1990.

It is difficult to characterise Jakubisko's style but, alongside an admiration for such contemporary directors as Godard and Fellini, he deliberately drew on his roots in Eastern Slovakia. Strong elements of folk culture manifest them-selves in his work, though he also deals quite explicitly with 'big' themes: apocalypse, war, 'liberations' by foreign powers and issues of Slovak identity. The films of his friend Elo Havetta (*Party in the Botanical Garden, Lilies of the Field* (*L'alie pol'né*), 1972) show similar folk influences, but he preserves his own distinctive approach. Dušan Hanák's bleak and modernist art movie, *322*, which ostensibly tells the story of a man suffering from cancer, provided a powerful allegory of contemporary social life. It was banned, together with his later, now classic, feature documentary, *Pictures of the Old World* (*Obrazy starého sveta*, 1972).

THE LEGACY OF THE WAVE

There is no question that the Czechoslovak new wave constituted a significant film movement, being directed towards both cultural and social change. While few of the leading filmmakers were members of the Communist Party, their politically critical and artistically innovative work can be viewed as an important development in the revitalisation and reform of socialism rather than its destruction. It was *glasnost* twenty years before Gorbachev. Providing a powerful and arguably unique episode in film history, the Czech new wave lasted about seven years (much longer than the movement's French and British counterparts) and played a more crucial, active role in social transformation. Suppressed by the post-invasion government, the new wave became a model for what could be achieved in filmmaking, and, for its former participants, it soon came to signify a lost golden age.

The established new wave directors were unable to regain the pre-eminence they had once enjoyed after the 'Velvet Revolution' of 1989[6] and, for many, after years of struggle with bureaucracy, a continued struggle to make films compromised by market pressures cannot have provided a very attractive option. Some of the directors have died (Jireš, Schorm, Juráček, Máša, Vláčil, Kachyňa, Kádar and Klos, Sirový), while others have remained abroad (Forman, Passer, Jasný). Menzel has opted to concentrate on theatre production. But others, such as Chytilová, Němec, Bočan, Vachek and Vihanová, remain active. Low-budget films such as Chytilová's documentary *Flights and Falls* (*Vzlety a pády*, 2000) and Němec's digitally-shot personal essay *Late Night Talks with Mother* (*Noční hovory s matkou*, 2001) reveal the world of what might have been.

The Czech new wave continues to exert great influence as a tradition and, while some younger directors quite naturally wish to forge their own paths, it makes its presence felt in such films as Jan Svěrák's Oscar-winning *Kolya* and Jan Hřebejk's Oscar-nominated *Divided We Fall* (*Musíme si pomáhat*, 2000), the low-key studies of Alice Nellis (*Eeny Meeny* (*Ene bene*), 2000, *Some Secrets* (*Výlet*), 2002) and the methodical works of Saša Gedeon (*Indian Summer* (*Indiánské léto*), 1995; *Return of the Idiot/The Idiot Returns* (*Návrat idiota*), 1999). These influences come primarily from Forman, Passer, and Menzel. Many of the younger filmmakers admit to an admiration for these directors, but it is less a matter of conscious homage than the inheritance of a similar world-view, of senses and perceptions.

Internationally, the influences are less obvious, although the references to *Closely Observed Trains* in Kieślowski's Polish film *Camera Buff* (*Amator*, 1979) and to *A Blonde in Love* in Pál Erdőss's Hungarian *The Princess* (*Adk király katonát*, 1982) are clearly not fortuitous. British director Ken Loach is a great admirer of Forman, Passer and Menzel – and, in particular, of the film *A Blonde in Love*. He once wrote: 'It made a great impression on me when it first came out; its shrewd perceptiveness, irony, warmth. It allowed characters time to reveal themselves'.[7] The influences on Loach are apparent in a number of his films but a number of other British pictures reveal a similar flavour (such as *Gregory's Girl*, 1981; *A Private Function*, 1984; *Brassed Off*, 1996). In some cases, there is a direct connection. Cinematographer Miroslav Ondříček (who worked with Němec and Forman) also shot three Lindsay Anderson films: *The White Bus* (1967), *If. . .* (1968), and *O Lucky Man!* (1973). The Czechoslovak new wave also had an impact outside of Europe, and includes many Asian directors among its admirers. Moreover, Forman and Passer brought a Czech flavour to their American films (*Taking Off*, 1971; *One Flew Over the Cuckoo's Nest*, 1975; and others).

But it is perhaps less a conscious working within a tradition that is important for contemporary Czech filmmakers than the bare *fact* of that tradition. The new wave indicated not merely what could be achieved, but also the role that cinema might play in society and culture. In a market of only ten million (less than the size of Greater London), filmmakers could easily be tempted to give up and submit to the global dominance of English-language cinema. Surprisingly, in the period 1991–2001, seven of the top ten best-attended films in the Czech Republic were Czech. Czech film culture is demonstrably strong, and it also indicates what can be achieved on shoestring budgets. Many of the films also show how to conduct a dialogue with an audience and address serious subjects in an accessible form. The cinemas of small nations will perhaps make a mark on the New Europe and, as the Hungarian director István Szabó has put it, give expression to the variety without which people will otherwise lose their identity and culture.[8]

NOTES

1. See Larry Wolff, *Inventing Eastern Europe: The Map of Civilization on the Mind of the Enlightenment* (Stanford, CA: Stanford University Press, 1994).
2. Herbert Eagle, 'Andrzej Wajda: Film Language and the Artist's Truth', in Ladislav Matějka and Benjamin Stolz (eds), *Cross Currents 1: A Yearbook of Central European Culture* (Ann Arbor, MI: University of Michigan, 1982), p. 339.
3. Herbert Eagle, 'Dadaism and Structuralism in Chytilová's *Daisies*', in Ladislav Matějka (ed.), *Cross Currents 10: A Yearbook of Central European Culture* (New Haven, CT: Yale University Press, 1991), p. 225.
4. Milan Kundera, interviewed by George Theiner, *The Guardian* (London), 12 October 1977, p. 10.
5. Karel Kosík, interviewed in Antonín J. Liehm, *The Politics of Culture*, trans. Peter Kussi (New York: Grove Press, 1973).
6. On 17 November 1989, an anti-regime march led to the subsequent collapse of the Communist government and the forming of a government with a Communist minority role on 10 December. Václav Havel, who had been in jail two months previously, was elected President on 29 December. The peaceful transference of power became known as the 'Velvet Revolution'.
7. Ken Loach, quoted on the video cover of *A Blonde in Love* (London: Connoisseur Video, 1993).
8. István Szabó, unpublished interview by Peter Hames (London: Institute of Contemporary Arts, 1999).

RECOMMENDED FILMS

All My Good Countrymen (*Všichni dobří rodáci*, Vojtěch Jasný, 1968)
Closely Observed Trains/Closely Watched Trains (*Ostře sledované vlaky*, Jiří Menzel, 1966)
Daisies (*Sedmikrásky*, Věra Chytilová, 1966)
Diamonds of the Night (*Démanty noci*, Jan Němec, 1964)
The Firemen's Ball (*Hoří, má panenko*, Miloš Forman, 1967)
Intimate Lighting (*Intimní osvětlení*, Ivan Passer, 1966)
The Joke (*Žert*, Jaromil Jireš, 1969)
A Blonde in Love/Loves of a Blonde (*Lásky jedné plavovlásky*, Miloš Forman, 1965)
The Party and the Guest/A Report on the Party and the Guests (*O slavnosti a hostech*, Jan Němec, 1966)
A Shop on the High Street/The Shop on Main Street (*Obchod na korze*, Ján Kadár and Elmar Klos, 1965)

RECOMMENDED READINGS

Biró, Yvette (1983) 'Pathos and Irony in East European Films', in David W. Paul (ed.), *Politics, Art and Commitment in the East European Cinema*. London: Macmillan.

Eagle, Herbert (1991) 'Dada and Structuralism in Chytilová's *Daisies*', in *Crosscurrents 10: A Yearbook of Central European Culture*. Ann Arbor, MI: University of Michigan, pp. 223–34.

Forman, Miloš, and Jan Novák (1994) *Turnaround: A Memoir*. New York: Villard Books, London: Faber.

Hames, Peter (1994) 'Forman', in Daniel J. Goulding (ed.), *Five Filmmakers: Tarkovsky, Forman, Polanski, Szabó, Makavejev*. Bloomington, IN: Indiana University Press, pp. 50–91.

Hames, Peter (2000) '*The Good Soldier Švejk* and After: The Comic Tradition in Czech Film', in Diana Holmes and Alison Smith (eds), *100 Years of European Cinema: Entertainment or Ideology?* Manchester: Manchester University Press/New York: St. Martin's Press, pp. 64–76.

Hames, Peter (ed.) (2004) *The Cinema of Central Europe*. London and New York: Wallflower Press.

Hames, Peter (2005) *The Czechoslovak New Wave*, 2nd edn. London and New York: Wallflower Press.

Iordanova, Dina (2003) *Cinema of the Other Europe: The Industry and Artistry of East Central European Film*. London and New York: Wallflower Press.

Liehm, Antonín J. (1974) *Closely Watched Films: The Czechoslovak Experience*. New York: International Arts and Sciences Press.

Liehm, Antonín J. (1975) *The Miloš Forman Stories*, trans. Jeanne Němcová. New York: International Arts and Sciences Press.

Liehm, Antonín J. (1983) 'Miloš Forman: the Style and the Man', in David W. Paul (ed.), *Politics, Art and Commitment in the East European Cinema*. London: Macmillan.

Škvorecký, Josef (1971) *All the Bright Young Men and Women: A Personal History of the Czech Cinema*, trans. Michael Schonberg. Toronto: Peter Martin Associates.

Škvorecký, Josef (1982) *Jiří Menzel and the History of the Closely Watched Trains*. Boulder, CO: East European Monographs/New York: Columbia University Press.

6. DANISH DOGMA

'Truth' and cultural politics

Linda Badley

INTRODUCTION

Dogma began audaciously, with a manifesto that renounced the current art of filmmaking and called for an oppositional movement with its own doctrine and rules. As movements go, this one was not born but staged. At Paris's Odéon Théâtre, on 20 March 1995, at an international symposium marking cinema's first century, Danish auteur, former Communist and renowned prankster Lars von Trier pronounced recent cinema 'rubbish', read from a red leaflet, showered copies into the audience and abruptly departed. The name of the movement ('Dogme', from the French) referred to a strict tenet or philosophy, and the manifesto, signed by von Trier and Thomas Vinterberg on behalf of a collective of four filmmakers, required abstinence from Hollywood-style indulgences and high-tech 'cosmetics'. The Dogma logo, a large blinking eye staring out of the rear end of a bulldog (or is it a pig?), said more. A mixture of post-modern irony, punk belligerence and serious confrontation, it was not easy to puzzle out. Was Dogma a practical joke? A crazy publicity stunt? A marketing strategy? Eventually all these and more, its aesthetic was as politically moti-vated as it was ironic.

Gathering energy throughout the second half of the 1990s, the movement drew international attention to a tiny country, jump-started a Danish new wave, revived the Scandinavian film industry and resonated with independent film-makers around the world. Dogma's minimalist, hand-held aesthetic and guerilla-style rhetoric coincided with the arrival of consumer-level digital technology and the DIY (do-it-yourself) movement. 'A technological storm [was] raging', which meant that cinema was 'up for grabs', the Dogma 95 manifesto asserted. Now, 'anyone c[ould] make movies', and Dogma offered a praxis – in 'punk', apolitical disguise.

Currently the movement has resulted in some forty-nine films and stimulated production of over 150 Danish features since 1998. It is partly responsible for the fact that Danish audiences now consume a significantly larger percentage of locally made films than any other European country except France.[1] It has also spurred a Scandinavian film revival, especially in Sweden, whose industry had lain dormant after Ingmar Bergman's achievements. Even so, Dogma's lasting importance may be in its role as an international initiative, public forum and transmedia phenomenon that has rippled out from film and television through the arts and beyond. The term is now used to refer to at least five things: (1) the concept, as outlined by the manifesto and the 'rules' for making Dogma films; (2) the collective of four 'Dogma brothers' and their films certified by a document that appears in place of the director's credit and designated by number; (3) certified international feature films from fifteen countries (ten from Denmark); (4) Scandinavian and international Dogma-*style* films such as *Lilja 4-Ever* (Sweden, 2002), *Full Frontal* (USA, 2002) and nearly any offbeat, low-budget, low-tech film made offshore of Hollywood; and (5) global transmediary Dogma, or initiatives across the arts and sciences that have adopted the concept.

ORIGINS

At their Cannes premiere in 1998, the first two films did not disappoint. Dogma no. 1, Vinterberg's *The Celebration* (*Festen*), exhilarated and shocked the audience and took the Jury's Special Prize. Dogma no. 2, von Trier's *The Idiots* (*Idioterne*), the festival's most coveted ticket, provoked controversy. Shot and edited on video, then transferred to 35 mm, these films proved the digital revolution was underway and directly challenged cinematic practice as it had not been challenged since the 1960s. Their impact was followed by no. 3, Søren Kragh-Jacobsen's popular, prize-winning *Mifune* (*Mifune sidste sang*, 1999), welcomed for steadying and 'humanising' the movement, while the fierce and visually arresting no. 4, Kristian Levring's *The King Is Alive* (2000), returned to the risk-taking of *The Idiots* while demonstrating the aesthetic potential of the digital medium. Beginning with no. 5, Jean-Marc Barr's *Lovers* (France, 1999), the first of some two dozen entries from a dozen countries, Dogma became a global movement.

Dogma coincided with a burst of pre-millennial energy from American independents, sharing with Tod Solondz, Jim Jarmusch and Harmony Korine a mood of anarchic disaffection and fuelling the DIY rebellion of the late 1990s led by Robert Rodriguez, Kevin Smith and Quentin Tarantino. The success of *The Blair Witch Project* (1999) validated the Dogma aesthetic, which in turn offered the indies a coherent anti-Hollywood stance, a European edge and a technique. The connection became official when the collective asked Korine to make the first American Dogma film, resulting in the movement's (and Korine's) most radical visual experiment to date, *julien donkey-boy* (no. 6, 1999).

Dogma also capitalised on the re-emergence of Danish cinema in the 1980s, the first since the 1910s and 1920s, when Nordisk Films Kompagni and film-makers August Blom, Benjamin Christensen and Carl Theodore Dreyer made some of the world's most acclaimed films. A cycle of Danish period pieces began in 1987 with the Academy Award-winning *Babette's Feast* (*Babettes gæstebud*, Gabriel Axel) and *Pelle the Conqueror* (*Pelle erobreren*, Bille August). This was diversified with Ole Bornedal's 1994 thriller *Nightwatch* (*Nattevagten*, remade in Hollywood by the same director in 1996) and led to a brief wave of stylish urban genre films including Nicholas Winding Refn's *Pusher* (1996). In the interim, Von Trier's postmodern/expressionistic 'European trilogy' (*The Element of Crime* (*Forbrydelsens element*), 1983; *Epidemic,* 1987; and *Europa* (*Zentropa*), 1991) together with his internationally acclaimed proto-Dogma film *Breaking the Waves* (1996) had made an indelible impression on European art cinema. Talk of 'A Danish New Wave' ushered in the first Dogma films, with the 1997 Toronto Film Festival featuring a 'Northern Encounters' retrospective of the work of von Trier, Dreyer, Finland's Aki Kaurismäki and Iceland's Fridrik Thor Fridriksson, and New York City's Lincoln Center sponsoring the series 'Danish Cinema Then and Now: Dreyer, von Trier and Beyond'.

Making these trends possible was the support of the provident and enlightened Danish Film Institute (DFI), created in 1968 and buttressed by a series of Film Acts including one that established the National Film School. Dogma became perhaps the only film movement to have sprung almost wholly from a single school, one that bred close relationships, enabled dialogue and fostered long-term mentor-partnerships such as between instructor and screenwriter Mogens Rukov and a host of Dogma writer-directors. The DFI favoured Danish contexts and social realism and insisted on fully developed scripts, but once approved, the filmmaker had relatively unlimited control. This system nourished von Trier but also provoked him to form Zentropa Productions with Peter Aalbæk Jensen in 1992 (and annex the fledgling company Nimbus) as the core for numerous collaborations. When the DFI balked at underwriting the first four Dogma films as a package, Zentropa and Nimbus were joined by several media outlets to foot the bill.[2] These negotiations have since provided talented young Danish filmmakers with a range of sources for funding and inspiration.

The members of the Dogma collective brought diverse perspectives and talents to the table. Vinterberg, who came from a family prominent in Danish cultural circles, had won awards for his 'diploma film' and the television drama *The Boy Who Walked Backwards* (*Drengen der gik baglæns*, 1995) and would make only one feature before *The Celebration* turned him into the movement's poster boy. Prague-educated veteran Søren Kragh-Jacobsen was known for his award-winning children's films and a distinguished songwriting career, while Kristian Levring, who had spent fifteen years making commercials around the world, was virtually unknown.[3] But the mastermind was undoubtedly von Trier, whose brilliant early films showed a technical mastery he needed to go beyond, and he invented Dogma as a necessary stage in his career. His television series *The Kingdom* (*Riget*, 1994) and *The Kingdom II* (1997) taught him to work without a safety net, using hand-held digital cameras and improvising with a large cast. The development of Dogma was concurrent also with his 'Gold Hearted Trilogy' of intense, spontaneously acted melodramas about tormented, self-sacrificing women: *Breaking the Waves* (1996), *The Idiots* (1998) and *Dancer in the Dark* (2000).

Dogma thus forced two tendencies into a productive tension. On the one hand, it imposed on the Danish welfare state and on a postmodern, post-Freudian, desire-manufacturing culture – and, of course, on von Trier – a repressive principle, the 'Vow of Chastity'. On the other, it theorised and forced filmmakers to practise, under rigorous strictures, a *loss* of control described in quasi-religious terms as a 'purification'.

THE MANIFESTO AND 'THE VOW OF CHASTITY'

To release filmmaking from a market-driven aesthetic based in technology, the movement sought, much like the leftist European new waves, to restore the creative anarchy of early filmmaking. The manifesto, composed (as legend has it) by von Trier and Vinterberg in 25 minutes, began in a hectoring pastiche of Marx, the Surrealists and the major documents of the new waves of the 1960s. Pitched in high-church rhetoric, this was followed by the ten-rule 'Vow of Chastity', which climaxed in a volley of pledges to 'refrain from personal taste', to 'regard the instant' over the whole, and 'to force the truth out of . . . characters and settings . . . at the cost of any good taste and any aesthetic considerations'. Coming up with the rules was 'easy', claims Vinterberg: 'We asked ourselves what we most hated about film today, and then we drew up a list banning it all.'[4] The idea was 'to put a mirror in front of [the movie business] and say we can do it another way as well'.[5] Thus, while deconstructing McMovie, Dogma provided a recipe for making low-budget feature films: the rules prohibited sets and required on-location shooting with hand-held cameras, direct sound and natural light. They had to be made in colour and 'in the here and now' – to capture a sense of real time, space and emotion. Genre films involving 'superficial action' (weapons and murders) and 'temporal and geographical alienation' (costume drama, science fiction, westerns) were forbidden. The film had to be calibrated or transferred to old-fashioned, almost square 35 mm Academy format. The director could *not* be credited.

The manifesto called for a return to authenticity, situating itself in relation to Soviet revolutionary cinema, Italian neorealism, *cinéma vérité* and the films of John Cassavetes and Stan Brakhage – with special reference to the *nouvelle vague*. It claimed (in the language of François Truffaut) to be a 'rescue' action aimed at counteracting a 'certain tendency' in current cinema. Flaunting its many heritages (with tongue in cheek), Dogma never meant to be original. It was the context that was new, making a particular mode of truth-seeking the issue. The European new waves, the French in particular, had invented the auteurist aesthetic that inspired the New American directors of the late 1960s and early 1970s, only to be co-opted in the 1980s as one more form of brand-name merchandising. Thus Dogma's primary targets were the Hollywood genre film and the 'romantic' aesthetic of the *nouvelle vague*. The cult of film as art, now compromised by market values, had led to the current malaise in which the technical mastery had obliterated any sense of the Real. Thus Dogma's revolutionary rhetoric evoked a grassroots, collectivist, situated *and* international challenge to Hollywood and corporate mergers such as Dreamworks.

DOGMA ELEMENTS AND TROPES

The rule forbidding the director's signature, laughable from a grandstanding von Trier, underscored Dogma's intention to decentre the filmmaking process. Two underlying goals were to 'liberate' experienced filmmakers from professional and genre conventions and their own personal styles, and to remove technological barriers between filmmakers, actors and settings. Celebrity culture and CGI technology threatened to turn acting into little more than image lending; Dogma required actors to improvise costumes, makeup, gestures, movements and lines. The film, unencumbered by a large crew and uninterrupted by long set ups, followed the actors over time, allowing them to sustain momentum and interact naturally in a location, which in turn the camera could use to advantage – the golden fields and candlelight in *Mifune* or the sand-filled rooms and dunes of *The King is Alive*. For filmmakers and actors, all this represented a recovery of the 'joyful' realism and experimental spirit of the earliest cinema. For young viewers brought up on MTV, it was both familiar and a revelation.

Dogma is celebrated for adapting documentary style to fiction film, but it represents equally a return to cinema's roots in theatre. Vinterberg's *The Celebration* was constructed around a wealthy Danish patriarch's sixtieth birthday celebration at which the elder son Christian (Ulrich Thomsen) discloses to the assembled family (at strategic moments in the sequence of the evening's courses, toasts and speeches) the father's sexual abuse of himself and his twin sister (a recent suicide). An Aristotelian tragedy down to unities of time, place and action, the story might have been filmed as a theatre piece by Ibsen or Strindberg; instead, it has the discomforting intimacy of a home movie filmed in real time. *The Celebration* furnished a stage not only for actors but for cinematographer Anthony Dod Mantle. Wielding a consumer-level Sony PC7 E, the smallest digital camera available, Mantle mingled and zoomed in like a paparazzi, grabbing close-ups, jump-cutting to snatch the revealing moment – at a crucial point taking us into Helene's (Paprika Steen) tampon case, where she shoves her sister's suicide note. In the economic choice of video, which fudged the 35 mm rule, Vinterberg and Mantle had put Dogma at the vanguard of the digital revolution, convincing sceptics like Spike Lee that the digital camera had powerful *aesthetic* advantages for a certain kind of film.

For all of Dogma's radical pretensions, the original films seemed resolutely apolitical. True, child abuse and racism provoked conflict and moments of recognition in *The Celebration* and *The King Is Alive*, as did disability, sexuality and discrimination in *The Idiots*. Issues were present but rendered peripheral or metaphorical, in service to some melodramatically revealed, intuitive 'truth'. In imposing minimalist austerity upon explosive situations, however, Dogma exploited a form of psychodrama that, widely perceived as 'Scandinavian', had considerable international cachet and was subversively different from McMovie. Aimed well below the Hollywood radar, Dogma's campaign was understood in quite political terms by European and American indie filmmakers. The foundational Dogma films, which the filmmakers talked out in a series of meetings before any shooting started, shared three formal and thematic elements:

1. the ensemble and the family melodrama;
2. the 'holy idiot', a damaged or disabled character(s) whose hysteria or radical innocence blows the cover of convention and exposes the emotional and aesthetic 'truth'; and
3. self-reflexiveness or metacinematic performance.

1. The ensemble: family melodrama and the group ethic

Nearly all the early Dogma films are ensemble films or family/alternative family melodramas including (in addition to the first four) *julien donkey-boy*, the Danish films *Italian for Beginners* (*Italiensk for begyndere*, no. 12, 2000), *Truly Human* (*Et rigtigt menneske*, no. 18, 2002), *Kira's Reason – A Love Story* (*En kærlighedshistorie*, no. 21, 2001), *Open Hearts* (*Elsker dig for evigt*, no. 28, 2002) and *Old, New, Borrowed and Blue* (*Se til venstre der er en svensker*, no. 32, 2003), as well as *Fuckland* (no. 8, Argentina, 2000), *Diapason* (no. 11, Italy, 2000), *Joy Ride* (no. 14, Switzerland), *Reunion* (no. 17, USA, 2001) and *Once Upon Another Time* (*Era Outra Vez*, no. 22, Spain, 2000). With Dogma's emphasis on collectives, location and actors, and its opposition to auteurism and hero-centred genre films, this is hardly a wonder. Another reason is a Danish 'group ethic' in one of the world's smallest and most provident welfare states in which, with high employment rates and 100 per cent literacy, there are theoretically no outsiders. At the same time, as in any extended family, outsiders do exist: the disabled, children, the elderly, ethnic minorities and members of the lower middle-class.[6] Dogma films both reflected the group ethic and put it to the test, focusing on outings, outsiders, alternative families or on complex and explosive situations that arise out of relationships.

Dogma exploited group dynamics, exposing secrets and repressed issues and bringing potential factions into open conflict. *The Celebration* is an oedipal family melodrama reminiscent of Bergman's films but situated within the house of a (specifically) Danish father, signifying the fatherland. *The Idiots* explores the limits of socially and politically 'safe' behaviour, as a commune of young urban professionals use Stoffer's (Jens Albinus) uncle's mansion as a platform for a series of attacks on middle-class values. Well off, with respectable family connections, they are insiders who identify with outsiders partly to protest against bourgeois hypocrisy, partly to find a pre-socialised subjectivity, and more often for a complex variety of psycho-social reasons. Where their enterprise fails, the film succeeds. Although in strikingly different locations and ways, in *Mifune* and *The King Is Alive*, the group becomes an alternative family or a redemptive experience for purposeless individuals.

2. Disability as subversion: the 'idiot technique'

To take on Hollywood without the latter's high-tech arsenal, Dogma needed powerful medicine. The movement also aimed to rout a tradition of Danish 'modesty' or, as Dogma filmmaker Lone Sherfig calls it, a 'fear of being over-expressive',[7] to which urban postmodern culture had added a layer of irony. To breach this, the original Dogma films (and many thereafter) featured a 'holy fool', often a literally disabled person, but just as often a dramatisation or metaphor of disability reinforced by a conspicuously stripped or 'disabled' film technique. While derived from Gnostic mystical traditions, the trope had regional roots in Calvinism, existentialism and a cinema of catharsis inherited from Danish philosopher Søren Kierkegaard. Most obviously, the Dogma 'brothers' capitalised on their own Scandinavian art-film tradition of perverse, ascetic psychodrama. In the films of Dreyer and Bergman, for example, 'Nordic' repression was pitted against itself to produce moments of naturalistic transcendence. Less obvious but equally powerful medicine was a maudlin theme from Danish kitsch. Thus von Trier's 'Gold Hearted' and American trilogies, with which Dogma has overlapped, were inspired not only by Dreyer's harrowing *The Passion of Joan of Arc* (*La Passion de Jeanne d'Arc*, 1928) but also a beloved Danish fairy tale about a little girl so good that she gave away all her food and clothing.

The 'idiot technique', which von Trier has equated with the Dogma 'method' of relinquishing technical control,[8] attempted to break through aesthetic and social artifice to recover the 'Real' as naked emotion. The idiot's presence – for example, in *The Kingdom*'s chorus of two dishwashers played by actors with Downs syndrome, or *Breaking the Waves*' sexual martyr Bess (Emily Watson) – creates moments of grotesque awkwardness and 'political incorrectness'. Commenting on his 1999 *Quiet Waters* (television project based on the sentimental pastoral stories of Danish writer Morten Korch), von Trier speaks of a need to 'dare to cry and to let ourselves be moved. We rely on this huge superstructure consisting of all kinds of artificial crap'.[9] The subversive tension between this need to cry and its ironic deflection is characteristically Dogmatic.

The Idiots is about a group of young urban professionals who 'perform' mental impairment, referred to as 'spassing', in public places in an absurdist quest for psychic authenticity, thus to break through to some pure emotional truth – 'the inner idiot' lost beneath the urban professional façade. *The Celebration* is a pressure cooker of concealed histories and repressed hysteria. In *Mifune*, a peasant passing as an urban careerist is called home to the family farm upon his father's death to reclaim the courage, curiosity and emotional vitality of his mentally disabled brother Rud (Jesper Asholt). In *The King Is Alive*, a group of tourists undergo extreme physical and psychological disorientation. It is no coincidence that *julien donkey-boy* was based on the experiences of Korine's schizophrenic Uncle Eddie and features a raving Werner Herzog as Julien's father or that Jennifer Jason Leigh's and Alan Cummings's all-but-Dogma film *The Anniversary Party* (2001) involves an all-night Hollywood 'family' gathering and an Ecstasy-induced orgy of truth-telling. Idiocy, mental illness, hysteria as truth serum, real and performed, is a key trope in the Danish films *Italian for Beginners*, *Truly Human*, *Kira's Reason*, *Open Hearts* and *In Your Hands* (*Forbrydelser*, no. 34, 2003), but it also appears in international films such as *Joy Ride* and *Diapason*.

3. Film as theatre: metacinema and metaculture

Together with the 'idiot technique', the certificate that appeared at the beginning of the film, the 'confessions' signed by the first six filmmakers and the hype surrounding the movement worked something like the theorising and placards that Marxist playwright Bertolt Brecht used to create his *Verfremdungseffeckt*.[10] They created a metacinematic space in which the conflict between the film's artifice and its much advertised search for 'truth' became highlighted. Also, the absence of what usually constituted a film (for example, non-diegetic music) caused audiences to attend the more closely to what was left, to focus on technique and message. The first four films played to this expectation through overt theatricalism which, accentuated by technical minimalism and hyperrealism, extended to a Dogma 'play within the play'. With the acerbic wit of a latter-day Hamlet, *The Celebration*'s Christian performs madness to catch the conscience of the incestuous patriarch. Engaging servants' and siblings' complicity in converting the occasion into a stage, he directs an oedipal docu-soap within and against the official family drama. The film is about the replacement of one set of rules – those of the Danish father whose traditions ground the film's dignified classical structure – with a regime of revolutionary truth-telling. Against this structure, *The Celebration* pitted Mantle's camera which, described as the size of a fist, seems charged with the repressed rage and desire of the younger generation, the servants, the film's audience and ultimately Dogma's deconstructive aesthetic, epitomised in what Mantle has called 'an image tending toward decomposition'.[11] The film spoke to the world of the erosion of the Hollywood 'family' and an impending digital revolution.

The Idiots, which von Trier has called 'the truest and most genuine thing [he has] made',[12] is, however, the testamental Dogma film, a documentary about its own making and a performance of the Dogma principles. Liberally improvised, the film was shot primarily (and with celebrated ineptness) by von Trier, with boom occasionally in view. The 'idiots', like the 'brothers', are a collective whose spassing performances are followed by analysis and further improvisation. Punctuated by a series of interviews (conducted three weeks after the group's dissolution) by an off-screen interrogator voiced by von Trier, the film has a visible surrogate in Stoffer, the idiots' alternately cynical and hysterical agent provocateur. This metanarrative was complemented by von Trier's audio diary, published in Danish when the film was released, and Jasper Jargill's revealing 'making of' documentary, *The Humiliated* (*De ydmygede*, 1998).

Like Dogma in general, *The Idiots* was deliberately offensive, breaking down barriers between public and private, fake and real, and creating confrontations that allow audiences no safe – rational or political – space, particularly in a scene in which the 'idiots' are visited by a group of authentically disabled people, plunging the pretending idiots (*and* the cast members who played them) into depression and disarray. As Stoffer ups the ante, fake spassing yields to real hysteria and becomes threatening. When the idiots are unable to pass the ultimate test, which demands that individuals (selected via a kind of Russian roulette) spass in their workplaces and homes, the group disperses and the experiment fails. Thus exposing the film's (and Dogma's) *lack* of authenticity, *The Idiots* seems able only to force a negative version of the 'truth' from its characters until the devastating final scene, which connects the group and the film with the authentically damaged outcasts of lower middle-class life.[13] The 'moral', says von Trier, is that 'you can practise the technique – the Dogma technique or the idiot technique – from now to kingdom come without anything coming out of it unless you have a profound, passionate desire and need to do so'.[14]

Metacinema continued in an understated way in *Mifune*, where Kragh-Jacobson employed a popular Morten Korch trope – the conflict between city and country values – with the latter triumphing. The film's centrepiece is the protagonist's 'idiotic' performance as the Japanese actor Toshiro Mifune, bringing him 'down' to the level of Rud, who believes Mifune lives in the cellar. Nevertheless the performance forces the 'truth' out of the situation.

But if *The Idiots* approximates guerrilla theatre and performance art and *Mifune* gives a nod to Japanese Noh plays, *The King Is Alive* draws on Shakespeare, Beckett and Brecht to make Dogma's most direct statement about film as theatre and as 'truth'. The hostile grandeur of the location, manifested in stunning, golden-toned desert panoramas, becomes supremely ironic: a scarcely compatible group of tourists stranded in a Nambian ghost town are persuaded by Henry (David Bradley), a former actor, to perform *King Lear* as a co-operative diversion or, as Levring has termed it, 'a Dogma play within a play'.[15] Via this endgame – exiled from their normal lives, limited by the rules for survival, their bodies burnished by the sun – the characters undergo a process of 'purification' just as Dogma is a process of purification of cinema. The characters stumble through their lines and, in increasing disorientation, lose themselves; they fuse with their performances in situated ways and find something authentic. It is the sensual, cynical *and* 'gold-hearted', horrifically abused (urinated upon) Gina (Jennifer Jason Leigh) who plays Lear's Cordelia. The suggestion is that Gina's passion to perform Cordelia transcends both her performance and herself and puts irony to shame. Her death provokes the moment of truth as the survivors huddle over her funeral pyre and, for the first time, speak their lines with 'found' meaning.

Numerous other Dogma films are about performance or filmmaking, or are 'making of' films about themselves, including *Strass* (no. 20, Belgium, 2001), *Camera* (no. 15, USA, 2000), *Interview* (*Intyebyu*, no. 7, Korea, 2000), *Fuckland* and Dogma derivations *The Anniversary Party* and *Full Frontal*. Through insistent self-referentiality, Dogma stirred up what Mette Hjort calls a metaculture, a context in which films were perceived as theorisations put into practice, requiring 'political' analysis and debate.[16] Thus Dogma became an international public forum whose very existence presented an alternative to global Hollywood. *The Idiots*, for example, created controversy locally over its treatment of disability and the Søllerød community, and internationally over nudity and foreign censorship – which led inevitably to the discussion of cinema, professionalism or its lack, and Dogma rules observed and broken. Demystifying itself and the filmmaking process, Dogma was also, perhaps most importantly, a global workshop.

SECOND WAVE AND POST-DOGMA

One often hears that Dogma is dead, that it ended as the idiots did when they realised they couldn't take their game of spassing home. Closer to the truth is the fact that it was invented as a kind of reality check and, like all movements, it was not intended to last. In 2000, the 'brothers', immersed in other projects, gave control over to the honour system, making the Dogma certificate available to any filmmaker who applied for one; and in 2002, the Secretariat closed. Yet acclaimed and popular (and certified) Dogma films continue to be made. A second wave of young Danish filmmakers use the Dogma rules to develop and authenticate something already implicit in their films. Lone Sherfig, Suzanne Bier, Annette K. Oleson, Natasha Arthy and Åke Sangren all bring the 'idiot technique' – the tragicomic humour, intensity and naturalness of early Dogma – to what might have been soap operatic material (*Open Hearts* and *In Your Hands*), romantic comedy (*Italian for Beginners, Old, New, Borrowed and Blue*) or an unsuccessful case study (*Kira's Reason*). Characters, already damaged, undergo yet more painful, purifying ordeals. Many of the pretensions, theatrical ensembles, self-referential elements and deep ironies early Dogma was known for, however, had served their purposes and flown.

Recently, the most celebrated international successes have been written and directed by women, notably Sherfig, Bier, Olesen and Arthy, whose characters are ordinary people in extraordinary circumstances, intimately rendered and, ultimately, survivors. And so Nikolaj Lie Kaas, who played *The Idiots*'s pinch-faced, angst-filled childlike 'idiot' Jeppe with devastating conviction, becomes *Open Hearts*' equally anguished, self-pitying, bitterly ironic paraplegic who emerges stronger through his pain. The plots are as melodramatic as ever: here a paraplegic loses his girlfriend to the husband of the woman who ran him over. Although mellower, several of the 'second wave' films (notably *Open Hearts* and *Kira's Reason*) are radically poised in the moment, in a way that, of the Dogma originals, only *The Idiots* managed to be. Thus Dogma fuelled the careers of an ambitious, talented gang of young filmmakers. After the international success of no. 13, *Italian for Beginners*, Sherfig has ventured into yet more emotionally honest territory with the Danish/Scottish collaboration *Wilbur Wants to Kill Himself* (2003). In this fashion, Dogma has been the force behind 'a golden age' in Danish cinema, or so claims a five-week Danish film series featured in February 2004 at the National Gallery of Art in Washington, DC.

Meanwhile, the Dogma brothers have been accused of abandoning their posts, but a longer look demonstrates just how Dogmatic they continue to be. Most still work out of Zentropa or Nimbus on projects that extend Dogma's emphasis on character, emotion and 'truth' in interesting ways. Post-Dogma, they made films in English with international casts, starting with von Trier's DV musical *Dancer in the Dark*, set in America, and Kristian Levring's *The Intended* (2002), an expressionistic and densely textured revisitation of *The Heart of Darkness* in the jungles of Malaysia that extended his use of on-location digital photography. Von Trier's *Dogville* (2003) and *Manderlay* (2005), the first two films of his US trilogy, were filmed (like *Our Town*) on an empty sound stage with chalk marks for streets and buildings, and were his most Brechtian theatre pieces yet, the culmination of his quest for a 'pure' cinema of emotion and provocation.[17] Reflecting America's 'true' face in its minimalist, European mirror, the US trilogy extends the Dogma mission (and much of its aesthetic) into more overtly political territory. Vinterberg's *It's All About Love* (2003) attempted futuristic fantasy without high-tech special effects, literalising a view of the twenty-first century as an emotional ice age and thus, like von Trier, continued searching for some lost human essence. And if the visceral and intellectually challenging Vinterberg/von Trier collaboration *Dear Wendy* (2005), a commentary on American gun culture, seems Dogma inspired on several levels, so does von Trier's Cannes 2005 announcement of his imminent return to his roots to make a second Dogma film, *Direcktøren for det hele* ('Managing Director of It All').

Zentropa studios is credited by *Screen* as 'the creative and business power-house that has reinvigorated an industry with its Dogma 95 concept'.[18] The spirit that launched Zentropa and Dogma has led to regional centres now helping young, iconoclastic directors change the way films are made. In 1996, Zentropa joined Swedish independent Thomas Eskilsson's Film i Väst and Memfis Films to diversify the depressed economy of Trollhätten, a run-down industrial town in southwest Sweden, into a flourishing film-production centre now known as 'Trollywood', where *Dancer in the Dark*, *Dogville*, *It's All about Love* and Lukas Moodysson's *Lilja 4-Ever* were all made as Danish-Swedish co-productions. Thus, a new Danish wave is helping to generate a pan-Scandinavian renaissance.

GLOBAL DOGMA

The number of non-Danish Dogma films is remarkable, thirty-nine out of forty-nine, from seventeen countries: USA, Canada, UK, Norway, Sweden, Finland, France, Belgium, Spain, Italy, Switzerland, Korea, Chile, Argentina, Mexico, Luxemburg and South Africa. A younger generation of Latin Americans such as José Luis Marquès, director of the Argentine hit *Fuckland*, have used Dogma to enhance a bare-bones tradition borne of necessity while deriving from earlier Third cinemas.[19] During the digital 'boom', Dogma became an art-house brand name that enabled productions such as the micro-budget, one-day shoot *Bad Actors* (no. 16, 2000), inspired by improvisational early Dogma, to finance a 35 mm print to show at festivals. It also created international audiences for films about local politics, such as *Fuckland* and *Resin*, which would otherwise have not been distributed. In these ways, Dogma has sparked a global cinema that may not conform to all or even many of the 'rules', but is founded in a search for authenticity, creativity and collaboration as opposed to a blockbuster mentality – in short, a subversive agenda.

The Dogma style has infiltrated Hollywood, genre film, the indie fringes and international film in unexpected ways. Steven Soderberg presented Hollywood stars (for instance, Julia Roberts) interested in *Full Frontal* with a manifesto requiring them to do their own makeup, drive to the set, eat together and improvise, and Dogma cinematographer Anthony Dod Mantle's digital camera lent a rawness and urgency to Danny Boyle's *28 Days Later* (2002), infusing the zombie/sci-fi/action film with a humanism that hit the right tone in the aftermath of 9/11. More broadly and importantly, Dogma has lent inspiration to a widespread 'new punk' movement that, shaped by DIY anti-professionalism, experimental digital camera work and computer-based editing, has been rewriting the Hollywood formula and includes international filmmakers such as Darron Aronofsky (*Requiem for a Dream*, 2000), Paul Thomas Anderson (*Magnolia*, 2000), Alejandro Gonzales Inniaritu (*Amores Perros*, 2000) and Mike Figgis (*Time Code*, 2000).[20]

More broadly yet, the Dogma concept has spawned a plethora of manifestos and initiatives across the disciplines: not only Denmark's *D-Dag* (*D-Day*, 2001) – a radical cross between cinema, live television and collaborative performance art – and Dogumentary (von Trier's 2000 documentary film movement), but a half-dozen other documentary manifestos/movements, a writers' movement (The New Puritans), a theatre movement,[21] a dance movement, an educational movement that returns to the 'unplugged' classroom, game-design manifestos including 'The LARP (Live Action Role Play) Vow of Chastity', a 'WebDogma' film movement and Vogma (Vertov with a Mac). Dogma hailed the 'technological storm' of the dawning century, and both sides of the 'digital revolution' have been inflected with Dogmaspeak. Although Vinterberg has said that the Dogma idea was to reflect – to 'put a mirror in front of the industry', *not* to provide 'another colour' – movements have a way of getting beyond their inventors' control.[22]

NOTES

1. For example, the 2002 Danish box office market share was 27.1 per cent, second to France's 33 per cent, even though France produces ten times the number of films per year as Denmark. See Louise Hagemann, 'Danish Film Year 2003 in Figures', *Danish Film Institute* December 2003, at: http://www.dfi.dk/sitemod/moduler/index_english.asp?pid=18100 (accessed 12 February 2005).
2. Jack Stevenson, *Dogme Uncut: Lars von Trier, Thomas Vinterberg, and the Gang that Took on Hollywood* (Santa Monica, CA: Santa Monika Press, 2003), pp. 77–8.

3. Dogma originally included one 'sister', Anne Wivel, a respected documentary film-maker.
4. Richard Kelly, *The Name of This Film is Dogme 95* (London: Faber & Faber, 2000), p. 7.
5. *The Name of This Film is Dogme 95* (dir. Saul Metzstein, writ. Richard Kelly, Minerva Pictures, UK, 2000).
6. Jack Stevenson, *Lars von Trier* (London: BFI, 2002), pp. 128–31.
7. Kelly, *The Name of This Film is Dogme 95*, p. 130.
8. Peter Øvig Knudson, 'The Man Who Would Give up Control', *Dogme95*, n.d., at: http://www.dogme95.dk/news/interview/trier_interview.htm (accessed 25 March 2004).
9. Mette Hjort and Ib Bondebjerg, *The Danish Directors: Dialogues on a Contemporary National Cinema* (Bristol: Intellect Books, 2001), p. 214.
10. See Berys Gaut, 'Naked Film: Dogma and Its Limits', in Mette Hjort and Scott MacKenzie (eds), *Purity and Provocation: Dogma 95* (London: BFI, 2003), pp. 89–101; Paisley Livingston, 'Artistic Self-Reflexivity in *The King is Alive* and *Strass*', in Hjort and MacKenzie, *Purity and Provocation*, pp. 102–10; and Murray Smith, 'Lars von Trier: Sentimental Surrealist', in Hjort and MacKenzie, *Purity and Provocation*, pp. 111–21, on self-reflexivity in selected films.
11. 'Frequently Asked Questions', *Dogme95*, n.d., at: http://www.dogme95.dk/faqu/faq.htm (accessed 25 March 2004).
12. Peter Schepelern, 'Film According to Dogme: Restrictions, Obstructions and Liberations', *Dogme95*, n.d., at: http://www.dogme95.dk/news/interview/schepelern.htm (accessed 12 February 2005).
13. Smith, 'Lars von Trier', p. 120.
14. Knudsen, 'The Man Who Would Give up Control'.
15. *De Lutrede* (*The Purified*), dir. Jesper Jargil. Jesper Jargil Film/Danish Film Institute, Denmark, 2002.
16. Mette Hjort, 'The Globalisation of Dogma: The Dynamics of Metaculture and Counter-Publicity', Hjort and MacKenzie, *Purity and Provocation*, pp. 133–57.
17. Similarly experimental was his documentary *The Five Obstructions* (*De fem benspænd*, 2004), a game of restrictions and an exercise in creativity in which von Trier challenged his idol Jorgen Leth to remake his 'perfect' twelve-minute film *The Perfect Human* (*Det perfekte menneske*, 1967) five times, with five different sets of limitations.
18. 'Zentropa', *Det Danske Filminstitut/Danish Film Institute*, 5 May 2003, at: http://www.dfi.dk/sitemod/moduler/index_english.asp?pid=13190 (accessed 25 March 2004).
19. Hjort and MacKenzie, 'Introduction', Hjort and MacKenzie, *Purity and Provocation*, p. 22.
20. Nicholas Rombes (ed.), *Post-Punk Cinema* (Edinburgh: Edinburgh University Press, 2005).
21. Dogma's influence on theatre extends most recently to *Festen*, David Eldridge's acclaimed 2003 stage adaptation of *The Celebration*, currently produced by Rufus Norris and playing at the Lyric Theatre in London to rave reviews.
22. *The Name of This Film Is Dogme 95*.

RECOMMENDED FILMS

The Celebration (*Festen*, Dogma no. 1, Thomas Vinterberg (uncredited), 1998)
Dancer in the Dark (Lars von Trier, 2000)
The Idiots (*Idioterne*, Dogma no. 2, Lars von Trier (uncredited), 1998)

Italian for Beginners (*Italiensk for begyndere,* Dogma no. 12, Lone Scherfig (uncredited), 2000)

julien donkey-boy (Dogma no. 6, Harmony Korine (uncredited), 1999)

The King Is Alive (Dogma no. 4, Kristian Levring (uncredited), 2001)

Kira's Reason – A Love Story (*En kærlighedshistorie,* Dogma no. 21, Ole Christian Madsen (uncredited), 2001)

Lilja 4-Ever (Lukas Moodysson, 2002)

Mifune (*Mifune sidste sang,* Dogma no. 3, Søren Kragh-Jacobsen (uncredited), 1999)

Open Hearts (*Elsker dig for evigt,* Dogma no. 28, Suzanne Bier (uncredited), 2002)

RECOMMENDED READINGS

Combes, Richard, and Durgnat, Raymond (2000) 'Rules of the Game', *Film Comment,* 36, 5 (September/October), 28–32.

Hjort, Mette, and Bondebjerg, Ib (eds) (2001) *The Danish Directors: Dialogues on a Contemporary National Cinema.* Bristol, UK, and Portland, OR: Intellect Books.

Hjort, Mette, and MacKenzie, Scott (eds) (2003) *Purity and Provocation: Dogma 95.* London: British Film Institute.

Kelly, Richard (2000) *The Name of this Book is Dogme95.* London: Faber & Faber.

Raskin, Richard and Christensen, Claus (eds) (2000) *Aspects of Dogma* (special issue), *p.o.v.: A Danish Journal of Aesthetics,* 10 (December).

Rockwell, John (2003) *The Idiots.* London: British Film Institute.

Roman, Shari (2001) *Digital Babylon: Hollywood, Indiewood and Dogme 95.* Hollywood, CA: Ifilm.

Schepelern, Peter (n.d.) 'Film According to Dogme: Restrictions, Obstructions and Liberations', *Dogme95,* at http://www.dogme95.dk/news/interview/schepelern.htm (accessed 12 February 2005).

Stevenson, Jack (2003) *Dogme Uncut: Lars von Trier, Thomas Vinterberg, and the Gang that Took on Hollywood.* Santa Monica, CA: Santa Monica Press.

Stevenson, Jack (2002) *Lars von Trier.* London: British Film Institute.

Von Trier, Lars and Vinterberg, Thomas (1995) 'The Dogme 95 Manifesto', 13 March, at: http://www.dogme95.dk (accessed 12 February 2005).

7. POST-COMMUNIST CINEMA

The politics of gender and genre

Christina Stojanova

Introduction

The title of Anita Skwara's 1992 essay, ' "Film Stars Do Not Shine in the Sky over Poland": The Absence of Popular Cinema in Poland',[1] was a condensed evaluation of the state of affairs not only in the Polish but also in the other Central and Eastern European cinemas in the immediate aftermath of Communism's demise.[2] A counter-productive impasse had been reached at that time as popular cinema lovers eager for entertainment and increasingly desensitised to Central/Eastern European auteur cinema, looked to whatever Hollywood, Indian, Egyptian or Latin American genre films were allowed through the stern censorship grid.[3] The early 1990s had seen the dismantling of state-financed film industries due to the misguided excitement over privatisation and laissez-faire policies. Now, however, some sixteen years after the spectacular collapse of Communism in the fall of 1989, along with its totalitarian regimes and centralised economies, one could say that starlight has become visible across the skies of Central/Eastern Europe.[4]

Since those days, filmmakers have struggled to win viewers at home, as well as the attention of western producers and distributors. Their newly found concerns with accessibility, popularity and the spectacular have resulted in various efforts to revive popular genre cinema, to the extent that these efforts may be read as attempts to find ways of placating the drastic political and economic changes that have ruptured the fabric of post-Communist societies.[5] With the suspension of all other imperatives under the collapse of the totalitarian regime, these popular genres demonstrate, in the words of Peter Brooks, 'that it is still possible to find and show the operation of basic ethical imperatives . . . That they can be staged indeed "proves" that they exist'.[6]

Drawing on a representative corpus of films produced in the formerly Communist countries of Central and Eastern Europe during the last ten years, this chapter scrutinises films from three of the most prevalent, hence indicative genres: the melodrama; the 'Mafiosi thriller', a new post-Communist genre that is a curious, cross-cultural hybrid of American genre formulas, anti-Americanisation impetus and Central/Eastern European artistic sensitivity;[7] and the nationalist epic.[8]

MELODRAMA

During the 1920s and 1930s, melodrama was the most popular film genre in Central and Eastern Europe, successfully competing with the state-endorsed chauvinistic and educational documentaries, ethnographic shorts and historical epics, all of which were designed to boost the morale of the newly-founded nations. This is hardly surprising, since what Thomas Elsaesser defines as the nineteenth-century European all-embracing 'melodramatic conception of life'[9] found a fertile ground in the crisis caused by the difficult social and national integration of the newly emerged Central and Eastern European countries. Melodrama harnessed frustration and anxiety over rapid industrialisation and the destruction of traditional rural life and values, displacing it onto the 'moral polarization and dramatic reversals' of fortune that are typical of the genre.[10] As in theatre and literature, pre-Second World War film melodrama managed to serve diametrically opposed ideological purposes of the swiftly changing political landscape of Central and Eastern Europe, including right-wing nationalism, populist Fascism and proletarian socialism. The screen was dominated basically by two types of melodramas: sentimental stories about 'familial relations, thwarted love and forced marriages'[11] of the extravagant military and the upstart bourgeois elites, or pitiful tales about the downfall of their victims from the social depths. The clash of these mutually exclusive social and 'ethical imperatives' replaced the 'tragic vision'[12] of the prolonged struggles for national independence.[13]

Istvan Szekely's *Rakoczi March* (*Rákóczi induló*, Hungary/Germany, 1933), one of the decade's landmark Hungarian films, skilfully interweaves its chauvinist stance within a sentimental narrative. Set in the good old times of *fin-de-siècle* aristocratic military circles and richly garnished with Hungarian songs and dances, the picture was successful with audiences and was declared by the pro-Fascist dictator Horthy to be his favourite film. Another important Hungarian melodrama from the 1930s, this time contemporary, is the paradigmatic *Meseautó* ('Dream Car', 1934). Openly following the pattern of

1930s Hollywood lyrical melodramas about a working-class Cinderella finding her rich Prince Charming, Béla Gaál's film adds a 'celebratory and domestic dimension to the shots of Budapest', thus preserving the film's 'Hungarianness' in a 'strikingly artistic fashion' and transcending the 'mere escapist entertainment . . . of its fairy story'.[14] From 1934 through 1938, *Meseautó*'s immense popularity generated 'no fewer than 75 imitations'.[15]

The situation was not much different in the Czechoslovak cinema, where the polished Central European style of theatrical filmmaking was creatively adopted for melodramas. The expressionism of Karel Anton served his adaptations of popular literary plots remarkably well. Anton's best-known work, *Tonka Sibenice* ('Tonka of the Gallows', 1930), the first Czech sound film, 'portrays a woman whose downfall cannot be forgiven, her generosity of spirit leading directly to her destruction'.[16] The 'lyrical eroticism'[17] of the internationally renowned Gustav Machatý came to be considered a trademark style of the interwar Czech film industry and a highly exportable commodity, especially the melodramas he made in collaboration with the poet Vitezslav Nezval: *Erotikon* (1929) and *From Saturday to Sunday* (*Ze soboty na nedeli*, 1931).

Before 1948, nearly all of the sixty-three feature films made in Bulgaria and almost two-thirds of the fifty-odd films made in Romania were melodramas. Poland was perhaps the only country where, especially in the 1920s, melodramatic plots were usurped by films which Frank Bren appropriately calls 'grudge movies', i.e. films 'settling scores with Poland's old oppressor, Tsarist Russia',[18] and the villains in *Cud nad Wisla* ('Miracle of the Vistula', 1920, Ryszard Boleslawski) and *Huragan* ('Hurricane', 1928, József Lejtes) – two of the best-known films of that time – are Russians: Bolsheviks and Tzarist officers, respectively.

Dragoljub Aleksic's *Nevinost bez zastite* ('Innocence Unprotected', 1942), the first Yugoslav sound film and one of the few Yugoslav features made before the end of the war, was also a melodrama (as suggested by its generic title). Indeed, the genre's interwar success over the officially promoted and much better funded nationalist films 'indicates the ways in which popular culture had not only taken note of social crises . . . but also resolutely refused to understand social change in other than private contexts and emotional terms'.[19]

With Socialist Realism (which glorified the social and political ideals of Communism) in place by the end of the 1940s as the official aesthetic of the Soviet-backed regimes across the region, melodrama's domination was brought to an abrupt end, since it was considered not only bourgeois, but also subversive, even more so than comedy. Curiously enough, Communist authorities failed to take advantage of melodrama's power as master narrative for mediation of social/ideological crises, and its ability to bring 'characters and culture (and ideology, for that matter!) . . . into a manageable steady state . . . prescribed by the dominant values and myths of the [Communist] culture'.[20]

A plausible explanation can be found in the usual mix of ideological and aesthetic concerns shared by the decision-making authorities (or censors). The state shamelessly capitalised on the popularity of imported melodramas, monetarily and ideologically. Genre's capacity for social criticism made imported Hollywood, Indian and Egyptian melodramas welcome propagandistic illustrations of capitalism's evils, but at the same time this rendered indigenous melodramas dangerous. The centralised and closely watched film industries could never accuse 'the [Communist] system of greed, wilfulness, and irrationality'[21] without violating ideological taboos. The contempt for melodrama was additionally fuelled by the authorities' 'subconscious fear of free-flowing emotions'[22] that, once unleashed, could threaten the precarious psychological balance of a repressed society.

Moreover, as Christine Gledhill argues, melodrama – with its 'search for something lost, inadmissible, repressed'[23] – found itself unwanted because of its nostalgic preoccupations. The genre's propensity for idealisation of an 'atavistic past', associated by authorities with the legacy of the bourgeoisie and the 'ancien régime', came to be considered anachronistic in an artistic environment interested mainly in legitimising the Communist regime and its vision of the future. Melodrama's 'inherent wailing' was in direct contrast to historical optimism, the dominant mood of socialist realist art. The social and emotional 'gestural rhetoric' of melodrama had no chance next to the 'positive', superego-driven characters and their rationalised, ideologically motivated behaviour 'associated with (masculine) restraint' and 'carried in verbal discourse and dialogue'.[24]

Irina Shilova points out another key reason for the decline of melodrama under Communism, and by extension of popular genres in general. In her view, 'sentimental education' was never high on the agenda of Central and Eastern European filmmakers, as it 'somehow escaped their didactic preoccupations with enlightenment and education, with 'high' art as opposed to the 'low' art of entertainment'.[25] Therefore, despite melodrama's general tendency to benefit from periods of 'intense social and ideological crisis',[26] it was not before well into the 1990s that the first successful melodramas began to appear.

Another, and more important, explanation for the difficulties encountered in post-Communist attempts to revive melodrama lies in the continuous absence of a nominal consensus as to what the basic values of post-Communist society are: what is socially acceptable and what is not; what is prestigious and what is not; essentially, what is good and what is evil. Neo-liberalism provided ideological justification for the post-Communist transition in the public sphere, but failed miserably in the private. Unlike its nineteenth-century ancestor, bourgeois capitalism, which burst into the social and cultural scene with its particular set of ethical values 'staged' in genres like melodrama, post-Communist neo-liberalism refused to provide evidence for its viability in other than macroeconomic terms. Apart from some vaguely implied miraculous interdependence between western-style affluence, market economy and democratisation, no justification was offered in either ethical or aesthetic terms for the pains of transition. The emotional void, once again, has been left open to foreign products – American and Latin American soap operas.

Following Elsaesser's distinction between the eighteenth-century 'pre-revolutionary sentimental novels' and the nineteenth-century 'Restoration melodramas', post-Communist melodramas could roughly be divided into two categories – antagonistic and reconciliatory. While the former often end 'tragically . . . focused on suffering and victimization . . . recording the struggle of a morally and emotionally emancipated bourgeois consciousness against the remnants of feudalism', the latter 'with the bourgeoisie triumphant' end happily, 'reconciling the suffering individual to his social position, by affirming an open society, where everything [is] possible'.[27]

The first post-Communist melodramas tackling contemporary issues were aesthetically the weaker ones in spite of their ambition to 'stage' melodramatic 'conflictual oppositions' about thwarted love and complicated family relations on the backdrop of acute social evils – xenophobia, abuse of newly acquired power and money, drug-related prostitution – emerging on the dreary post-Communist landscape. Eastern European filmmakers, whose professional skills were shaped in a manner more suitable for the management of ideas than of emotions, indulged in foregrounding the social at the expense of the personal 'excess of emotion, ecstatic woe, sobs and tears'.[28] Marek Piwowski's *Uprowadzenie Agaty* ('The Kidnapping of Agatha', Poland, 1993), Maciej Slesicki's *Tato* ('Daddy', Poland, 1995), Krystyna Janda's *Pestka* ('Seed', Poland, 1996) and Metod Pevec's *Carmen* (Slovenia, 1996) are among the few contemporary antagonistic melodramas that enjoyed a decent run in the international festival circuit, albeit a rather modest success with critics and audiences at home. They display the masochistic and paranoid tendencies of the woman's film, where the heroine – the innocent maiden, the fallen woman or the professional – is punished for her transgressive strive for independence, thus 'mediating in private context'[29] the evolving drama of post-Communist social and financial deprivation, coupled with the advent of the so called 'male democracies'. The realities of 'shock marketisation' quickly dissuaded Eastern European women from their facile belief that democracy would automatically relieve them from their Communist predicament, known as the 'double burden' – the need to handle a full-time job and fully care for the family – and by the mid-1990s the majority of the unemployed (60–70 per cent) across the region were women.[30] But it was too late as they were already trapped between resurgent patriarchy and poverty. Young Agatha's love for a poor Gypsy musician is thwarted by her powerful *nouveau riche* father, who arranges for a 'police bullet to end the[ir] misalliance'.[31] Pevec's Carmen is a prostitute and drug addict, the illegitimate daughter of a cleaning woman, punished for her mismatched passion for a writer and intellectual, who first takes advantage of her and then watches helplessly her demise. In the more decisively conservative context of Polish cinema, independent career women are openly accused for the disintegration of the family, viewed as the worst legacy of Communism. In what he believes to be a noble gesture to protect his daughter, the hero of *Tato* declares his career-oriented wife as mentally unstable and deprives her of custody over their child. In *Pestka*, a surprisingly uninspired directorial debut by Janda – an actress famous for her dissident stance during the Solidarity crisis in the late 1970s and early 1980s – the heroine (played by Janda herself) is a successful professional who jumps under a tram in a self-sacrificial attempt to redeem herself and save her deeply religious lover from the complications of his extra-marital affair. Unfortunately, the filmmakers remain ideologically apprehensive whether to focus their accusations on the 'wilful and irrational' Communist legacy or on the post-Communist 'greed'[32] thus failing to personalise pure evil and fully harness the melodramatic energy of the conflict.

Marta Meszaros's *A Magzat* ('Foetus', Hungary, 1993) moves from what Susan Hayward calls the 'excess and unresolved contradictions' of the female melodrama to the 'masculine melodrama and its function of reconciliation'.[33] The film is a melodramatic rendition of the grand themes from Meszaros's golden period of the 1970s: motherhood and female bonding. Following the genre's paradigm, the director 'sides with the powerless'[34] in the person of a young mother who cannot afford to keep her third child and reluctantly agrees to an elaborate scheme for its adoption. Evil, coupled with social power, is epitomised by a childless *nouveau riche*, who believes that she can buy herself motherhood. In the name of female solidarity, however, Meszaros blurs the edges of the social conflict, indulging our visual pleasure with the erotic allure of female bonding in beauty parlours and expensive restaurants. In the happy ending, the poor woman decides to keep her baby and the rich one, moved by her predicament, generously repudiates the contract. By constructing them both as emotionally disenfranchised and sisters in suffering, Meszaros transforms their social antagonism into an affective symbiosis. Yet this compromise between the male sphere of power and money, represented by the *nouveau riche*, and the female sphere of motherhood and family, represented by the poor woman, remains rather precarious both aesthetically and ideologically.

The much-celebrated, Oscar-winning films *Kolya* (Jan Svĕrák, Czech Republic, 1996) and *Burnt By the Sun* (*Utomlyonnye solntsem*, Nikita Mikhalkov, Russia, 1995) as well as András Salamon's Sundance Festival-supported debut, *Close to Love* (*Közel a szerelemhez*, Hungary, 1999) are male melodramas of the reconciliatory kind, where public tensions are, to quote Elsaesser once again, 'resolved in a personal, emotional space . . . reconciling the suffering individual to his social position'. The story is situated on the eve of the relatively peaceful collapse of Communism in Czechoslovakia or what came to be known as the 'Velvet Revolution'. As the result of a bogus marriage to a Russian woman, Louka (Zdenek Svěrák), a seasoned, middle-aged Prague bachelor and womaniser is stuck with a charming five-year-old boy who does not speak a word of Czech (*Kolya*). In the late 1990s, Karcsi (Ferenc Hujber), a young and promising Budapest cop, meets a lovely Chinese immigrant woman who is pregnant, in trouble with the law and does not speak a word of Hungarian (*Close to Love*). What follows is the predictable emotional involvement of the protagonists with their carefully selected 'other'. The otherness of the Russian boy and the Chinese woman are defined along age, gender, language and ethnic/racial lines, thus binding these otherwise simple stories to such powerful socio-cultural sentiments as post-totalitarian blame and guilt, misogyny, anti-Russian feelings and racism.

To justify the protagonists' transformation to a gentler and kinder form of masculinity, the directors of *Kolya* and *Close to Love* foreground the 'myth-making function' of melodrama, the significance of which 'lies in the structure and articulation of the action and not in any psychologically motivated . . . individual experience'.[35] The emotionally ignorant protagonist attains knowledge of love, but not before overcoming the trials that lead to reconciliation with social change 'in private contexts and emotional terms'. In other words, Louka moves from the nonchalant existence of an oversexed bachelor to the mundane responsibilities of a single parent in trouble with the Communist authorities. The gradual deconstruction of one myth – that of care-free bachelorhood – simultaneously with the construction of another – that of self-sacrificial parenthood – is the universally appreciated aspect of *Kolya*, which, in the finest traditions of Czech literature and cinema, is saturated with a large dose of (self-) irony. The myth-making quality of the protagonists' actions benefits from activating the archetype of the biblical Joseph, husband of the Virgin Mary. This patriarchal symbolism is ironically reiterated at the finale: after his painful separation from Kolya, Louka discovers that his lover is pregnant, and we are left with the comforting anticipation that, like Joseph, he will raise the child. *Close to Love* ends with a more straightforward rendition of the biblical analogy: after exchanging a successful career for love, Karcsi and his racially mixed 'holy family' leave the maternity ward and disappear into the uncertainties of a frosty Budapest dawn.

In *Burnt By the Sun*, the simple story about a day in the life of a 1917–22 Civil War hero activates an even more powerful national sentiment and, within the confines of a love triangle, deals with grave public issues and national complexes. The film's very existence 'affirms an open society', allowing free discussion of the long-repressed trauma of the Stalinist purges of the 1930s. It is about an emotionally excessive confrontation between the male protagonists – Kotov (Nikita Mikhalkov) and Mitya (Oleg Menshikov) – over the love of Marusia (Ingeborga Dapkunaite), played out in five acts observing the classical unities of time and space. Their clash epitomises two irreconcilable ideological positions (whether 'right' or 'wrong' depends on the viewer's own *Weltanschauung*) and two traditionally antagonistic types of Russian masculinity: the *bogatyr*, a mythic Russian hero of peasant origin, and the urban *intelligent*, a relatively new historical construct. In the face of an arbitrary totalitarian system, however, their ideological allegiances are rendered equally worthless, and the tragedy of their confrontation, in Peter Brooks's words, is replaced by an ethical imperative which defines them both as accomplices in their own destruction. Kotov's 'Christ-like suffering'[36] at the finale – severely beaten and humiliated – and Mitya's Judas-like suicide after having delivered him to the NKVD[37] evoke equally passionate empathy. Thus the 'tragic' vision is replaced by an ethical imperative, where the powerful melodramatic myth-making devices serve the moral purpose of vindicating both the monolithic *bogatyr* and the malleable *intelligent* as helpless victims of Stalin's ruthless tyranny. The long-awaited reconciliation of two antagonistic Russian archetypes of masculinity in the face of history's cruel unpredictability turns into a so much needed absolution for contemporary Russian males in their struggle for reconciliation with maybe not as deadly, but similarly incomprehensible social change.

Typically, the post-Communist male melodramas marginalise their female protagonists, but they do so elegantly. In *Kolya*, the boy takes over the narrative space usually occupied by the female protagonist, while Louka's beloved is a secondary personage. In *Burnt by the Sun*, Marusia is no more than a symbol of the noble Russian woman. It is obvious, however, that this sort of femininity has irretrievably sunk into the collective unconscious, and even Dapkunaite, specially imported from Finland for the role of Marusia, is unable to resuscitate this image rooted in Russian literature. Like Natasha Rostova from Tolstoy's *War and Peace*, Marusia is torn between two men. And like Natasha, she stands for everything that is beautiful and pure, her love the highest endorsement of the protagonist's righteousness. Unlike Natasha, however, Marusia does not have a life of her own, and, after having served as a catalyst for the confrontation of the two male leads, her death is inconsequentially reported in the final titles.

In *Close to Love* the female protagonist also serves as a catalyst for the male hero's noble actions, but her marginality is here justified by the mysterious aura of the exotic 'other'. It is interesting to note that while the other damsels-in-distress discussed above are left (by ineffective or equally helpless men) at the mercy of the 'willfulness and irrationality' of fate, she is the only one saved by Karcsi's 'selfless heroism'.[38]

Once again, it should be noted that the success of these melodramas is predicated on transliteration of traditionally invincible masculinities into more vulnerable ones, and on the cathartic effect it brings to bear on male audiences' post-Communist frustrations and idiosyncrasies. In their nostalgia for stability, (male) melodrama and the nationalist epic (as we shall see below) also reach for Communist and pre-Communist role models, when it was clear who was the villain and who the victim. In order to validate Karcsi's self-sacrificial gesture, for example, the filmmaker activates the historical archetype of the chivalrous lover – popularised by Hungarian operettas and interwar melodramas – whose durability was assured after the success of the latest, albeit rather bland, contemporary rendition of the original *Meseautó* ('Dream Car'), Barna Kabay's *Meseautó* (Hungary, 2000). Indeed, when the Old is no more and the New has not yet emerged, traditional values, albeit transliterated and amended, seem to be the only ones that are stable.

The appearance of Lidia Bobrova's *Granny* (*Baboussia*, Russia-France, 2003), a powerful, antagonistic and contemporary Russian melodrama, demonstrates the filmmakers' growing confidence in handling emotional excess. What is more, the film underscores the consolidation of the post-Communist value system around the growing consensus that the source of all evil is the post-Communist, post-Soviet change, while propagating a nostalgic return to the good old 'atavistic past' – that of Brezhnev's stagnation in the 1970s. *Granny* is liable to provoke 'ecstatic woe, sobs and tears' featuring the grim final voyage of its elderly heroine, who after being rejected by all of her children proceeds to her predictable suicide by exposure. The contemporary wintry episodes are juxtaposed with reminiscences of the beautiful sunny days in the 1970s when everyone lived in harmony. Through a representative selection of the children's social status, Bobrova pushes the metaphor even further, heavily implying that Baboussia is no other but Mother Russia, who has been kicked out in the cold by her ungrateful, *nouveau riche* children and is dying desperate with her inability to help the really deserving ones – the refugees from Chechnia.

THE MAFIOSI THRILLER

Conservatism in the construction of gender roles is even more manifest in the second genre under discussion, the Mafiosi thriller. While melodrama reflects post-Communist confusion by showing both women and men as victims of Communism and/or post-Communism, the Mafiosi thriller, with its 'code of action, honour, success and failure . . . accommodates the symbolic functioning of masculinity'[39] in the brave new world of post-Communism. As is to be expected of such a male genre, it uses female protagonists sparingly and as functions of the hero.

The unprecedented commercial success of Wladyslaw Pasikowski's *Pigs* (*Psy*, Poland, 1992) and Aleksei Balabanov's *Brother* (*Brat*, Russia, 1997) set the stage for the Mafiosi thrillers, and while a few have been produced elsewhere (e.g. Hungary and Romania), the genre remains most popular in Poland and Russia.

The evolution of the Mafiosi thriller, like that of the melodrama, is both predicated on and contained by the post-Communist ideological and moral interregnum. As a mixture of elements borrowed from classical Hollywood gangster films, *noir* thrillers and more recent generic mutations like the vigilante movie, the Mafiosi thriller calls to mind John Woo's pre-1997 Hong Kong oeuvre, and like its antecedents, it appears in times of trouble. Its formulaic content could be summarised as the struggle of the lonely hero against the forces of evil. Its obvious intention is to exploit what Leo Braudy calls the 'generic expectations'[40] of the audience, created and cultivated over the years by American cinema. It features similar villains – mostly former members of the Communist secret services turned Mafiosi – and follows them through their deadly struggle with their rivals: local, Russian, Eastern European, even Italian. The reason for the blood spilled is not so important, but it usually involves some shady deals in arms, narcotics, radioactive materials, etc. The authorities, if present at all, are either corrupt or helpless in the face of lawlessness and organised crime. The Mafiosi thriller focuses, therefore, on the hero's efforts to restore justice. In psychoanalytic terms, his plight is a projection of the male's repressed desire to exorcise pent-up frustrations accumulated during his regimented existence under Communism. These films also mirror male fantasies about dealing with new post-Communist anxieties.

Franz Mauer (Boguslaw Linda), the hero of *Pigs*, is reassigned to the police force after a post-Communist downsizing of the Secret Service, while his best friend Olo (Marek Kondrat) is hired as a hit man by one of their former bosses turned Mafioso. The turning point comes when several of Franz's new colleagues are shot dead by Olo's gang, and while Franz takes the road towards justice and turns against his former cronies, Olo sinks deeper into moral decadence. The parallel development of Franz's positive and Olo's negative apprenticeship reveals two antagonistic codes of 'action, honour, success and failure',[41] and two types of masculinity epitomising the fundamental moral and social dilemma of post-Communist existence: the clash between very real evil and intangible good.

Against the backdrop of this realistic, at times brutally naturalistic conflict, Olo's betrayal is as inevitable as it is common. Far from an acrimonious Hollywood villain, he is just another guy, pragmatic and cynical like Franz before his transformation. He dies without understanding Franz's remark about killing him 'out of principle'. Viewers would probably also have their doubts if it were not for the brilliant manner in which Pasikowski resolves the most contentious issue in the film: Franz's moral awakening.

Unlike Olo, Franz's character is an intertextual construct. He is drawn along the lines of the introverted private eyes from Humphrey Bogart's crime films of the 1940s, whose ethos of predestined suffering and sacrifice in the name of a noble cause happens to be a basic trait of the Polish national ethos, of its romantic literary heroes and certainly of the Polish Film School heroes of the 1950s. The actor, Boguslaw Linda, who has recently turned 50, is still an undisputed star in Poland. His modernised 'Polishness', a mixture of romanticism, fatalism, and defiance, made him a symbol of the 'Cinema of Moral Concern'[42] and one of Krzysztof Kieslowski's favourite actors. In fact, Linda's dark charisma – strongly reminiscent of Bogart's existential resignation – elevates his Franz Mauer to the status of tragic hero. The actor did so well in *Pigs* that he has been associated with his screen persona ever since, earning him half a dozen roles in the same vein.

Like Linda, the much younger Sergei Bodrov Jr is no action hero; neither of them displays the extroverted flamboyance and physical aptitude so typical of their Hollywood counterparts. Emulating the latter would be culturally implausible, therefore both Linda and Bodrov Jr invest in a rare commodity these days – the creation of local heroes who are easy to identify with. Unlike Linda, however, Bodrov Jr is not a romantic hero; he is the boy-next-door, and this is what makes his unforgiving characters so attractive to Russian male viewers. His breakthrough role came with the Oscar-nominated anti-war film *Prisoner of the Mountains* (*Kavkazkii Plennik*, Russia, 1996), directed by his father, Sergei Bodrov. Capitalising on his son's understated screen presence, Bodrov Sr cast him as an amiable POW who befriends his Chechen captors. His role in *Brother*, another smart career choice, made him a leading star of the New Russian Cinema (hence his returning role in Balabanov's sequel, *Brother 2* (*Brat 2*, Russia, 2000)). His Danila, who, after having fought in Chechnya, returns home to become a champion of the down-and-out against the Mafiosi, represents a further evolution of the same screen persona. Danila's character does not take narrative time to *become* a hero – he already *is* the hero from *Prisoner of the Mountains*. Not unlike the Socialist Realist cinema of the 1930s and 1940s, this structure precludes character transformation, thus enabling the cycle of conflicts to be prolonged indefinitely.

The Mafiosi thriller's Manichaean structure determines the division of secondary characters into friends and enemies of the hero. To be sure, this dichotomy is better suited to urban mythology than to sociology; as Lévi-Strauss once commented, 'nothing resembles mythic thought more than ideology'.[43] The friends – homeless pensioners, helpless women, veterans from the Afghan War, all victimised by the Mafia and forgotten by the state – belong to the well-publicised margins of Russian society. The enemies are also the usual suspects: former party and KGB *apparatchiks* turned Mafiosi, a bunch of undifferentiated thugs and 'persons of Caucasian origin'.[44] The clash with the latter ensures the continuity of Bodrov's patriotic image, evoking strong xenophobic sentiment in Russian audiences angered by the endless wars in the Caucusus.

As both *Pigs* and *Brother* demonstrate, the theme of betrayal is very important for the Mafiosi thriller. After the decades of terror, institutionalised lies and divisive manipulation, the worst legacies of totalitarianism are the frustrating feelings of guilt and blame. Sooner or later, therefore, the Mafiosi hero is faced with the urgent need to avenge or forgive an act of betrayal. In contrast to Franz, Danila chooses to forgive his brother, a Mafiosi hit-man, who has used and betrayed him. *Brother* vindicates the call of blood, an important motif in Russian culture, long-buried under pseudo-allegiances to Party and Communist ideology.

The representation of women in the Mafiosi thriller reflects the idiosyncrasies of post-Communist gender representation. The women in Franz's life are beautiful and treacherous; however, in accordance with the predominant values of post-Communist society, their destructive behaviour is not irrational or passion-driven like that of the *film noir*'s *femme fatale*, but practical and materialistic. Franz's wife has left him for a better life in America, and his girlfriend leaves him for Olo – after all, in democratic Poland a Mafia hit-man is much better off than a police officer. These women epitomise the rapidly changing representation of female gender on post-Communist screens, which could be summarised as a change from the 'self-sacrificing to the self-investing woman'[45] – from that of a devoted mother, wife and/or shock worker[46] under Communism to a post-Communist harlot.

Brother accommodates male chauvinism as carefully as it does other populist sentiments. In accordance with the genre (and with Russian patriarchal, or *domostroi*, culture), women are the hero's most valuable acquisitions. They are supposed to be protected and respected, but never trusted or allowed into his inner sanctum.

Danila's girlfriends are selected with female viewers in mind. They represent two entirely different social and generational milieus: Cat (Mariya Zhukova) is a fashionable St Petersburg downtown junkie, and Sveta (Svetlana Pismichenko) is an older, married, working-class woman. Catering to the predominant conservatism of Russian viewers, sexual intimacies are only suggested, yet Sveta's rape by the Mafiosi is graphically explicit. In the context of *Brother*'s narrative, the rape is supposed to be vengeance for Danila's actions (it does trigger his rage and the final shoot-out), but in a de facto sense it works as a ritual punishment for Sveta's marital infidelity, and as such signals yet another concession to patriarchy.

The modification of a well-known genre formula to an entirely new social and cultural environment serves as magnifying glass of predominant social mores, all the more revealing of hidden evils. The Mafiosi thriller's *raison d'être* as a cross-cultural hybrid is predicated on this transparency, which, however, could often be hampered by incompatibilities of the foreign antecedent with the aesthetic and ethical requirements of the indigenous modes of representation. The legacy of Soviet cinema is a case in point here, since its aesthetic traditions largely shaped Central/Eastern European filmmaking for almost half a century.

This cinema favours slow-paced narration and the so-called 'psychological camera' – almost static, with a preference for meticulously lit indoor locations. Classical Soviet montage was used mainly for making ideological points and very rarely for building up suspense. The success of *Pigs* and *Brother* rests on the ability of their respective directors to turn these apparent constraints into virtues. Car-chase sequences, special effects and exotic locations are avoided, as they would have been forbiddingly expensive, not to mention risky, as any clumsy emulation of Hollywood would be disastrous with the highly critical domestic audience.

In *Pigs 2*, for example, the characteristic preoccupation of Eastern European cinema with the didactic over the poetic brings the action to a standstill. This tendency comes to a head in some new Mafiosi thrillers like Abai Karpykov's *Fara* (Russia/Khazakhstan, 1999), where the words suffocate the action thus mercilessly exposing not only the film's structural and stylistic deficiencies, but also the ethical ambiguity of the whole enterprise.

Post-Communist filmmakers are still ambivalent concerning whether or not to condemn the Mafiosi as greedy and ruthless villains killing mainly for hire, or to represent them as knights of a sort, or even contemporary Robin Hoods. As *Brother* and *Pigs* demonstrate, the logic of the genre brings forth the negative aspects of society and its mores. Western viewers have a hard time digesting episodes and comments suggestive of bigotry, misogyny, homophobia and anti-Semitism. As a character in *Brother* puts it, 'What is good for a Russian can kill a German'. In *Brother 2*, therefore, in order to circumvent the motivation of all that blood and violence in local social and moral terms, the director goes global and takes the Mafiosi chase to Chicago.

However, there are limits that cannot be trespassed even during this current confusion of values, and the genre's success remains predicated on the ability of filmmakers to take a rigorous, albeit risky stand on grave social issues. One of the latest Russian Mafiosi thrillers, *Sisters* (*Syostry*, 2001), Sergei Bodrov Jr's directorial debut, is more than a canny emulation of *Pigs* and *Brother*. Like them, it owes its popularity at home and with festivals world-wide to the carefully observed balance between appreciation and condemnation, between myth and reality. But, unlike its predecessors, *Sisters* offers a balanced gender representation by following the growing affection between two estranged sisters, who are caught between Mafiosi settling their accounts and who become the film's only 'rational and moral agents'.[47] The genre's evolution is consistent with the escalating social pessimism, emphasised here via the director's cameo appearance. This innocent, narcissistic gesture links Bodrov Jr's screen persona as the good Mafioso-cum-(possible)-saviour with the *Brother* films, suggesting that while law and order in Russia are in ever-shorter supply, his vigilante heroes and the entire Mafiosi genre will continue to be very much in demand.[48]

THE RETURN OF THE REPRESSED: NATIONALIST EPIC

From the discussion thus far, one could rightfully conclude that the more successful a post-Communist film genre is, the more powerful its conservative tendencies will be. In this context, the recent revival of another traditional Central/Eastern European genre, the nationalist epic, seems perfectly logical. As a rule, the nationalist epic supports the political status quo and, therefore, has been the genre favoured by the authorities from its inception in the late 1910s to the present. Its propensity to find justification for current policies and exorcise collective frustrations by conjuring up the ghost of the 'glorious past' has made it a suitable vehicle for strengthening the national spirit. In its more atrocious versions this genre has also functioned as an expression of state-induced, chauvinistic attitudes and territorial claims, hence the so-called 'grudge films'.

Between the wars, nationalist epics were most popular in Romania, Poland, and Bulgaria, countries whose national integration was traumatic due to complex internal and external historical factors, and where they remained popular under Communism. After the decline, in the early 1960s, of the Polish School associated with the innovative filmmaking style of Andrzej Wajda, Kazimierz Kutz and Andrzej Munk, most of this movement's directors found refuge in nationalist epics based on the rich Polish literary tradition and in the lucrative budgets that went with them. In Romania and Bulgaria, nationalist epics reflected, among other things, the megalomaniac ambitions of the Communist dictators, who wanted to see themselves as part of the indigenous monarchic succession.

Not surprisingly, immediately following the collapse of Communism expensive nationalist epics were unaffordable. It took seven years for the Russian film *Yermak* (1996, Vladimir Krasnopolsky and Valeri Uskov) to see the light of day, and when it finally did, the audiences' tastes had radically changed. There was no place for expensive cinematic expressions of historical sentiments at that time. And when Emir Kusturica's rather costly *Underground* (France/Yugoslavia, 1995) appeared, it was meant not to boost, but to deconstruct, the genre's traditionally chauvinistic perspective.

Over the past few years a cluster of nationalist epics have appeared in quick succession in Poland and Hungary. Jerzy Hoffman's *With Fire And Sword* (*Ogniem i mieczem*, 1999), Andrzej Wajda's *Pan Tadeusz* (1999), Filip Bajon's *The Spring to Come* (*Przedwiośnie*, 2000), and Jerzy Kawalerowicz's *Quo Vadis?* (2001) are made by the four colossi of postwar Polish cinema. All based on renowned literary classics, most of which have enjoyed more than one screen adaptation at home and abroad, these films are reported to be 'the most expensive' and 'the most popular ever' in Polish film history.[49]

In contrast, the Hungarian output comes as a real surprise, since the genre has not seriously been on the filmmakers' agenda in that country. Made to commemorate the millennial anniversary of the Hungarian state, Gábor Koltay's *Sacra Corona* (2001), Csaba Káel's *Bánk Bán* (2001) and Géza Bereményi's *The Bridgeman* (*A hidember*, 2002) do not sport the literary or artistic credentials of their Polish counterparts, but they too are reportedly 'the most expensive and popular Hungarian films ever made'.[50] When we add to the list Agnieszka Holland's contribution, *Jánosik* (aka *The True Story of Janosik and Uhorcik*),[51] a Slovak-Polish blockbuster threatening to wipe out Slovakia's lean film budget for years to come, it becomes obvious that we are dealing with an important socio-cultural phenomenon. From a strictly pragmatic point of view, this phenomenon could be explained with reference to the generous budgets such films command. From a socio-cultural point of view, it could be seen as a symptom of the agonising Romantic idea of nationhood and as a beleaguered defiance of globalisation in general, and of Hollywood in particular. In the present context, this phenomenon can be read as a displaced reaction to the deep frustration with the growing social tensions of post-Communism and its ever-shifting cultural and moral codes, and as another expression of the longing for stability of gender representation, as discussed above.

With Fire and Sword, the first part of Henryk Sienkiewicz's trilogy, is made in the style of its second and third part, also directed by Hoffman.[52] The film reinterprets the seventeenth-century Polish-Cossack wars as fairy tale (or as Hollywood kitsch), where the very real and long-existing ethnic tensions between Ukrainians and Poles serve as the backdrop to a pumped-up love triangle. *Sacra Corona* gravitates to the same stylistic pole in its glorification of the eleventh-century Hungarian kingdom and Christianity's stabilising role in the interregnum after the death of King István, the founder of the Hungarian state. *Quo Vadis?*, meanwhile, deviates a bit from the nationalist epic's traditional preoccupation with national history as it is set in the times of Emperor Nero in the first century AD, but it is as epic as they come, running the highest-ever film budget in Poland at US$ 18 million, and nationalist, too, in its Catholic piety, epitomised by the suffering of its Polish heroine Lygia (Magdalena Mielcarz) and her family at the hands of the pagan Romans.

Wajda's *Pan Tadeusz*, the uncontested gem among the latest apparitions of the nationalist epic, is situated at the opposite end of the stylistic range with its bitter romantic playfulness reminiscent of Wajda's ironic-nostalgic 1972 rendition of Stanisław Wyspianski's poem *The Wedding* (*Wesele*). Unfortunately, its most significant artistic accomplishment (the organic integration of Mickiewicz's verse) remains inaccessible to foreign viewers. Similarly obscure to non-Hungarians (due primarily to the film's confused script and pretentious style) is the tragic and controversial persona of the 'Greatest Hungarian count' of the nineteenth century, Széchenyi István, one of the builders of Budapest (*The Bridgeman*). Further high-gloss attempts to come to terms with controversial historical facts and figures take as their subjects the theory and practice of the Bolshevik Revolution throughout the Russian Empire and in Poland (*The Spring to Come*), as well as the activities of Juraj Janosik, an eighteenth-century highway rogue, claimed as a national hero in Poland and Slovakia (*Jánosik*).

The above films offer escapist identification par excellence with role models sanctified by tradition. They flaunt 'real', unproblematised heroes, committed to sacrosanct nationalist goals: either accomplished leaders of a patriotic war (*Sacra Corona*, *With Fire and Sword*) or undergoing apprenticeship to lead a struggle for social or national emancipation (*Jánosik*, *Pan Tadeusz*, *The Bridgeman*, *Bánk Bán*, *The Spring to Come*). The women in the wings are wise mothers, sublime objects of courtly love or romanticised desire, sometimes home wreckers or even witches, who in general 'know' their inspiring, supportive or destructive place in the life of the hero and society. His enemies are mercilessly destroyed for their cowardice and betrayal, or else generously forgiven.

If the post-Communist melodrama, as argued above, 'resolutely refuses to understand social change in other than private contexts and emotional terms', and if the Mafiosi thriller offers cathartic relief by 'accommodating the symbolic functioning of masculinity' in the public realm, the nationalist epic seeks to resolve both individual and collective anxieties in the context of history. The above-mentioned films display striking similarities in reaching back through the centuries for stable social and moral values and for long-forgotten collective archetypes, hence their success with audiences. In so doing, the nationalist epic serves a conciliatory, albeit ideologically controversial, social and ideological function. It goes without saying that their melodramatic tendencies, brought to the extreme in *Bánk Bán*, a lavish screen adaptation of a romantic nationalist opera, are very strongly felt, as the genre relies heavily on emotional excess and sentimental sensationalism, as well as on 'melodrama's search for something lost' and its 'ties to an atavistic past', to quote Christine Gledhill once again.

Nationalist epics offer their viewers – as an alternative to the standardised and ubiquitous Hollywood dream – an escape to a dream-world familiar from nursery tales and national literary classics. This explains the kind of aesthetic lenience demonstrated by the viewers of these films, and to a large extent by their critics, who, seemingly blinded by their unprecedented popularity, fail to notice the films' regressive (including xenophobic and misogynistic) tendencies. Thus what was originally conceived as an effective remedy by various nation-states during times of crisis may very well become a divisive agent in a liberal, ethnically diverse and increasingly emancipating global environment. It seems that the ever-brighter film stars in the sky over Central and Eastern Europe are bringing to light not only charismatic heroes but also some embarrassing idiosyncrasies, collective as well as individual.

NOTES

1. Anita Skwara, ' "Film Stars Do Not Shine in the Sky over Poland": The Absence of Popular Cinema in Poland', in Richard Dyer and Ginette Vincendeau (eds), *Popular European Cinema* (London: Routledge, 1992), p. 220.
2. The geopolitical concept of Eastern Europe was established in the late nineteenth century, was reconfirmed by the peace treaties after the First World War and, after the Second World War, was sealed by the Iron Curtain. According to Churchill's 1946 famous Fulton speech, the Iron Curtain divided the continent into totalitarian East and free West. Until 1989, Eastern Europe consisted (in alphabetical order) of Albania, Bulgaria, Czechoslovakia, Poland, Romania, Hungary and Yugoslavia. With the GDR added and Yugoslavia (and later Albania) subtracted, Eastern Europe became synonymous with terms like 'Soviet', 'Eastern' or 'Communist' Bloc, and, along with them, was discarded as artificial after the fall of Communism.
3. See Christina Stojanova, 'The Most Important Art', in *Correspondence*, Council of Foreign Relations, US, No. 8 (2002), pp. 11–12, also at *Correspondence: An International Review of Culture and Society*, 8 (Summer/Fall 2001), pp. 11–12, http://www.cfr.org/press/publications/correspondence.php (accessed 5 March 2005), and in *Filmkultura*, Budapest, Hungary, at: http://www.filmkultura.hu/2000/articles/essays/index.hu.html (accessed 5 March 2005); Geo Saizescu, Dana Duma, Calin Caliman (eds), *Cinema 2000* (Buchuresti, Romania: Editura VICTOR, 2000), pp. 287–303; in *Kino*, 6 (1999), Sofia, Bulgaria, pp. 3–14. See also Christina Stojanova, *Dual Vision: Eastern European Cinema and the Totalitarian State 1948–1989* (London: I. B. Tauris, forthcoming).
4. Throughout this chapter the term 'Central/Eastern European' is used interchangeably with 'post-Communist'.
5. My knowledge of the films has been acquired first-hand by travelling extensively across the region since 1993; by sitting on juries (Cottbus IFF, Germany, 2004; Karlovy Vary IFF, Czech Republic 2002; Sochi European FF, Russia 2001; Documentary Jury, Karlovy Vary IFF 2000; Moscow IFF, Russia 1999; Sochi IFF, Russia 1997), and by curating numerous retrospectives of Central/Eastern European cinema throughout Canada.
6. Brooks, *The Melodramatic Imagination*, p. 201.
7. Christina Stojanova, 'Le film de genre américain dans le cinema post-communiste: "le Mafiosi Thriller" ', in *Ciné-bulles*, 17, 2 (Été/Summer 1998), pp. 38–43.
8. The latest films to come out from Central and Eastern Europe further sustain the argument that the tendencies outlined below are paradigmatic and endemic across the region.
9. Thomas Elsaesser, 'Tales of Sound and Fury', in Christine Gledhill (ed.), *Home Is Where the Heart Is* (London: BFI, 1987), p. 50.
10. Christine Gledhill, 'The Melodramatic Field: An Investigation', in Gledhill, *Home Is Where the Heart Is*, p. 30.
11. Susan Hayward, 'Melodrama', in *Key Concepts in Cinema Studies* (Routledge: London, 1999), p. 200.
12. Ibid., p. 200.
13. The countries that came to constitute Eastern Europe or the 'Soviet' Bloc after 1945 gained their independence either as a side-effect of the Russian-Turkish wars from the second half of the nineteenth century (Bulgaria, Romania and Serbia) or emerged as sovereign entities as a result of the piece treaties signed after the First World War (Czechoslovakia, Hungary, Poland and Yugoslavia).
14. Bryan Burns, *World Cinema: Hungary* (Cranbury, NJ: Associated University Presses, 1996), p. 10.

15. According to Istvan Nemeskurty, 205 feature-length melodramas were produced between 1939 and 1943 in Hungary (Istvan Nemeskurty, *Istorija vengerskogo kino 1896–1966* (Moscow: Izdatelstvo Isskustvo, 1969), p. 94).
16. Peter Hames, *The Czechoslovak New Wave* (Berkeley, CA: University of California Press, 1985), p. 1.
17. Ibid., p. 23.
18. Frank Bren, *World Cinema I: Poland* (Urbana, IL and Chicago: University of Illinois Press, 1989), p. 13.
19. Elsaesser, 'Tales of Sound and Fury', p. 47.
20. Robert Kolker, *Film, Form, and Culture* (New York: McGraw-Hill, 1999), pp. 110–11.
21. Elsaesser, 'Tales of Sound and Fury', p. 46.
22. Irina M. Shilova, 'Emotions as the Source of a Genre', trans. Christina Stojanova, in *Kinovedcheskie Zapiski*, 11 (1991), p. 70.
23. Gledhill, 'The Melodramatic Field', p. 24.
24. Ibid., pp. 32–4.
25. Shilova, 'Emotions as the Source of a Genre', pp. 67–71.
26. Elsaesser, 'Tales of Sound and Fury', p. 45.
27. Ibid., pp. 45–6.
28. Linda Williams (1991), 'Film Bodies: Gender, Genre, and Excess', in Leo Braudy and Marshall Cohen (eds), *Film Theory and Criticism*, 5th edn, eds Leo Braudy and Marshall Cohen (Oxford and New York: Oxford University Press, 1999), p. 711.
29. Hayward, 'Melodrama', p. 202.
30. Raya Staikova, Assen Yossifov and Zoya Gadeleva, *Losses with or without Indemnity: People's Expectations and the Responsibility of the State. Final Report 1998–2–134. SOCO (Social Consequences of Economic Transformation in East-Central Europe) Program* (Vienna: Institute for Human Sciences, 1999). Raya Staikova, Assen Iossifov and Zoya Gadeleva, *Risk and Indemnity? Society's Expectations of State Responsibility in the Bulgarian Transition*, SOCO (Social Consequences of Economic Transformation in East-Central Europe) Project Paper no. 64 (Vienna: Institue for Human Sciences, 1999).
31. Marek Haltof, *Polish National Cinema* (New York and Oxford: Berghahn Books, 2002), pp. 6–11.
32. Elsaesser, 'Tales of Sound and Fury', p. 46.
33. Hayward, 'Melodrama', p. 204.
34. Martha Vicinus (1981), qtd in Gledhill, 'The Melodramatic Field', p. 21.
35. Elsaesser, 'Tales of Sound and Fury', p. 44.
36. Ibid., pp. 44–6.
37. Abbreviation of the Soviet Secret Police in the 1930s, predecessor of the KGB.
38. Elsaesser, 'Tales of Sound and Fury', pp. 44–6.
39. Christine Gledhill, 'The Melodramatic Field', p. 10.
40. Leo Braudy (1976), 'From *The World in a Frame*', in *Film Theory and Criticism*, p. 618.
41. Gledhill, 'Introduction', *Home Is Where the Heart Is*, p. 10.
42. An iconoclastic trend in Polish cinema between the mid-1970s and the imposition of martial law in the country in 1981, characterised by its open criticism of the moral status quo of the Communist regime.
43. Susan R. Suleiman, *Authoritarian Fictions* (Princeton, NJ: Princeton University Press, 1993), p. 4.
44. An officially accepted, somewhat ironic, Russian reference to people from Chechnya, Georgia, Abhasia and Armenia.

45. Mira Marody and Anna Giza-Poleszczuk, 'Changing Images of Identity in Poland: From the Self-Sacrificing to the Self-Investing Woman?', in Susan Gal and Gail Kligman (eds), *Reproducing Gender: Politics, Publics, and Everyday Life after Socialism* (Princeton, NJ: Princeton University Press, 2000), pp. 151–75.
46. Shock workers contributed most hours of unpaid labour to the fulfilling of the plan.
47. Vaclav Havel, 'The Power of the Powerless', in John Kean (ed.), *The Power of the Powerless* (Hutchinson: London, 1978), p. 65.
48. Unfortunately, without Bodrov Jr, who died tragically in 2002 during the first week of shooting of his second film, *The Messenger*.
49. Jerzy Peltz, *A Report on the Polish Cinema*, paper presented at East European Film Today, FIPRESCI Conference, 4–6 October, 2002, Szolnok, Hungary.
50. György Baron, moderator's remarks from East European Film Today, FIPRESCI Conference, 4–6 October, 2002, Szolnok, Hungary.
51. Co-directed with her daughter Kasia Adamek, to be released in 2005.
52. *Pan Wolodyjowski* (Poland, 1969) and *The Deluge* (*Potop*, Poland, 1974, Oscar nomination 1975) were until recently 'the most popular and expensive films of all time' made in Poland (F. Bren, p. 88: promotional materials for *With Fire and Sword*).

RECOMMENDED FILMS

Melodramas

Burnt By the Sun (*Utomlyonnye solntsem*, Nikita Mikhalkov, 1995, Russia)
Erotikon (Gustav Machatý, 1929, Czechoslovakia)
Granny (*Baboussia*, Lidia Bobrova, 2003, Russia-France)
Kolya (Jan Svěrák, 1996, Czech Republic)
Meseautó ('Dream Car', Béla Gaál, 1934, Hungary)

Mafiosi thrillers

Brother (*Brat*, Aleksei Balabanov, 1997, Russia)
Pigs (*Psy*, Wladyslaw Pasikowski, 1992, Poland)
Sisters (*Syostry*, Sergei Bodrov, Jr, 2001, Russia)

Nationalist epics

Khan Asparoukh ('681 The Glory of the Khan', Ludmil Staykov, 1981, Bulgaria)
Pan Tadeusz (Andrzej Wajda, 1999, Poland)
With Fire and Sword (*Ogniem i mieczem*, Jerzy Hoffman, 1999, Poland)

RECOMMENDED READINGS

Allan, Seán and Sandford, John (eds) (1999) *DEFA: East German Cinema 1946–1992*. New York and Oxford: Berghahn Books.
Burns, Bryan (1996) *World Cinema: Hungary*. London: Flicks Books.
Goulding, Daniel J. (1985) *Liberated Cinema: The Yugoslav Experience*. Bloomington, IN: Indiana University Press.
Goulding, Daniel J. (ed.) (1989) *Post New Wave Cinema in the Soviet Union and Eastern Europe*. Bloomington, IN: Indiana University Press.

Haltof, Marek (2002) *Polish National Cinema*. New York and Oxford: Berghahn Books.

Hames, Peter (1985) *The Czechoslovak New Wave*. Berkeley, CA: University of California Press.

Holloway, Ronald (1985) *The Bulgarian Cinema*. London and Toronto: Associated University Press.

Iordanova, Dina (2003) *Cinema of the 'Other' Europe: Industry and Artistry of East Central European Film*. London: Wallflower Press.

Kenez, Peter (2001) *Cinema and Soviet Society: From the Revolution to the Death of Stalin*. London: I. B. Tauris.

Liehm, Antonin J. and Liehm, Mira (1988) *The Most Important Art: Central and Eastern European Film after 1945*. Berkeley, CA: University of California Press.

Michalek, Boleslaw and Turaj, Frank (1988) *The Modern Cinema of Poland*. Bloomington, IN: Indiana University Press.

Paul, David W. (ed.) (1983) *Politics, Art, and Commitment in the East European Cinema*. New York: St. Martin's Press.

Petrie, Graham (1978) *History Must Answer to Man*. Budapest: Corvina Books.

Stoil, Michael (1982) *Balkan Cinema: Evolution after the Revolution*. Ann Arbor, MI: UMI Research Press.

PART III

SOUTH AMERICAN TRADITIONS

8. POST-*CINEMA NOVO* BRAZILIAN CINEMA

Randal Johnson

INTRODUCTION

Film industries around the world depend on diverse forms of state support for their very existence. Brazilian cinema is no exception. When former president Fernando Collor de Mello did away with government programmes of film production financing and distribution shortly after taking office in 1990, Brazilian cinema plunged into one of the worst crises of its history. After Collor's impeachment for corruption in 1992, the administration of Itamar Franco implemented a new mode of government support through the use of tax incentives and deductions. The Audiovisual Law (1993) allowed Brazilian cinema to begin the slow process of re-emerging from the crisis.[1] Since that time, Brazil has produced more than 200 feature-length films. Audiences around the globe have greeted with applause such pictures as *Central Station* (*Central do Brasil*, Walter Salles Jr, 1998) and *City of God* (*Cidade de Deus*, Fernando Meirelles and Kátia Lund, 2002). Such films, in turn, have expanded Brazilian cinema's share of its own market.

Numerous critics have attempted to describe, categorise or analyse the major currents of post-crisis production. Since many if not most of the films in question reveal a quite natural interest in exploring diverse facets of Brazilian society (something that has characterised major tendencies of Brazilian cinema from its very inception) critics have frequently attempted to understand recent production in comparison or contrast with the *Cinema Novo* movement of the 1960s and 1970s. Lúcia Nagib, for example, has argued that contemporary Brazilian cinema's approach is national, but not nationalist, and that *Cinema Novo*'s focus on the political has been replaced by a predominant interest in the personal.[2] Kleber Mendonça Filho sees a certain continuity between the two periods, suggesting that with such films as *City of God*, *Madame Satã* (Karim Anouiz), *The Trespasser* (*O Invasor*, Beto Brant) and *Bus 174* (*Ônibus 174*, José Padilha), all of which were released in 2002, Brazilian cinema has rediscovered the 'social tensions' of Nelson Pereira dos Santos's *Rio, 40 Degrees* (*Rio 40 Graus*, 1955) and Glauber Rocha's *Land in Anguish* (*Terra em Transe*, 1967).[3] Ivana Bentes, on the other hand, arguing that *Cinema Novo*'s 'aesthetic of hunger' has given way to a 'cosmetics of hunger', has criticised numerous recent films for not living up to Glauber Rocha's aesthetic and political radicalism.[4]

In this chapter I will discuss some of the most significant trends of the new Brazilian cinema, particularly in relationship to *Cinema Novo*, thus attempting to offer a somewhat different perspective on the debate. As a central part of Brazilian film history, *Cinema Novo* is an obligatory point of reference in any discussion of modern cinema in Brazil. At the same time, one must recognise that both Brazil and its motion pictures have changed in numerous ways since the 1960s. Although some filmmakers associated with the movement continue to be active (e.g. Eduardo Coutinho, Carlos Diegues, Ruy Guerra and Nelson Pereira dos Santos), the re-emergence of Brazilian cinema since the early 1990s has been due in large part to the appearance of a new generation of filmmakers who have moved beyond *Cinema Novo*'s considerable aesthetic and political legacy.

GENERAL TENDENCIES

The major challenge faced by Brazilian cinema since the crisis of the early 1990s has been to reoccupy the portion of its own market (long dominated by Hollywood) that it previously held. This obviously means attracting the public to its movies and developing in them the habit of seeing Brazilian films. To this end, filmmakers have explored a broad diversity of aesthetic and thematic proposals and strategies. Comedy has been particularly significant for rebuilding Brazilian cinema's public. Carlota Camurati's *Carlota Joaquina, Princess of Brazil* (*Carlota Joaquina, Princesa do Brasil*, 1995) – the first film of the post-crisis period to attract more than a million spectators – draws from the comic tradition of the *chanchada* in a rather caricatured and grotesque portrait of the Portuguese royal family in the early nineteenth century.[5] In *Little Book of Love* (*Pequeno Dicionário Amoroso*, 1997) and *Possible Loves* (*Amores Possíveis*, 2001), Sandra Werneck explores the pitfalls of relationships in modern Rio de Janeiro. *A Dog's Will* (*O Auto da Compadecida*, 2000), Guel Arraes's adaptation of Ariano Suassuna's well-known play, is a fast-moving comic morality tale with roots in medieval theatre, *autos*. Based on a true story, Andrucha

Waddington's *Me You Them* (*Eu Tu Eles*, 2000) deals with a woman with three husbands living in the same house and features a splendid soundtrack of northeastern music by popular singer and songwriter Gilberto Gil. Also set at least partially in the northeast, Carlos Dengues's *God Is Brazilian* (*Deus É Brasileiro*, 2003) tells what happens when God comes to Brazil looking for a saint to replace him while he is on vacation.[6]

Dramatic films of diverse inclinations have also been important. Laís Bodansky's *Brainstorm* (*Bicho de Sete Cabeças*, 2001) is a powerful movie that focuses on a young man who is committed by his father, and against his will, to a mental institution. Luiz Fernando Carvalho's *To the Left of the Father* (*Lavoura Arcaica*, 2001), an adaptation of Raduan Nassar's homonymous novel, tells the story of a prodigal son from a patriarchal Lebanese-Brazilian family. Roberto Santucci's *Bellini and the Sphinx* (*Bellini e a Esfinge*, 2002) and Flávio Tambellini's *Bufo & Spallanzani* (2001), based on novels by Tony Belotto and Rubem Fonseca, respectively, venture into the terrain of detective thrillers. Walter Salles Jr's black-and-white *Foreign Land* (*Terra Estrangeira*, 1995), filmed partially in Portugal, deals beautifully with exile, displacement, and identity. Karim Anouiz's *Madame Satã* reconstructs the bohemian underworld of 1940s Rio de Janeiro in his portrait of the black transvestite known as Madam Satan. Carlos Diegues's *Orfeu* (1999) brings the story of Orpheus back to Rio de Janeiro's Carnival in a film based less on Marcel Camus's 1959 version than on its literary source, Vinícius de Moraes's drama *Orfeu da Conceição*.

Other filmmakers have opted for period projects or what Mendonça Filho calls 'obituary films', that is, movies about great political or artistic figures from Brazil's history (e.g. Sérgio Rezende's *Mauá: O Imperador do Rei* (1999), Zelito Vianna's *Villa-Lobos: A Life of Passion* (*Villa-Lobos: Uma Vida de Paixão*, 2000) and André Sturm's *Sonhos Tropicais* (2001)). Some, with an eye on the international market, have made films partially or entirely in English. In pictures such as Murilo Salles's *How Angels Are Born* (*Como Nascem os Anjos*, 1996), Bruno Barreto's *Four Days in September* (*O Que É Isso, Companheiro?*, 1997), Luiz Carlos Lacerda and Buza Ferraz's *For All: Springboard to Victory* (*For All – O Trampolim da Vitória*, 1997) and Bruno Barreto's *Bossa Nova* (2000), the use of English is important for the story's dramatic development, while in others, such as Monique Gardenberg's *The Interview* (*Jenipapo*, 1995) and Walter Lima Jr's *The Monk and the Hangman's Daughter* (1996), one gets the sense that its use is either arbitrary or imposed as a condition of co-production.[7]

Documentary production has been particularly rich since the crisis of the early 1990s. João Jardim and Walter Carvalho's beautiful *Janela da Alma* (2002) deals with sight and features interviews with such people as Wim Wenders, José Saramago and Oliver Sacks. Paulo Caldas and Marcelo Luna's

The Little Prince's Rap Against the Wicked Souls (*O Rap do Pequeno Príncipe*, 2000) traces the divergent trajectories of two young men from the same poor neighbourhood in Recife, one of whom becomes a musician, the other an assassin. Erik Rocha's *Stones in the Sky* (*Rocha que Voa*, 2002) and Sílvio Tendler's *Glauber – Labirinto do Brasil* (2003) both deal with *Cinema Novo* leader Glauber Rocha. The former, made by Glauber's son, is constructed around footage Glauber himself shot in Cuba; the latter uses footage taken both during Glauber's illness in Portugal shortly before his death in 1981 and during his wake and burial as its points of departure. The most important documentary filmmaker in Brazil continues to be Eduardo Coutinho, whose *The Mighty Spirit* (*Santo Forte*, 1999), *Babilônia 2000* (2000), and *Edifício Master* (2000) deal with popular views of religion, the millennium as seen in a Rio de Janeiro urban slum (or *favela*) and the diverse community residing in a building in Copacabana. Coutinho consistently gives voice to those who are rarely heard, thus offering compelling views of contemporary Brazilian society.

Through this very brief and obviously incomplete overview, the difficulty of attempting to fit contemporary Brazilian cinema into any simple category should be clear. Recent production clearly cannot be understood by focusing exclusively on the movement's legacy, nor should it be judged by *Cinema Novo*'s aesthetic and political imperatives. Points of contact, however, do in fact exist, and it is to them that I now turn, beginning with a brief summary of some of the movement's primary concerns.

CINEMA NOVO AND POST-CINEMA NOVO

Cinema Novo emerged at a specific historical moment and it confronted specific challenges and issues with the responses and strategies that were then possible. Ideologically associated with the political left, the movement espoused a radical nationalist, anti-imperialist and anti-capitalist political perspective. It sought, above all, to use the cinema as a tool for consciousness-raising in the process of social transformation rather than as a form of entertainment. As Glauber Rocha wrote in his seminal manifesto 'The Aesthetics of Hunger', with their 'sad, ugly . . . desperate films', *Cinema Novo* directors sought to 'make the public aware of its own misery' in the hope that they would participate in the struggle for national liberation.[8]

To reach that end, *Cinema Novo* sought a revolutionary aesthetic posture in radical opposition to the easily digested narrative transparency of mainstream cinema, and particularly of so much American cinema. In this sense, the movement was aligned with an international vanguard involving such filmmakers as Jean-Luc Godard, Jean-Marie Straub and Pier Paolo Pasolini that sought to transform cinematic language, linking aesthetics and politics. Rocha's writings are filled with reflections on the possibilities of 'decolonising' cinema, recognising, in a tradition that goes back at least to Vladimir Mayakovsky, that 'without revolutionary form there can be no revolutionary art'.[9] However, *Cinema Novo* also sensed that it would be impossible to create such a language within the traditional structures of the Brazilian film industry. To this end, the movement sought out alternative models of film production, largely inspired by postwar Italian neorealism and the French *nouvelle vague* and summarised in the oft-repeated strategic slogan 'a camera in your hand and an idea in your head'.[10]

Unlike the 1960s, contemporary Brazilian cinema is not guided, unified or constrained by grand political narratives such as those which guided *Cinema Novo* and other contemporaneous fields of cultural production. Today there is no unifying movement, common cause or hegemonic political discourse, and the cinema is no longer seen as a tool for consciousness-raising in a broader process of social transformation. Rather, it is a form of artistic or cultural expression and, yes, a form of entertainment. As Carlos Diegues, one of the founding members of *Cinema Novo*, has recently put it, the social importance of the cinema is its 'ability to entertain, to move and excite people, to make them think, to bring them together, promoting their spiritual progress, their identification with the other'.[11] This is obviously a far cry from the political radicalism of *Cinema Novo*.

By the same token, with few exceptions (e.g., Júlio Bressane, Carlos Reichenbach), experimentation with film language – at least in feature-length films – takes place largely within parameters that are accessible to a mainstream audience. The often-unstable handheld camera of *Cinema Novo* has been replaced by the steady-cam, the stark photography by increasingly sophisticated cinematography, and digital technology that frequently draws from the language of television, advertising and video clips. This is perhaps not surprising given the advances that have taken place in audio-visual technology since the 1960s, as well as the fact that three of the most important production companies to emerge since the crisis of the early 1990s – Conspiração (*Eu Tu Eles*), O2 (*Cidade de Deus*) and Videofilmes (*Central do Brasil*) – also make commercials, video clips or other modes of television programming. Some critics see this as a sign of globalisation and the imposition of Hollywood's standards while others are more sanguine. Cinematographer Affonso Beato, for example, suggests that 'Brazilian photography is beautiful not because of the influence of advertising, but rather because we have good photographers. Today's public wants well-made films, and we have the obligation to give them that'.[12]

The question of the production model that Brazilian cinema should take has still not yet been fully resolved, primarily because of Hollywood's continuing domination of the domestic market, which renders production difficult under any circumstances. Whereas many 'independent' filmmakers (who are in fact dependent on government financing) continue to adhere to a relatively low-cost, auteur model of production, others opt for a more explicitly 'commercial' model, often in association with Globo Filmes (the film subsidiary of the powerful Globo television network) or American distributors such as Columbia, Fox and Warner Bros, under the auspices of the provisions of the Audiovisual Law.[13] After the crisis of the early 1990s, Brazilian filmmakers almost by necessity had to explore diverse ways to bring the public back to the theatres where their movies were showing. Films that reject at least some level of commercial appeal and insist on an iconoclastic or experimental discourse draw very few spectators. This fact in itself goes a long way toward explaining the greater accessibility of most of today's films when compared with those of *Cinema Novo*, whose public was largely composed of students, liberal professionals intellectuals and artists.[14] As Eduardo Escorel has written, 'Rejecting commercial criteria implies accepting our relegation to a ghetto, or, put another way, it means passively accepting our exclusion from our own market'.[15] And the fact of the matter is that Brazilian cinema will only become truly self-sustaining when it can occupy a significant portion of its own market.

BACK TO THE BACKLANDS

With this general backdrop in mind, one must recognise that since the emergence of *Cinema Novo* in the early 1960s, social concerns have never ceased to exist in Brazilian cinema. What no longer exist are the didacticism and the ideological dogmatism of early *Cinema Novo*. We no longer see mythic struggles between good and evil or history and destiny, as in the films of Glauber Rocha. Many films do in fact return, as numerous critics have pointed out, to what Bentes refers to as *Cinema Novo*'s 'territories of crisis': the impoverished northeastern backlands (the *sertão*) and *favelas*.[16] Others deal with questions of poverty, violence, and corruption. To establish points of convergence and divergence between *Cinema Novo* and contemporary Brazilian cinema, I will briefly examine a number of different films that deal precisely with these 'territories' or issues.

Numerous films of the 1990s and early 2000s are indeed set in the *sertão*: Waddington's *Me You Them*, Diegues's *God Is Brazilian*, Salles Jr's *Central Station* and *Behind the Sun* (*Abril Despedaçado*, 2002), Rosemberg Cariry's *Corisco & Dadá* (1996), Lírio Ferreira and Paulo Caldas's *Perfumed Ball* (*Baile Perfumado*, 1997), José Araújo's *O Sertão da Memória* (1997) and Sérgio Rezende's *The Battle of Canudos* (*Guerra de Canudos*, 1997), to mention only the most widely discussed. These and other films are not necessarily set in the northeast *because* of *Cinema Novo*, although they do often render homage to the movement. In fact, the northeast has long played an important role in Brazil's creative imagination, so it is not at all surprising that numerous contemporary films would be shot there.

The *sertão* that appears in these films, however, is generally not the mythical 'territory' of Glauber Rocha, where archetypical figures act out larger-than-life struggles. Rather, as Nagib and others have pointed out, the recent films set in the *sertão* tend to focus on the personal, rather than the political. *Corisco & Dadá*, for example, deals as much with the relationship between these two historical characters as with the struggle in which they are engaged. The same goes for *Perfumed Ball*, which provides a more 'intimate' look at the *cangaceiro* (gangster) Lampião and his gang, and *The Battle of Canudos*, which follows the drama of a family caught up in the Canudos war. The comedies *Me You Them* and *God Is Brazilian* (see above) both deal with diverse aspects of Brazilian society and the Brazilian personality. Rather than *Cinema Novo*, the latter movie's journey from the northeast to central Brazil evokes Diegues's earlier film *Bye Bye Brazil* (*Bye Bye Brasil*, 1980), which does include an important subtext dealing with the evolution and transformations of *Cinema Novo*.[17]

Perhaps surprisingly, the most controversial of these pictures has been Salles Jr's award-winning *Central Station*, a film that some have described as resuscitating *Cinema Novo*'s original objective of showing the true face of Brazil. But the Brazil that *Central Station* reveals is not the pre-revolutionary Brazil of early *Cinema Novo*. It is a country still plagued by poverty, violence, injustice, inequality and cynicism, but it is also a Brazil characterised by hope, compassion and solidarity. Dora (Fernanda Montenegro) and Josué's (Vinícius de Oliveira) search for the boy's father is also a search for self and for Brazil itself. As the director has stated, *Central Station* is 'the story of a boy searching for a father he has never met . . . of a woman searching for the feelings she has lost . . . and, in a way, it's a film searching for a certain human and geographical territory . . . a territory of solidarity . . . and fraternity'.[18] *Central Station* is a complex, eloquent and sensitive portrait of contemporary Brazil, without being didactic or paternalistic. This profoundly universal humanistic statement, which values solidarity and compassion over what Salles Jr has called a 'culture of indifference [and] cynicism',[19] has obviously had great resonance both domestically and internationally.

Why the controversy? Perhaps because *Central Station* has been *too* successful, *too* accessible to broad audiences and not sufficiently 'politically correct' or 'Glauberian'. Gilberto Vasconcelos, for example, denounced the film as an expression of globalised, neoliberal standards dictated by Hollywood and as 'a publicity icon of the FHC [Fernando Henrique Cardoso] era', suggesting that 'we would be better off watching a documentary about the Central Bank'.[20] Bentes argues that films such as *The Battle of Canudos* and *Central Station* transform *Cinema Novo*'s 'territories of poverty' into 'exotic gardens' or historical museums.[21] *Central Station*, in Bentes's view, presents a romanticised *sertão*, an 'idealised return to the roots', a 'territory of conciliation and pacification', offering a 'melancholic and conciliatory "happy ending" that is distant from Rocha's utopian gesture toward transcendence and freedom'.[22]

Both Vasconcelos and Bentes seem to have difficulty breaking free from the ideological strictures of *Cinema Novo* and recognising that the political does not always have precedence over the personal. Perhaps the most important thing about *Central Station* – and the reason for its broad success – is that it is an intensely Brazilian story expressing universal values that audiences around the world can understand and relate to. It is clearly one of the high points of post-crisis Brazilian cinema.

URBAN VIOLENCE

Another important current in contemporary Brazilian cinema involves urban violence, which has reached crisis in several major cities, with well-organised and heavily armed drug traffickers challenging police in increasingly daring ways, particularly in Rio de Janeiro. Journalist and filmmaker Arnaldo Jabor has noted that for his generation – the *Cinema Novo* generation – 'misery was one of the contradictions of capitalism, to be eased through social justice . . . But misery was "out there somewhere", in the hillside slums, in the northeastern droughts, somewhere far away, and it gave rise to crime as a deviation from "normal" behaviour. Casual crime legitimated our "good" little world'.[23] But things have changed since then, and now the periphery has invaded the centre with its own laws and logic. 'Today, misery is another nation, in the center of the Unsolvable, untouched by salvation and political hope . . . Crime surrounds and implicates us; and there are no innocents'.[24] According to Jabor, it no longer makes sense to talk about class struggle, consciousness-raising or citizenship. Some marginalised segments of the population have raised their own consciousness, and in an entirely different direction than what his generation had hoped for.

Violence, be it personal, political, social or institutional, has long been represented in Brazilian cinema, and it would be surprising were it not a feature of contemporary films. José Joffily's *Who Killed Pixote?* (*Quem Matou Pixote?*, 1996) focuses on police violence against the poor and particularly on the killing of Fernando Ramos da Silva, who played the lead role in Hector Babenco's *Pixote* (1980). Beto Brant's *Belly Up* (*Os Matadores*, 1997) deals with loyalty and betrayal among professional assassins working for a wealthy drug trafficker along the Brazil–Paraguay border. In his *Chronically Unfeasible* (*Cronicamente Inviável*, 2000), Sérgio Bianchi paints a devastating portrait of Brazil as a country in which there is no solidarity and in which no one is entirely free from blame. It is a society permeated by corruption, self-interest, brutality and violence. The film points toward an almost absolute social impasse that can only result in violence. Using a fragmented narrative with a voice-over that ranges from ironic to cynical, *Chronically Unfeasible* is perhaps the most uncompromising and hard-hitting of all of the films produced since the crisis of the early 1990s.

More than any others, two feature-length films – Meirelles and Lund's *City of God* and Brant's *The Trespasser* – and two documentaries – Padilha's *Bus 174* and João Moreira Salles and Kátia Lund's *Notícias de uma Guerra Particular* (1999) – exemplify what Jabor means when he talks about the periphery invading the centre. Perhaps the starting point for this tendency is the documentary by Moreira Salles and Lund. *Notícias de uma Guerra Particular* focuses on the war between drug traffickers and the police in the Dona Marta *favela* that rises above the Rio de Janeiro district of Botafogo. Based on two years of interviews, the documentary contrasts the perspectives of drug traffickers (some of whom are no more than twelve or thirteen years old), the police and residents of Dona Marta. Through its juxtaposition of such perspectives, the film reveals different aspects of an undeclared civil war, which a military policeman interviewed describes as a seemingly endless 'private war', in Rio de Janeiro. What it does not offer is a vision of hope for the future of Brazil.

Bus 174 looks at a crime that took place in the Jardin Botânico district of Rio in June 2000 when a man hijacked a bus and kept a young woman hostage for several hours before the police killed both of them. Padilha examines both the kidnapper's background and police incompetence in his attempt to gain some understanding of these tragic events. The kidnapper had seen his mother murdered when he was ten, and he later survived the police massacre of street children outside the Candelária church in downtown Rio. He was subsequently confined to Rio's notoriously violent prison system. Given the lack of any kind of effective social services net, he was clearly on a road of despair and hopelessness starting at a very early age. The police, on the other hand, were totally unprepared for the hostage situation and unable to negotiate a peaceful solution. In his review for *The New York Times*, A. O. Scott writes that the film offers 'an extraordinarily detailed, horribly sad portrait of a life shaped by the cruelty and indifference that seem endemic in urban Brazil'.[25]

Youth such as the drug traffickers in *Notícias de um Guerra Particular* and the hijacker in *Bus 174* become the protagonists of Meirelles and Lund's *City of God*, which is based on a novel by Paulo Lins and a screenplay by Bráulio Mantovani. With few exceptions, *City of God* features non-professional actors, a number of whom belong to Nós do Morro, a non-governmental organisation that works with theatre in the Rio de Janeiro *favela* known as Vidigal. *City of God*, named for a low-income housing project outside of Rio, portrays, over a period of three decades, the lives of children and young adults who are caught up in a web of violence from which there appears to be no escape. Shot in a very fast-moving and fluidly edited cinematic language that draws heavily from advertising and video clips, the film combines extremely graphic images of violence with a certain sense of humour expressed by the narrator, a boy from the City of God who wants to become a professional photographer. The film was very popular at the time of its release, attracting more than three million spectators in Brazil and an even larger international audience, and it has generated the television series *Cidade dos Homens* (2002, 2003), using some of the same actors and focusing on the lives of two young men both in the *favela* where they live and in their interactions with diverse segments of Rio de Janeiro society (e.g. the school, the postal service, the beach, middle-class youth).

City of God has also provoked a heated debate about cinema's responsibility in the representation of violence. Bentes, for example, condemns the film for transforming violence into a spectacle without offering the necessary contextualisation and without indicating the underlying causes of violence. Others, such as Susana Schild, counter that by focusing only on the housing project and the violence within it. *City of God* 'could not have been more explicit in the 'contextualisation' of the violence', which only exists because of the omission of the government, the indifference of the elite and much of the media, and the drug consumption of the privileged classes. Schild notes that between 1987 and 2001, 467 young people under the age of 18 were killed in the Israeli-Palestinian conflict, whereas 3,937 were killed in the undeclared war in Rio de Janeiro. In this context, the film is simply realistic.[26]

The feature film that perhaps best exemplifies Arnaldo Jabor's comment about the periphery invading the centre is Brant's *The Trespasser*, which tells the story of three partners in a successful construction firm, two of whom hire an outsider to kill the third. He does so, and he also murders the partner's wife. The problem begins after the feigned grieving has subsided. The killer, played by Paulo Miklos – vocalist of the rock group Os Titãs – appears at their firm one day and insinuates himself into the business, suggesting that he can take care of the company's security. He even ends up having an affair with the daughter of the couple he has murdered. And no matter how hard the partners try, the man won't go away. As Jabor puts it, the low-budget and hard-hitting *The Trespasser* is 'exceptional in the way it shows how the "dirty" world invades the tranquil sordidness of bourgeois society'.[27] There is no Manichaeanism here; everyone is implicated in Brant's grim and frightening vision of contemporary Brazilian society, where the marginalised – which were the focus of many *Cinema Novo* films – seem to have tired of the margins.

Contemporary Brazilian cinema explores multiple avenues of artistic expression as it attempts, with growing success, to re-establish its position in the domestic market. Its diversity and its filmic exploration of diverse aspects of Brazilian society are its strengths. The *Cinema Novo* movement of the 1960s and 1970s is and will continue to be an important point of reference, but today's filmmakers are not – and cannot be – constrained by its considerable legacy.

NOTES

1. The crisis reached its peak in early 1990, when Brazil's new (and soon to be impeached) president, Fernando Collor de Mello, did away with government support for the nation's film industry and other fields of cultural production. For an overview of the crisis, see Randal Johnson, 'The Rise and Fall of Brazilian Cinema, 1960–1990', in Randal Johnson and Robert Stam, *Brazilian Cinema*, expanded edition (New York: Columbia University Press, 1995 [1991]), pp. 362–86. For a brief discussion of the re-emergence, see Randal Johnson, 'Departing from *Central Station*: Notes on the Reemergence of Brazilian Cinema', *The Brazil e-Journal*, a publication of the Brazilian Embassy in Washington, DC (Spring 2000), http://www.brasilemb.org/profile_brazil/brasil_ejournal_randal.shtml (accessed 4 February 2005).

2. Lúcia Nagib, 'Cinema Novo Meets the New Cinema', *Framework*, 42 (Summer 2002), pp. 12–42.

3. Kleber Mendonça Filho, '2002, O ano em que o Brasil voltou a ser filmado', *CinemaScópio*, 6 December 2002, http://cf.uol.com.br/cinemascopio/artigo.cfm?CodArtigo=66 (accessed 5 March 2005).

4. See Ivana Bentes, ' "Cosmética da fome" marca cinema do país', *Jornal do Brasil*, 8 July 2001, http://jbonline.terra.com.br/destaques/glauber/glaub_arquivo4.html (accessed 7 March 2005); and Ivana Bentes, '*Cidade de Deus* promove turismo no inferno', *O Estado de São Paulo* 31 August 2002, http://www.consciencia.net/2003/08/09/ivana.html (accessed 7 March 2005).

5. The comedy or musical comedy known as the *chanchada* was a popular cinematic genre in Brazil from the mid-1930s until the late 1950s. It gave rise to such stars as Carmen Miranda and Grande Otelo.

6. Eight of the top ten Brazilian films since the re-emergence are comedies, and six of those feature children's stars Xuxa or Renato Aragão.

7. More successful at reaching the international market have been films such as *Central Station* and *City of God*, which tell Brazilian stories in Portuguese using an international *film* language rather than English. Perhaps not surprisingly, both Walter Salles Jr and Fernando Meirelles have been invited to direct films outside of Brazil. Salles's *The Motorcycle Diaries* (2004) involves production companies from Argentina, Peru and Chile, as well as France, Great Britain and the United States. Its executive producer, Robert Redford, is American. Salles is obviously Brazilian, but the film is not. More recently, Salles has directed the American production *Dark Water* (2005), based on a novel by Kôji Suzuki. Meirelles, on the other hand, has directed the Anglo-American production of *The Constant Gardener* (2005), based on the novel by John Le Carré.

8. Rocha's manifesto, 'Uma Estética da Fome', was originally published in the *Revista Civilização Brasileira*, no. 3 (julho de 1965). An English-language version appears in Randal Johnson and Robert Stam (eds), *Brazilian Cinema*, 3rd edn (New York: Columbia University Press, 1995), pp. 68–71.

9. Along with artist Alexander Rodchenko and filmmaker Sergei Eisenstein, poet Vladimir Mayakovsky formed part of LEF, the Left Front for the Arts, in early Soviet Russia. LEF believed that artistic form was a vehicle for ideology, and that art could contribute to the construction of a new society only through the creation of revolutionary artistic forms.

10. See Randal Johnson, 'Brazilian Cinema Novo', *Bulletin of Latin American Research*, 3, 2 (1984), pp. 95–106; and Johnson and Stam, *Brazilian Cinema* (1991).

11. In Arnaldo Bloch, ' "A cultura está sob intervenção" ' [interview with Carlos Diegues], *O Globo*, 3 March 2003.

12. Cited in Alexandre Werneck, 'Estética Polêmica', *Jornal do Brasil*, 11 June 2002, http://jbonline.terra.com.br/jb/papel/cadernob/2002/07/16/jorcab20020716001. html (accessed 7 March 2005). Beato is cinematographer of Glauber Rocha's *Antônio das Mortes* (*O Dragão da Maldade contra o Santo Guerreiro*, 1968) and Carlos Diegues's *Orfeu* (1999), among many others.

13. See Randal Johnson, 'TV Globo, the MPA and Contemporary Brazilian Cinema', in Lisa Shaw and Stephanie Dennison (eds), *Latin American Cinema: Essays on Modernity, Gender, and National Identity* (Jefferson, NC: McFarland, 2005), pp. 11–38.

14. G. Dahl, 'Cinema Novo e seu público', *Revista civilização brasileira*, 11/12 (December/March 1966/1967), p. 194.

15. Eduardo Escorel, 'Quadrilha – Não Há Cinema sem Consumo', communication presented at the symposium on *O Cinema como Expressão Cultural*, Centro Cultural Banco do Brasil, Rio de Janeiro, 27–29 May 2003, www.criticos.com.br (accessed 7 March 2005).

16. Bentes, ' "Cosmética da fome" marca cinema do país'.

17. Randal Johnson, 'Film, Television and Traditional Folk Culture in *Bye Bye Brasil*', *Journal of Popular Culture*, 18, 1 (Summer 1984), pp. 121–32.

18. Qtd in Anthony Kaufman, 'Sentimental Journey as National Allegory: An Interview with Walter Salles', *Cineaste*, 24, 1 (1998), p. 20.

19. Ibid., p. 20.

20. Gilberto Vasconcelos, ' "Central do Brasil"/Outra Visão', *Folha de São Paulo*, 12 February 1999.

21. Bentes, ' "Cosmética da fome" marca cinema do país'.

22. Ibid.

23. Arnaldo Jabor, 'Nas periferias, a "pós-miséria" cria outro país', *O Estado de São Paulo*, 16 April 2002.

24. Ibid.

25. A. O. Scott, 'Dissection of a Crime Leaves Brazil Exposed', *New York Times*, 27 March 2003, http://query.nytimes.com/gst/fullpage.html?res=980DE6D61030F93 4A15750C0A9659C8B63 (accessed 7 March 2005).

26. Susanna Schild, '*Cidade de Deus*: O Tiro que não Saiu pela Culatra', 26 September 2002, www.criticos.com.br (accessed 7 February 2005).

27. Jabor, 'Nas periferias, a "pós-miséria" cria outro país'.

RECOMMENDED FILMS

Behind the Sun (*Abril Despedaçado*, Walter Salles Jr, 2001)
Bossa Nova (Bruno Barreto, 2000)
Bus 174 (*Ônibus 174*, José Padilha, 2002)
Central Station (*Central do Brasil*, Walter Salles Jr, 1998)
Chronically Unfeasible (*Cronicamente Inviável*, Sérgio Bianchi, 2000)
City of God (*Cidade de Deus*, Fernando Meirelles and Kátia Lund, 2002)
Foreign Land (*Terra Estrangeira*, Walter Salles Jr, 1995)
Four Days in September (*O Que É Isso, Companheiro?*, Bruno Barreto, 1998)
God Is Brazilian (*Deus É Brasileiro*, Carlos Diegues, 2003)
Me You Them (*Eu Tu Eles*, Andrucha Waddington, 2000)
Orfeu (Carlos Diegues, 1999)
Possible Loves (*Amores Possíveis*, Sandra Werneck, 2001)
Tieta of Agreste (*Teita do Agreste*, Carlos Diegues, 1996)

RECOMMENDED READINGS

Foster, David William (2000) *Gender and Society in Contemporary Brazilian Cinema*. Austin, TX: University of Texas Press.

Johnson, Randal (1984) *Cinema Novo x 5: Masters of Contemporary Brazilian Film*. Austin, TX: University of Texas Press.

Johnson, Randal (1987) *The Film Industry in Brazil: Culture and the State*. Pittsburgh, PA: University of Pittsburgh Press.

Johnson, Randal, and Stam, Robert (eds) (1982, 1988, 1995) *Brazilian Cinema*. New York: Columbia University Press.

Nagib, Lúcia (ed.) (2003) *The New Brazilian Cinema*. London: I. B. Tauris.

Stam, Robert (1997) *Tropical Multiculturalism: A Comparative History of Race in Brazilian Cinema and Culture*. Durham, NC: Duke University Press.

Xavier, Ismail (1997) *Allegories of Underdevelopment: Aesthetics and Politics in Modern Brazilian Cinema*. Minneapolis, MN: University of Minnesota Press.

9. NEW ARGENTINE CINEMA

Myrto Konstantarakos

In a country whose cultural scene has always been prominent but is now close to bankruptcy, there is no future for middle-class kids studying law or medicine. So they might as well turn to what they like. The second half of the 1990s saw the eruption onto the scene of a generation of enthusiastic film students who transformed the Argentine filmscape by rebelling against the existing industry, radically renewing the aesthetics and themes of local cinema, bringing back young audiences and film critics, and provoking a true boom of festivals and events centred around the unclear notion of 'independence'. But what are the characteristics of these films and what do they have in common? In what way have they rekindled the indigenous film industry? What is their aesthetic importance? To what are they opposed and how can one distinguish between those who belong and those who do not? This chapter attempts a definition of the so-called 'new Argentine cinema' and endeavours to investigate the validity of this label.

CONTEXT

In Argentina after dictatorship and the initial euphoria accompanying the return of democracy in 1983, there followed many long years of economic instability. It was only in 1996, therefore, that the Festival de Mar del Plata reopened its doors and the local film industry started to get back on its feet. Until then the study of film had been split between the school of the Institute of Cinema (the CERC), which taught only technicians, and the cinephiles belonging to clubs such as the famous Nucleo of Salvador Sammaritano. It was not until 1984 that the University of Buenos Aires launched its first degree in film. Five years later, the 'Image and Sound' section was established in the Faculty of Architecture, again for technicians but with some theoretical modules as well. The initial impetus thus had schools of cinema springing up from the end of the 1980s and becoming widespread throughout all the large towns. Eventually more than 7,000 students were attending some twenty schools – numbers previously unheard of in South America. One of the private institutions, the prestigious Universidad del Cine run by the well-known 1960s director Manuel Antín (b. 1926), was also set up as a production house.

Nowadays, the first generation of graduates from these schools have made their first or second films, or else set up parallel channels to promote, produce and distribute the works of their peers. These directors and producers receive support from the elders of their profession, intellectuals as well as critics. A network with the mission of showing these films free of charge has grown up as these filmmakers have had no access to conventional distribution, and shorts competitions have blossomed. New cinema reviews have been launched: both *Haciendo Cine*, which helps the making of independent films, and *Film* (edited by Fernando Peña, who also runs the Filmoteca) now compete with the slightly more established *El Amante de cine*.

The Argentine film legislation of 1995 is the envy of South America. This is so despite its imperfections – in particular the fact that it allows for only one source of funding and renders investment in filmmaking unattractive to television companies (which is not, for example, the case in France or Italy). Despite this and other weaknesses, it would be the best film legislation in the region if only it were respected. In 1998 the Director of the Institute of Cinema, Julio Mahárbiz, was accused of embezzlement when he withdrew financial support from all of the productions then underway. But it was in 1995 that, thanks ironically to the much-despised Institute, the local film industry was rejuvenated with the launch of *Brief Stories* (*Historias Breves*), a competition of short films seen by some 12,000 spectators. It was during this competition that Bruno Stagnaro and Adrián Caetano met and set out on the path to making *Pizza, Beer, Smokes* (*Pizza, Birra, Faso*, 1998), and that Lucrecia Martel managed to secure funds for *The Swamp* (*La ciénaga*, 2001). *Brief Stories* was deemed so successful that it was held again in 1997 and 1999.

With the unexpected success of the New Iranian film Abbas Kiarostami's *A Taste of Cherry* (*Ta'm e guilass*, 1997) – believed to be a hard sell in Argentina but which still managed 150,000 sales in its one cinema, where it played for almost a year – the domestic film industry came to firmly believe in the public's appetite for independent cinema. The capital's first film festival in April 1999 was billed as 'independent' and, though little advertised, brought in an enthusiastic crowd as soon as tickets went on sale and was sold out daily. Within a year of this, the 'independent' label no longer applied, as both the national and local governments were on the same side. Nevertheless, the festival's success rapidly overtook the more established and glamorous Mar del Plata Film Festival and was moved from November to March.

URBAN SETTINGS

Despite receiving praise and recognition from critics and the public alike, the new crop of Argentine filmmakers refuse to be labelled as a movement because they lack a declaration of principles and a single set of ideas. Nor is it accurate to call them a new 'generation', given the very different ages of the filmmakers.[1] One can, though, distinguish two main trends and influences. The first is a reactualisation of the French New Wave in the work of Martín Rejtman and Esteban Sapir. Despite their great originality, however, both Rejtman's *Rapado* (1992) and Sapir's *Fine Powder* (*Picado fino*, 1998) went unnoticed by the public, and only *Pizza, Beer, Smokes* generated interest in them. The main second trend and influence is Italian neorealism, albeit without the Italian filmmakers' compassion for the suffering of others.

There is a deficit in the visual representation of Buenos Aires, in photography for example. Traditionally this was left to literature, but at the moment only in film can the city be found as it truly is, and not as it is portrayed by television. Is it then the theme – of marginality – and the location – a mostly urban setting – which creates the novelty? In the first years of the movement, the films in question focused on the social exclusion of the capital's outskirts and shantytowns (one notable early exception is Gregorio Cramer's *Winter Land* (*Invierno mala vida*, 1997), shot among the sheep of Patagonia but still focusing on a couple of marginals).

It was Alejandro Agresti's *Buenos Aires Vice Versa* (1996), with its depiction of the city as woven together from the enmeshed lives of its diverse inhabitants (à la Robert Altman's *Short Cuts* (1993)), which brutally introduced viewers to the Buenos Aires of today – with its slums, seedy hotels and violence, remnants of the years of bloody dictatorship. An old couple who have lost their daughter during the years of the Junta have locked themselves away and never venture out. Through an advertisement, they hire a young girl to film the town for them and will only pay her if they like what they see. It is through the girl's footage that her patrons discover the town as it is some fifteen years after the dictatorship, and their reaction is to violently reject it (perhaps anticipating the public's reaction to this new style of filmmaking?), their objection being that the slum dwellers are not 'people'. With the help of her film and a child from the shantytowns who guides her through the streets, the girl herself discovers a side of the capital she did not know.

Agresti's declared intention in the picture is to hold a mirror to his audience and to the city because, as he says, there has as yet been no film of contemporary Buenos Aires. Rather than the moment of their watching it, it is his audience's reaction afterwards, when being plunged back into the city and the locations depicted on screen, which interests the director. This is the lesson Caetano and Stagnaro seem to have followed in *Pizza, Beer, Smokes* as they send their actors (illegally) into the very symbol of the capital city, the giant obelisk. *Buenos Aires Vice Versa* received much acclaim and marked the return of Agresti, a director who had emigrated to Holland and whose earlier works such as *Secret Wedding* (*Boda secreta*, 1989) have not all been released in his native land. Through this film he has become an 'agent of transformation',[2] with students flocking to gawk at him. Making movies with very little means, eschewing television clichés, using new faces, handheld camerawork, a mixture of fiction and documentary, the direct recording of reality, improvisation and digressions in storytelling, Agresti is the precursor to the young independent cinema.

Most Argentine student shorts are also focused around the same gritty, urban themes as *Buenos Aires Vice Versa*. So is *Bad Times* (*Mala época*, 1999), which consists of four segments, shot by four different directors (Nicolás Saad, Mariano De Rosa, Salvador Roselli and Rodrigo Moreno), in which Buenos Aires is portrayed as a battle ground, a machine made to expel marginals. Furthermore, the countryside is no longer seen as a safe haven from the harshness of the city, and neither is the South (which has traditionally assumed this role). In Fernando Spiner's *The Sleepwalker* (*La Sonámbula*, 1999), the protagonists' escape to the south of the province leads them to their demise and, when Rulo (Luis Margani) gets to Comodoro Rivadavia – 2,000 kilometres south of the capital – in Pablo Trapero's *Crane World* (*Mundo grúa*, 1999), it is only to find himself again in the similar San Justo, his neighbourhood in Buenos Aires.

Is the urban theme then the defining quality of new Argentine cinema? Fernando Musa's *Fuga de cerebros* (1998) came out just after *Pizza, Beer, Smokes* and is situated in the slums of Buenos Aires, but it is not clear that he belongs to the movement. The difficulty with the 'new Argentine cinema' label is knowing to whom it applies; Musa's treatment of urban marginality, for example, is radically different from that of Trapero, Caetano and Stagnaro. Instead of the new realism, Musa prefers a magical realism: when the protagonist in *Fuga de cerebros* kisses the young girl with whom he has fallen in love by the river, night falls and stars shine all around. Quintín, meanwhile, defines the new generation in *opposition* to the magical realism of Eliseo Subiela (*Last Images of the Shipwreck* (*Últimas imágenes del naufragio*, 1985); *Don't Die Without Telling Me Where You're Going* (*No te mueras sin decirme adónde vas*, 1995)) and the allegories of Fernando Pino Solanas (*Tangos, the Exile of Gardel* (*Tangos, l'exil de Gardel*, 1985); *The South* (*Sur*, 1988)): 'The first element dividing the generations is that people don't fly in Argentine films any more'.[3] Moreover, the financing of *Fuga de cerebros*, which came in part from the privately-owned Channel 13, had an effect on the film's aesthetic, rendering it more conventional than the others, as well as on the choice of actors, who came from television series or *telenovelas*.

AESTHETICS

It is therefore partly in their method of finance that the new Argentine directors have broken with the past, resigning themselves to filming without money, be it from the government (INCAA) or television. If they do, it is only once the project is finished, as with Pablo Trapero or Adrián Caetano, who each contacted established producer Lita Stantic to distribute *Crane World* and *Bolivia* (2000), respectively. These low-budget pictures, which had seemed experimental and a financial risk, have turned out to be good value, recouping their initial investment. With no conventional financing, however, shooting takes a long time, for a longer shoot keeps costs down. Moreover, the arrival of digital video has noticeably reduced total production costs in comparison with shoots relying on traditional film equipment, and has made it possible to operate with smaller crews during filming and post-production, thereby favouring independent producers. Of course, new forms of production imply new aesthetics. Because of their limited means, the films in question tend to take on a neo-realistic air, with non-standard formats – 16 mm or digital video used and subsequently blown up – natural settings, non-professional actors, monochrome filming and little or no artificial lighting (as in Gustavo Corrado's *El Armario* (2000), for example) in a documentary style. But there can still be great differences in the aesthetics of these works. For example, many of the above films have very few cuts, whereas *Fine Powder* has 1,200.

Whereas Subiela's filmmaking is individualistic, the new style is primarily collective. As was the case in the 1960s and 1970s, directors, technicians, cinematographers (such as Esteban Sapir) and editors feel a common bond and help each other out: the post-production of *Pizza, Beer, Smokes* was completed in Trapero's studio and Lisandro Alonso's *Freedom* (*La libertad*, 2001) was produced by Trapero and Rejtman. In addition, a new star system based on physical types rather than actors has started to appear (consider, for example, Luis Margani, Hector Anglada, Dolores Fonzi and Daniel Hendler). Another characteristic of the new independent cinema is the expansion of feminine voices in its ranks – at least a dozen – and, more recently, its geographic explosion: Salta (Lucrecia Martel, Rodrigo Moscoso), Patagonia (Gregorio Cramer, Daniel Burman, Carlos Sorín), Rosario (Gustavo Postiglione, Héctor Molina, Fernando Zago), as well as road movies about *porteños* stranded in the middle of nowhere, thereby allowing for a series of unusual encounters and interwoven stories (e.g. Moreno's *The Resting Place* (*El descanso*, 2001) and Diego Lerman's *Suddenly* (*Tan de repente*, 2002)).

Finally, because most of the first features were made with their respective director's own money, these films 'were not born with expectations of a film industry, but with the need for expression and experiment'.[4] Also, because the directors in question have less interest in finding a mass audience, they do not feel the need to include either average or strongly metaphorical characters in order to secure audience identification, thus allowing them to be more specific: it is as though 'the independent had made an inventory of curiosities, a freaks cinema'.[5]

POLITICS

The developments mentioned above are taking place in the country that is said to have been the first to theorise and analyse a cinema which was nationalist, realist and popular, through the work of Fernando Birri (b. 1925) and the Litoral School. It was Birri who, with his films *Throw Us a Dime* (*Tire dié*, 1958) and *Flooded Out* (*Los inundados*, 1961), started mixing fiction and documentary. Influenced by Italian neorealist cinema, he followed the path of critical realism initiated by early Argentine filmmakers José Agustín Ferreyra (1889–1943), Mario Soffici (1900–77), Leopoldo Torres Ríos (1899–1960) and Hugo del Carril (1912–89), but went further than the mere portrayal of that which he witnessed. Instead, he set himself up as a militant. Birri was the first theorist of political film on the continent, an accomplishment that has earned him the honorary title of founding father, some would say 'pope',[6] of New Latin American Cinema.

However, Argentine movies today are not so much inspired by Birri, or by the celebrated committed films of the 1970s, as they are by the work of Leonardo Favio (b. 1938). Other than their affinity to Favio and Carlos Sorín (who had not made a film for twelve years until *Historias minimas*), the members of the new movement feel like 'orphans'.[7] Favio chose to depict the world of the marginalised with no pretence of mirroring the militant fervour of Birri. His films have an uncomplicated lyricism which liken them to the work of director Leopoldo Torre Nilsson (1924–78) and which contribute to the construction of a national physiognomy. Unlike other directors of the same period who chose to adopt European models of filmmaking, Favio sought to create his own aesthetic by touching on popular themes. Indeed the essence of his first film, *Chronicle of a Boy Alone* (*Crónica de un niño solo*, 1964), was to show that, while there was a difference between living at the margins of society and living as an outlaw, there was only a small step between the two. In contrast to the work of the Grupo, Cine Liberación centred around Pino Solanas (b. 1936) and Octavio Getino (b. 1935), who sought to provoke political change, Favio did not call into question the role of film in the fight for freedom, instead keeping within the confines of traditional cinematography.

Years of censorship have left people intimidated, no longer daring to put forward a political viewpoint; this is clearly illustrated in Andrés Di Tella's 1997 documentary on censorship, *Forbidden* (*Prohibido*). Furthermore the rampant corruption of the Menem regime contributed to the devalorisation of politics: any semblance of ideology was finally discarded when this initially Peronist president, who had spent five years in prison for his beliefs, set the country on a new liberal course, adopting the economic policies of his former foes.[8] Whereas in the 1960s and 1970s Argentine cinema was politically charged, directors today do not want to talk about politics, preferring the films themselves to stand as their political actions. Finding no party which gives voice to their ideas, and wary in general of party politics, they make their statements through other means, by showing the misery of urban marginalisation, for example. And this is all the more natural to them, since 'poverty is not a horror outside the frame or a postcard of a shantytown but is the material from which these films have been made'.[9]

Even those films which form part of the other current emanating from the French New Wave and which seem apolitical cannot help but reflect a new mindset: Rejtman's *Silvia Prieto* (1999), for example, shows Buenos Aires as being, much like contemporary politics, devoid of all meaning. The filmmaking of the group of directors discussed here all sets out with the same objective: to show that which is hidden, that which is unspoken, to give a voice to those who have lost their place in society and to concern itself with a confined milieu, suggesting that through the observation of small things in daily life one can reach an understanding of all else. Making movies thus becomes another way of promoting politics in a country that is barely beginning to find its feet after years of harsh dictatorship.

LANGUAGE

To date, the only book devoted to this topic in English is a collection of essays entitled *New Argentine Cinema: Themes, Auteurs and Trends of Innovation*, edited by Horacio Bernardes, Diego Lerer and Sergio Wolf. The book identifies an intermediate generation of filmmakers ten years older, mostly between the ages of thirty-five and forty-five – perhaps making them a 'bridge' – and giving them the label 'industry auteurs'.[10] Fernando Spiner (*The Sleepwalker*; *Gravedad* (*Adiós querida luna*, 2002)), Eduardo Milewicz (*Life According to Muriel* (*La Vida según Muriel*, 1997)) and Fabián Bielinsky (*Nine Queens* (*Nueve reinas*, 2000)) are the first generation of film students – now teachers as well – producing classical narrative structures within the industry but also integrating elements of the independent cinema. Even *The Swamp*, generally seen as the masterpiece of the new movement, is an 'industry film'; although Martel is the same age as the others, her picture from the start had

Lita Stantic as producer – which was not the case with the other films – and she was given more than a million dollars by well-known investment companies, enabling her to cast professional actors such as Graciela Borges and Mercedes Morán.

More than anything else, it is on that which it seeks to avoid that this new generation is mainly in agreement, namely the emphatic, slow, pompous style of post-dictatorship Argentine cinema, along with its bombastic and theatrical dialogue. As in the time of the French New Wave, young directors here have fought against the plodding and affected films made in their country over the previous twenty years, and that were better received abroad than at home. 'Argentine cinema', as Quintín has stated, 'used to be sententious, explanatory, omniscient and aspired to express consensus truths'.[11]

This is probably why the *Dogma 95* movement aroused so much interest in Argentina: Lars von Trier's *The Idiots* (*Idioterne*, 1998) and its making-of documentary were screened at the first Buenos Aires Independent Film Festival and were followed by a teleconference with the writer/director. A workshop led by the film's assistant director and lead actor helped local students – including Gregorio Cramer – to make their own Dogma films, shown at the end of the festival. A fierce debate raged in *La Nación* newspaper, where Eliseo Subiela wrote a harsh article containing such inanities as 'the rules of the Dogma movement prevent us from being free'. The response in the same paper from Alejandro Maci (director of *The Imposter* (*El impostor*, 1997)) two days later pulled no punches. A new generation had been born that, along with Dogma, extolled the virtues of a more natural style of filmmaking, although in Argentina this is determined more by scarcity of means rather than by the Danish movement's rigid rejection of Hollywood commercial cinema. Indeed, the *cinéma de papa* epistomised by Subiela and supported by the Institute of Cinema tends to leave newcomers feeling deprived and, much as in Thomas Vinterberg's *The Celebration* (*Festen*, 1998), truly 'fucked' by their elders. In fact, a few Dogma films were subsequently made in Argentina: the second and third parts of Gustavo Postiglione's 'home' trilogy (*The Birthday Party* (*El cumple*, 2000) and *The Flick* (*La peli*, 2000)), and José Luis Marquès's *Fuckland* (2000) – although Marquès only realised he had made a Dogma film once it was finished.

Unlike their elders, the younger Argentine directors choose to present small portraits and destinies, as Sergio Wolf explains: 'To limit, to lighten, to subtract, those are the verbs that energize these fictional worlds'.[12] But it is specifically, at least initially, language – or the absence of it – and the predilection for everyday life that sets these films apart from the ranting *film à thèse* of their predecessors. As Pier Paolo Pasolini used to do in the Roman *borgate*, Stagnaro and Caetano hung out in the streets around the capital's Obelisk to write the dialogue for *Pizza, Beer, Smokes*. The language of the marginalised Argentine youth – exemplified by the film's title – opaque to academics and difficult to translate, did not prevent the film from winning major awards at international festivals. Critics recall the first viewing of *Pizza, Beer, Smokes* at the 1997 Mar del Plata Film Festival: here was a film finally 'alive, original, vibrant, and sincere. Theirs was a film that did not smell of mothballs, that was not made according to a stereotypical formula or filled with old, often-repeated dialogue. . . Instead of declamations, there was strong, parched images, instead of stilted dialogue, a live voice'.[13] And language influences aesthetics: this roughness in the film's dialogue 'is translated into images no longer falsely beautified by photography or art direction'.[14]

Subsequently, characters talking as they do in real life have appeared in more technically polished commercial productions and television programmes made by a new generation of producers, such as Adrián Suar. The great variety of directly recorded speech also goes hand-in-hand with *Silvia Prieto*'s obscure forms of dialogue, *Fine Powder*'s sampled sounds and the few words and contemplative choice of extreme asceticism in Alonso's *Freedom*. These filmmakers find that, as Gustavo J. Castagna has said, 'Silence is the most powerful way to use sound'.[15] The new generation can claim to have rid Argentine cinema 'of all excess – nouns, adjectives, overacting, stridency, traumas, untruths; we have arrived at a nothingness'.[16] There is a direct connection here to the absence of costume dramas or flashbacks. The films in question are rigorously contemporary and concerned only with the present day – Postiglione's *The Barbeque* (*El Asadito*, 1998) is even constructed around the arrival of the new millemium – and, for the first time since the 1976–83 dictatorship, the trauma of *desaparecidos* is absent from the narratives (though not the case in Agresti's work).

Conclusion

Does cinema provide an answer to serious financial crisis? The question is rather whether 'independent films are the result of the only chance to make them or are they a matter of choice?'[17] Caetano's answer to this question is: 'I don't want to be an auteur. I am because I have to be. If no one calls me about making movies, I've got to do them on my own'.[18] Will the new generation of Argentine directors change their style once they integrate with the industry and are given the chance to make more expensive productions? It does not seem to be the case with such budget films as Caetano's *A Red Bear* (*Un Oso rojo*, 2002) and Trapero's *El Bonaerense* (2002), although it is too early to say for sure.

But even if, thanks to new technologies, both filming and post-production can be done at reduced costs, the same cannot be said about the stages following post-production, as a circuit for distributing these new Argentine films simply does not exist. Their creators still have to rely on the festival circuit, and the films are better known abroad than in the land in which they were made: Mariano Manzur's *Los Porfiados* (2001) and Lilian Morello's *Once* (1998) have still never been properly screened in Argentina. While these films can be made virtually without external funding, distribution and exhibition channels will have to be set up if this exciting movement is not to be confined solely to international festivals.

NOTES

1. Sergio Wolf, 'The Aesthetics of the New Argentine Cinema: The Map Is the Territory', in Horacio Bernardes, Diego Lerer and Sergio Wolf (eds), *New Argentine Cinema: Themes, Auteurs and Trends of Innovation* (Buenos Aires: Fipresci, Ediciones Tatanka, 2002), p. 30.
2. Ibid.
3. Quintín, 'From One Generation to Another: Is There a Dividing Line?', in Bernardes et al., *New Argentine Cinema*, p. 113.
4. Gustavo J. Castagna, 'From one Vanguard to Another: Is there a Tradition?', in Bernardes, et al., *New Argentine Cinema*, p. 109.
5. Wolf, 'The Aesthetics of the New Argentine Cinema', p. 29.
6. John King, *Magical Reels: A History of Cinema in Latin America* (London: Verso, 2000), p. 85.
7. Wolf, 'The Aesthetics of the New Argentine Cinema', p. 29.
8. For background, see Sarah Whitesel, 'Menem and the Ultramenemists Meet the Post-Menem Era', *Washington Report on the Hemisphere*, 18–16, http://www.coha.org/newsletter/18-16.html (accessed 5 December, 2003).
9. Quintín, 'From One Generation to Another', p. 114.
10. 'From Industry to Independent Cinema: Are There "Industry Authors"?', a conversation between Horacio Bernardes, Diego Lerer and Sergio Wolf, in Bernardes et al., *New Argentine Cinema*, p. 123.
11. Quintín, 'From One Generation to Another', p. 114.
12. Wolf, 'The Aesthetics of the New Argentine Cinema', p. 36.
13. 'From Industry to Independent Cinema', p. 121.
14. Quintín, 'From One Generation to Another', p. 114.
15. Gustavo J. Castagna, 'From One Vanguard to Another: Is There a Tradition?', in Bernardes et al., *New Argentine Cinema*, p. 54.
16. Diego Lerer, 'Pablo Trapero: Man of Suburbia', in Bernardes et al., *New Argentine Cinema*, p. 148.
17. 'From Industry to Independent Cinema', p. 125.
18. Castagna, 'From One Vanguard to Another', p. 59.

RECOMMENDED FILMS

Bad Times (*Mala época*, Nicolás Saad, Mariano De Rosa, Salvador Roselli, Rodrigo Moreno, 1999)
Buenos Aires Vice Versa (Alejandro Agresti, 1996)
Crane World (*Mundo grúa*, Pablo Trapero, 1999)
Fine Powder (*Picado fino*, Esteban Sapir, 1998)
Freedom (*La libertad*, Lisandro Alonso, 2000)
Historias mínimas (Carlos Sorín, 2002)
Nine Queens (*Nueve reinas*, Fabián Belinski, 2000)
Pizza, Beer, Smokes (*Pizza, Birra, Faso*, Bruno Stagnaro, Adrián Caetano, 1998)
Silvia Prieto (Martín Rejtman, 1998)
The Swamp (*La ciénaga*, Lucrecia Martel, 2001)

RECOMMENDED READINGS

The very 'newness' of the subject matter implies that very little has been written on it so far, except newspaper and magazine articles. To date, only two Argentine essays including interviews have been published, only one has been translated to English.

Bernardes, Horacio, Lerer, Diego and Wolf, Sergio (eds) (2002) *New Argentine Cinema: Themes, Auteurs and Trends of Innovation*. Buenos Aires: Fipresci, Ediciones Tatanka.

King, John (2000) *Magical Reels: A History of Cinema in Latin America*. London and New York: Verso.

Oubiña, David and Aguilar, Gonzalo Moisés (1993) *De cómo el cine de Leonardo Favio contó el dolor y el amor de su gente, emocionó a su cariñoso público, trazó nuevos rumbos para entender la imagen y otras reflexiones*. Buenos Aires: Nuevo Extremo.

Saad, Nicolás and Toledo, Teresa (eds) (2000) *Miradas: el cine argentino de los noventa*. Madrid: Casa de América.

PART IV

AFRICAN AND MIDDLE EASTERN TRADITIONS

10. EARLY CINEMATIC TRADITIONS IN AFRICA

Roy Armes

This chapter introduces the various strands of film production that already existed in Africa when post-independence feature filmmaking began in both the Maghreb and Sub-Saharan West Africa in the mid-1960s. One characteristic feature both before and after independence was the dominance of western films on screens throughout Africa. Speaking specifically about Cameroon, but describing a situation common throughout the continent, Richard Bjornson has noted that:

> Although foreign films and pulp fiction conveyed attitudes that were sharply criticised by government officials, religious leaders, and intellectuals, they appealed to large numbers of Cameroonians for the same reason that soccer matches attracted enormous crowds. All three forms of entertainment provide a vicarious escape from the monotony of everyday life. They also enabled people momentarily to forget the country's pressing social and economic problems.[1]

This fact forms the background for all the various attempts to create viable African filmmaking.

COLONIAL FILMS

The cinema reached Africa at much the same time as it spread across Europe and the United States. There were film shows in Cairo and Alexandria as early as 1896, in Tunis and Fez in 1897, Dakar in 1900 and Lagos in 1903. Little one-minute films were shot there too at the turn of the century, as the Lumière operators made a habit of shooting local 'views' (a comparatively easy procedure since Lumière's cinematograph was both camera and projector combined). The aim was both to increase the attractiveness of their local screenings and to provide films for subsequent world-wide distribution. The Lumière catalogue of 1905 contains over fifty such views shot in North Africa.

With the arrival in Tunisia in 1919 of the director Luitz-Morat – a former stage partner of both Sarah Bernhardt and Réjane – to shoot scenes for his feature film *Les cinq gentlemen maudits* (*The Five Accursed Gentlemen*, 1920)[2] a new stage in the exploitation of the African colonies began: their use as locations for foreign feature films. Though a few films, such as Léon Poirier's *Brazza ou l'épopée du Congo* ('Brazza or the Epic of the Congo', 1939) and Jacques de Baroncelli's *L'homme du Niger* ('The Man from Niger', 1939), dealt with West Africa, the overwhelming bulk of the colonial films were set in North Africa. Even the Pierre Loti novel *Roman d'un spahi* ('The Story of a Soldier'), which is set in Senegal, was filmed in 1935 by Michel Bernheim with the location changed to Southern Morocco.

A mythical North Africa thus became the location for a succession of notable films. As David Henry Slavin observes, 'colonial films are melodramas, simple stories of individual lives and loves. But they are suffused with racial and gender privilege'.[3] In comparison with other mainstream European and Hollywood films they also contain a very high proportion of tales of defeat. According to Dina Sherzer:

> The films, which took place in North Africa, presented the colonies as French directors imagined them, as territories waiting for European initiatives, virgin land where the White man with helmet and boots regenerated himself or was destroyed by alcoholism, malaria, or native women. They displayed the heroism of French men, along with stereotypical images of desert, dunes and camels, and reinforced the idea that the Other is dangerous.[4]

What is most remarkable about this body of films, however, is what they omitted: 'They did not present the colonial experience, did not attach importance to colonial issues, and were amazingly silent on what happened in reality. They contributed to the colonial spirit and temperament of conquest and to the construction of White identity and hegemony'.[5]

Though very little of the film was actually shot in North Africa – the casbah was reconstructed by designer Jacques Krauss at the Joinville studios in Paris – Julien Duvivier's *Pépé le Moko* (1936) is an archetypal French colonial film. Made by one of French cinema's most successful technicians then at the height of his powers, the film tells of the doomed love of the Parisian jewel thief

Pépé le Moko (Jean Gabin), who has taken refuge in the casbah, and Gaby (Mireille Balin), a high-class prostitute who is visiting Algiers with her rich champagne-merchant lover. Their meeting is contrived by the Arab police inspector Slimane (Lucas Gridoux). Pépé is aware of the dangers of the affair, and warned by Slimane that he will be arrested if he leaves the casbah, but nonetheless, when Gaby leaves, Pépé tries to accompany her. Handcuffed and facing long imprisonment, he stabs himself on the dockside, as the unsuspecting Gaby sails away. This, like most colonial films, is a purely European drama, to which the inhabitants of Algiers (and to a considerable extent the setting itself) are irrelevant.

In western gangster film terms, *Pépé le Moko* is remarkable for the basic passivity of its hero broken only by moments of violent rage (very characteristic of the roles Gabin played in French 1930s 'poetic realist' cinema). Gabin is very much the star and, particularly through the lighting, the film 'takes to unprecedented heights the glamorisation of his face and general allure'.[6] Balin is given similar photographic treatment, and it is typical of the film's stance that only the inhabitants of the casbah are shown to sweat – never the French lead performers. Though Pépé is allegedly responsible for thirty-five robberies and two bank raids, the sole external action sequence in the film is a desultory night-time shoot-out. There are, however, two killings of informers, one of which is the rightly celebrated scene in which the terrified victim inadvertently switches on a mechanical piano as he reels away from his executioner. Remarkably, though Pépé is the film's protagonist, he goes knowingly towards his own self-inflicted death. He is less a hero corrupted by the Orient, than a man bearing the seeds of defeat within him from the first.

What is more striking, however, particularly from a present-day standpoint, is the handling of the setting and the Arab characters. In the opening scene the local French police chief gives his visiting French-based colleagues a lecture on the casbah. Though nine national or racial types are mentioned as making up the casbah's 40,000 inhabitants, the word 'Arab' does not occur: there are, as most commentators on the film have noted, no Arabs in the casbah. Slimane is stereotyped as a wily and treacherous oriental, detested by his French superiors (though in truth he has to do little more than channel Pépé's pre-existing self-destructive impulses), and Pépé's girl friend Inès (Line Noro) is depicted not as an Arab, but as a gypsy, complete with dark make-up, black frizzy hair and large earrings. As the Algerian critic Abdelghani Megherbi notes, 'Duvivier did not think it worthwhile to give even the slightest role to Algerians. The latter, as was the custom, formed an integral part of the décor on which colonial cinema fed so abundantly'.[7] The sole Arab name in the credits is that of Mohamed Iguerbouchen, who supplied the 'oriental' music to supplement Vincent Scotto's effective but fundamentally western score.

SAMAMA CHIKLY

The only pioneer filmmaker to work independently in either the Maghreb or West Africa under colonialism was the Tunisian Albert Samama Chikly (1872–1934) – a remarkable figure in every respect to be a pioneer of Arab cinema. For one thing, Chikly was a Jew who had acquired French citizenship. Chikly's Italian wife and daughter both converted to Islam, and there can be no doubt about his personal sense of his Tunisian identity. But after running away to sea as a teenager, Chikly remained enthralled with the West and its technology. As an active photographer he was fascinated by Lumière's invention of the cinematograph in 1895, and it is believed that he organised Tunisia's first film show in 1896. When the First World War began, Chikly became one of the dozen cameramen employed by the French Army film service (along with Abel Gance and Louis Feuillade), filming at the front at Verdun in 1916. His services, in a war in which 10,000 Tunisian volunteers and conscripts died in the trenches, earned him the Military Medal.

The extensive use of North African locations by French filmmakers began towards the end of the First World War, and Chikly served as cameraman of one of these films, *The Tales of a Thousand and One Nights* (*Les contes des mille et une nuits*, 1922), by the Russian émigré director Victor Tourjansky. The same year Chikly directed his first fictional film, *Zohra*, scripted by and starring his daughter. This short film tells the story of a young French woman shipwrecked on the coast of Tunisia and rescued by Bedouin tribesmen, with whom she lives for a while. Captured by bandits while travelling in a caravan taking her to a French settlement, she is again rescued, this time by a dashing French aviator, and restored to her parents. This simple tale reflects two of Chikly's passions, Bedouin life and aviation, and Haydée's performance earned her a part in Rex Ingram's *The Arab* (1924), alongside Ramon Navarro.

Chikly's second feature-length film, *The Girl from Carthage* (*La fille de Carthage/Aïn El-Ghazel*, 1924) was also scripted by Haydée who again took the leading role and also edited the film. If *Zohra* was a 'semi-documentary',[8] *The Girl from Carthage* is the full fictional story of a young woman pressured into agreeing to her father's choice of husband (a rich and brutal landowner), who runs away to the desert, followed by the gentle young teacher she loves. When he is killed by their pursuers, she stabs herself and falls dead across his body. The film's theme of forced marriage and the use of a female protagonist make *The Girl from Carthage* a fascinating ancestor of the kind of Tunisian cinema which would come into being over forty years later.

SOUTH AFRICAN CINEMA

At the time of independence in the Maghreb and French colonial Africa – when the new African cinemas were about to come into being – there were only two film industries in Africa. One of these – that located in South Africa – could obviously be of no relevance, despite the state subsidy scheme established in 1956 and the existence of 1,300 or so feature films produced there between 1910 and 1996,[9] since it was a white cinema constructed for a white audience. Writing in 1989, Keyan Tomaselli notes:

> The strategic ideological importance of South African cinema – indeed, of the media in general – is rarely appreciated, when concern is directed to the more pressing issues of repression. However, repression has to be legitimised in some way, and cinema has historically played an important role in presenting apartheid as a natural way of life.[10]

South African cinema during the apartheid era continued the traditional role of cinema in colonial societies. To quote Tomaselli once more:

> South Africa's filmmakers feel that their films lie outside politics, that they are merely entertainment. But this is not the case. Their class position, their underlying social and cinematic assumptions, their emphasis on commerciality, their Hollywood inspired models, their working 'within the rules', and their displacement of actual conditions by imaginary relations which delineate an apartheid view of the world, make their films susceptible to the propagandistic intentions of the state.[11]

Yet things could have been very different, since a form of black capitalism – a 'brash and vigorous African capitalism'[12] – did emerge in South Africa in the mid-nineteenth century, only to be defeated by the 1890s by white politicians. As John Iliffe puts it, 'White missionaries and officials gave black South African capitalist farmers the security they needed in order to succeed; white governments destroyed them when they succeeded too well'.[13] Instead, in the twentieth century white governments and white businessmen came together in schemes which involved 'a deliberate attempt by the state to create an economy in which at least substantial areas of enterprise would be in the hands of private capitalists'.[14] This model of capitalism, which had worked well in nineteenth-century Japan, succeeded too in South Africa, where it reflected the belief that 'it was the most expedient means to achieve rapid modernisation'.[15] Thus, successful industrialisation – initiated by whites for the benefit of whites – lies at the base of South Africa's film industry and allowed it to exist without an export market.

The white Zimbabwean (then, before independence, Rhodesian) filmmaker, Michael Raeburn, has provided an interesting introduction to South African cinema:

> The films which are made in South Africa by South Africans (all of them white) are not shown abroad. So it is not surprising that few people know that the country has been producing feature films regularly since 1916. These films are made by whites, for whites. The financing of this production is made possible by the extremely high standard of living of the white minority privileged by shameful racial laws.[16]

Raeburn characterises the one hundred features shot since 1945 as 'just pale imitations of anglo-american archetypes',[17] noting a striking resemblance to western colonial cinema: 'in the white films, the non-white are only extras. If the script requires a non-white to talk to or touch a white, the role has to be played by a blacked-up white'.[18]

The one South African feature film to become an international success was *The Gods Must Be Crazy* (1980), made by Jamie (Jacobus Johannes) Uys, a former school teacher who had been active as a film director for thirty years and who was to be awarded South Africa's highest civil award, the Order of Merit, for services to the film industry, in 1983.[19] On the surface, the film is simply a very amusing comedy about a bushman, !Ky, who sets out to return an empty Coke bottle which he thinks is a gift from the gods. The other plot strand concerns a white scientist (whose speciality is elephant dung), who involves !Ky to help save a white school teacher, who has been kidnapped – along with her class of black schoolchildren – by a black guerrilla leader.

Though the film is seemingly innocuous, poking fun at blacks and whites alike, it is in fact 'impregnated with the spirit of apartheid'.[20] The film masquerades as a Botswanan production, but the 'Botswana' which forms its setting, where the bushmen lead their idyllic life, in no way resembles the real landlocked republic of the same name. Significantly, the film could not have been set in South Africa, since there the pass laws restricting the movement of blacks would have rendered its plot impossible. The commentary accompanying the opening travelogue is highly condescending, and the name of the black guerrilla villain, Sam Boca, has curious connotations, since the *sambok* is the leather whip regularly used by white South African police to disperse black demonstrations. The name also recalls that of Sam Nujoma, leader of the SWAPO liberation movement in neighbouring Namibia, and indeed the film has disturbing echoes of the actual political situation there, since the South African authorities had enlisted the bushmen in their fight against SWAPO.[21] Peter Davis concludes that, whatever his intentions, Uys has created 'an imaginary country which the architects of apartheid would like us to believe in, a

South Africa well-intentioned to all',[22] through a plot in which, if it is read metaphorically, 'the blacks are like children led astray by agitators coming from outside (the black liberation forces). But they are not the only ones under threat: the white race, personified by the heroine, is also threatened'.[23]

Three years later, however (though still nine years before the end of apartheid in 1994), filmmaker John van Zyl could already look towards the emergence of a very different South African cinema, which would relate more closely to developments elsewhere in the continent:

> The future of South Africa's film industry does not lie in the same mould as that of Australia. Its vigour and its inspiration will have to come from the same roots as the vigour and inspiration of its theatre. The real industry of the future will be a predominantly black one, and will link itself to the energy of other Third World film industries.[24]

There were indeed interesting co-production links with West African filmmakers (Soulymane Cisse, Idrissa Ouedraogo and Jean-Pierre Bekolo) in the mid-1990s, and by the beginning of the new millennium, some steps at least had been taken to transform South African cinema itself.[25]

EGYPTIAN CINEMA

The second African film industry was that in Egypt, which, like South Africa, had a very different political and economic history from that of its neighbours. Notionally independent since 1922 – though with British dominance persisting from 1882 until the 1952 military coup against King Farouk – Egypt had a history of industrial development going back to the early part of the nineteenth century, when, as Tom Kemp points out, Mohamed Ali 'initiated a state programme, designed to strengthen the economy of his country, not unlike that of Peter the Great in Russia a century before'. For various reasons, not least the Anglo-Turkish Treaty of 1838 which insisted on the ending of state monopolies, Mohamed Ali's project failed and 'for the rest of the 19th century Egypt became a primary-exporting, predominantly agricultural country'.[26] But with the attempts at industrialisation came – for the elite at least – a growing sense of national identity. Fresh attempts at modernisation were made in the twentieth century, when 'some import-substitution industries were established', the trend being 'assisted by the two world wars and the slump in export prices during the 1930s'.[27] This was the context in which Egyptian cinema came into being, first through a handful of silent films made by isolated pioneers, many belonging to Cairo's thriving expatriate communities. As Kristina Bergman puts it, 'at first financed by Lebanese and Greeks, shot by Italians, designed and acted by the French, films then became Egyptian'.[28]

The key date was the founding of the Misr Studios in 1935, after which Egyptian cinema became a genuine film industry, capable of producing a dozen pictures in 1935 and building continuously so as to reach over forty a year by 1945. The vision and drive behind this development was that of Talaat Harb, director of the Bank Misr, who envisaged a company 'capable of making Egyptian films with Egyptian subjects, Egyptian literature and Egyptian aesthetics, worthwhile films that can be shown in our own country and in the neighbouring countries of the East'.[29] The film industry was thus at the heart of the development of Egyptian capitalism, since the Bank Misr was the leading Egyptian bank, dominating the country's entire economy until nationalisation in 1960.[30] A year later, the film industry itself was nationalised, to become the General Organisation for Egyptian Cinema.

In her foreword to a volume celebrating one hundred years of Egyptian cinema, Magda Wassef notes the existence of:

> . . . 3,000 fictional feature films, several dozen unforgettable titles, some outstanding filmmakers and above all an impact that exceeds the aim fixed at the outset: 'entertainment'. Indeed a real phenomenon of identification is created for millions of Arabs from the Atlantic to the Persian Gulf . . . For millions of Arabs who were moved by the voices of Oum Kaltoum and Farid al-Atrache, who shared the sorrows of Faten Hamama and who laughed at antics of Ismaïl Yassine, Egyptian cinema is an object of Arab desire and pride. Through it they feel reconciled with their identity, ridiculed and crushed by the destructive and often castrating colonial presence.[31]

Egypt's dominant genre, the melodrama, is worth considering briefly, not because of its influence on post-independence filmmakers elsewhere in Africa, which was nil, but as a fascinating contrast to the European colonial film, and as one kind of baseline against which the particular approaches of the post-independence filmmakers North and South of the Sahara can be assessed.

Three basic features of melodrama are common to both the Egyptian film and the European or Hollywood colonial feature. The first is the focus on emotional intensity, which forms the basis of Ali Abu Shadi's very useful definition of melodrama from an Egyptian perspective:

> Melodrama is a form more than a genre. It differs from tragedy, comedy, and farce in its emotional intensity, calamitous events, and one-dimensional characters. The plots are marked by the sudden movement between highly exaggerated situations in which coincidence plays a major role . . . The melodramatic style uses emotionalism in the writing and the directing and exploits any device to manipulate the feelings of the audience.[32]

The second shared element is the use of stereotypic characters. For the Tunisian-born critic Khémais Khayati the ideology which forms the basis of Egyptian film melodrama is 'a succession of stereotypes and clichés'.[33] Similarly the colonial film may be about individualised characters, but their progress and relationships are structured – so as to meet the needs of accessible dramatic patterns – into clearly defined stereotypic roles.

The third shared feature is the Manichaean world, which Khayati sees as characteristic of Egyptian cinema:

> There is good and evil. There is God and the Devil. Between them no reconciliation is possible. Values are total and never relative. Just like the unfolding of the seasons and work in the fields, ideological and sentimental life is predetermined. Nothing usurps the absolute nature of God.[34]

There is immense comfort for the audiences – in the West as much as in the Arab world – in such a black-and-white world of certainties. We know how people should behave and can appreciate when the accepted norms are violated. There is no ambiguity about how the world should be, the ambiguity comes from our empathy with characters who transgress. We can do this comfortably because we know that they will, in the end, have to face up to the consequences.

The key difference between Egyptian melodrama and the colonial film, whether European or Hollywood, lies in the treatment of character. In Egyptian cinema, the characters 'do not change or grow emotionally, and the lines between good and evil are clearly demarcated. There is a relative absence of human will, with fate determining the outcome of events'.[35] This is supported by Abbas Fadhil Ibrahim in his analysis of three melodramas from the years 1959–1960: 'Fatality, fate and chance make and undo the happiness and misfortune of the characters. Accidents, incidents and slips multiply, modifying the course of their lives'.[36] Khayati further notes that in Arab-Muslim culture, 'the submission of the individual is complete and the allegiance of the community to God is total. Every revolt against the community is a revolt against God. And every revolt against God is an assault on the immutable order of the world and, for this reason, merits punishment'.[37] He sees the maintenance of this set of traditional (or rural) values in Egyptian cinema as the reason for the diminished role of the individual since:

> . . . the drama is above all a collective drama and of necessity rooted in the past. This collective drama is in contradiction to individual drama in so far as the individual is not a unity within the whole, but represents the whole. Rural ideology and its dramatic expression are therefore reduced to a collectivity where individual freedom is never established as either a given or a result. It is inconceivable on its own.[38]

This is the very opposite of the western ideology underlying Hollywood and European films, colonial or not, where the key assumption about characters is that they are individuals, able to make choices as the basis for action. Whatever the pressures or dangers, these choices are ultimately freely made by the individual, and cannot be blamed on background, family upbringing, heredity or even social or economic pressures.

For Khayati, Egyptian tradition-based drama is 'a drama of fatality and happy endings, a drama which does not know the anguish of free choice and which works in blocks and never by nuances'.[39] By contrast, in the colonial film, as an exemplar of western cinema, there are *only* individuals who make choices and act upon them. There is always a space for individual decision-making and an opportunity to turn thought-through decisions into the individual actions, by which we – the spectators – can recognise the worth of the character in question. These choices and actions have consequences that flow logically from them, and, in essence, a human being is the sum of his or her free individual choices and actions. In Egyptian cinema, on the other hand, there are grave restrictions on the actions a character can take and still retain the sympathy of the audience. As Ibrahim notes:

> The woman's adultery never goes beyond platonic love because a sexual relationship outside marriage remains taboo . . . The audience cannot sympathise with characters who seriously transgress the collective morality. That explains how Faten Hamama [one of the great stars of Egyptian cinema] managed to keep her angelic image while continuing, in one film after another, to take husbands from their wives.[40]

The colonial film, like much conventional Hollywood drama, differs from this in being essentially a drama of individual human redemption, with the three acts of its dramatic action dealing successively with personal transgression (or some form of misrecognition) by the protagonist, a long period of (often misguided) action leading to an ultimate recognition of the truth, which in turn allows for the final act to show the character's struggle for redemption (leading, in its turn, to the reward of social integration, often symbolised by marriage with the romance figure who has been shown, as the narrative has unfolded, to be worthy of love).

A perfect example of the Egyptian approach to melodrama is Henry Barakat's *The Sin* (*Al-haram*, 1965), produced by the newly-established state monopoly, the General Organisation for Egyptian Cinema. *The Sin* is widely regarded as the prolific Cairo-born director's best work, and figures in at least one list of the best ten Arab films of all time.[41] Adapted from a novel by Youssef Idriss, the film deals with the sufferings of migrant farm workers, whose lives are precarious, since they are hired only by the day at crucial seasons of the year and forced to work far from their homes. Though filmed on location and including many villagers in its cast, the film's stance is far from that of the Italian neorealists: the subject is softened and sentimentalised, the action is set safely back in 1950 (the Farouk era) and, in the central role, Faten Hamama gives a glittering star performance. What is fascinating is the way in which the film shapes its story of a woman who inadvertently kills her own new-born child, so that while its personal emotional impact is maintained, it is, at the same time, swallowed up, as it were, in the eternal, unchanging life of the peasantry.

The Sin begins, as it will end, with almost documentary-style images of the arduous life of the Egyptian peasantry, accompanied by an explanatory voice-over commentary. Social hierarchies of a virtually feudal kind are shown, as well as a real hostility between settled villagers and the migrant seasonal labourers, but all these tensions are resolved as the film unfolds and the disparate sections of society come together with a common purpose. The action is triggered by the discovery of a child's body under a tree near the fields where the migrant labourers are employed, and the opening section follows the search for the child's mother, both within the village and among the migrant peasants. Eventually the mother is found, a peasant woman working to support two small children and a disabled husband. She is now is sick and has been hidden by the community of migrants.

The film's central portion is a long flashback depicting the woman's life up to this point in time. Of course, even the scenes of her early hopes and happiness are coloured by what we know of her eventual decline. Her descent into poverty has a fatal inevitability – it is certainly not in any way her fault or her husband's. Her 'sin' is no more than stealing sweet potatoes to feed her sick husband: caught by the brutal landowner, she is raped and made pregnant. The child's death is depicted as similarly beyond her control. Sick, worn out and alone, she kills the child by clumsily trying to stifle its cries, which she fears will reveal her situation. This central section of the narrative is shaped so as to increase the film's emotional impact: the woman's labour pains are emphasised by repeated drum rhythms, and her lonely birth ordeal is intercut with a joyous peasant celebration.

The final section of *The Sin* begins as her story comes nearer to the film's present, and we re-see events in the film's opening sequence, this time from her point of view. There can be only one outcome, her death, and though her first attempt at suicide is foiled, she eventually dies under the very tree where she gave birth. But the narrative does not end with this harrowing personal tragedy. The village and migrant communities come together to reclaim her as part of the community. They conceal her 'sin' (so that her husband will not die of shame), and the narrative pattern too works to erase the personal disasters (rape and infanticide) by retuning to the eternally suffering peasantry. Even the tree, the final voice-over narration tells us, is now not a place of sin and death, but a shrine visited by married women seeking legitimate children. In this way, *The Sin* brings together all the key elements of Egyptian melodrama: a circular narrative structure using a long central flashback through which the past weighs down upon the present, a pattern of images and music that enhances the audience's emotional response, a protagonist who suffers but lacks any individual responsibility for what happens to her, an overall sense of unchallengeable fatality, and the portrayal of an unchanging traditional community which is barely touched by the ripple of personal tragedy.

ALGERIAN FILMMAKING

The final model of pre-independence filmmaking in Africa is to be found during the bitter Algerian war for independence (1954–62), when 16 mm militant film was used as part of the liberation struggle. The catalyst for this was the French Communist documentary filmmaker René Vautier (b. 1928), who had been decorated with the *croix de guerre* at the age of 16 for his resistance activities against the German occupiers in his native France. In 1952 he had also been imprisoned by the French government for violating the 1934 Laval law by filming without authorisation in Africa, where he had made the first French anti-colonialist film, *Afrique 50* (1950).[42] Vautier had already made an independent short (now lost), *Une nation, l'Algérie*, when he began filming with Algerian resistance fighters in 1957–58 under the auspices of the National Liberation Front (FNL) leader Abbane Ramdane. The result was the widely seen 25-minute documentary *Algeria in Flames* (*Algérie en flammes*, 1959), of which the technicians in East Germany, where it was edited, made 800 copies.[43] Unfortunately for Vautier, however, by the time the film was complete, Ramdane had been murdered in one of the internecine disputes which characterised the FLN, and he himself was imprisoned, without trial and largely in solitary confinement, by the Algerians for twenty-five months.

The first film collective which Vautier set up in the Tebessa region in 1957, the Farid group, comprised a number of Algerians. It aimed to 'show the methods used by the French administration and army to deal with the Algerian population'.[44] In 1958 the group was transferred to Tunis, then the base for the leaders of the Algerian liberation movement, where it became the film service of the Algerian Republican Provisional Government in exile (GPRA). The GPRA thought the role of film important enough for it to send another young filmmaker, Mohamed Lakhdar Hamina, to study film at FAMU in Prague in 1959. Vautier himself, who was wounded three times in his various frontier crossings into Algeria, set up a film school, whose pupils made two collective documentaries in 1957–58. Before the end of the hostilities, however, four of his five students had been killed. Other documentaries of 1957–58 include

The Refugees (*Les Réfugiés*), which earned its maker, Cécile Decugis, two years' imprisonment upon her return to France, and two films made for the Service Cinéma FLN by Pierre Clément, *Refugees* (*Réfugiés*) and *Sakiet Sidi Youssef*, before his capture and imprisonment by the French forces.

Also shot in the resistance struggle during 1961 were four films made for the Service Cinéma GPRA by Mohamed Lakhdar Hamina (now returned after a year in Prague) in collaboration with Djamel Chanderli: *Our Algeria* (*Djazaïrouna/Notre Algérie*), *The Guns of Freedom* (*Banâdiq al-hûria/Les Fusils de la liberté*), *The People's Voice* (*Saout echaab/La Voix du peuple*) and *Yasmina*. In addition, Yann and Olga Le Masson (with the collaboration of Vautier) made *I'm Eight-Years-Old* (*J'ai huit ans*), showing the horrors of the war by means of the drawings and stories of refugee children in Tunisia. The following year, 1962, Vautier completed *Five Men and One People* (*Cinq hommes et un peuple*) and Abdelhalim Nacef made *The Koranic Teacher* (*Le Taleb*).[45] As the Algerian sociologist Mouny Berrah notes, these were all 'collective and committed films, immediate films devoted to their project and intention of rehabilitating a self-image deconstructed and devalued by the occupier and arguing for the justice of a war condemned as "butchery" by the enemy'.[46]

For Algerian film historian Lotfi Maherzi these films have a double value: recording the exact reality of the situation in Algeria and showing the close support of the Algerian people for the struggle.[47] They found an audience not only in the Arab countries and eastern Europe, but also on western television, where they served to counter French propaganda efforts. Though they could not, of course, be shown at the time in Algeria, they were frequently projected there during the first years of independence.[48] It is interesting to note that, despite the demands of their militant filmmaking, both Vautier and Lakhdar Hamina made other kinds of films while in Tunisia. Vautier directed the fictional short, *Golden Chains* (*Chaînes d'or*, 1956), which saw the first screen appearance of Claudia Cardinale, while Lakhdar Hamina made three short documentaries with his FAMU professor, François Sulc, one of which won a prize at the Venice Film Festival.

In Algiers in 1962 Vautier and Rachedi went on to set up the short-lived audio-visual centre (CAV), in the context of which *A People on the March* (*Peuple en marche*, 1963) was made, and in 1963 Lakhdar Hamina became head of the Algerian newsreel organisation (OAA), where he eventually produced his own first three features. But their particular form of committed militant filmmaking had no part to play in the totally bureaucratised mode of film production that emerged in Algeria in the mid-1960s. Considering the post-liberation career of Ahmed Rachedi, Claude Michel Cluny notes what he considers a 'fundamental error' in Algeria cinema: 'They had not worked out what role cinema could play in the elaboration of a new society; they gave priority to a celebration of past battles, rather than to a militant cinema with a revolutionary vocation'.[49] Both Rachedi and Lakhdar Hamina became prominent feature filmmakers and bureaucrats after independence, but only Vautier retained his stance as an independent militant filmmaker (making, among other committed films, the highly praised *Being Twenty in the Aurès Mountains* (*Avoir vingt ans dans les Aurès*) in 1972).

CONCLUSION: POST-INDEPENDENCE AFRICAN FILMMAKING

Foreign producers from Europe and the United States still use the rural landscapes of the Maghreb as locations for their films and, though the old colonial ideology no longer prevails, the works produced have as little relevance as ever to the realities of African life. A number of filmmakers in Morocco and Tunisia have taken the opportunity to gain some experience by working on these foreign features, but only very subordinate roles – as production managers or assistant directors – are open to them. In any case this is a form of production beyond their aspirations, since the sheer size of the financial resources behind international productions such as *Lawrence of Arabia* (1962), *Raiders of the Lost Ark* (1981) or *The English Patient* (1996) makes this model of production irrelevant to indigenous African producers.

The nature of the African industries that emerged in Egypt and South Africa show clearly how filmmaking is of necessity shaped by ideological factors: Islamic beliefs about morality, social responsibilities and gender relations, on the one hand, apartheid assertions and assumptions about race, on the other. Both film industries continue with varying degrees of success to face new challenges in a very different world: confronting the very real threats to freedom of expression posed by Muslim fundamentalism in Egypt, and responding to the equally real opportunities of shaping a black cinema for a black-governed society in the new South Africa. But in the absence of the kinds of industrial infrastructures which were developed in Egypt and South Africa, the models of production developed there are again irrelevant to African filmmakers North and South of the Sahara.

Equally, the increasingly autocratic one-party states that emerged after independence throughout Africa made the Vautier model of militant documentary filmmaking – a perfect example of the 'third cinema' advocated by Fernando Solanas and Octavio Getino and theorised by Teshome Gabriel[50] – totally impossible. The situation of post-independence filmmakers instead echoes that of Samama Chikly in Tunisia in the 1920s, in that they have no option other than to work totally independently but within strict, state-defined limits, finding finance where they can, working as total creators (producing, directing, scripting) in a context lacking in technically trained local collaborators.

NOTES

1. Richard Bjornson, *The African Quest for Freedom and Identity: Cameroonian Writing and the National Experience* (Bloomington, IN: Indiana University Press, 1994), p. 311.
2. Maurice-Robert Bataille and Claude Veillot, *Caméras sous le soleil: Le Cinéma en Afrique du nord* (Algiers: Victor Heintz, 1956), pp. 13–14.
3. David Henry Slavin, *Colonial Cinema and Imperial France, 1919–1939: White Blind Spots, Male Fantasies, Settler Myths* (Baltimore, MD: Johns Hopkins University Press, 2001), p. 18.
4. Dina Sherzer, *Cinema, Colonialism, Postcolonialism: Perspectives from the French and Francophone Worlds* (Austin, TX: University of Texas Press, 1996), p. 4.
5. Ibid.
6. Ginette Vincendeau, *Pépé le Moko* (London: BFI Publishing, 1998), p. 29.
7. Abdelghani Megherbi, *Les Algériens au miroir du cinéma colonial* (Algiers: SNED, 1982), p. 247.
8. Guillemette Mansour, *Samama Chikly: Un Tunisien à la rencontre du XXème siècle* (Tunis: Simpact Editions, 2000), p. 254.
9. Samuel Lelièvre (ed.), *Cinémas africains, une oasis dans le désert?* (Paris: Corlet – Télérama, 2003), p. 252.
10. Keyan Tomaselli, *The Cinema of Apartheid* (London: Routledge, 1989), p. 11.
11. Ibid., p. 81.
12. John Iliffe, *The Emergence of African Capitalism* (London: Macmillan, 1983), p. 18.
13. Ibid., p. 22.
14. Ibid.
15. Iliffe, *The Emergence of African Captalism*, p. 82.
16. Michael Raeburn, 'Prétoria veut construire un "Hollywood" sud-africain . . .', in Guy Hennebelle (ed.), *Les cinémas africains en 1972* (Paris: Société Africaine d'Edition, 1972), p. 261.
17. Ibid., p. 263.
18. Ibid.
19. Keyan Tomaselli, 'Le Rôle de la Jamie Uys Film Company dans la culture afrikaner', in Keyan Tomaselli (ed.), *Le cinéma sud-africain est-il tombé sur la tête?* (Paris: L'Afrique littéraire, 1986), p. 78.
20. Peter Davis, '*Les dieux sont tombés sur la tête*, de Jamie Uys: Délices et ambiguités de la position du missionnaire!', in Tomaselli, *Le cinéma sud-africain est-il tombé sur la tête?*, p. 53.
21. Ibid., p. 57.
22. Ibid., p. 56.
23. Ibid., pp. 57–8.
24. John van Zyl, cited in Tomaselli, *The Cinema of Apartheid*, p. 127.
25. Gibson Boloko, 'La Situation de l'Industrie Cinématographique Sud-africaine (1980–2000)', in Lelièvre, *Cinémas africains, une oasis dans le désert?*, pp. 258–63.
26. Ibid.
27. Tom Kemp, *Industrialization in the Non-Western World* (London and New York: Longman, 1983), p. 189.
28. Kristina Bergmann, *Filmkultur und Filmindustrie in Ägypten* (Darmstadt: Wissenschaftliche Buchgesellschaft, 1993), p. 6.
29. Samir Farid, 'Les six générations du cinéma égyptien', *Écran*, 15 (Paris, 1973), p. 40.
30. Patrick Clawson, 'The Development of Capitalism in Egypt', *Khamsin*, 9 (1981), p. 92.

31. Magda Wassef (ed.), *Egypte: Cent ans de cinéma* (Paris: IMA, 1995), p. 14.
32. Ali Abu Shadi, 'Genres in Egyptian Cinema', in Alia Arasoughly (ed.), *Screens of Life: Critical Film Writing from the Arab World* (St. Hyacinthe, Quebec: World Heritage Press, 1996), p. 85.
33. Khémais Khayati, *Cinémas arabes: Topographie d'une image éclatée* (Paris and Montreal: L'Harmattan, 1996), p. 204.
34. Ibid., p. 202.
35. Shadi, 'Genres in Egyptian Cinema', p. 82.
36. Abbas Fadhil Ibrahim, 'Trois mélos égyptiens observés à la loupe', in Mouny Berrah, Victor Bachy, Mohand Ben Salama and Ferid Boughedir (eds), *Cinémas du Maghreb* (Paris: CinémAction 14, 1981), p. 123.
37. Khayati, p. 203.
38. Ibid., p. 204.
39. Ibid.
40. Ibrahim, 'Trois mélos égyptiens observés à la loupe', p. 123.
41. Khayati, pp. 77–87.
42. René Vautier, *Afrique 50* (Paris: Editions Paris Expérimental, 2001).
43. René Vautier, *Caméra citoyenne* (Rennes: Éditions Apogées, 1998), p. 156.
44. Lotfi Maherzi, *Le cinéma algérien: Institutions, imaginaire, idéologie* (Algiers: SNED, 1980), p. 62.
45. This listing is taken from the chronology established in Mouloud Mimoun (ed.), *France-Algérie: Images d'une guerre* (Paris: Institut du Monde Arabe, 1992), pp. 68–71.
46. Mouny Berrah, 'Histoire et idéologie du cinéma algérien sur la guerre', in Guy Hennebelle, Mouny Berrah and Benjamin Stora (eds), *La guerre d'Algérie à l'écran* (Paris: Corlet/Télérama/CinémAction 85, 1997), p. 160.
47. Maherzi, *Le cinéma algérien*, p. 64.
48. Abdelghani Megherbi, *Les Algériens au miroir du cinéma colonial* (Algiers: SNED, 1982), p. 269.
49. Claude Michel Cluny, *Dictionnaire des nouveaux cinémas arabes* (Paris: Sindbad, 1978), p. 264.
50. See Fernando Solanas and Octavio Getino, 'Towards a Third Cinema', in Michael Chanan (ed.), *Twenty-Five Years of the New Latin American Cinema* (London: BFI Publishing, 1983) and Teshome H. Gabriel, *Third Cinema in the Third World* (Ann Arbour, MI: UMI Research Press, 1982).

Recommended films

Africa 50 (*Afrique 50*, René Vautier, France, 1950)
Algeria in Flames (*Algérie en flammes*, René Vautier, Algeria, 1958–59)
Being Twenty in the Aurès Mountains (*Avoir vingt ans dans les Aurès*, René Vautier, France, 1972)
Les cinq gentlemen maudits (*The Five Accursed Gentlemen*, Luitz-Morat, France, 1919)
The Girl From Carthage (*La fille de Carthage/Aïn El-Ghazel*, Albert Samama Chikly, 1924)
The Gods Must Be Crazy (Jamie Uys, South Africa, 1980)
The Man of the Niger (*L'homme du Niger*, Jacques de Baroncelli, France, 1939)
A People on the March (*Peuple en marche*, Collective, Algeria, 1963)
Pépé le Moko (Julien Duvivier, France, 1936)
The Sin (*Al-haram*, Henry Barakat, Egypt, 1965)

RECOMMENDED READING

Benali, Abdelkader (1998) *Le Cinéma colonial au Maghreb*. Paris: Éditions du Cerf.
Hennebelle, Guy (ed.) (1972) *Les Cinémas africains en 1972*. Paris: Société Africaine d'Edition.
Hennebelle, Guy, Berrah, Mouny and Stora, Benjamin (eds) (1997) *La Guerre d'Algérie à l'écran*. Paris: Corlet/Télérama/CinémAction 85.
Lelièvre, Samuel (ed.) (2003) *Cinémas africains, une oasis dans le désert?* Paris: Corlet/Télérama/CinémAction 106.
Maherzi, Lotfi (1980) *Le Cinéma algérien: Institutions, imaginaire, idéologie*. Algiers: SNED.
Mansour, Guillemette and Chikly, Samama (2000) *Un tunisien à la rencontre du XXième siècle*. Tunis: Simpact Éditions.
Megherbi, Abdelghani (1982) *Les Algériens au miroir du cinéma colonial*. Algiers: SNED.
Slavin, David Henry (2001) *Colonial Cinema and Imperial France, 1919–1939*. Baltimore, MD: Johns Hopkins University Press.
Tomaselli, Keyan (1989) *The Cinema of Apartheid*. London: Routledge.
Wassef, Magda (ed.) (1995) *Egypte: Cent ans de cinéma*. Paris: IMA.

11. ISRAELI PERSECUTION FILMS

Nitzan Ben-Shaul

INTRODUCTION

This chapter deals with the diachronically shifting formal and thematic implementation of the Jewish tradition of being a persecuted people as presented
in Israeli films. This translates for secular Israeli Jews into a self-conception
of living in a besieged state facing a hostile world. Considered by many to
have become central to Israeli culture,[1] it inheres in films dealing with issues
perceived by Israelis to threaten the state's existence, namely films about war
with the Arab world, films about the Israeli-Palestinian conflict and films
dealing with inter-ethnic tensions among Israeli Jews. This tradition, whose
formal and thematic cinematic implementation constructs a threatening
reality from which there is no escape, fashions to varying degrees the overall
structure of the films, their plots, their cinematic visual and aural compositions and the constitution of the characters populating them. This chapter will
focus upon three films, cardinal and comprehensive in their respective
periods, all dealing with the issue of war: *Hill 24 Doesn't Answer* (*Giv'a 24
Eina Ona*, 1955), *Siege* (*Matzor*, 1969)[2] and *Kippur* (2000). It also briefly
places the films within the context of their production and the extratextual
reality forging their embedded conceptions, while incidental mention is made
of films addressing the Israeli-Palestinian conflict or the inter-ethnic tensions
among Israeli Jews.[3]

A PERSECUTED NATION

The notion of Israel being a persecuted nation, as held by Israeli Jews, derives from historical experiences, religious traditions and Israel's predominant state ideology. It stems from Israelis' recent experiences of conventional war and acts of terror, as well as from sporadic condemnations of Israel by world organisations. This often evokes for Israeli Jews the long history of anti-Semitism culminating in the Holocaust, a history constituting traumatic past experiences both for the individual and the collective. This history is memorised in relation to deeply ingrained biblical religious tenets having to do with Jews being a chosen people (*Am Nivchar*), alone among the nations (*Am Levadad Yshkon*), with no one but god almighty and their own resources to protect them in a hostile world seeking their destruction. The biblical people of Amalek who sought to destroy the Jews have become the symbolic (read also a-historical) name given in Jewish religious circles, but also in the secular discourse, to Israel's enemies, past, present and future. Amalek's a-historical symbolisation as such already occurs in the Bible. Furthermore, as has been shown, Israel's dominant state ideology since the late 1950s has used the collective remembrance of past atrocities inflicted upon the Jewish people to maintain the idea that the world is against Israel because it is a Jewish state.[4]

ISRAELI PERSECUTION FILMS

A look at some of the cardinal films produced in Israel during distinct sequential periods on the subject of war shows the recurrence of compositions and figurations whose interrelations evoke notions of claustrophobia or agoraphobia, violence, threatening encirclement and suspicion. These are often expressed as follows:

1. shadowy patterns of lighting;
2. visual and aural configurations composing closed and labyrinthine spatial formations;
3. open threatened spaces where there is no refuge;
4. unexpected, abrupt editing patterns and camera movements creating violent surprises;
5. temporal circular structures whose synchronic framework disjoints their diachrony;
6. fatalistic or bounded story structures;
7. recurrence of suspicious and violent interactions among characters;
8. conspiratorial modes of action;
9. thematic and formal isolation of threatened individuals or groups.

These configurations, whose dominance varies in different periods, formally and thematically embed in these films the notion of Israel being a persecuted nation. This notion, to a varying degree, semantically colours the films' problematic subjects as being unresolvable, dead-ended and threatening.

1948–67: BETWEEN PERSECUTION AND PEACEFUL COEXISTENCE

The conflict between Israeli and Arab communities, a feature of early twentieth-century life in Palestine, climaxed in what Israelis call the War of Independence, referred to by the Arabs as *al nakba* – the catastrophe. In this war Israel fought off the combined armies of several Arab states immediately following its declaration of independence on 14 May 1948. The war resulted in the expansion of Israel's territories beyond the UN partition decision of 1947, the flight and/or expulsion of 600,000 Palestinians, mainly into the West Bank and Gaza Strip territories, and the signing of ceasefire agreements between the hostile countries, thus maintaining a state of suspended war.

Within Israel, the establishment of the state generated deep changes in the socio-economic and political structure developed during the pre-state period. These changes were due to the doubling of the Jewish population within three years of independence (1949–51) following a massive immigration of Jews – mostly from Islamic countries – as well as to Israel's new political position within the region. These changes shifted the general productive focus towards rapid industrialisation, leading in turn to drastic alterations in Israel's socio-political structure.

Providing leadership for these changes, even as it underwent a correlated political and ideological transformation, was the Mapai (Hebrew acronym for Workers Party of the Land of Israel) political party, headed for many years by David Ben-Gurion. Once the war had been won, the Mapai exchanged its pre-state hegemonic yet sectarian Zionist-Socialist policy for a form of statism (*mamlachtiyut*). Statism depended on a centralising strategy designed to achieve the consolidation of Mapai's hegemony over the entire population. It led to the political oppression of opposing factions, particularly the extreme left and right parties, through a coalition with religious parties, and to the shift from the pre-state socialist economic party orientation to a quasi-socialist formation. Politically, it led to Israel aligning with the western bloc of states, a foreign policy that led to, among other things, the Sinai Campaign against Egypt in 1956. In that war, Israel joined with France and Britain in an attempt to overthrow Egypt's president Nasser and defeat his anti-colonialist initiatives.

Statist policy resulted in the consolidation of Mapai's dominance over the state apparatus through the constitution of a unified statist educational system and a unified statist army. The pre-state paramilitary organisations, in contrast, had been ideologically aligned. Control over the economy was achieved through the Histadrut (the general worker's union) – at that time the most powerful socio-economic organisation. This hegemony endured until the overturning of Mapai in 1977.

On the ideological level, statist policy manifested itself in the difference between Mapai's pre-state and post-independence construction of the term Sabra (the term used by Israelis to describe their native born, based on the local prickly pear fruit by the same name, which is tough on the outside and soft and sweet on the inside). Thus, in Mapai's pre-state Zionist-Socialist ideology, the Sabra had been the native-born revolutionary agent of Zionism, characterised primarily by his labouring to redeem the land and himself through participation in a socialist collective. In Mapai's post-independence statist ideology, the Sabra now became the Israeli soldier fighting for the state's independence, a native though ethnically mixed Jew divorced from his Diaspora past (yet, notwithstanding 2,000 years of history, directly connected to his biblical past). Thus the idea of an independent Israeli state and its ideal Sabra citizen became the primary symbols of the statist ideology.

Hence, the War of Independence soon became a central subject in Mapai's statist ideology. The cultural establishment of the time generally incorporated and reproduced its own conception of the war as a struggle for national survival against overwhelming odds,[5] a conception most developed and obvious in the national cinema. While other cultural forms, particularly literature, remained somewhat independent of the political establishment because of their moral authority, strong traditions and widespread readership, the underfinanced film industry was totally dependent on state support. Most films of the period were documentaries commissioned by various state agencies to promote statist ideology, while the few fiction films that managed to get made depended heavily on governmental funding and were under strict scrutiny by government officials. The period's most ambitious and comprehensive cinematic treatment of the War of Independence can be found in *Hill 24 Doesn't Answer* (1955), directed by Thorold Dickinson.[6]

The film opens with a strategic map showing the various fronts on which Israel was attacked by the different Arab forces during the war. The image is, in effect, a state of siege. There is a quick cut to close-ups of four dead Israeli soldiers, each of which is intercut with a brief image of the soldier when he was alive. This formal device alludes to the ultimate threat of the war – total annihilation of the Israeli people. At the same time, this introduction prefigures the individual fates of the film's protagonists, narrated in a long flashback that traces how the four came to occupy the hill they subsequently defend from Arab attack.

A further set of flashbacks tells the stories of the three male protagonists: an Irishman who, while serving in the British police force in Mandate Palestine and persecuting Jewish underground fighters and illegal immigrants, falls in love with a Jewish Sabra woman and eventually joins the Israeli army after the

British leave; a Jewish American tourist who, after having encountered Arab aggression while touring the country, joins the Israeli army and takes part in the failed attempt to liberate the besieged Jewish quarter in Jerusalem; and a Sabra who, fighting on the Egyptian front, captures an ex-German Nazi soldier in Egyptian army uniform. The fourth soldier, a woman Israeli fighter of Yemeni origin, has no episode of her own, nor can she be considered one of the film's major protagonists. In effect, she replaces the film's major female protagonist – the Irishman's beloved (as will be discussed further below). Each personal flashback concludes with a brief return to the four fighters on their way to the hill. After the last flashback, we return to Hill 24 which the soldiers had set out to climb and take possession of at night. We hear gunfire and then the film cuts to a panning shot of a stretch of land seen on a silent and tranquil day.

The focus then shifts to a jeep carrying three officers: a Jordanian, an Israeli and a UN peacekeeper. They climb up Hill 24 where they find the dead soldiers, framed identically to the film's opening sequence. The UN officer finds the Israeli flag in the woman's hand and proclaims the hill to be Israeli territory. As dramatic music plays, we see a series of aerial panning shots of Israel's agricultural and industrial topography with the words 'The Beginning' superimposed.

Thus the overall narrative structure of the film stretches along two formal and thematic trajectories. One is circular: the reiterative flashback formation returns us to the drive to the hill each time, while the film's concluding images return us to the beginning. The disparate narrative spaces connect to the different fronts on which Israel had to fight, offering visual correlatives to the map of the state of siege that serves as the film's preface.

The other trajectory is, however, progressive: the forward march to conquer the hill, interrupted by three flashbacks, creates a motion that carries the narrative beyond the tragic destiny of its protagonists in order to connect with the ceasefire and the peaceful resolution of Israel's border dispute. The enclosed car moving in the night towards Hill 24, its motion interrupted by flashbacks that show the soldiers fighting on three different fronts, metaphorically carries the spectator beyond the actual scene of the night-time battle to the following bright day. A tranquil panning shot of the surrounding land ends with a framing of Hill 24, a quiet place where four dead heroes lie.

These two trajectories, the one expressing the idea of persecution and annihilation through a condensation of time (past and present) and narrative space (different fighting fronts), and the other suggesting an eventual peaceful survival through a correlation of time (present with future) and narrative space (abstract dark with concrete lighted space), find their formal and thematic reflexes in the three flashback episodes.

The first episode is structured by these two overlapping yet distinct trajectories. The Irishman's experience as a military policeman emphasises his undercover chase after Jewish underground fighters and illegal immigrants through a claustrophobic labyrinthine space that suggests deception and constant danger. Narrow alleys leading nowhere, suspicious glances, chiaroscuro lighting, jerky camera movements and dramatic music dominate stylistically. The chase reaches its formal and thematic zenith with the capturing of an underground Jewish fighter, revealed as such by his concentration camp tattoo. This subtle correlation of Israel's adversaries with the Nazi regime is elaborated in the other episodes. Thus the third episode focuses on the Sabra's encounter with an ex-Nazi in Egyptian army uniform. The correlation of British and Egyptians with the Nazis substantiate the never-ending persecution of the Jews, which is passed from one enemy culture to the next. A similar theme is present in the second episode, which focuses upon the failed attempt to liberate the besieged Jewish quarter in Jerusalem. Thus the American, along with other soldiers, infiltrates Jewish Jerusalem where he is wounded and trapped by the Jordanian army. We see him in a darkened room full of wounded men and frightened women, children and elderly people. His dialogue with an elderly rabbi articulates in words what the scene articulates in image and sound – that there have always been forces of evil seeking the destruction of the Jewish people. Thus the siege by the Jordanians is simply another expression of this desire for the annihilation of the Jews.

Providing counterpoint to this theme in the other episode is the love story between the Irishman and the Sabra woman. Their romance unfolds within a series of peaceful spaces, as their developing passion creates a milieu of love and happiness: her cozy and artsy apartment, the Druse village to which she retreats to study and meditate, a café where soft music is played and loving couples dance. These sequences are filmed with even or realist lighting and slow and continuous camera movements as peaceful ethnic music plays on the soundtrack. This movement reaches its formal and thematic zenith with the couple's kiss. The image of the woman metonymically represents the future of the state. Born in the country, she is glimpsed dressing, living and moving within an authentically Israeli space (as contrasted with the *noirish* Jerusalem episode, the image of a hostile Diaspora in the territory of the *goyim*). Tellingly, her costume blends Bedouin, Russian and Israeli elements within her Israeli clothing, while European-style cafés are juxtaposed harmoniously with Oriental (Druse) villages. She shelters the underground Jewish fighter, seen briefly towards the end in army uniform, which suggests her patriotism, yet she has no problem whatsoever in falling in love with a non-Jewish foreigner. She lives in peace with both East and West – Druse and British. Finally, and this is most important though often overlooked,[7] she does not die, as do the other main characters. Instead, she implicitly survives the war to live in the state as it moves towards a brighter future.

This 'peaceful' trajectory appears in the other episodes as well. Its formulation within the third episode is particularly interesting. The Sabra fighter is seen from the deluded point of view of the dying Nazi he encounters as the anti-Semitic prototype of the East European Jew (bearded, long nosed and so on).[8]

This Diaspora stereotype then dissolves into the actual, and substantially different, image of the Sabra as objective reality is restored. The complex dissolve and exchange of viewpoints implies among other things the Zionist's 'positive' use of anti-Semitic imagery to differentiate the Israeli-born from the Diaspora Jew, demonstrating the restorative power of nationhood. Most important, perhaps, the Sabra, no longer what 'a Jew' used to be, demonstrates how his fight for independence will change the rest of the world's attitude towards the Jewish people, replacing a negative stereotype with a positive one.

Hill 24 Doesn't Answer conceives the War of Independence in a contradictory fashion. On the one hand, the war is legitimated by its correlation with the never-ending history of Jewish persecution; it becomes a 'no choice' and 'no way out' situation, yet another crisis to be survived. On the other hand, the war becomes the means through which the historical situation of the Jewish people will change because of Israel's military strength, its independence and the evolving Jew (in whom nativist and Diaspora identities condense), who exemplifies this emancipatory process.[9]

1967–77: COPING WITH PERSECUTION – FROM COLLECTIVISM TO INDIVIDUALISM

This triumphalist yet persecutory conception of war found in *Hill 24 Doesn't Answer* and other films throughout the 1950s and early 1960s underwent significant transformation in the films produced following what Israelis term the Six Day War in June 1967. In that war, Israel did not wait to be attacked but launched pre-emptive strikes against the Egyptian, Syrian and eventually the Jordanian armies, who were massing for attack.[10] The brief war resulted not only in a successful defence of the nation but in the expansion of Israel's territories beyond the ceasefire borders established after the War of Independence. Israel began an occupation that largely endures to the present day of the West Bank of the Jordan River and the Gaza Strip with its million Palestinian inhabitants and post-1947 refugees (who subsequently became subject to Israeli military rule), the Egyptian Sinai desert to the Suez Canal and the Syrian Golan Heights.

In contrast to the relatively stable ceasefire agreements that followed the War of Independence and the 1956 Sinai Campaign, the 1967 war was followed not by negotiations but by Egypt's War of Attrition against Israel (1967–71). This consisted of sporadic but continual military clashes along the ceasefire border by the Suez Canal, as well as guerrilla and terrorist activity by the various Palestinian organisations, operating mainly from Jordan and the occupied territories of the West Bank and Gaza Strip. These intermittent military and guerrilla activities continued until the next major war in October 1973. This later war will be dealt with in the next section; it was for the most part avoided by Israeli filmmakers as a subject until 1981.

What characterises the cinematic representation of the Six Day War in this period (1967–77) is a narrative structure that can be imagined as two concentric circles – the outer circle dealing with Israel at war and the inner circle portraying the conflict between the individual and society. Two different causal connections are generated within the films between the two circles. One depends on the argument that because the Arab world (and consequently the world at large) is against Israel, the aspiration to lead a private, non-collective life is impossible or irrelevant for circumstances do not allow individuality to flourish. The other, by way of contrast, claims that individuality is not only possible but also necessary if Israel is to survive the persecution that presumably threatens it.

This concentric structure and the two correlating arguments find expression in the focus upon individualistic – and sometimes idiosyncratic – characters, who are at odds with the conformist society around them because of their successful attempt to assert their personal freedom. This conflict constitutes the film's inner circle. When these characters are drawn into the outer circle where the fact of war is inescapable, they prove not only their allegiance to society but also demonstrate that western-style individualism is necessary to Israel's survival.

The trajectory traversed by the characters in these films shifts the focus away from the earlier social collectivist paradigm that characterised the 1950s, whereby collective military and civilian efforts along with socio-ethnic condensation were considered the answer to Israel's persecuted situation. The new trajectory suggests an individualistic social paradigm as a better social coping mechanism than the collectivist one. The rationale offered is that only the individualistic initiative and personal qualities of the Israelis will save tiny Israel from the collective masses in the Arab world.[11] This shift is supported by the films' overall structure. Characterised by reflexivity and marked western cinematic intertextual quotations, it articulates a mosaic-like, episodic narrative that references French New Wave films.[12] Such a formal strategy matches liberal democratic civilian existence, promulgating the attitude that life can continue even though sporadic terrorist warfare and constant wars threaten.

The optimism and individualism evidenced in films of this period can be attributed to the swift military victory of the Six Day War as well as to the relative economic improvement resulting from growing American political and financial support. These films promoted the individualistic, capitalist derived ideology that accompanied such strong American influence. Coincidentally, this change contributed to the expansion of the film industry. Beyond economic improvements which found expression in the volume of production and in the production values of some films (for example, the combat scenes in Uri Zohar's 1968 film *Every Bastard a King* (*Kol Mamzer Melech*)),[13] the liberalisation process led to the government's perception of film as more of an industry than a propaganda venue, a change reflected in the transfer of film matters to the ministry of commerce. Gilberto Toffano's *Siege* (1969), whose theme is Israel's isolated and constantly threatened existence, offers a good illustration of the pattern that films of this period generally follow.

A widow whose officer husband was killed in action begins a love affair with another man, a civilian who operates a tractor. Just when they are about to begin a new life, he is called to reserve duty on the Jordanian front during the War of Attrition. The film ends with a news bulletin reporting that a tractor operator was hit on the Jordanian front, leaving the woman in a state of fearful suspense regarding the fate of her lover.

Siege opens with documentary footage showing civilians being called up to fight or waiting to get on a plane back to Israel, while the news reports announce the failure of diplomatic efforts, the imminent outbreak of war and coded signals calling up different units to report for duty. The coarse black and white documentary images, the nervous faces, the jerky editing and the loud grating voice of the news announcer articulate a strong sense of anxiety. The story begins as we see an officer leaving his wife and child and driving off to war.

Following this brief opening, we are presented with recurring images of the woman's loneliness, isolation and anxiety, such as in a long shot unevenly split into black and white where we see her against the background of a lighted room while most of the frame is black. This opening articulation of a state of siege shifts from the public feeling of siege to the woman's private anxious isolation. However, the correlation of private and public, focalised through the woman, weakens as the film develops, only to strengthen as the story moves toward the War of Attrition.

Through much of the film the public feeling of siege recedes thematically into the background. The narrative traces the woman's successful attempt to break free from her husband's friends and her neighbours. Her mourning, loneliness and claustrophobia (personal expressions of the state of siege) alter to boredom, defiance and disrespect for the social conventions others try to impose upon her, robbing her of individuality. This theme is prominent in a swish pan of the woman riding her bicycle through empty streets that is synchronised with a voice-over of murmuring, gossiping voices; or in a sequence that features radio reports of terrorists playing over repetitive shots of her alone in her apartment, where she is seen leafing through magazines or speaking on the phone to a friend in Paris, clearly oblivious to the reports. This formal transvaluation is enhanced by the other space the film constructs, in which her slowly evolving new love affair becomes the main focus.

This other narrative space expresses the idea that Israel is primarily a western country, sharing ideals of western liberal individualism. The first transition to this space occurs in a busy city street, where we see the widow wearing European-style clothes, sporting dark sun glasses, and smoking a cigarette while rock music can be heard in the background. This is when she first encounters the tractor driver. Later, as their love affair develops, we will intermittently see rapid montage sequences featuring shots of various western 1960s' symbols (Beatles records, Piccadilly Square, fashion magazines with girls in mini skirts, film billboards, supermarkets, rows of Coca-Cola bottles, coffee shops in gasoline stations). We follow the pair of lovers as they tour the territories occupied after the Six Day War – presented as an exotic market in the eastern part of Jerusalem, for example – where tourists buy mementos, acting out western neo-colonialism. The tourists are seen speaking about her husband 'as a human and not as a symbol' and about his death as the result of a mistaken bullet, while the new, civilian, lover outlines his world-view, which is focused on the little day-to-day but nonetheless important things in life: achieving personal happiness, being independent, and so on.

Yet this private space makes room for meditations on the ways in which military differs from civilian life: that soldiers and civilians have distinct functions – that the army fights and civilians build, that ultimately Israel is a western democratic country where the army follows and serves civil life, and that unfortunately it is located in the third world where national anti-colonialist struggles for freedom (justified in other third world countries) are taking place and generating unrest in the region. It would take too long to locate each of these ideas within the film, but what concerns us is their shared formal implementation, which is characterised by reflexivity and western cinematic intertextual quotation. Thus they include reflections on the relation between life and art (through the docudrama model), a strong formal concern (varied forms of intercutting between scenes emphasising rhythm, playing with objective and subjective streams of consciousness shots, complex – though not innovative – sound/image combinations), reflections on television (news reports in which we see various third world places and leaders, eliciting a sense of wonder about how available the world has become), and quotations of film genres (such as in an interview of the husband's friend – also an officer in the army – who appears wearing a cowboy hat in the midst of an army drill in a field reminiscent of the American West, describing the merits of the distinct, individualist, highly professional and devoted Israeli soldier, which the dead husband – his commanding officer – had epitomised).

Towards the end, after the drafting of her civilian lover in the midst of the War of Attrition, and the consequent news report of a tractor operator severely wounded along the Jordanian border where he has been posted, the film shifts again to a formal conception of siege. This is done through a series of intermingled documentary and fictional shots reiterating the feeling of anxiety developed in the beginning, while also explicitly (and clearly for ideological purposes) articulating the idea that the whole world is against Israel. The latter is achieved by referring to world leaders condemning Israel and by showing the shared anxiety of the multi-ethnic constituents of Israeli society.

This shift returns us to the beginning (the outer circle), creating a correlation between public and private siege. This is preceded by the resolution of the conflict between the civilian lover – private individualism – and the dead husband's friends – collectivism – through a man-to-man talk in which it becomes clear that the civilian had also taken part in the Six Day War and that friends of his had also been killed. This return, however, leads to the subordination of individualism to the dominant perception of persecution. In this way, *Siege* marks the transition from a collectivist social paradigm to an individualistic one, even as it maintains the underlying notion of Israel being a persecuted nation. Individualism, so the film argues, is in fact a better strategy to cope with constant persecution than collectivism.

1977–2003: Outer and Inner Persecution in a Threatened, Split Society

The theme of persecution in films on war produced up to 1977 underwent a radical change in films of the 1980s, establishing a new paradigm that has endured until the present. Whereas in pre-1977 films persecution, while accepted as a given, coexists with other notions and is modified by them (peaceful coexistence in 1947–67 and individualism in 1967–77), after that year persecution thematically dominates Israeli war films as never before, along with the often vague suggestion that Israel is somehow responsible for the persecution it suffers. In these later films, war is a constant threat, erupting out of nowhere only to suddenly end. It figures as an event whose different elements – terror, mines, explosions, violent military encounters and death – sporadically invade the narrative trajectory, disrupting the plot. In turn, narratives sometimes gain coherence by being framed by war. (For example, *The Vulture* (*Ha'Ayit*, 1981) begins with the October 1973 war and ends with preparations for another, unspecified conflict.) War is posited as the sole origin for a society that is presented as morally, emotionally, aesthetically and mentally corrupt. Society is anxious and suspicious, its members either malicious and violent, or naive and therefore lost, confused and in despair. This confusion, anxiety and despair are supported by disjointed plot lines articulated within an entrapping narrative space.

These films protest against their fabricated reality. This is sometimes expressed by characters who articulate a vague desire for peace. However, this protest and desire are presented as imaginary, lacking resonance in the overall structure of the films (as a kind of Job's complaint to God). This lack of resonance derives primarily from the representation of war as the sole source of societal corruption, while war itself, repeatedly reappearing, does so for no apparent reason. Thus relevant protest and a realisable desire for peace are foreclosed as possibilities.

Films like *Late Summer Blues* (*Blues Lahofesh Hagadol*, 1987, dir. Renen Schorr) which deals with the War of Attrition, *Avanti Popolo* (1986, dir. Rafi

Bukai) dealing with the Six Day War, or even *Ricochets* (*Shtei Etzbaot M'Tzidon*/'Two Fingers From Sidon', 1986, dir. Eli Cohen), an Israel Defense Forces subsidised film dealing with the Lebanon War, all feature and even focus upon characters who seek to evade the reality of war either through political subversion (*Late Summer Blues*), solidarity with the enemy (*Avanti Popolo*), or passive resistance (*Ricochets*). However, the desire of these subversive characters to evade the reality of periodic war is undermined by the narrative (and other formal and thematic strategies), leading either to their awareness that war is a natural and necessary evil (*Late Summer Blues, Ricochets*) or to their deaths (*Avanti Popolo*).

This theme is particularly evident in films that address the 1973 October (or Yom Kippur) war, in which Egypt and Syria initiated a concerted attack from south and north leading to heavy casualties on the Israeli side. Although the 1973 war was eventually won by Israel, which re-established its pre-1973 ceasefire borders, the price paid in human lives was unprecedented for Israelis. It is significant that whereas the Six Day War in June 1967 quickly generated a series of war films that memorialised it, the Yom Kippur War did not find a place in Israeli films in the years immediately following.[14] In fact, the first fictional cinematic explicit consideration of the October war was in 1981 in *The Vulture*, directed by Yaki Yosha. The particular way in which the war is treated in this film is to be traced mostly to the changed political climate in Israel following the change in government that came about as a result of the 1977 national elections, which brought the right-wing Likud Party to power after a sixty-year-long hegemony of the left. Israeli filmmakers, as well as various artists and intellectuals aligned with the left, were dubious of the political climate that they feared the right wing would bring about; they felt deep anxiety about their own well-being and that of the state of Israel. Ironically, the fear of Israeli filmmakers for their professional future was misplaced, since under Likud the film industry received massive governmental support and suffered little censorship. In fact, the new government established the 'Committee for the Encouragement of Quality Films' that funded the highly critical and politicised films that were produced during this period.

Notwithstanding this perplexing situation, we might term the cinematic perception that evolved after 1977 as evidencing a double-binded notion of persecution: one, internal, having to do with the left's fear of now being persecuted by the right, who had attained political power; and the other, external, having to do with the long-held notion of persecution of the state by the Arab world. This is probably why we find in these films a contradiction between an explicit critique of Israeli society, along with the aesthetic grounding of this critique within a cinematic reality of persecution, making the vague critique irrelevant to what the films perceive to be Israel's real situation.

Of particular interest in this regard is Amos Gitai's film *Kippur* (2000), which follows this ongoing perception but also offers interesting formal configurations to powerfully articulate the notion of persecution. The film attempts to bring alive the director's personal experiences during the War of Atonement. It follows a group of soldiers haphazardly formed into a rescue unit amid the chaos of war. The film vaguely protests against warmongers and the horrors of war, apparently offering instead the option of sensuality. It opens with a long lovemaking scene between a soldier and his girlfriend, followed by his departure to the front with a friend. On the way, they meet a militant officer who leads his troops enthusiastically into the middle of a heavy bombardment in which all but he are killed. This is followed by the protagonists' rapid assignment to an airborne rescue unit and their various encounters with the wounded and dead soldiers they have to evacuate from the front. Their own helicopter is hit, and then they themselves are evacuated. The film ends with the hero's return from the hell of war to his lover's bed, to a lovemaking scene identical to that which had opened the film.

An analysis of *Kippur*'s formal structure reveals it is motored by the concept of persecution. Hence, beyond a narrative circularity, the recurring use of battlefield shots, long in distance and in duration, in which we witness failed rescue attempts by the protagonists, evokes a strong sense of agoraphobia. In the centre of the frame, a group of defenceless soldiers are seen in the middle of an open, muddy and cold battlefield, with bodies falling around them, casualties of the constant shelling and occasional bullets; this deadly gunfire seems to come out of nowhere. In a particularly powerful scene, the main characters are shown trying to carry a wounded soldier on a stretcher. They are unable to advance as they sink into the heavy mud, as the wounded soldier finally drops from the stretcher and dies in their arms. Their frustrated attempts to resuscitate him, as shells explode around them, are presented in long shots and are emblematic of the film's vague cry against a faceless constant state of war. To this agoraphobic feeling, a further sense of claustrophobia is added in the recurring close-ups of the protagonists within the confined space of a helicopter hovering above the battlefield, accompanied by the constant, monotonic and threatening soundtrack of the helicopter's propellor blades. Out of this represented hell emanates a strong sense of unidentified threat and futility.

These elements in the film form a counterpoint to the vague critique of war suggested in the portrayal of an aggressive officer held responsible for his troops' deaths, as well as in the apparent opposition of love to war. It turns the initial anger at the warmonger's irresponsibility into sorrow and pity for a tragic figure. This is effected largely by the visual rhyme between the circular, hallucinatory walking of the disillusioned officer among his dead troops and the protagonists' repeated, frustrated attempts to evacuate the wounded, portrayed as a Sisyphean task. Likewise, the film changes the lovemaking scenes from a vague but viable opposition to war into a temporary, shaky refuge from war's ongoing hell. The war is not over when the protagonist is finally released, and his desire and his embrace of his lover are now charged with the anxiety and fear of an experienced threatening outside. The calm and innocent atmosphere that had characterised the opening love scene is certainly no more.

CONCLUSION

A national cinema often reveals widespread beliefs and ideas. Israeli films offer evidence of the deeply ingrained notion of persecution shared by many Israeli Jews. Granted, the treatment of war over time changed from patriotic unquestioning to political criticism, and some films entertained competing notions of possible peaceful coexistence (1947–67), of Israel being a liberal powerful state (1967–77), while others even ridiculed and criticised the belief in persecution (1977–2000). Even so, an ongoing and underlying conception of Israeli political filmmaking has been that of a besieged, persecuted nation. While this cinematic conception may not be unique to Israeli films,[15] it does stem from longstanding Jewish tradition, one that has been transferred to the cinema. Moreover, this dominant notion is widespread in Israeli culture. It holds a prominent place in educational textbooks, in secular national monuments and holidays, and in literature.[16] It offers a form of cohesion to a society otherwise divided along class, ethnic, religious and ideological lines, influencing the ways in which Israelis evaluate fundamental socio-political and geo-political concerns and often blocking serious consideration of feasible solutions to the nation's political problems.

NOTES

1. Several scholars have considered this notion in relation to Israeli society using somewhat different terms and methods. See Daniel Bar-Tal and Dikla Antebi, 'Siege Mentality in Israel', *International Journal of Intercultural Relations*, 16, 3 (1992), pp. 251–75; Conor Cruise O'Brien, *The Siege* (New York: Simon & Schuster, 1986); Michael Brecher, *Decisions in Crisis, Israel, 1967 and 1973* (Berkeley, CA: University of California Press, 1980); Robert Alter, 'The Massada Complex', *Commentary*, July 1973, http://www.commentarymagazine.com/ (accessed 6 March 2005); Meron Benvenisti, *The Sling and the Club* (Jerusalem: Keter, 1988); Charles Liebman and Eliezer Don Yehiya, *Civil Religion in Israel* (Berkeley, CA: University of California Press, 1983); Yehoshafat Harkaby, *Facing Reality* (Jerusalem: Van Leer Foundation, 1981).
2. The analysis of the films *Hill 24 Doesn't Answer* and *Siege* is adapted from Nitzan Ben-Shaul, *Mythical Expressions of Siege in Israeli Films* (Lewiston, NY: Edwin Mellen Press, 1997), pp. 9–31. Printed by permission of Edwin Mellen Press.
3. For an expanded analysis of these films in this respect see Ben-Shaul, *Mythical Expressions of Siege*, pp. 47–120.
4. Liebman and Don Yehiya, *Civil Religion in Israel*.
5. See, for example, Dan Miron, *If There is No Jerusalem: Essays on Hebrew Writing in a Cultural-Political Context* (Tel-Aviv: Hakibbutz Hameuchad, 1987).
6. On the dependence of the period's sparse film industry upon the government as opposed to the literary establishment, see Nurith Gertz, *Motion Fiction: Israeli*

Fiction in Film (Tel Aviv: Open University of Israel, 1993), pp. 20–3. From 1948 to 1960 only seven feature films where produced, all of them evidencing a similar conception to that found in *Hill 24 Doesn't Answer*. See for example *Pillar of Fire* (*Amud H'Esh*, 1959, Larry Frisch); *A Stone on Every Mile* (*Even Al Kol Meel*, 1955, Aryeh Lahola); *B'Ein Moledet* ('Without a Homeland', 1956, Nuri Habib).

7. For example, see Ella Shohat, *Israeli Cinema: East/West and the Politics of Representation* (Austin, TX: Texas University Press, 1989), pp. 58–76.

8. The Nazi-Arab correlation in relation to the 1950's notion of siege has also been noted and analysed in Shohat, *Israeli Cinema*, pp. 69–73. For my discussion of Shohat's position on this see Ben-Shaul, *Mythical Expressions of Siege*, p. 20, n.18.

9. The notion of social condensation (*Mizug Galuiot*) that evolved during this period rests upon the notion that Jews gathered from different Diaspora communities will intermingle – culturally and biologically – and the result will be a new condensed Jew constituted by what is good from each of the different diasporas. This notion has shifted throughout the years. See Ben-Shaul, *Mythical Expressions of Siege*, pp. 83–120.

10. For an extensive analysis of the cognitive and extratextual factors (including what the writer terms the *Holocaust Syndrome*), leading to the Israeli government's decision to declare war in 1967 (as well as its decision to abstain from a pre-emptive strike during the October War in 1973), see Brecher, *Decisions in Crisis*.

11. The appearance of the liberal autonomy paradigm is further established in three other types of films produced during this period: auteristic films such as Yehuda Ne'eman's *The Dress* (*Ha-Simla*, 1970), where formal artistic reflexivity grounded the theme of the individual suffocated by societal conventions; the popular war action film that celebrated Israel's swift victory and valorised the elite commando unit fighters for their individuality and inventiveness while stereotyping the Arab fighters as vicious and stupid (for example, in *Azit Hakalba Hatzanhanit* ('Azit, the Paratrooper Dog', 1972, Boaz Davidson), a children's film focusing upon the heroic deeds of a German shepherd dog and her valiant paratrooper owner and trainer); and in the social comedy *Burekas* films, such as *Katz V' Carasso* ('Katz and Carasso', 1971, Menahem Golan), where ethnic diversity is celebrated as ethnic legitimate capitalist competition rather than tension. See Ben-Shaul, *Mythical Expressions of Siege*, pp. 103–12.

12. On the New Wave characteristics of these films see Shohat, *Israeli Cinema*, pp. 197–203; Ben-Shaul, *Mythical Expressions of Siege*, pp. 103–12; Nurith Gertz, *Motion Fiction*, pp. 97–175.

13. See Shohat, *Israeli Cinema*, p. 105.

14. The Yom Kippur War and the type of shock of recognition it generated (after the post-1967 euphoria), was one of the cardinal factors leading to the downfall of the Labor Alignment Party, and the rise to power of the right-wing Likud Party in the 1977 elections.

15. On the expression of persecution in films produced around the world see Ben-Shaul, 'Film Genres as Syndromes: The Genre of Siege', *Assaph Kolnoa: Studies in Cinema and Television*, Section D, no. 2 (2001).

16. See Daniel Bar-Tal, *Understanding Psychological Bases of the Israeli-Palestinian Conflict*, International Center for Peace in the Middle East, Discussion Paper 12, May 1984; E. Ben-Ezer, 'War and Siege in Israeli Literature 1948–1967', *Jerusalem Quarterly*, 2 (Winter 1977) and E. Ben-Ezer, 'War and Siege in Hebrew Literature after 1967', *Jerusalem Quarterly*, 9 (Fall 1978), pp. 20–45; Nurith Gertz, *Social Myths in Literary and Political Texts*, Research Report, Open University of Israel, Working Paper no. 712/86.

RECOMMENDED FILMS

Avanti popolo (Rafi Bukai, 1986)
Beyond the Walls (*Me'Ahorei Hasoragim*, Uri Barbash, 1984)
Every Bastard a King (*Kol Mamzer Melech*, Uri Zohar, 1968)
Fellow Travellers (*Magash Hakesef*, Yehuda Ne'eman, 1983)
He Walked Through the Fields (*Hu Halach B'Sadot*, Yosef Millo, 1967)
Hill 24 Doesn't Answer (*Giv'a 24 Eina Ona*, Thorold Dickinson, 1955)
Kippur (Amos Gitai, 2000)
Siege (*Matzor*, Gilberto Tofano, 1969)
The Vulture (*Ha Ayit*, Yaki Yosha, 1981)
They Were Ten (*Hem Hayu Asarah*, Baruch Dienar, 1961)

RECOMMENDED READINGS

Bar Tal, Daniel (1984) *The Massada Syndrome: A Case of Central Belief*, The International Center for Peace in the Middle East, Discussion Paper 3.

Ben-Shaul, Nitzan (1997) *Mythical Expressions of Siege in Israeli Films*. Lewiston, NY: Edwin Mellen Press.

Friedman, Regine-Mihal (2001) 'Images of Destruction/Destruction of Images', *Assaph Kolnoa: Studies in Cinema and Television*, Section D, no. 2, pp. 247–56.

Gertz, Nurith (2001) 'Gender and Nationality in the New Israeli Cinema', *Assaph Kolnoa: Studies in Cinema and Television*, Section D, no. 2, pp. 227–46.

Liebman, C. and Don Yehiya, E. (1983) *Civil Religion in Israel*. Berkeley, CA: University of California Press.

Neeman, Judd (1995) 'The Empty Tomb in the Postmodern Pyramid: Israeli Cinema in the 1980s and 1990s', in Charles Berlin (ed.), *Documenting Israel*. Cambridge, MA: Harvard College Library, pp. 117–51.

O'Brien, Connor Cruise (1986) *The Siege*. New York: Simon & Schuster.

Raz, Yosef (2003) *Beyond Flesh, Queer Masculinities and Nationalism in Israeli Cinema*. New Brunswick, NJ: Rutgers University Press.

Segev, Tom (1995) *The Seventh Million: The Israelis and the Holocaust*. New York: Hill & Wang.

Shohat, Ella (1989) *Israeli Cinema: East/West and the Politics of Representation*. Austin, TX: Texas University Press.

12. NEW IRANIAN CINEMA

1982–present

Negar Mottahedeh

INTRODUCTION

Iranian cinema experienced substantial growth after the Islamic Revolution of 1978–79 and gained wide popularity in international film festivals in the decades that followed. In 1992, the Toronto International Film Festival called Iranian cinema 'one of the pre-eminent national cinemas in the world', a verdict that was echoed years later by a *New York Times* reviewer who concurred that the New Iranian cinema was 'one of the world's most vital national cinemas'.[1] In 1998, Iranian cinema ranked tenth in the world in terms of output, surpassing Germany, Brazil, South Korea, Canada and Australia, and far exceeding the high-volume traditional Middle Eastern film producers, Egypt and Turkey.[2]

Few had such expectations from a newly established theocratic state. Soon after the Shah of Iran, Reza Shah Pahlavi, was overthrown in 1979, the country's spiritual and revolutionary leader, Ayatollah Ruhollah Khomeini – who had been forced into exile by the Pahlavi regime – returned from Paris and assumed the role of political and religious leader. Upon his arrival Khomeini made his first public address, in which he laid out the regime's relation to cinema:

> We are not opposed to cinema, to radio, to television . . . The cinema is a modern invention that ought to be used for the sake of educating the people, but as you know, it was used instead to corrupt our youth. It is the misuse of cinema that we are opposed to, a misuse caused by the treacherous policies of our rulers.[3]

The new policies established by the Khomeini regime ensured that the film industry would be used on a broad national scale to educate the population in Islamic citizenship. They aimed thereby to stimulate and propagate a new and vital national culture, both locally and globally.

Cinema was to be used to create an Islamic culture through a new conception of Islamic citizenship. According to Hamid Naficy, what 'Islamic culture' frequently meant in the rhetoric of the clergy could be classified under the following categories:

> Nativism (return to traditional values and mores), populism (justice, defense of . . . the disinherited), monotheism, anti-idolatry, theocracy (. . . rule of the supreme jurisprudent), ethicalism and Puritanism . . ., political and economic independence, and the combating of arrogant world imperialism, a concept often condensed in the slogan 'neither East nor West'.[4]

The Islamic Republic entrusted cinema with promoting these fundamental aspects of Islamic culture. Ali Akbar Hashemi-Rafsanjani, the Iranian President, emphasised this responsibility in an address to Iranian film directors by telling them, 'If you . . . make good films, there will be no need for pulpits'.[5] The regime's goal was to create a national film industry devoid of foreign influences and, by extension, to create a national culture that would remain detached from both East and West. Thus, under threats of censorship, Iranian filmmakers have produced a cinema that has purported to represent 'the national' and 'the local' in some pure form. Although the parameters of Islamic culture were laid down through the effort to bring film under the control of dominant state ideology, what it would mean to create a national film industry and to constitute a new cinematic culture was as yet unclear.

THE RULE OF MODESTY

The regulations put into effect in 1982 mainly targeted the representation of women and heterosexual relations on screen, with the film industry obliged to abide by 'the rule of modesty'. Imposed on the cinema, this law necessitated the wearing of scarves, veils and loose-fitting tunics by women. Women were constrained to portrayals that upheld their dignity, and were to avoid activities and movements that would reveal the contours of their body. Men and women would have no physical contact and were prohibited from looking at each other with desire on screen.

In *The White Balloon* (*Badkonake sefid*, 1995), one of the first post-revolutionary films to achieve international success, we see an interesting instance of the attempt to conform to modesty laws. In this film, the father of Razieh

(Aida Mohammadkhani), the main protagonist, is absent throughout the visual track. Though he is a significant figure in the narrative, he speaks his lines off-screen, from a shower window that opens onto an interior courtyard. He remains there and speaks through that window for the length of the film. Director Jafar Panahi thus manages to avoid showing any physical contact whatsoever between the actors who play Razieh's mother and father, and in this way circumvents possible censorship.

Post-revolutionary modesty laws addressed themselves not only to the representation of heterosexual relations, but to the representation of bodies as well. As a consequence of the restrictions placed on Iranian films, cinematic desexualisation became the rule in the 1980s and early 1990s. Women's bodies, seen as vehicles of sexual desire (even when fully veiled), were represented as static and sexually undifferentiated.

Modesty laws enforced the veiling of women in all circumstances. Although Islamic traditions encourage the veiling of women in public and in the company of unrelated men, the introduction of veiling in the cinematic representation of private spaces and activities involving only women contradicted the conventional perception of film as representing reality. Because even the most religious women did not veil in front of their husbands in real life, the representation of veiled women in private, familial spaces seemed unrealistic to Iranian audiences. While Islamic laws affected many areas of social and cultural life, such as consumption, entertainment and sartoriality, the veil came to stand for the disproportionate intrusion of Islamic cultural policies on private practices in cinema.

The Legend of a Sigh (*Afsane-Ye – Ah*, 1991), for example, is about a female novelist who suffers from a writer's block and, through the agency of Ah, a handsome young man who materialises when he hears a heartfelt sigh, experiences the lives of four women from widely different strata of Iranian society. In this film, director Tahmineh Milani includes a bedroom scene in which Feresteh, an architecture student, redrafts her work as her sister Firoozeh sleeps. At one point the sister sits up in bed to complain about the light. The oddity of the existing modesty laws is emphasised here, as the young girl is shown wearing her veil to bed. Of course this scene was both unnecessary and avoidable in the context of the film narrative as a whole. It must be read, then, as a form of silent protest by the feminist director, whose meticulous attention to modesty laws throughout the film forces her to construct highly unrealistic, even comic scenarios.

Stressing the perception of the female body as the site of heterosexual potency, modesty laws not only affected the representation of women – they also affected film form. Close-ups of women and point-of-view shots which, through the gaze of the camera, allow unrelated men (in the theatre) and women (on screen) to look at each other directly were thought to violate Islamic modesty by censors. The eye-line matches and shot patterns that are said to be constitutive of the system of suture configure a threat to male piety in relation to a female body in which heterosexual desire itself is said to reside in Muslim belief.[6] The close-up is capable of objectifying female beauty and sexualising the visual relationship between a man and a woman; this 'naked' interrogation of the female body implies the disintegration of Muslim male identity. In Iranian cinema, then, the viewing subject himself is at risk. Vision itself, therefore, must be proscribed.

In dominant Hollywood cinema, narrative continuity depends largely on visual cues. These visual cues allude to spatial and temporal continuities outside the visual frame. Thus limitations on vision that subvert eyeline matches between characters and shot-reverse shot patterns that link characters together also unravel spatial and temporal continuities between shots, and in doing so disrupt narrative continuity which relies on the exchange of glances to trigger the viewer's own imagination of contiguous spaces outside the frame. The proscription of vision as it informs Iranian cinema tends to subvert conventionally unquestioned cinematic systems that give a sense of cohesion and meaning to the narrative through spatial and temporal continuities. The desexualised look, the unfocused gaze and the long shot – all instances of the inscription of modesty in Iranian cinema, as Hamid Naficy has argued – thus problematise western cinematic theories which rely on audience identification and implication achieved through the operations of 'suture'.[7]

NEW CODES AND CONVENTIONS

Confined by the inscription of modesty in cinema, Iranian filmmakers of the 1980s and 1990s were forced to think more carefully about cinematic grammar and the language of film itself. If Iranian cinema could not speak in the conventionalised language of Hollywood realism, if it could not make use of the filmic codes that have habitually rendered time and space continuous, then another cinematic grammar – a new language, in fact – had to be developed. What would this language look like?

Elaborating on the difference between Iranian cinema and other world cinemas, Mohsen Makhmalbaf – one of the best-known Iranian filmmakers – made the following observation:

> I see that whenever we use montage or a metaphor that denotes a single meaning, then the [Iranian] spectator is capable of grasping the meaning of the image . . ., but as soon as the representation carries a plurality of meaning . . . the spectator fails to understand . . . Sometimes the language of cinema is spoken by using shadows . . . Sometimes the language of the image rests in the use of the (camera) lens . . . It is the effect of repetition

and pedagogy and the becoming cliché [of a technique] that [allows] the majority [of the audience] to get it . . . But when the language of cinema speaks through framing, by way of broken [sight] lines or direct ones, or by using colour or mise-en-scène, or through the relationship between objects within the frame, or by [the use of] light, or by [the use of visual] concept[s], not one person understands. This is because the language of cinema arrives by way of, and is borrowed from [Western traditions of] painting. And Iranian film audiences are not familiar with painting. This is why Iranian filmmakers must be answerable to the fact that a whole people are uneducated in the history of Western visual arts.[8]

If Iranian cinema is to communicate to all Iranians about the new nation, then the audience must at least be literate in the language of film to understand it. But when limitations imposed on vision exclude globally accepted codes and conventions that constitute the dominant grammar of cinema, filmmakers are forced to ask what an alternate grammar would look like.

If the mediation of meaning among a diversity of national citizens is made possible through the production of and literacy in a standardised language, how is the mediation of meaning from screen to audience possible under conditions of cinematic censorship? Iranian filmmakers came up with numerous solutions to these issues by creating allegorical figures, displacing plots and deferring cinematic closure. Repetition standardised many of these new innovations in cinematic grammar, transforming them into codes and conventions that made Iranian cinema look, but more importantly speak, differently than other major film cultures. This has resulted in cinematic opportunities as well as problems of legibility.

In *Del Shodegan* ('The Enamored', 1992), director Ali Hatami narrates the story of a group of traditional musicians who are invited to go abroad in order to record their music on the newly invented gramophone. The scenes representing the musicians' farewells are instructive in that they show the expression of emotion between fictive family members. None of the actors are related in real life, so they must by law avoid physical contact. How is an emotional farewell communicated between family members in Iranian post-revolutionary cinema? One scene in *Del Shodegan* is particularly provocative here in that it makes use of a symbolic figure to convey the stirring farewell between a filmic husband and wife (see Figure 12.1).

The scene opens with a long shot of the musician's wife packing her husband's clothes. She is donned in a headscarf and is outfitted in the clothing worn in harem interiors in late nineteenth-century Iran. The musician and his wife then sit down by a round table on which rests a set of books, a santoor (a string instrument) and a cat. The couple discuss the things that join them in their affections for one another and review the promises and sacrifices they have

Figure 12.1 *Del Shodegan*, scene 17, frames 1–8

made in their devotion to music. The wife speaks to her husband with an averted gaze while she strokes the musical instrument – the signifier of their common love – with her palm.

The scene's opening long shots are followed by nine shot-reverse shots at medium length in which the wife is framed with the santoor looking obliquely to the right of the frame, and the husband, shot with the cat resting by his arm, alternately looking to the right, looking down and finally gazing directly to the left of the frame (in shot 6), as if looking at his wife. Contrary to the conventions governing the depiction of a conversation in classical Hollywood cinema – in which a series of close-ups are edited together in a shot-reverse shot pattern – the closing shot in this sequence from *Del Shodegan* is the *only* close-up to appear in the scene. The close-up frames the cat, who we first see being stroked by the musician's hand, and then by his wife's hand as they exchange their vows to stay bound by the music that unites them (shots 7 and 8).

Under the guidelines for modesty in Iranian cinema, this scene, depicting a heterosexual relationship, gives shape to a convention that aims to express an intense bond of love on the post-revolutionary screen. The cat becomes a symbol of displacement and a representational cue for the common bond of love in *Del Shodegan*. With the strong presence of the *Kanun-e Parvaresh-e Fekri-ye Kudakan va Nowjavanan* (Centre for Intellectual Development of Children and Adolescents) in the film industry, children too have became symbols of displacement in many post-revolutionary films. In films like *Bashu* (*Bashu, The Little Stranger*, 1989), *The Mirror* (*Ayneh*, 1997), *Homework* (*Mashgh-e Shab*, 1990) and *Sokout* (a.k.a. *The Silence*, 1998), child characters give their directors figures who can sing, dance and portray adult relations and heterosocial emotions that were otherwise strictly censored according to the rule of modesty. The depiction of disciplinary relations between parents and their children, or between teachers and their students, have also provided some directors – such as Abbas Kiarostami – with displaced sites for the critique of a restrictive society, while highlighting the callous treatment of children by adults in Iranian society.

Despite their differences, dominant cinema's preoccupation with 'realism' continued to exert an influence on Iranian filmmakers. For most directors in this country, shifting the camera away from urban settings allowed for a more 'believable' depiction of the 'new' ideal of Islamic Iran. In making 'village films' set in fictive rural and actual village locations,[9] the directors in question avoided the problem of having to maintain modesty in dress. In contrast to urban women, who would need to be screened in interior spaces wearing large outer garments in conformity with modesty laws but contrary to actual contemporary practice, toiling peasants and rural women could be imagined outdoors in rural spaces, wearing headscarves and colourful garments that were nevertheless congruent with the existing regime's dictates of modesty.

The authoritarian language of Islam that was to give shape to the new language of Iranian cinema by resituating vision itself was thereby displaced to a fantasmatic site where it could have little ideological effect. New conventions developed as symbolic embodiments of state-imposed regulations,[10] and village films which fabulated the life and labour of fictive primitives were one adaptation of these new embodiments. They enabled Iranian filmmakers to create realistic scenarios, while ushering in a cinema that was more linguistically and scopically diverse, more brilliant and colourful, than ever before.

This turn to location filming, the use of a mobile camera and the reliance on available light and sound (which was markedly differed from studio-style lighting and dubbing), coupled with an increased self-reflexivity within Iranian films concerning the role of cinema in the production of the social world, links new Iranian cinema with the *nouvelle vague*, the French New Wave that emerged in France in the 1950s and early 1960s. Filmmakers associated with this movement, such as Godard, Truffaut, Rivette, Chabrol and Rohmer, developed or adhered to a much more casual style of filmmaking than was typical at the time, using Parisian streets and coffee bars as locations. Freed from the confines of the studio sets, the mobile *nouvelle vague* camera would often follow a character around the city or look over his or her shoulder merely to watch life go by. Films made as part of this movement, like the films associated with the Italian neorealist movement a few decades earlier, were immersed in the quotidian, and were self-reflexively interrogating the effects of the medium on the construction of everyday reality.

In Iranian cinema, the characteristic blending of documentary and fiction, of the everyday and the extraordinary, in films such as Mohsen Makhmalbaf's *Gabbeh* (1996), Samira Makhmalbaf's *The Apple* (*Sib*, 1998) and Abbas Kiarostami's *Close Up* (*Nema-ye Nazdik*, 1990), emphatically forces viewers to contemplate the relation between the cinematic and the real. This makes the comparison between new Iranian cinema and the *nouvelle vague* more tenable. The proximity of this blended genre to 'what is really there', however, has raised questions among Iranian feminists concerning the representation of Iranian women's lives on the screen. Watching the success of the industry in film festivals around the globe, feminists and other critics have repeatedly argued that the films in question present unrealistic views of Iran and its way of life.[11]

FEMINIST DEBATES AND THE QUESTION OF REALISM

Perhaps the most dominating marker of new Iranian cinema in the West is its designation as an industry attached to colour; that is, to the abundant use of colour in representing sweeping landscapes, peasant life and nomadic existence. These representations, promoted by the national film industry in such pictures as Makhmalbaf's *Gabbeh* and *Kandahar* (2001), Abbas Kiarostami's *Where Is the Friend's Home?* (*Khane-ye doust kodjast?*, 1987), *Through the Olive Trees* (*Zire darakhatan zeyton*, 1994) and *The Wind Will Carry Us* (*Bad ma ra khahad bord*, 1999) and Majid Majidi's *Color of Paradise* (*Rang-e khoda*, 2000) and *Baran* (2001), have come under scrutiny both within the country and in the diaspora. Central to these critiques, once again, is the industry's problematic representation of women, as colourful, fetishised spectacles of native primitivism or as domesticated urban housewives.

Iranian feminists articulate this problematic in terms of the shift from pre-revolutionary cinematic depictions of women as 'unchaste dolls' to the 'chaste dolls' of the post-revolutionary period in Iranian cinema. Shahla Lahiji's work on the representation of women in Iranian films stands at the forefront of these critiques, as she suggests that the 'unchaste dolls' of the pre-revolutionary cinema were banished from the cabaret stage and confined within the interior walls of the kitchen, where they are engaged in domestic chores.[12] However, Lahiji claims that the stereotypical depiction of women on screen has been challenged recently by the work of female filmmakers who 'object to the unrealistic image of women in Iranian cinema' by presenting their female characters in a more realistic light. She argues that 'the international reception of [their] approach has finally persuaded their male colleagues to reappraise their own work'.[13] This more realistic portrayal of women and their role in Iranian society is attributed by Lahiji to the widespread positive reception of Iranian films around the globe.

While such critiques of the stereotypical depictions of women in Iranian cinema may be seen as progressive in the context of a national film industry that is charged by its government to propagate 'proper' standards of Islamic life among a vastly illiterate population, they become quite problematic in a transnational context, such as an international film festival, in which Iranian films often circulate. Lahiji's critique of the stereotypical female in the new cinema evokes, albeit negatively, Steve Neale's discussion of stereotypes in his study of race and ethnicity in film.[14] Drawing on theoretical traditions within cinema studies, Neale suggests that the study of stereotypes requires a comprehensive approach in which narrative structure, genre conventions and cinematic styles are analysed, and attention gets paid to broader practices of filmic production. This is because, as Robyn Wiegman has argued, positive images can be 'as pernicious as degrading ones'.[15]

In the context of an industry that has sought to produce a national cinema steeped in local traditions and values that resist interpretations of national identity from the outside, it seems crucial to attend to the codes, conventions and effects specific to this cinema itself. Rather than focusing on the question of realism, which is fundamental to the logic of western film practice, the more relevant question for a cinema like Iran's – one that consciously distances itself from outside influences – concerns the specific conventions used to construct Iranian women on screen in the first place. An analysis of Makhmalbaf's *Gabbeh* will provide us with some insights into the language of Iranian film-making and its relation to realism when it comes to the representation of women.

Originally conceived as a documentary about the Qashqa'i nomads and their practice of weaving *gabbeh* rugs, the film revolves around the courtship of a young nomad, Gabbeh (Shaghayeh Djodat), and her horseback-riding lover who are prevented by a dominating tribal father from forming a union. The central obstacle to the union between Gabbeh and her lover is the arrival of Gabbeh's older uncle. An urban schoolteacher whom we first encounter in a nomadic school tent giving a lesson on colour, Gabbeh's uncle comes to the tribe to visit his mother after many years of absence, and to find a suitable bride. The uncle's arrival coincides with the death of his mother, who is also Gabbeh's grandmother. The tribe proceeds to mourn the woman's death by weaving a rug that narrates the day of the event and of the uncle's arrival. His mother lost, the uncle goes in search of a wife; and being Gabbeh's elder, the young nomad's courtship with her lover is, by rite, delayed.

Gabbeh's mother then gives birth. A kid goat disappears in the mountains and Gabbeh's younger sister dies in search of it. It rains and the rugs must be collected and protected. Each of these events delays Gabbeh's union. Furthermore, they are not represented in chronological order. Rather, seen in terms of the 'past' or the 'future', each one is intercut with sequences staged in a seemingly timeless 'present' that takes place on a river front where an elderly couple engage Gabbeh in a conversation about her life. Gabbeh's story thus becomes an atemporal cinematic narrative that is structured formally by the storytelling practices of the *gabbeh*-weavers themselves. As the women and children weave the rugs, they intermittently turn to the camera with a celebratory cry: 'Life is colour!'; 'Woman is Colour!'; 'Man is Colour!'

In the key sequences where the narrative attempts a forward movement towards the consummation of at least two heterosexual relationships, what interrupts the narrative telos is colour. In one scene, girls carrying bouquets (responsible for the processes of colour extraction from prairie plants) interrupt Gabbeh's impassioned attempt to run away with her courting horseback-rider (see Figure 12.2). The dye-making processes engaged in by Gabbeh and the younger tribeswomen halt the consummation of Gabbeh's marriage by deferring the scene of the uncle's union. Scenes representing the procedures of spinning and weaving coloured threads used by the nomadic tribeswomen to produce narrative patterns on the *gabbeh* rugs postpone the scene of the uncle's marriage. The production and spectacle of colour thus disrupt narrative continuity in *Gabbeh*, and in doing so fracture the film's reliance on the habitual touchstone of realism in dominant (western) cinematic discourse.

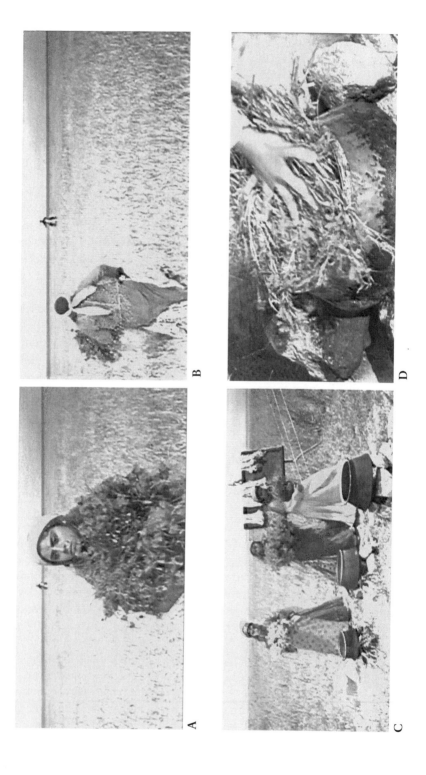

A

B

C

D

Colour functions in *Gabbeh* to escape, subvert and disrupt the conventional organisation of plot. The film's use of colour disrupts temporal and spatial continuities upon which *conventions* of narrative realism rely. Thus colour in the film unsettles commodification and fetishisation of the fictive nomadic primitive as a coherent and unified identity that is accessible beyond the fiction and the film's own spatio-temporal boundaries. While Makhmalbaf's film shatters conventional modes of representation, it does not do so to reveal the truth behind false illusions, to identify stereotypical representations as fraudulent, or alternately to represent the nomad in her true form. Instead, the film's strategic use of colour, conceived as a disruptive spectacle, serves to undermine the formal structures and cinematic conventions that have repeatedly fetishised and exoticised other cultures by relying on the cinematic *conventions* of realism as a coefficient of cultural truth. *Gabbeh* boldly ties itself to an unruly cinematic practice that is disruptive not only for its production of unusual temporalities but also for its dislocation of realist cinematic codes – codes that have encouraged the perception that representations of the unusual and the exotic in films about other cultures and in third world films are actual.

When Iranian films and their colourful fictive primitives meet their audiences in film festivals around the globe they do not attempt to represent the real beyond the realm of representation. Instead, they self-consciously question the standardised narrative forms and cinematic conventions that have structured the representation of third world women as authentic and indexical to the real in dominant cinemas.

NOTES

1. *Toronto International festival of festivals catalogue* (4 September 1992), p. 8, and Judith Miller, 'Movies of Iran Struggle for Acceptance', *New York Times*, 19 July 1992, H9, H14.
2. See Hamid Naficy, 'Iranian Cinema', in Oliver Leaman (ed.), *Companion Encyclopedia of Middle Eastern and North African Film* (New York: Routledge, 2001), pp. 130–222.
3. Ruhollah Khomeini, *Islam and Revolution: Writings and Declarations of Imam Khomeini*, trans. Hamid Algar (Berkeley, CA: Mizan Press, 1981), p. 248.
4. Hamid Naficy, 'Islamizing Film Culture in Iran: A Post-Khatami Update', in Richard Tapper (ed.), *The New Iranian Cinema: Politics, Representation and Identity* (London: I. B. Tauris, 2002), p. 29.
5. Akbar Aalami, 'Twenty Years of Iranian Cinema', *Donya-ye Sokhan*, 83–4 (1999), p. 67.
6. As an effect of certain filmic codes such as shot-reverse shot patterns which establish the point of view of two characters in conversation, and eye-line matches that 'stitch' the spectator into the film text by positioning the viewer as a film character (or alternately as the one looking at the character from a previously off-screen space), the system of suture is said to give film a sense of seamlessness. In film theory, suture is conceived as the use of conventions that produce the film universe as a safe place in which the spectator finds him or herself comfortably inscribed. Cf. Kaja Silverman, *The Subject of Semiotics* (New York: Oxford University Press, 1983).

7. Hamid Naficy, 'Veiled Vision/Powerful Presences: Women in Post-Revolutionary Iranian Cinema', in Mahnaz Afkhami and Erika Friedl (eds), *In the Eye of the Storm: Women in Post-revolutionary Iran* (Syracuse, NY: Syracuse University Press, 1994), pp. 131–50.
8. Mohsen Makhmalbaf, 'Dastfurush: Interview', *Gong-e Khab-dideh*, 3 (Tehran: Nashrani, 1996–97), p. 137.
9. Jamsheed Akrami, 'Cinema II: Feature Films', in *Encylcopaedia Iranica*, Vol. 5, ed. Ehsan Yashater Costa (Mesa, CA: Mazda Publishers, 1991).
10. For more on Iranian films as allegories informed by the conditions of the country's film industry, see Shohini Chaudhuri and Howard Finn, 'The Open Image: Poetic Realism and the New Iranian Cinema', *Screen*, 44, 1 (Spring 2003), pp. 38–57. I would also like to thank the graduate students in my Contemporary Iranian Cinema class in the Literature Program at Duke University (Spring 2003), Arnal Dilantha Dayaratna, Abigail Lauren Salerno and Shilyh Warren, for their insights on Iran's film industry and for giving shape to this reading.
11. See, for example, Azadeh Farahmand's essay, 'Perspectives on Recent (International Acclaim for) Iranian Cinema', in Tapper, *The New Iranian Cinema*, pp. 100–1.
12. Shahla Lahiji, 'Chaste Dolls and Unchaste Dolls: Women in Iranian Cinema since 1979', in Tapper, *The New Iranian Cinema*, pp. 215–26.
13. Ibid., p. 224.
14. Steve Neale, 'The Same Old Story: Stereotypes and Difference', *Screen Education*, 32–3 (1979), pp. 33–7.
15. Robyn Wiegman, 'Race, Ethnicity and Film', John Hill and Pamela Church Gibson (eds), *The Oxford Guide to Film Studies* (Oxford: Oxford University Press), p. 165.

RECOMMENDED FILMS

Close-up (*Nema-ye Nazdik,* Abbas Kiarostami, 1990)
The Color of Paradise (*Rang-e khoda*, Majid Majidi, 1999)
The Cyclist (*Bicycleran*, Mohsen Makhmalbaf, 1988)
Gabbeh (Mohsen Makhmalbaf, 1996)
Killing Mad Dogs (*Sagkoshi*, Bahram Beizai, 2001)
Taste of Cherry (*Ta'm e guilass*, Abbas Kiarostami, 1997)
Through the Olive Trees (*Zire darakhatan zeyton*, Abbas Kiarostami, 1994)
Two Women (*Do zan*, Tahmineh Milani, 1998)
Under the Skin of the City (*Zir-e poost-e shahr*, Rakhshan Bani-Etemad, 2001)
The Wind Will Carry Us (*Bad ma ra khahad bord*, Abbas Kiarostami, 1999)

RECOMMENDED READINGS

Dabashi, Hamid (2001) *Close-up: Iranian Cinema Past, Present and Future*. New York: Verso.
Issa, R. and Whitaker, S. (eds) (1999) *Life and Art: The New Iranian Cinema*. London: British Film Institute.
Khalili Mahani, Najmeh, 'Bahram Baizai, Iranian Cinema, feminism, art cinema', at: http://www.horschamp.qc.ca/new_offscreen/baizai.html (accessed 7 March 2005).
Mottahedeh, Negar (2000) 'Bahram Baizai's Maybe Some Other Time: The un-Presentable Iran', *Camera Obscura*, 15, 1, pp. 162–91.
Naficy, Hamid (1994) 'Veiled Vision/Powerful Presences: Women in Post-Revolutionary Iranian Cinema', in Mahnaz Afkhami and Erika Friedl (eds), *The Eye of the Storm: Women in Post-Revolutionary Iran*. Syracuse, NY: Syracuse University Press, pp. 131–50.

Naficy, Hamid (2000) 'Self-Othering: A Postcolonial Discourse on Cinematic First Contacts', in Fawzia Afzal-Khan and Kalpana Seshodri Crooks (eds), *The Preoccupation of Postcolonial Studies*. Durham, NC: Duke University Press, pp. 292–310.

Naficy, Hamid (2001) 'Iranian Cinema', in Oliver Leaman (ed.), *Companion Encyclopedia of Middle Eastern and North African Film*. New York: Routledge, pp. 130–222.

Naficy, Hamid (2003) 'Theorizing "Third World" Film Spectatorship: The Case of Iran and Iranian Cinema', in Anthony Guneratne and Wimal Dissanayake (eds), *Rethinking Third Cinema*. New York: Routledge, pp. 183–201.

Saeed-Vafa, Mehrnaz and Rosenbaum, Jonathan (2003) *Abbas Kiarostami*. Urbana, IL: University of Illinois Press.

Tapper, Richard (ed.) (2002) *The New Iranian Cinema: Politics, Representation and Identity*. London: I. B. Tauris.

PART V

ASIAN TRADITIONS

13. POPULAR HINDI CINEMA AND THE FILM SONG

Corey Creekmur

While popular Indian films – especially the pan-Indian Hindi language movies produced in Bombay (now officially Mumbai) commonly and condescendingly known as 'Bollywood' cinema – typically share a number of stylistic characteristics and narrative conventions, the inclusion of film songs is their most persistent feature and an element of South Asian film culture which extends far beyond the boundaries of cinema halls. Film songs enjoy massive popularity and long-term relevance for audiences, and so frequently exceed their original significance within the films for which they were composed and performed. Although the claim is slightly overstated, popular music in India *is* film music, and the success of many films depends upon the popularity of their songs, usually 'launched' in advance of a film's opening: if the music isn't first a hit, the film is unlikely to then succeed. Circulated through other media such as radio, television and commercial as well as pirated recordings, film songs permeate daily life in India; they can be heard at weddings as well as political rallies, in slums and in five-star hotels. The popular party game of *antakshari*, also played within films and on television quiz shows, depends upon players who can quickly recall and sing a large catalogue of film songs.

While pop music soundtracks have become increasingly crucial to the marketing and success of American films across genres, popular Indian cinema as a whole has been a thoroughly musical cinema since the arrival of film sound, serving a massive audience in India and abroad that has come to expect songs in films which might otherwise be identified as romances, comedies, thrillers or melodramas. Because songs are a common feature of almost all popular Indian films, the distinct Hollywood genre of 'the musical' is rarely used to designate films in India, though the pervasive use of songs has led some critics to claim, misleadingly, that *all* popular Indian films are musicals: one might just as persuasively assert that *no* Indian films are musicals, since songs are used across genres and thus a distinct category of 'musicals' cannot be clearly distinguished from other forms. The tradition of the film song in Indian cinema insists that almost all popular films should balance narrative with spectacle, speech with singing, and the gestures of acting with the choreography of dance. Rather than constructing a special but isolated genre for the presentation of musical performances, popular Indian cinema obscures any significant difference between the experience of cinema and of musical entertainment.[1]

THE 'EVERGREEN' FILM SONG: 'MERA JOOTA HAI JAPANI'
('MY SHOES ARE JAPANESE')

Film songs are not just a common attraction added to the other pleasures of popular cinema in India but serve as key components in the Indian mass audience's popular memory and cultural traditions. The way in which film songs function as a modern tradition might be demonstrated by a convenient example from the South Asian diaspora, which traces the movement of South Asians as well as their popular culture across the globe. In an early sequence of Mira Nair's *Mississippi Masala* (1992), as an Indian couple and their daughter are forcibly ejected from Uganda, an armed soldier seizes one of the few items the family is attempting to carry to the United States, a portable cassette player with a tape the soldiers play briefly before smashing the machine: though its lyrics are subtitled for the English-language audience, the song we hear is probably unfamiliar to most of Nair's western viewers. Less directly, another Indian artist working in and on the South Asian diaspora cites the same song at the beginning of another text. As the Bombay film star Gibreel Farishta falls through the sky toward England to begin Salman Rushdie's novel *The Satanic Verses* (1988), he sings and translates 'the old song into English in semi-conscious deference to the uprushing host-nation': 'O, my shoes are Japanese, These trousers English, if you please. On my head, red Russian hat; my heart's Indian for all that'. Almost a half-century after the first appearance of the 'old song', the final Hindi line of its refrain provided the title for a 2000 film, *Phir Bhi Dil Hai Hindustani* ('But the heart is still Indian'), produced by and starring current Bombay superstar Shah Rukh Khan. But the song was already being cited by Hindi films as early as *Chori Chori* ('Sneaky Sneaky', 1956), a loose remake of Frank Capra's *It Happened One Night* (1934) and the last film featuring the legendary 1950s screen couple Raj Kapoor and Nargis as a romantic duo. The hit song is briefly heard playing on the popular Radio Ceylon (at a time when All India Radio did not play film songs) to introduce the main male character played by Raj Kapoor.

Whereas the last two examples, though from films produced almost fifty years apart, obviously rely on their assumed Indian audience's early and ongoing familiarity with the song, Nair and Rushdie's presumably more cosmopolitan, international audiences must be sharply divided by either knowledge or ignorance of the song. As an especially prominent example, 'Meera joota hai japani' ('My shoes are Japanese'), composed by the legendary team of Shankar-Jaikishen with lyrics by Shailendra and performed by the famous 'playback' singer Mukesh, first appears in director-star Raj Kapoor's 1955 classic *Shri 420* ('Mr 420', the number ironically referring to the section of the Indian Penal Code defining cheats after the honorific *Shri*). As an upbeat declaration of a character's core identity despite global (albeit shabby) trappings, the song was immediately popular and especially relevant for Indians still revelling in their recently achieved national independence. As its clever reprisal in *Chori Chori* only a year later affirmed, the song was instantly associated with Raj Kapoor, especially in his frequent screen persona as an Indian version of Charlie Chaplin's little tramp. For later generations of Indians, whether at 'home' or in 'the world' (to invoke Nobel laureate Rabindranath Tagore's famous distinction), the song has provided a shorthand affirmation of national and cultural identity, serving an ongoing symbolic function that is the ostensible purpose, if not always the effect, of national anthems rather than mere pop songs. Known to millions of average Indians before its later circulation through art films and serious fiction, the song's lack of familiarity among western audiences demonstrates a persistent cultural gap between the popular entertainment of South Asia and western recognition and appreciation of those traditions.

If the example of 'Mera joota hai japani' (which, like many Hindi film songs, simply derives its title from its first line) demonstrates both the decades-long and international circulation of an 'evergreen' – to use the popular Anglo-Indian term – film song, as well as the cultural division between a mass audience familiar with a large repertoire of Hindi film songs and a (largely western) audience oblivious of such artefacts, we should recognise that such imbalances have historical and cultural explanations. Historically, film songs have travelled along with South Asians, of course, but have also circulated wherever Hindi films were distributed, including China, the Soviet Union, Greece, parts of Africa and the Middle East, where Hindi lyrics were often replaced with local languages, sometimes obscuring the Indian origins of the song. To this day 'Awara hoon' ('I'm a vagabond'), the title song of Raj Kapoor's *Awara* ('The Vagabond', 1951) remains well known throughout Russia, which the director-star visited, and China, where both the song and film were said to be Chairman Mao's favourites. (As evidence of the song's resonance, director Jia Zhang-ke's 2000 film *Platform* includes a scene of young adults attending a late 1970s screening of *Awara* in a small town in western China while the title song plays.)

However, popular Hindi film songs have only recently come to the attention of American and most European filmgoers, through snippets in such self-consciously hip films as *Moulin Rouge* (2001), *Ghost World* (2000) and *Eternal Sunshine of the Spotless Mind* (2004), or through samples mixed into recent rap recordings. At the same time, the prevalence not just of Hindi songs but of what both Indian filmmakers and fans call 'picturised' song and dance sequences in almost all popular Indian films has probably prevented their success in some international markets. For American audiences whose taste for the traditional film musical (featuring musical performances as opposed to the now ubiquitous song-filled compilation soundtrack) has diminished since the early 1960s, the promise that almost every popular Indian film includes from five to seven lengthy musical sequences may seem a threat rather than an attraction. The fact that such songs stretch mainstream Indian films to a running time of around three hours (with a marked intermission or 'interval') may also be unattractive to audiences used to shorter films. The use of clever and often highly poetic Hindi and Urdu lyrics that resist easy translation perhaps most obviously alienates audiences who rarely consume popular vocal music not performed in English. Within India, and with an impact on the international circulation of Indian films, the presence of songs has, again, typically divided films into the art cinema that does not contain 'picturised' songs, and the popular cinema which now seems almost unthinkable without them. For decades, this fundamental distinction encouraged the international distribution and acclaim of the realist Bengali films of Satyajit Ray, which were not widely viewed in India, whereas massively popular Indian films remained unknown to audiences as well as critics in Europe and the United States.

In India, as elsewhere, the arrival of film sound immediately suggested the opportunity to include music as well as dialogue (with the latter suddenly reinforcing India's linguistic diversity and the growth of regional cinema industries). India's rich musical heritage had been intimately tied to its theatrical traditions for centuries, and more recent forms like the nineteenth-century Parsi theatre, which incorporated western stage techniques and Indian narratives and music, directly influenced early cinema. The first Indian sound film, *Alam Ara* ('The Light of the World', 1931), included seven songs and effectively established subsequent Indian cinema as a musical form. By the mid-1930s the 'singing star' K. L. Saigal became legendary for his performances in films such as *Devdas* (1935) and *Street Singer* (1938) whose songs remain revered. In the next decade, the female singers Suraiya and 'Melody Queen' Noorjehan, who appeared onscreen together in *Anmol Ghadi* ('Precious Time', 1946), dominated popular music before the latter migrated to Pakistan following Indian independence and the violent partition of the subcontinent in 1947.

THE STARS: PLAYBACK SINGERS, COMPOSERS AND LYRICISTS

In the early sound era, the practice of synchronous sound recording meant that a star's singing skills took precedence over their appearance or acting until the film and recording industries discovered the possibilities of 'playback', in which a prerecorded voice might accompany a glamorous star (or talented actor) lacking singing skills. While many national cinemas (including of course Hollywood) have secretly relied upon dubbing for attractive but vocally limited stars, in India this practice was eventually acknowledged with credits, and the voices of the most popular – and astonishingly prolific – off-screen 'playback singers' soon became as famous as the stars who borrowed their voices on-screen. Popular male playback singers such as Mohammed Rafi, Mukesh, Manna Dey, Talat Mahmood and Kishore Kumar (the rare playback singer who also starred in films) were often closely associated with specific stars but regularly supplied the musical voices for dozens of actors. A smaller group of female playback singers has been dominated for almost fifty years by the voice of Lata Mangeshkar, who has virtually defined the female singing voice in popular Indian cinema. Lata's impact and popularity have perhaps only been rivalled by her sister Asha Bhosle, known for singing the sexier 'bad girl' songs that do not fit Lata's more proper image. Although estimates of her recording output have been routinely inflated, Lata's career is in any case astonishing, resulting in thousands of songs recorded in various languages and styles. Though now semi-retired, Lata's voice can still be heard on recent hits such as the title song from the blockbuster *Kabhi Khushi Kabhie Gham* ('Sometimes Happy, Sometimes Sad', 2001) at a time when most of her rivals – and the starlets she lends her voice to – are decades younger than her.

India's classical music tradition is best known to modern audiences through the master sitarist Ravi Shankar, the sarod player Ali Akbar Khan or tabla star Zakir Hussain. Based on an intricate system of scales and melodic patterns called *raags* or *ragas* and rhythmic cycles called *taals*, Indian classical music often informs film music, though film music often extends from light classical forms to increasingly electronic disco beats, an eclecticism that has often led to film music's easy dismissal in spite of its immense popularity. Given the pressures on musicians to annually produce hundreds of songs for India's steady stream of films, accusations of repetition, 'borrowing' and outright plagiarism are common. Like most commercial music industries, even original songs are produced within generic conventions that, again, draw upon Indian as well as international styles. Unsurprisingly, most Hindi film songs, like pop music everywhere, are love songs that often rely upon and update the poetic tradition of the (originally Persian Muslim) *ghazal*, which articulates the pains and pleasures of love, usually from a male perspective and often in the elevated language of legendary Urdu poets. (A 'light classical' Hindi counterpart, focused on romance from a female perspective, is the *thumri*, often associated with *kathak* dance.) In a cinema that has usually shunned explicit demonstrations of sexuality or physical romance – kissing is famously rare in Hindi cinema – love songs typically embody the passion and heartbreak of lovers more powerfully than dramatic scenes. Other only slightly less common subgenres include collective songs (especially popular during festive village scenes); friendship songs often celebrating male companionship or *dosti*, as in the massive hit film *Sholay*'s ('Flames', 1975) famous song 'Yeh dosti' ('This friendship'); patriotic songs (stirring in the years after independence, and more troubling in the context of recent Hindu nationalism or religious 'communialism'); and devotional songs, often with sources located in the traditional forms of the Hindu *bhajan* or the *qawwaali*, the Sufi devotional music best known outside South Asia through the late singer Nusrat Fateh Ali Khan. Identified by form as well as content, even these traditional categories are often 'impure' in so far as they maintain India's musical heritage while simultaneously invoking western popular styles.

Alongside the most famous playback singers, the composers and lyricists of film songs are often celebrated in their own right and followed closely by dedicated fans. Music directors such as Naushad, the teams of Shankar-Jaikishen and Laxmikant-Pyarelal, and S. D. Burman drew upon Indian light classical and folk music as well as western styles, often creating controversies over the 'purity' of Indian film music. Inevitably, most Indian film music is an eclectic hybrid of eastern and western styles and instruments produced for an audience that simultaneously seeks familiarity and novelty. Following in his father's path, the composer R. D. Burman drew upon American rock music as well as Ennio Morricone's innovative scores for Italian 'spaghetti Westerns' in many of his 1970s scores. Contemporary film scores commonly mix traditional Indian instruments with electronic beats and are perhaps best represented through the compositions of A. R. Rahman (whose film songs formed the basis for the stage musical *Bombay Dreams*). Like the best of his predecessors, Rahman's work is both deeply rooted in South Asian musical traditions and fully attentive to international trends, styles and new technologies. Many of the most successful film song lyricists, including Sahir Ludhianvi, Shailendra, Kaifi Azmi and Javed Akhtar (also a notable screenwriter) have notable careers as poets, especially in Urdu, the official language of Muslim Pakistan that is deeply intertwined with spoken Hindi. Although many film songs are castigated by critics for their 'vulgar' or inane lyrics, through such figures the film song has also sustained many of the literary and poetic traditions of South Asia.

SONG PICTURISATION

In conjunction with the musical and vocal styles of film songs, playback recording opened up the visual and cinematic opportunities of song picturisation, allowing directors to dramatically animate what had once been relatively static on-screen performances. Although in the hands of lazy directors song sequences can become tediously conventional (leading to equally lazy claims that all song sequences look the same), for more inventive or ambitious filmmakers, the presentation of film songs demands innovation and experimentation (which of course is often then copied in turn). While uninspired filmmakers often have young lovers sing and dance as they gambol among trees, or stage yet another song in the downpour of India's annual monsoons, even otherwise average films often feature remarkable or clever song sequences; while urban dramas since the 1950s typically locate musical numbers in relatively realistic western-style nightclubs, song sequences in films such as *Chandralekha* (1948) thrilled audiences with massive sets filled with hundreds of dancing and singing extras atop huge drums. Classic films like *Mughal-e-Azam* (1960) shifted from black and white to dazzling colour to highlight the spectacle of their most elaborate song sequences, including an elaborately choreographed sequence shot in an ornate hall of mirrors. By the 1960s song sequences often transported actors and narratives outside of India to depict exotic locales: Raj Kapoor's romantic drama *Sangam* ('Confluence', 1964) famously, and influentially, carried its stars to European locations for song sequences. Hindi films are also fond of self-reflexive song sequences that parody or pay homage to earlier examples, or which playfully reveal the techniques of playback recording in the manner of Hollywood's *Singin' in the Rain* (1952). In fact, a relatively early sound film like director V. Shantaram's *Aadmi* (1939) includes a sequence that anticipates, by over a decade, the comic revelation in that famous Hollywood musical that a character is lip-synching while another person actually sings, while *Padosan* (1968) plays equally clever games with an audience fully aware of the convention of playback singing that allows one performer's voice to serve another actor's body.

More recent Hindi films inevitably demonstrate an MTV aesthetic (though the Indian version of MTV relies almost entirely on songs taken directly from films rather than fully autonomous music videos), with rapid cutting, sudden changes in costume (often marked by prominent brand logos) and settings, and increasingly sexualised dancing. In a few cases, film songs have been the most controversial parts of otherwise innocuous films: the actress Madhuri Dixit shot to stardom after performing a sexy dance to the hit song 'Ek do teen' ('One two three') in *Tezaab* (1988), and subsequently generated even more controversy by 'pasteurising' a song entitled 'Choli ke peeche kya hai' ('What's behind my blouse?') in the film *Khalnayak* (1993). Although the answer to the question was 'my heart' and the song was comically reprised by the film's male lead, the number generated a heated debate in the Indian Parliament about the decline of taste in popular Indian film and music. Though easily criticised as vulgar and commercial, such numbers have also energised the Hindi film song, which had been reduced to a few perfunctory numbers in many male-oriented action films of the late 1970s and early 1980s. Teen-oriented hits such as 1997's *Dil to Pagal Hai* ('The Heart's Crazy') (which, unusually, advertised itself as a musical) and 2001's *Dil Chahta Hai* ('The Heart Yearns') feature athletic dance numbers by young people living exciting lives as explicit consumers of fashion and leisure activities, with pulsating dance tracks generating more attention than the pretty love songs of earlier decades. At the same time, *Dil Chahta Hai* includes an affectionate parody of the picturisation styles of the past few decades, simultaneously mocking and paying tribute to the tradition it inherits.

GURU DUTT'S *PYAASA* ('THE THIRSTY ONE', 1957)

While all Hindi filmmakers are faced with the pressure of incorporating film songs for an audience that has seen and heard almost every variation, a number of directors have distinguished themselves with their unusually creative song sequences. As one of the crucial figures of the post-Independence era now celebrated as the 'golden age' of Hindi cinema, the actor-director-producer Guru Dutt is frequently celebrated for his inventive and distinctly cinematic talents for song picturisation. His masterpiece *Pyaasa*, which tells the story of a sensitive poet (played by the director) whom the world celebrates only after he appears to have died, contains a number of innovative song sequences which together demonstrate an impressive range of narrative, stylistic and emotional options for the use of popular songs in Hindi cinema. With music by S. D. Burman (known for his reliance on Bengali folk tunes) and lyrics by the progressive Urdu poet Sahir Ludhianvi, the songs of *Pyaasa* are richly varied in style and mood. The playback singers Geeta Dutt (the director's wife), Mohammed Rafi and, for one song, Hemant Kumar supply the voices for the film's stars. A comic song, 'Sar jo tera chakaraaye ('If your head aches . . .') playfully mimics, with the sharp sound of the Indian drum (*tabla*), the flashing fingers of the street masseuse played by comedian Johnny Walker. The film's most haunting, anguished songs, by contrast, rely on minimal orchestration: 'Ye kooche ye neelaam ghar dilkashi ke' ('These streets, the auction-houses of pleasure . . .') starts and stops as the drunken, disillusioned poet lurches through a just-independent India that still prostitutes its daughters. He persistently asks 'Jinhen naaz hai Hind par vo kahaan hai' ('Where are those that take pride in India?') as he witnesses the new nation's persistent failures. The film's final song, 'Ye mehalon, ye takhton, ye taajon ki duniya' ('This world of thrones, palaces, and crowns . . .') in which the presumed dead poet Vijay is resurrected to accuse those who have exploited him, builds from a whisper to a scream, and from a quiet protest at the back of an auditorium to a full-scale riot as the crowd storms out. The editing of the sequence is determined by musical phrases, with the motion of actors and of the camera fully choreographed to interact with the movements of the score and singer Mohammad Rafi's rising vocals. An earlier dream sequence constructed around the duet 'Hum aap ki aankhon mein' ('I will set my heart in your eyes') resembles a number from a Hollywood musical and so appropriately uses a western waltz tempo, whereas a scene between Vijay and the prostitute Gulab (who recognises the poor poet's work as the product of a great soul) relies upon a group of local musicians performing 'Aaj sajan mohe ang laaga lo' ('Hold me in your arms today . . .') a *kirtan* (devotional song) sung by Geeta Dutt which, in contrast to the number echoing Hollywood musicals, transforms the human sexuality of the scene into divine love through its roots in Hindu religious traditions. Boldly challenging the easy claim that the songs and song sequences in Hindi films all sound and look alike, films like *Pyaasa* are most formally inventive and daring precisely in their presentation of songs.

Whereas the traditional Hollywood musical has been, to a large extent, displaced by the compilation of distinct pop songs on the film soundtrack (then marketed as a collection of often heterogeneous artists and musical styles), the popular Hindi film has continued to foreground musical performance for a large international audience that has not tired of this convention. For contemporary western audiences, even the Hollywood musical, a genre devoted to presenting singing and dancing to audiences, is now easily viewed as a narrative 'interrupted' by musical numbers; the full appreciation of popular Indian cinema might only begin when one begins to recognise that this cinema might be best understood and appreciated as the presentation of songs which are occasionally 'interrupted' by a narrative.

NOTE

1. This chapter concentrates on the dominant Hindi language cinema produced in Bombay. However, India supports equally large regional cinemas in the South Indian languages of Tamil and Telegu, as well as smaller popular cinemas in approximately half a dozen other languages, most of which also feature film songs. Broadly, Indian art films are in part defined by the absence of film songs, whereas Indian 'middle cinema' is a realistic form that includes songs.

RECOMMENDED FILMS

Awara ('The Vagabond', Raj Kapoor, 1951)
Devdas (Bimal Roy, 1955)
Dilwale Dulhania Le Jayenge ('The Brave One Takes the Bride', Aditya Chopra, 1995)
Hum Aapke Hain Koun . . .! ('Who Am I to You?', Sooraj Barjatya, 1994)
Lagaan ('Tax', Ashutosh Gowarikar, 2001)
Mother India (*Bharat Mata*, Mehboob Khan, 1957)
Mughal-e-Azam ('The Emperor of the Mughals', K. Asif, 1960)
Pyaasa ('The Thirsty One', Guru Dutt, 1957)
Satya ('Truth', Ram Gopal Varma, 1998)
Sholay ('Flames', Ramesh Sippy, 1975)

RECOMMENDED READINGS

Chakravarty, Sumita S. (1993) *National Identity in Indian Popular Cinema 1947–87*. Austin, TX: University of Texas Press.

Dwyer, Rachel and Patel, Divia (2002) *Cinema India: The Visual Culture of Hindi Film*. London: Reaktion Books.

Gopalan, Lalitha (2002) *Cinema of Interruptions: Action Genres in Contemporary Indian Cinema*. London: British Film Institute.

Kabir, Nasreen Munni (2001) *Bollywood: The Indian Cinema Story*. Oxford: Channel 4 Books.

Majumdar, Neepa (2001) 'The Embodied Voice: Song Sequences and Stardom in Popular Hindi Cinema', in Pamela Robertson Wojcik and Arthur Knight (eds), *Soundtrack Available: Essays on Film and Popular Music*. Durham, NC: Duke University Press, pp. 161–81.

Manuel, Peter (1993) *Cassette Culture: Popular Music and Technology in Northern India*. Chicago: University of Chicago Press.

Mishra, Vijay (2002) *Bollywood Cinema: Temples of Desire*. London: Routledge.

Rajadhyaksha, Ashish and Willemen, Paul (1999) *The Encyclopedia of Indian Cinema*, New rev. ed. Delhi: Oxford University Press.

Vasudevan, Ravi S. (ed.) (2001) *Making Meaning in Indian Cinema*. New Delhi: Oxford University Press.

Virdi, Jyotika, (2003) *The Cinematic ImagiNation: Indian Popular Films as Social History*. New Brunswick, NJ: Rutgers University Press.

14. CHINESE MELODRAMA

The wenyi genre

Stephen Teo

The *wenyi pian*, a name which denotes the melodrama in Chinese cinema, is an enigmatic nomenclature even to the Chinese. Taken literally, the words *wenyi* mean literature (*wen*) and art (*yi*), but how does such a combination with *pian* (film) imply melodrama? In a sense, the term is deliberately imprecise and can refer to conventional melodramas in terms of a highly sentimental and exaggerated story usually with song numbers thrown in, as well as love stories and 'women's pictures' focusing on female protagonists as long-suffering heroines. This chapter will focus on the *wenyi pian* as a discernible melodrama genre as it developed within Chinese filmmaking traditions, recognising the terminology as incorporating a broad spectrum of melodrama including the romantic film or love story, the 'woman's picture' or the literary adaptation (for example, films based on the novels of Eileen Chang and Qiong Yao, two authors commonly regarded as *wenyi* specialists). Previous writings in English on Chinese melodrama, such as those by E. Ann Kaplan, Paul Pickowicz, Nick Browne and Ma Ning,[1] have focused on the melodramatic representation of ideology and subjectivity in mainland Chinese films (the 'progressive melodramas' of the 1930s, the films of Xie Jin and other directors in the 1980s) rather than pursue the notion of the melodrama as a pre-existing Chinese genre. While these writers speak of a *melodramatic mode* in Chinese cinema, I will analyse a specific *type* of melodrama rather than a mode and representation of melodrama in Chinese cinema.

For reasons of space, this chapter is neither an exhaustive nor a definitive discussion of the *wenyi pian*. I focus on one strand of the genre – the romantic film or love story – that I deem to be the most common form of Chinese melodrama. I deliberately avoid discussing the left-wing melodramas of Chinese cinema in the period 1932–37, not only because the above-mentioned scholars have already covered this ground quite extensively,[2] but also because the *wenyi pian* as a discernible genre developed mainly in the postwar period, flowering briefly in Shanghai from 1946 to 1949 (as exemplified by the films of the Wenhua Company). After the civil war, the genre was transplanted to the Hong Kong cinema and then to Taiwan, but I have put aside discussing the Taiwanese cinema's development of *wenyi* films, opting instead to focus on the Hong Kong cinema. Ideally, experts in the field will eventually take up the discussion on those Taiwanese directors who worked in the genre, ranging from largely unknown veterans such as Li Hsing, Pai Ching-jui and Liu Chia-chang to celebrated names such as Hou Hsiao-hsien and Edward Yang. They merit an entire essay unto themselves which, when written, will attest to the scope and complexity of the *wenyi* film in Chinese cinema.

WENMING XI AND THE ORIGINS OF WENYI PIAN

When the Chinese began making films at the turn of the twentieth century, melodrama developed out of theatrical precedents such as *wenming xi* (literally, 'civilised dramas') which were popular in Shanghai and which the Chinese adopted from the Japanese *shimpa* ('new drama'). *Wenming xi* were modern plays with melodramatic content, emphasising love affairs, adventure and crime. The form allowed some room for improvisation – as opposed to operas and plays performed in the traditional theatre according to a prescribed text – although it later became distorted due to the inclusion of many traditional elements.[3]

The Shanghai film industry in the 1920s incorporated *wenming xi*, using many of its dramas and co-opting many of its actors to appear on screen. Chinese film directors also created a variant of realism out of *wenming xi*, as exemplified by *Gu'er jiuzu ji* ('Orphan Saves His Grandfather', Zheng Zhengqiu, 1923), which initiated a cycle of so-called 'society films' (*shehui pian*) stressing contemporary social themes rather than the mythic-historical subjects of costumed dramas. The 'society films' were the precursors of the 1930s' 'progressive melodramas', films that dealt with themes of poverty and social deprivation and attempted to look at its root causes in society – exemplified by such classics as Wu Yonggang's *The Goddess* (*Shen nü*, 1934) about a Shanghai prostitute bringing up her child, and Shen Xiling's *Crossroads* (*Shizi jietou*, 1937) about unemployed youth. The 'progressive melodrama' tradition faded by the time of the Sino-Japanese War which erupted in 1937. After the Japanese occupied Shanghai, the Chinese film industry relocated to the 'Orphan Island', referring to those zones in the city unoccupied by Japan and administered by western powers from 1937 to 1941. During this period, the term *wenyi pian* referred to adaptations of Chinese and foreign novels; a popular source in the latter category was Alexandre Dumas fils' *Camille* (*La Dame aux camélias*, 1848) which best strikes the tone of the sort of melodrama that *wenyi pian* came to signify.

In the 1940s – after the war – the term was used to refer to the crop of films produced by the production company Wenhua (established in 1946), which drew upon artistic literary sources and indeed employed literary talent such as the playwright Cao Yu to write and direct films. In latter years, the term has sometimes been used to refer to the art film, and at other times to all contemporary films as opposed to historical period films. The word *wen* can also mean 'civil', so that films labelled as such are therefore distinguished from martial arts films, which are classed under the *wu* (martial) designation. But in so far as *wenyi pian* is used to denote the melodrama, it matches the broadness and abstraction of the English word itself, which originates from the Greek *melos* (music) and *drama*.

CHARACTERISTICS OF *WENYI PIAN*

It wasn't until after the Second World War that Chinese cinema came up with the exemplar of *wenyi pian* as an all-encompassing contemporary melodrama: Fei Mu's *Spring in a Small Town* (*Xiao cheng zhi chun*, 1948). Fei Mu began his career in the 1920s. He was as indebted to *wenming xi* as were other directors from that dawning period of Chinese cinema, but by the 1930s, he developed *wenming xi* as a form of modern drama that could reflect contemporary life, in contrast to the costumed drama (*guzhuang xi*) which tended to regress into fantasy and supernaturalism. By the time he made *Spring*, he had realised very nearly a new genre. *Spring*, a Wenhua production, describes the postwar melancholy of a husband and wife living in a Chinese-style home destroyed by the war. The film can reasonably be described as a 'woman's picture', a 'family melodrama' with a didactic focus on *lunli* (Confucian family ethics and moral principles), or a 'romance' entailing a triangular love tangle. To this day the film remains a compelling example of the *wenyi pian*, partly because of its theatrical and literary qualities – fundamental characteristics of 'civilised drama' made visually interesting by its director.

Tian Zhuangzhuang's 2002 remake, which adhered closely to the original plot, evokes these very same qualities, though arguably to a lesser degree. The literary nature of the *wenyi pian* is conveyed in both versions – as is often the case in films of the genre – through the cultivated good taste of the heroine. Additionally, in Fei Mu's version, the narrative is framed by mesmerising voice-over narration (an ingredient that is missing in Tian's remake), which also decisively reorients the film to the heroine's (Wei Wei) perspective. Apart from the literary device of the narration and the theatrical nature of Fei Mu's piece, *Spring in a Small Town* is a microcosm of the genre: it contains music in the form of several songs, though in 1948 when the film was made, these songs were culled from the existing repertoire of folk melodies rather than newly composed popular songs (as is the practice of *wenyi pian* today). It could also be considered a 'realist' work, as it deals with the manners and mores of Chinese family life and depicts emotions realistically.

The broad, all-encompassing application of *wenyi* as seen in the example of *Spring* is in keeping with its bias towards modernity and contemporary society. From time to time, the term *wenyi pian* has been further broadened to describe slice-of-life conscience pictures (such as contemporary youth problem movies) and has also been combined with other genres – for example, the comedy-melodrama (such as the Peter Chan films of the 1990s, *He's a Woman, She's a Man* (*Jinzhi yuye*, 1994), *Comrades, Almost a Love Story* (*Tian mi mi*, 1997)) and the musical-melodrama (such as the series of late-1940s movies starring torch singer Zhou Xuan). In the main, however, the classic convention of the *wenyi pian* requires that the male and female heroes be romantically involved, and this therefore indicates that the *wenyi pian* is at heart a romance picture – which makes Fei Mu's *Spring in a Small Town*, Tian Zhuangzhuang's remake of the same, as well as Wong Kar-wai's evocative *In the Mood for Love* (*Huayang nianhua*, 2000) all classics of the kind.

The main ingredient of the romance picture is that of *qing*, an emotion that involves sentimentality but is not confined to it. Chinese artists have tended to emphasise *qing* as the purest form of human feeling and expression of emotion, but superior artists have operated on the dictum: 'fahu qing, zhihu li' (roughly translated, this means 'begin from emotion, end in humility'). In other words, desire should be bound by ethics.[4] This was the dictum that Fei Mu abided by when making *Spring in a Small Town*. Wei Wei's heroine is married to a weak, sickly man. One day, the heroine's ex-lover shows up as a house guest and she tries to rekindle their romance. Their mutual desire is obvious but they are restrained by certain social proprieties that both pro-tagonists observe.

In the *wenyi* melodrama, the hero and the heroine are not rebels against society. They may suffer the impact of conservative social conventions but they take care to observe them. In the case of the husband and wife in *Spring*, desire may be well and truly dead, but a sense of mutual duty, devotion and obliga-tion remains – one could say a 'purer' kind of love. The woman's husband is bedridden for the most part and conjugal sex is a duty that he is unable to fulfil. The husband acknowledges his impotence by trying to do away with himself, thus releasing his wife from the bondage of marital union. The ex-lover, a doctor, saves him. In the end, the woman is compelled to return to her husband as her ex-lover walks out of her life, voluntarily and because of his loyalty to his friend. There is mutual sacrifice on all sides and the integrity of the family is preserved. Desire has been restrained by ethics, although viewers may be struck by the fact that the female character displays more boldness in the matter of sexual desire. To modern eyes, the ex-lover appears somewhat impotent. He restrains the woman's attempts at seduction rather than succumbs to them. The two male characters are 'weak' in contrast to the female, as if she offsets the traditional strength of the male sex. It is worth considering why this is so.

THE WEAK AND THE STRONG

The 'weak hero' archetype is a standard of the *wenyi* film that remained popular for nearly twenty years in Chinese-speaking cinemas from the time of *Spring in a Small Town*'s release in 1948. But the mould had been around since the early days of Chinese film, principally manifested through the 'Mandarin Duck and Butterfly School', a genre of popular fiction consisting of classical-style love stories featuring the pampered sons (or *gongziger*) of the scholastic nobility. These characters were essentially bookworms and playboys, as exemplified by the role models Jia Baoyu (the leading male character of the classic novel *Dream of the Red Chamber*) and Tang Bohu of *The Three Smiles*. According to early Chinese critics, the *gongziger* of literature were made over for the cinema, and the most idolised models of the early screen were the *fengliu caizi* (unconventional, libertarian, but still talented men of letters) who bore a feminine stamp. The male stars of 1930s Chinese cinema conformed to this scholar-playboy-pampered son heroic archetype from literature.

The *gongziger* archetype in postwar Chinese cinema is symbolised by the sick husband in *Spring in a Small Town*. The Wenhua Company productions revitalised this postwar cinema with an artistic-literary (*wenyi*) injection, exemplified not only by *Spring* but also by films such as *Bright Day* (*Yanyang tian*, 1947), scripted and directed by the dramatist Cao Yu. By 1948, when *Spring* was released, the *wenyi* picture was frowned upon as the civil war between the Communists and the Nationalists raged in China, bringing about another reappraisal of the socio-political sensibilities that cinema was supposed to impart to society. *Spring in a Small Town* was criticised by leftist critics at the time for being too negative and for 'assiduously playing up the decadent emotions of the declining class'.[5] After the Communist victory, the film was put in cold storage where it remained for over thirty years until it resurfaced in a retrospective of Chinese films in Hong Kong in 1983.

When China closed in on itself after the Communist victory, Hong Kong movie-making inherited the styles and traits of the *wenyi* film (and all other Chinese film genres). The anguished male hero faint of heart and weak in physique was a characteristic figure in Hong Kong's Mandarin cinema. From the 1950s to the 1960s, male leads played straight men weighed down by too much sentiment for the fairer sex. Their hearts were so tender and their minds so romantic that tears sprang forth from their eyes as readily as flowers in spring. Hong Kong's Mandarin cinema was a virtual abode of male homebodies who appeared to do nothing more than mope and weep and wax nostalgic in the typical *wenyi pian*: examples are Guan Shan in *Love Without End* (*Bu liao quing*, 1961) and *The Blue and the Black* (*Lan yu hei*, 1966, in two episodes), Zhang Yang in *Sun, Moon and Star* (*Xing xing yeu liang tai yang*, 1961) and Peter Chen Hou in *Till the End of Time* (*He ri jun zai lai*, 1966). The weakling-hero was also prevalent in Cantonese cinema, as witnessed by the careers of Ng Cho-fan, Cheung Ying, Cheung Wood-yau and Patrick Tse Yin: all actors who typified unrequited lovers and wimpish husbands.

Female audiences were particularly attracted to these 'soft' leading men. There was also a tradition in Cantonese cinema of cross-dressing females, exemplified by Yam Kim-fai, who hardly ever appeared in her real sex in more than 300 films and whose legions of fans were women. Yam Kim-fai symbolised the dominance of the female star. Think of the 1950s and 1960s and it is likely that images of female icons will prevail: Li Lihua, Bai Guang, Zhou Xuan, Grace Chang, Jeanette Lin Cui (in the Mandarin cinema); Yam Kim-fai, Pak Suet-sin (Yam's partner in many films and in real life: she played her own sex as a counterfoil to Yam's male impersonations), Fong Yim-fun, Hung Sin-nui, Josephine Siao and Chan Bo-chu (in the Cantonese cinema). The dominance of women on the screen reflected the social realities that women tended to go to the movies more often than men during this time, and that the *wenyi* film was a haven of the female ideal.

The female ideal characterised by gentility, kindness, softness and frailty is manifested in what I have elsewhere called the '*wenyi* madonna'.[6] The *wenyi* madonna is weak in power because of her inferior social status predetermined by society. But she possesses her own kind of strength – a strength derived from weakness, so to speak. Hence, innate strength of character contrasted with social weakness typifies the figure of the *wenyi* madonna, and this is precisely the quality exuded by the greatest female stars during Shanghai cinema's golden age of the 1930s: stars such as Ruan Lingyu, Butterfly Wu, Wang Renmei, Zhou Xuan, Yuan Meiyun, Nancy Chan and Li Xianglan (the China-born Japanese actress Yoshiko Yamaguchi, also known as Shirley Yamaguchi). Of this group, it was perhaps Ruan Lingyu who best symbolised the spirit of women in Chinese society; she personified female resolve, intelligence and forbearance, so much so that her characters became deeply etched into the popular imagination as *the* image of the Chinese woman – an image recreated in Stanley Kwan's endearing homage to the star, *Actress* (1991), with Maggie Cheung giving a magnificent interpretation of Ruan.

The dominance of women in Hong Kong cinema was considered an unnatural phenomenon by director Zhang Che, who strove to break the trend in his creation of martial arts leading men in 1965. Zhang came up with the slogan 'yang gang' ('staunch masculinity') to describe the new heroic man, incorporating the tenets of martial arts and the physique of the slim but muscular warrior, who often appeared naked to the waist. Such an image, typified by Bruce Lee, has now become the standard in Hong Kong film. On the other hand, there is also a tradition of the female warrior: the *xia nü* (chivalrous woman). *Xia nü* is in fact the Chinese title of King Hu's 1969 classic *A Touch of Zen* (*Xia Nü*) in which actress Xu Feng plays a knight-lady who is the equal of any male fighter but who still possesses all the feminine graces and talents in art, poetry and song. The character subsumes her fighting qualities when in the company of a lover, adopting the stereotypically 'gentler' qualities of her gender. According to the critic Sek Kei, this conjoining of both martial and civilian qualities, both in support of the male sex, is a manifestation of 'the classic ideal Chinese woman'.[7]

Hu's martial arts masterpiece is an instructive example of *wenyi* elements crossing over to other genres. There are differentials of emotion (or *qing*) as the plot turns from one level to another; and there are two classic types of the *wenyi pian* represented: the weak male scholar who knows nothing about fighting, and the strong woman who is both feminine and beyond feminine – a model for the character played by Zhang Ziyi in Ang Lee's recent hit, *Crouching Tiger, Hidden Dragon* (*Wo hu cang long*, 2000). While it is not usually described as such, *A Touch of Zen* is effectively both a martial arts film and a *wenyi pian*, or, in other words, a martial arts melodrama.

THE *WENYI PIAN* IN THE POSTMODERN AGE

As time has passed and social mores have changed, the male persona in Chinese cinema has undergone a dramatic turnaround. In the mid-1960s, the sensitive romantic hero began giving way to the macho warrior as the 'new school' martial arts movie was born. The *wenyi* film fell into a decline as Hong Kong cinema concentrated on the resurgent martial arts genre. But the *wenyi* film survived, and it has proven itself as durable a genre as the martial arts film. At the end of the twentieth century, Hong Kong cinema experienced a *wenyi* revival with the release of films like Sylvia Chang's *Tempting Heart* (*Xin dong*, 1999), Jingle Ma's *Fly Me to Polaris* (*Xing yuan*, 1999), Yee Chung-man's *Anna Magdalena* (*On na ma dut lin na*, 1998) and Wong Kar-wai's *Happy Together* (*Chunguang zhaxie*, 1997) and *In the Mood for Love* (2000) – all consummate examples of the union of literature, art, music (in the form of song inserts) and romance.

In the Mood for Love is the high point of this classical resurgence. Wong endows his film with a mnemonic, nostalgic quality to evoke a past embedded with *wenyi* references. For example, he raises the emblem of Zhou Xuan, whose classic rendition of the song 'Huayang de Nianhua' (a phrase indicating 'those wonderful varied years') is heard in the film. Moreover, the plot recalls that of Fei Mu's *Spring in a Small Town* in both its romantic and ethical dimensions. Tony Leung and Maggie Cheung play two people thrown together while grappling with the infidelities of their respective spouses. Leung and Cheung develop a relationship of their own, one built upon mutual sympathy and apparently unconsummated. The unfolding of this central relationship forms the film's backbone, but the nature of it is only hinted at – and therein lies the mystery and fascination. Referring to the affair of their respective spouses, Maggie Cheung's character declares, 'We will never be like them!', a statement which acts as an aphorism of the film as a whole. With it, Wong signals his own distinctive treatment of the archetypes of the *wenyi* genre.

Tony Leung's character may exhibit the classic feebleness of the *wenyi* male hero and Maggie Cheung may seem the put-upon *wenyi* madonna. But all is not as it seems. A fondness for martial arts novels leads to rendezvous in hotel rooms. The use of the martial arts device raises interesting levels of association; there is, for example, a linkage with the idea of the romantic knights-errant and the associated concepts of honour and chivalric behaviour. It is well known that martial artists are required to practise discipline and celibacy, a norm that holds a clue to the manner of the film's central relationship. The association of martial arts with Leung suggests that he is not a weak hero but rather someone with strength of character, displaying the same kind of noble self-denial as the ex-lover in *Spring*.

The other aspect of the recent *wenyi* revival revolves around the question of gender and sexuality, exemplified by Wong's *Happy Together* and Stanley Kwan's *Hold You Tight* (*Yue kuai le, yue duo luo*, 1998) and *Lan Yu* (2000), all of which belong to a class of gay *wenyi* movies, a relatively recent phenomenon that one can identify with Kwan more than any other director. Prior to his coming out as a gay director, Kwan had made 'women's pictures' where the director projected his own homosexuality in the form of a transformed female sensibility.[8] *Rouge* (*Yanzhi kou*, 1989) is a good example of how Kwan treats the sexual archetypes of the traditional *wenyi pian*, with his lead players Leslie Cheung and Anita Mui personifying respectively the qualities of male weakness and female strength. Cheung is the prerequisite passive male character while Mui's character alternates between innate strength and physical weakness – exactly the qualities of the *wenyi* madonna as represented in the figure of Ruan Lingyu. Yet Cheung and Mui can also be seen as two sides of a single character. Their blurred genders make *Rouge* a fascinating study of the way in which the *wenyi* genre has passed into the postmodern era of mixed gender traits.

In *Hold You Tight* and *Lan Yu*, Kwan attempts to break out of the 'woman's picture' mould to achieve a more direct identification with his male protagonists. Chingmy Yau plays double roles in *Hold You Tight*, first as Moon, a wife alienated from her husband and having an affair with a young lifeguard, and then as Rosa, a businesswoman in the process of getting a divorce whom the young man later meets. Both characters are imbued with disenchantment, a result of their being alienated from their male partners, but the disenchantment ultimately arises from Kwan's real motivation – a coming to terms with his homosexuality. In the intimate moments between Moon and her husband, Kwan displays a voyeuristic interest in the latter. This same voyeurism is evident in his treatment of the lifeguard, and in Eric Tsang's closeted gay, a real-estate agent who becomes friends with Moon's husband. Kwan has stated that 'the Yau character does not belong to the personal world of Stanley Kwan'.[9] It is on such a premise that *Hold You Tight* shifts the locus away from the female to accentuate the gay sensibility, but the film suffers from the shift. No longer does Kwan show his sympathy for the female, and indeed the film could be attacked for its patronising view of women and the institution of heterosexual marriage. *Lan Yu*, on the other hand, is a touching film that functions purely on the level of a straightforward gay romance, shot in mainland China (which gives it the distinction of being possibly the first overtly gay *wenyi* film made in the country).

Like Wong Kar-wai, Kwan obviously has a feel for the genre, his revisionist treatment in *Hold You Tight* notwithstanding. Kwan's recent films are really variations of an old theme, which is that romance may be eternal but the conflict between partners is always present and ever changing. Kwan's most evocative *wenyi* picture remains *Rouge*, because, like Wong's *In the Mood for Love*, it is a film about the history of the genre (and more besides – it attempts to recreate the vanishing spaces and localities of Hong Kong's history) while assuming the guise of a modern film dealing with universal questions of marital fidelity, love and remorse, and sexual identity. In this way, the genre reorients and adapts itself to changing sensibilities; the films themselves become historical texts of the times but they also rebound on history. The films of Wong and Kwan – the modern *wenyi* masters – prove the norm that the more a genre adapts to modern sensibilities, the more it retains the characteristics of the well-tried genre.

NOTES

1. On the various discussions of Chinese melodrama, see E. Ann Kaplan, 'Melodrama, Subjectivity/Ideology: Western Melodrama Themes and their Relevance to Recent Chinese Cinema', in Wimal Dissanayake (ed.), *Melodrama and Asian Cinema* (Cambridge and New York: Cambridge University Press, 1993); Paul G. Pickowicz, 'Melodramatic Representation and the "May Fourth" Tradition of Chinese Cinema', in Ellen Widmer and David Der-wei Wang (eds), *From May Fourth to June Fourth: Fiction and Film in Twentieth Century China* (Cambridge, MA: Harvard University Press, 1993), pp. 295–326; Ma Ning, 'Spatiality and Subjectivity in Xie Jin's Film Melodrama of the New Period', in

Nick Browne, Paul G. Pickowicz and Esther Yau (eds), *New Chinese Cinemas: Forms, Identities, Politics* (New York: Cambridge University Press, 1996); and Nick Browne, 'Society and Subjectivity: On the Political Economy of Chinese Melodrama', in *New Chinese Cinemas*.

2. For a more extensive discussion on the subject of the left-wing cinema, readers are advised to refer to a newly published monograph: Laikwan Pang's *Building a New China in Cinema: The Chinese Left-wing Cinema Movement 1932–1937* (Lanham, MD: Rowman & Littlefield, 2002).

3. For a brief account of the genesis of *wenming xi*, see A. C. Scott, *Literature and the Arts in Twentieth Century China* (New York: Anchor Books, 1963), pp. 36–7.

4. Stephen Teo, *Hong Kong Cinema: The Extra Dimensions* (London: British Film Institute, 1997), p. 209.

5. Cheng Jihua (ed.), *Zhongguo dianying fazhan shi* (*A History of the Development of Chinese Cinema*) (Beijing: Zhongguo Dianying, 1963), Vol. Two, p. 271.

6. See Stephen Teo, 'Wenyi Madonna', *Cinemaya*, 25/26 (1994–95), p. 7.

7. Sek Kei, 'The War between the Cantonese and Mandarin Cinemas in the Sixties, or How the Beautiful Women Lost to the Action Men', in Law Kar (ed.), *The Restless Breed: Cantonese Stars of the Sixties* (Hong Kong: 20th Hong Kong International Film Festival, 1996), p. 31.

8. See 'Interview with Stanley Kwan', *Hong Kong Panorama 97–98* (Hong Kong: Hong Kong Provisional Urban Council, 1998), p. 70.

9. Ibid., p. 70.

RECOMMENDED FILMS

Comrades, Almost a Love Story (*Tian mi mi*, Peter Chan, 1997)
Fly Me to Polaris (*Xing yuan*, Jingle Ma, 1999)
Happy Together (*Chunguang zhaxie*, Wong Kar-wai, 1997)
He's a Woman, She's a Man (*Jinzhi yuye*, Peter Chan, 1994)
Hold You Tight (*Yue kuai le, yue duo luo*, Stanley Kwan, 1998)
In the Mood for Love (*Huayang nianhua*, Wong Kar-wai, 2000)
Lan Yu (Stanley Kwan, 2000)
Rouge (*Yanzhi kou*, Stanley Kwan, 1989)
Springtime in a Small Town (*Xiao cheng zhi chun*, Tian Zhuangzhuang, 2002)
Tempting Heart (*Xin dong*, Sylvia Chang, 1999)

RECOMMENDED READINGS

Bordwell, David (2000) *Planet Hong Kong*. Cambridge, MA and London: Harvard University Press.

Browne, Nick, Pickowicz, Paul, Sobchack,Vivian and Yau, Esther (eds) (1996) *New Chinese Cinemas: Forms, Identities, Politics*. Cambridge and New York: Cambridge University Press, 1996.

Dissanayake, Wimal (ed.) (1993) *Melodrama and Asian Cinema*. Cambridge and New York: Cambridge University Press.

Cheuk-to, Li (ed.) (1986) *Cantonese Melodrama 1950–1969: The Tenth Hong Kong International Film Festival*. Hong Kong: Hong Kong Urban Council.

Cheuk-to, Li (1994) 'The Melodrama Strikes Back: Hong Kong Cinema 93–94', *18th Hong Kong International Film Festival* (catalogue), Hong Kong.

Stokes, Lisa Odham and Hoover, Michael (1999) *City on Fire: Hong Kong Cinema*. London and New York: Verso.

Teo, Stephen (1994–95) 'Wenyi Madonna', *Cinemaya*, Autumn–Winter, pp. 25–6.

Teo, Stephen (1997) *Hong Kong Cinema: The Extra Dimensions*. London: British Film Institute.

Teo, Stephen (2001) 'Wong Kar-wai's *In the Mood for Love*: Like a Ritual in Transfigured Time', *Senses of Cinema*, 13 (April–May), http://www.sensesofcinema.com/contents/01/13/mood.html (accessed 12 January 2005).

Widmer, Ellen and Der-wei Wang, David (eds) (1993) *From May Fourth to June Fourth: Fiction and Film in Twentieth Century China*. Cambridge, MA and London: Harvard University Press.

15. JAPANESE HORROR CINEMA

Jay McRoy

Horror cinema has long been a vital component of the Japanese film industry. During the politically and socially turbulent decades following the end of the US military occupation of Japan, directors like Honda Ishirō[1] (*Godzilla* (*Gojira*, 1954), *Attack of the Mushroom People* (*Matango*, 1963)), Shindo Keneto (*Onibaba*, 1964) and Kobayashi Masaki (*Kwaidan* (*Kaidan*, 1964)) created compelling cinematic visions that met with assorted critical and financial success both domestically and in foreign markets. Often informed by folklore and frequently indebted to the aesthetics of Japanese Noh and Kabuki theatre, these films engage a myriad of complex political, social and ecological anxieties, including – but by no means limited to – apprehensions over the impact of western cultural and military imperialism and the struggle to establish a coherent and distinctly Japanese national identity. Over the last decade, however, Japanese horror cinema has reached new levels of popularity, with representatives of the genre appearing everywhere from the programmes of prestigious international film festivals to the shelves of even the most overtly commercial video stores. Such visionary directors as Kurosawa Kiyoshi, Miike Takeshi, Tsukamoto Shinya and Nakata Hideo have produced some of the world's most innovative, thought-provoking and visually arresting works of cinematic horror.

In 2002 alone, Japanese horror films not only reached increasingly wider audiences through satellite and cable television services like the Sundance Channel, but also received remarkably expansive critical and theoretical consideration in venues as diverse as academic journals dedicated to film and cultural studies, internationally distributed periodicals such as *Film Comment* and *Asian Cult*

Cinema, and a plethora of Internet sites committed to everything from informed cultural investigations of the genre to enthusiastic fan-based appreciation of the films and directors most frequently associated with this new 'new wave' of Japanese cinema. If one factors in the success of Gore Verbinski's *The Ring* (2002), the recent Hollywood remake of Nakata's extraordinarily successful 1998 supernatural thriller *Ringu*, as well as the hype surrounding Nakata's US produced *The Ring Two* (2005), the influence of Japanese horror cinema becomes even more apparent. Indeed, with both a US remake of Kurosawa's *Kaïro* (a.k.a. *Pulse*, 2001) and a British remake of Nakata's *Chaos* (*Kaosu*, 1999) looming on the horizon, it is quite likely that Japan's latest renaissance in filmic terror will continue to shape the direction of Japanese and world cinema for years to come.

This chapter examines the current national and international appeal of Japanese horror cinema, locating this 'explosion of [Japanese] horror films'[2] within what Jeffrey Jerome Cohen would describe as an 'intricate matrix of relations (social, cultural, and literary-historical)'[3] – a socio-political cauldron from which emerge constructions of monstrosity and horror, both progressive and reactionary. In the process, I will highlight some of the genre's major thematic and aesthetic trends, positioning them within a specifically Japanese cultural context that takes into account both the radical economic and political fluctuations of the last half century, and an ever-emerging politics of identity informed by a logic akin to what H. D. Harootunian describes as 'relationalism (*aidagarashugi*)'.[4]

'A JAPANESE THING': SOCIAL BODIES, CINEMATIC HORROR

Western horror films have long been obsessed with bodies – both corporeal and social – and the rhetoric (visual, philosophical, etc.) of embodiment. Frequently marked by a thematic preoccupation with monstrosity in all its polymorphic, anthropomorphic and 'all-too-human' manifestations, horror films provide insight into not only a culture's dominant ideologies, but also those multiple subject positions that question or contest the status quo. This has particularly been the case in much of western culture, where analytical approaches from the 'psychoanalytic' critiques advanced by scholars like Robin Wood, Barbara Creed and Steven Jay Schneider, to the 'Marxist' inquiries set forth by theorists like Christopher Sharrett and Tania Modleski have offered valuable insights into the extents to which horror literature and film facilitate or challenge the circulation of capitalist disciplinary power. In short, western horror films, whether progressive or ideologically recuperative, function metaphorically, participating in a larger discourse of embodiment by mobilising notions of containment, flexibility and identity (individual, national, etc.). In the process, these texts reveal volumes about the socio-political geometries from which, and against which, they arise.

How, then, might Japanese horror cinema differ from and/or resemble its western counterpart? To what extent can we understand images of corporeal cohesion and radical or 'monstrous' alterity in Japanese horror films as allegories for larger socio-political concerns?

To answer these questions, we must first acknowledge the importance of the body as a metaphorical construct in Japanese society. However, before embarking upon such a discussion, it is important to note that the following paragraphs are by no means intended to serve as an exhaustive analysis of this complex discursive phenomenon. Such an exploration would certainly constitute a valuable contribution to Japanese cultural studies, but it is also an avenue of inquiry far beyond the scope of this introductory chapter. Rather, my object in the following paragraphs is to illustrate the presence, within Japanese cultural and political discourse, of the consolidated and fragmented body as an operative allegorical motif. By extension, the subsequent paragraphs aim to provide a historical basis from which one may understand contemporary Japanese horror cinema and the models of embodiment that so frequently accompany conceptions of the horrific (and 'monstrous').

In discussions of modern and contemporary Japanese society, western sociologists and historians frequently articulate the island nation's often turbulent past via a discursive paradigm that foregrounds a propensity for adaptability[5] and change in the face of socio-political crises and transformation. However, since at least the mid-nineteenth century and the Meiji restoration, numerous Japanese scholars have imagined the construction and maintenance of a consolidated – and distinctly Japanese – cultural and national identity in both implicitly and explicitly physiological terms. Thus the application of the body as metaphor for larger socio-political formations is by no means the exclusive domain of western culture. As scholars as varied in their critical methodologies as Marilyn Ivy, Ramie Tateishi, Darrell William Davis and H. D. Harootunian demonstrate, Japanese artists and intellectuals often employ the image of the body, and the integrity of its 'boundaries', within a larger allegorical framework; as such, it frequently provides a vital component for imagining modern and contemporary notions of 'Japanese-ness'.

For instance, one can clearly discern a discourse of 'monstrosity' and dangerous transmutations underlying contesting interpretations of Japan's so-called 'modernisation' in the years following the Meiji restoration of 1868, a tumultuous period during which Japan emerged from a relatively isolationist paradigm as a response to not only the impact of western cultural and military imperialism, but also the rapid process of industrialisation it engendered.[6] As Tateishi notes, Inoue Tetsujiro, in his writings on 'monsterology' during the 1890s, merges metaphors of monstrosity with a pathologisation of pre-'modern' Japanese theological (or 'superstitious') precepts in an attempt to reify convictions that 'the conflict between the past and the modern' represented 'a battle against monstrous forces', and that the 'eradication of superstition . . . was instrumental to the constitution of a healthy, modern Japanese state'.[7] Marilyn Ivy advances a similar thesis in her description of the construction of an increasingly discrete Japanese social body during the mid- to late-nineteenth century. In particular, Ivy links Japan's self-identification as a 'nation-state' with 'the threat of domination by European and American powers'.[8] In this sense, one can understand the very idea of a 'Japanese culture' as 'entirely *modern*'.[9] A response to colonialist overtures, the creation and maintenance of a definitive Japanese social body evolved within the cultural imaginary even as the trappings (both material and ideological) of western culture became progressively familiar.

In contrast to writers like Inoue, twentieth-century Japanese scholars and cultural theorists like Kamei Katsuichirō and Hayashi Fasao perceived the introduction/incursion of western (largely US) culture as a dissolution of a 'sense of "wholeness" in life among the Japanese'.[10] From this perspective, westernising forces are a deforming and disintegrating influence;[11] the impact of western culture disrupts a spiritually and socially coded 'Japanese-ness' that, as Darrell William Davis asserts, had been shaped and reshaped 'for a very long time, even before Japan's mid-nineteenth-century encounter with American gunboats and the Meiji restoration of 1868'.[12] Even to this day, over a half century after the Allied occupation further facilitated the proliferation of western cultural hegemony, this impulse to recover a perceived sense of social cohesion can still be observed:

> In contemporary Japan there has been a relentlessly obsessive 'return' to 'origins': an orchestrated attempt by the state to compensate for the dissolution of the social by resurrecting 'lost' traditions against modernism itself, and by imposing a master code declaring 'homogeneity' in a 'heterogeneous' present.[13]

Like Inoue's 'monsterology', which depicts enduring religious models (or 'superstitions') as a 'monstrous' pre-'modern' past threatening the emergence of a newly modernist, industrial and internationally engaged Japan, discourses that call for a resistance of western cultural and military imperialism through the restoration of a conspicuously unified and 'Japanese' past promote a narrative in which a return of a 'repressed' and/or 'oppressed' identity figures prominently.[14] Both ideologies, informed by metaphors of imperilled social bodies, coexist in the larger cultural imaginary. Likewise, as Davis shows, both positions depend upon an understanding of nationalism as an invention made possible only through the acknowledgement of a 'relative' (as opposed to binary) difference that reaffirms the inescapability and permanence of cross-cultural 'syncretism'/contamination.[15] Furthermore, the contesting ideologies discussed above can be understood as having achieved varying degrees of metaphorical translation through the iconography and dominant scenarios of Japanese horror cinema, particularly those texts created in the tumultuous decades following the Second World War.

Indeed, to contextualise not only the recent 'explosion' of Japanese horror cinema, but also the general popularity of horror films in Japan over the last fifty years, one cannot underestimate the impact of such crucial events as Japan's catastrophic defeat in the Second World War (and the subsequent years of foreign occupation), the decades of dramatic economic recovery and the similarly spectacular financial recession of the 1990s upon both the national psyche and, consequently, the artistic creations that inevitably emerged. In addition, it is equally essential to recognise how these larger social transformations inform the shape and significance of those institutions and behavioural codes central to the development and preservation of a sense of national and cultural identity. As Tim Craig notes, large-scale political and economic shifts invariably produce 'new social conditions', including 'urbanisation, consumer cultures, changing family structures and gender roles, and lifestyles and values that are less purely traditional and more influenced by outside information and trends'.[16] Correspondingly, given the influence of such novel 'social conditions' and transformations upon the cultural imaginary, it seems only fitting that they would find reflection within the 'popular culture'[17] as well.

As a substantial product of Japanese popular culture, horror films provide one of the more valuable and flexible avenues through which artists can apply visual and narrative metaphors to engage a changing social and cultural terrain. Furthermore, given Japan's aforementioned complex, and often contradictory, responses to the 'permanence of imprints left by the contact with the West',[18] the liminal physiognomies that frequently populate Japanese horror films (be these corporeal formations traditionally monstrous, phantasmagoric or representations of the human form dismantled) are ideal models for interrogating Japan's 'cultural particularity', a malleable 'relationalism (*aidagamshugi*)'[19] that 'reflects the diversity of Japanese society at a given moment', as well as its ability to 'accommodate change throughout time'.[20] Therefore, it is to these works of cinematic terror that I now turn, endeavouring, over the next several pages, to distinguish some of Japanese horror cinema's most prominent and enduring subgenres while noting the extent to which their themes and motifs may reveal a culture at once increasingly nationalistic and global/syncretic.

NIGHTMARE JAPAN: SOME MAJOR TRENDS

Categorising films by genre (horror, science fiction, romance, etc.) is a perilous exercise, as is any attempt at providing an even remotely 'exhaustive' introduction to a cinematic genre or tradition, be it the Japanese horror film or the American Western. In this sense, what many scholars understand as 'generic conventions' are, like the 'monstrous' embodiments that often populate those texts traditionally designated as 'horror' films, resistant to easy classification. Genres and subgenres, then, are slippery and frequently hybrid constructions that bleed through and across both related and seemingly unrelated filmic categories in a perpetual process of cross-pollenisation.

In the case of Japanese horror cinema, representations of fear, horror and monstrosity can be evidenced in texts commonly assigned to such established, yet by no means impermeable film traditions as *pinku eiga* (the 'pink' or 'softcore' film), *chanbara eiga* (the samurai film) and *yakuza eiga* (the Yakuza or 'gangster' film).[21] Similarly, prominent conventions from these established film cycles appear within the plots of Japanese horror films, though usually to a degree that renders them subordinate to the development of terror. A film like Kitamura Ryuhei's *Versus* (2000), for example, features dead Yakuza rising – zombie-like – to pursue the film's hero and love interest through a magical, albeit blood-drenched, forest. In addition, a horror film that contains elements of the *kaidan* or 'ghost story' tradition may also include features that audiences usually associate with apocalypse narratives or works of postmodern body horror. Hence, the following outline of major trends in Japanese horror cinema offers a provisionary (and always already conditional) guide to some of the genre's more common motifs. As such, it is my hope that it will not only reveal something of the breadth and diversity of the Japanese horror film over the last half decade, but also show how cinematic horror, in the words of Harmony Wu, 'offers a highly charged and usefully pliable framework for articulating diffuse, intangible and various anxieties'.[22]

The *kaidan*/'avenging spirit' film

Representative texts include: the *Ghost Cat* (*kaibyo*) films (Arai Ryohei et al., 1953–68); *Onibaba* (Shindo Keneto, 1964); *Kwaidan* (1964); *Sweet Home* (*Suito homu*, Kurosawa Kiyoshi, 1989); Nakata Hideo's *Ghost Actress* (*Joyū-rei*, 1996), *Ringu* (a.k.a. *Ring*, 1998) and *Dark Water* (*Honogurai mizu no soko kara*, 2001); *Audition* (*Ōdishon*, Miike Takashi, 1999); and *Freeze Me* (Ishii Takashi, 2000).

Although a broader interpretation of the 'avenging spirit' motif incorporates films that rely less on the spiritual and the uncanny to unsettle viewers (e.g. Miike's *Audition* or Ishii's *Freeze Me*), most cinematic texts designated as *kaidan* depict the incursion of supernatural forces into the realm of the ordinary, largely for the purposes of exacting revenge. To relate the tale of a 'wronged', primarily female entity returning to avenge herself upon those who harmed her, films like *Onibaba*, *Kwaidan* and *Ringu*, to name only a select few, draw on a multiplicity of religious traditions (Shintoism, Christianity, etc.), as well as the plot devices from traditional literature and theatre (including Noh theatre's *shunen-* (revenge-) and *shura-mono* (ghost-plays), and Kabuki theatre's tales of the supernatural (or *kaidan*)). Prominent features associated with the woman as 'avenging spirit' include long black hair and wide staring eyes (or, frequently, just a single eye), as long black hair is often symbolic of feminine beauty and sensuality, and the image of the gazing female eye (or eyes) is frequently associated with the vagina.[23] Furthermore, while valid arguments can be advanced that the haunted house occupies its own generic category, linking depictions of haunted houses (see, for example, Obayashi Nobuhiko's *House* (*Hausu*, 1977) and Kurosawa's *Sweet Home*) with the trope of the 'avenging spirit' seems particularly appropriate for this introductory chapter, especially if one considers the dominant societal coding of the domestic realm as feminine.

Similarly, recent films such as *Audition* and *Freeze Me*, in a manner reminiscent of both *kaidan* and western rape-revenge films like *I Spit on Your Grave* (Meir Zarchi, 1978) and *Ms. 45* (Abel Ferrara, 1981), recall and, especially in the case of more contemporary offerings, articulate the complex, paradoxical and increasingly protean role of women within Japanese culture. Depicted as 'both a source of danger to the norm and the very means of perpetuating that norm', such texts frequently position women as 'both symbolically dangerous . . . as well as the source of all that is Japanese';[24] through their vengeance, they simultaneously balance the scales of a perceived sense of justice, evoke fears of social change or the return of a 'monstrous past'[25] and expose the inequities inherent within a largely patriarchal culture. With recent transformations in the national economy begetting an influx of women in the workforce, as well as radical changes in both family dynamics and the conceptualisation of domestic labour, the 'avenging spirit' motif remains profoundly popular. As Susan Napier and Ann Allison posit, in a transforming national and international landscape informed by increasingly reimagined gender roles, Japanese men have 'apparently suffered their own form of identity crisis',[26] resulting in a panicked cultural reassessment in which contemporary manifestations of the 'avenging spirit' motif can be understood as symptomatic.

The *daikaiju eiga* (the giant monster film)

Representative texts include: Honda Ishirō's *Godzilla* (*Gojira*, 1954) and its over twenty sequels, *Rodan* (*Sora no daikaijū Radon*, 1956), *Mothra* (*Mosura*, 1961), *Dogora the Space Monster* (*Uchu daikaijū Dogora*, 1965); *Gamera* (*Daikaijū Gamera*, Yuasa Noriaki, 1965) and its sequels; *Majin: Monster of Terror* (*Daimajin*, Yasuda Kimiyoshi, 1966) and its sequels.

Among the most immediately recognisable films in Japanese cinema, *daikaiju eiga* provide the perfect arena for the mobilisation of numerous social anxieties, not the least of which constellate about the dread of mass destruction, mutation and the environmental impact of pollution resulting from rapid industrialisation.

As Japan remains the only nation to have suffered a direct nuclear attack followed by decades of exposure to US military exercises (including atomic tests) in the Pacific, the aquatic and heavenward origin of these mutated creatures seems only appropriate, as does their intentional, and sometimes unintentional, annihilation of major urban centers. Tokyo in particular endures repeated destruction in these narratives, a motif that has received notable critical attention in texts ranging from Darrell William Davis's *Picturing Japaneseness: Monumental Style, National Identity, Japanese Films* to Mick Broderick's recent edited anthology, *Hibakusha Cinema: Hiroshima, Nagasaki and the Nuclear Image in Japanese Film*.

Additionally, the recurring portrayal of friction between scientists and the military – conflicts that often delay the monsters' vanquishing – seems an ideal plot device for a cinematic tradition arising from a nation at once 'ground zero' for wide-scale industrial, technological and economic development and the victim of perhaps history's most deadly union of science and warfare. In this simultaneous dread of atomic disaster and rapid industrialisation, *daikaiju eiga* resemble American giant monster films of the 1950s, like Gorden Douglas's *Them!* (1954) and Bert I. Gordon's *The Beginning of the End* (1957), in that both cinematic traditions depict a socio-cultural dread over what Mark Jancovich, in his book *Rational Fears: American Horror in the 1950s*, describes as 'processes of social development and [scientific, technological, and cultural] modernisation'.[27] Additionally, even when openly marketed towards children and characterised as friendly protectors of the Japanese islands (a tropological shift suggestive of the notion that, despite their origins, monsters like Gojira and Gamera are profoundly products of Japanese popular culture), *daikaiju eiga* remain creative forums where very human fears over very human threats are projected onto fantastical physiognomies, battled but, in the majority of cases, never fully destroyed.

The apocalyptic film

Representative texts include: *The Last War* (*Sekai daisenso*, Matsubayashi Shuei, 1961); Fukasaku Kinji's *Virus* (*Fukkatsu no hi*, 1980) and *Battle Royale* (*Batoru rowaiaru*, 2000); *Burst City* (*Bakuretsu toshi*, Sogo Ishii, 1982); *Uzumaki* (Higuchinsky, 2000); *Kaïro* (a.k.a. *Pulse*, Kurosawa Kiyoshi, 2001).

Akin to *daikaiju eiga* in their depiction of contemporary civilisation under assault or in ruins, these 'ominous yet captivating'[28] films recall a history of destruction and reconstruction that has resulted, both nationally and internationally, in the correlation of the Japanese social body with 'not only apocalypse, but the fact of its transcendence: the finite and, through it, the infinite'.[29] The events that bring about the 'end of the world as we know it' can be secular (i.e. ushered in through technological means), religious (informed by any, or even a combination, of the multiple religions practised in Japan) or both. Fukasaku's dystopian bloodbath *Battle Royale*, for instance, places a class of students on a remote and heavily secured island, where they are compelled by the government to fight to the death in a highly publicised annual spectacle. A cross between *Lord of the Flies* (Peter Brook, 1963) and the American 'reality'-TV series, *Survivor* (2001–), the physical and philosophical struggle between the students becomes a frightening and starkly pessimistic metaphor for Japanese social and political concerns at the dawn of the new century.

With its final injunction to 'run', *Battle Royale* does offer a razor-thin sliver of hope as the film comes to a close; however, most apocalyptic narratives offer a somewhat more explicit implication that 'the end' is, perhaps, only a new beginning. The anime series *Neon Genesis Evangelion* (*Shin Seiki evangelion*, 1995–96), for example, merges the destructive power of technology with a multi-faceted composite of concepts harvested from numerous faiths in its futuristic account of global death and regeneration. Likewise, Kurosawa's *Kaïro* combines the technological and paranormal to craft a narrative with an eerily cataclysmic finale infused with threat and promise. Of the theme of apocalypse in his work, the director notes: 'In . . . my films . . . you see cities destroyed, and perhaps even hints that the end of civilisation is near. Many people construe those images and ideas as negative and despairing, but I actually see them as just the opposite – as the possibility of starting again with nothing; as the beginning of hope'.[30]

The techno-/body-horror film

Representative texts include: *Attack of the Mushroom People* (Honda Ishirō, 1963); *Horror of a Deformed Man* (*Kyofu kikei ningen*, Ishii Teruo, 1969); *Death Powder* (*Desu pawuda*, Izumiya Shigeru, 1986); Fukui Shozin's *964 Pinnochio* (1992) and *Rubber's Lover* (1997); Tsukamoto Shinya's *Tetsuo: The Iron Man* (1990), *Tetsuo II: Body Hammer* (1991) and *Denchu Kozo no boken* (a.k.a. *Adventures of Electric Rod Boy*, 1995).

Like the many texts that comprise the apocalypse genre and *kaiju eiga*, 'techno-/body-horror' films literalise the darker side of a process of nationwide industrialisation largely orchestrated as a result of, and in direct response to, western military and cultural imperialism. As horror films, they contribute to a discourse of boundary violation and body invasion, graphically enacting, in the process, perhaps the most dreadful apocalypse of all – the perpetual intimate apocalypse of the human body revealed not as a consolidated and impregnable citadel, but as a flexible assemblage that disallows for illusions of corporeal integrity or of the sovereignty of the human form. In their focus on issues of 'biological privation, technological instrumentality, and the loss of biological control',[31] these works closely resemble what Eugene Thacker describes as 'biohorror', a union of 'futuristic dystopia produced through science and technology' and 'the violent monstrosities that manifest themselves within the human body'.[32]

As scholars like Andrew Tudor, Philip Brophy and Kelly Hurley have illustrated, works of postmodern body horror – with their representations of 'the human body defamiliarised, rendered other'[33] – constitute a significant amount of contemporary horror cinema. Given that these themes of corporeal disintegration and the fusion of the organic with the mechanical within pervade some of the most influential works of western horror cinema by maverick directors like David Cronenberg, David Lynch and Clive Barker, it should come as little surprise that works like Tsukamoto's *Tetsuo: The Iron Man* and *Tetsuo II: Body Hammer* have found avid and devout audiences world wide. No matter how well these texts seem to travel, however, one should not lose sight of the films' cultural specificity. As Sharalyn Orbaugh reminds us, the Japanese cyborg differs from its western counterpart in that the 'other-'ing of the Japanese corporeal and social body by 'Western hegemonic discourse allows for an exploration of the hybrid, monstrous, cyborg subject from a sympathetic, interior point of view rarely found' in North American and European 'cultural products'.[34] Thus accompanying the horror of the physical body rendered/revealed as indiscrete in its multifarious hybridity is the notion of the Japanese social body as 'monstrous' both to itself and to an orientalist western imagination.

The torture film

Representative texts include: Ishii Teruo's *The Joy of Torture* (*Tokugawa onna keibatsu-shi*, 1968), *Oxen Split Torturing* (*Tokugawa irezumi-shi: Seme jigokui*, 1969); *Beautiful Girl Hunter* (*Dabide no hoshi: bishoujo gari*, Suzuki Norifumi, 1979); *Entrails of a Beautiful Woman* (*Bijo no harawata*, Komizu Kazuo, 1986); *Guinea Pig: Lucky Sky Diamond* (a.k.a. *Bloody Fragments on a White Wall*, Hashimoto Izō, 1989); *Urotsukidōji: Legend of the Overfiend* (*Chōjin densetsu Urotsukidōji*, Takayama Hideki, 1989); the *Guinea Pig* series (eight episodes, Satoru Ogura et al., 1988–93).

Often cited as some of world cinema's most notorious motion pictures, the torture genre, long popular in Japan, has become increasingly attractive to an ever-wider array of western horror fans hungry for films that push the portrayal of violence and gore to new extremes. Influenced by *chanbara eiga* and *pinku eiga*, the scenes of rape and ritualised brutality that infuse many of these narratives convey multiple aesthetic traditions and social concerns. The often deliberate and almost ceremonial evisceration of the (often eroticised) female body, for instance, is reminiscent of Japanese rituals like *hara kira*, 'an ancient act in which female votives would offer up the "flower" of their entrails and blood by a self-inflicted knife wound',[35] while the apportioning of gender roles addresses concerns about the stability of traditional sex – and, by extension, class-based divisions of labour.

This latter point is particularly evidenced when one recognises that it is primarily the men in these productions that do the abusing; correspondingly, it is largely women who prove the recipients of phallic assault via rape and other assorted forms of corporeal violation. Far and away the most infamous torture films, however, are those that comprise the *Guinea Pig* series. Primarily shot on video, and with unknown – and often disguised – actors cast in major roles, these texts, at times, resemble documentaries. As remarkable exercises in special effects technology, guerilla-style editing and gut-wrenching *mise-en-scène*, the look and feel of these films differ radically from virtually any work of western horror cinema, an aesthetic that prompted the American actor Charlie Sheen to mistake an episode of the series (Hino Hideshi's *Guinea Pig: Flowers of Flesh and Blood* (*Za ginipiggu 2: Chiniku no hana*, 1985)) for an actual snuff film.[36] Merging the aesthetics of *cinéma vérité* and *cinéma vomitif*,[37] these films are by turns sadistic and contemplative, gruesome and elegiac. Each text is its own 'flower of flesh and blood', sprouting forth and blooming its bloodiest shade of red where traditional conceptions and emerging notions of gender, class and nation intersect.

CINEMA VISCERA

Two final noteworthy (but comparatively minor) subgenres within Japanese horror cinema include, on the one hand, a collection of bleak, nihilistic films that depict what Thomas Weisser and Yuko Mihara Weisser describe as 'dove style violence',[38] and on the other, the serial killer film. The former, a filmic phenomenon best illustrated by Matsumura Katsuya's dark and controversial *All Night Long* (*Ooru naito rongu*) trilogy (*All Night Long*, 1992; *All Night Long 2: Atrocity*, 1994; *All Night Long 3: Atrocities*), are studies in postmodern alienation taken to its direst terminus: the affect-less, almost Darwinian destruction of the weak by the strong. The term 'dove style violence' stems directly from this expression of detached cruelty and refers to the practice of 'certain species of bird; when a flock member is *different* or weaker, the others peck at it dispassionately until it's dead'.[39] Focusing primarily on the lives of desperate, often jaded young people who perpetrate acts of deliberate cruelty upon those whose very isolation, timidity and frail physiques render them least capable of marshalling a defence, these films present viewers with protagonists that seemingly embody the most destructive and extreme consequences of scholastic competition, economic recession and recent shifts in gender dynamics.

Although a careful viewer can locate antecedents within the gory torture film tradition, the serial killer subgenre – as represented by suspenseful and complex narratives like Kurosawa's *Cure* (*Kyua*, 1997), Iida George's *Another Heaven*

(*Anazahevun*, 2000) and Ishii Sogo's *Angel Dust* (*Enjeru dasuto*, 1994) – is a relatively late development in Japanese horror cinema. Generally focusing on the complex relationship between a detective/law officer and her/his psychotic yet disquietingly comparable adversary, these films not only resemble American thrillers like *Manhunter* (Michael Mann, 1986), *The Silence of the Lambs* (Jonathan Demme, 1991) and *Se7en* (David Fincher, 1995), but also provide, through the figure of the serial killer, a distinctly human body upon which Japanese filmmakers, like their North American and European counterparts, may 'encode, deliberately or otherwise, many . . . cultural phobias in their polysemous narrative representation in . . . film'.[40] Curiously, in a trend that seemingly separates Japanese serial murder films from their western cousins, several of the genre's more prominent texts interweave the themes of murder and mesmerism (e.g. *Cure, Saimin* (Ochiai Masayuki, 1999)), or depict the force behind the slayings as a body-hopping supernatural entity (*Another Heaven*).[41] Such narrative devices render serial murder as a phenomenon that, arising within a modernised capitalist culture, perpetuates itself in an almost viral manner. Virtually no one is immune from the allure of violence; anybody is a potential killer.

The extent to which these sub-genres continue to develop will be interesting to watch in the years to come, but one fact remains certain. The Japanese horror film continues to exert a powerful influence upon world cinema, and if the current international prestige enjoyed by directors like Kurosawa Kiyoshi, Nakata Hideo and Miike Takashi is any indicator, their impact will surely be felt deep into the twenty-first century.

NOTES

1. Japanese names in this chapter are presented in the Japanese order, with the family name preceding 'first' name.
2. Alvin Lu, 'Horror: Japanese-Style', *Film Comment*, 38, 1 (January/February 2002), p. 38.
3. Jeffrey Jerome Cohen, 'Monster Culture (Seven Theses)', in Jeffrey Jerome Cohen (ed.), *Monster Theory: Reading Culture* (Minneapolis, MN: University of Minnesota Press, 1996), pp. 2–3.
4. H. D. Harootunian, 'Visible Discourses/Invisible Ideologies', in Masao Miyoshi and H. D. Harootunian (eds), *Postmodernism and Japan* (Durham, NC: Duke University Press, 1989), p. 80.
5. Such discussions of cultural adaptability as a particularly Japanese trait are, of course, reductive in that similar claims can be made about most cultures, especially when studied over many years or during periods of significant cultural, national or even ecological transition.
6. As Elizabeth Ann Hull and Mark Siegel note in 'Science Fiction', their contribution to the *Handbook of Japanese Popular Culture* (eds Richard Gid Powers and Hidetoshi Kato (New York: Greenwood Press, 1989)), '[t]he industrial revolution was not simply imported by the Orient; it was forced upon it, either through imperialistic exploitation or, in the case of Japan, as a defense against exploitation' (p. 245).

7. Ramie Tateishi, 'The Contemporary Japanese Horror Film Series: *Ring* and *Eko Eko Azarak*', in Steven Jay Schneider (ed.), *Fear Without Frontiers: Horror Cinema Across the Globe* (Guildford: Fab Press, 2003), p. 3.

8. Marilyn Ivy, *Discourses of the Vanishing: Modernity, Phantasm, Japan* (Chicago: University of Chicago Press, 1995), p. 4.

9. Ibid.

10. Harootunian, 'Visible Discourses/Invisible Ideologies', p. 70.

11. One manifestation of this 'disintegrating' effect was the apparent rise in individu-alised, 'autonomous disciplines', a system of social compartmentalisation in which an emerging concentration on specialised fields of 'knowledge' led to the establish-ment of 'barriers between different areas of culture, causing mutual isolation and preventing genuine self-understanding' (Harootunian, 'Visible Discourses/Invisible Ideologies', p. 74).

12. Darrell William Davis, 'Reigniting Japanese Tradition within *Hana-Bi*', *Cinema Journal*, 40, 4 (Summer 2001), pp. 60–1.

13. Harootunian, 'Visible Discourses/Invisible Ideologies', p. 66.

14. D. P. Martinez recognises the logic behind this narrative as a rhetorical (and fre-quently aesthetic) construct that presents an almost panicked reification of a illu-sory 'wholeness' through a depiction of the Japanese national identity as discrete and homogenous: 'Japan is similar to many modern nation-states in that it has had to construct a model of a unitary identity shared by all citizens. Identity no longer depends on religious models or on loyalty to one particular ruler/leader, but on the wider construct of the imagined national community. This nationalism depends on the mass production of mass culture and, while the logic of capitalism (late or other-wise) demands diversification, the underlying logic of one identity (the Japanese) as different from that of their neighbors (let us say, Korea or China) remains crucial to the nation state'. D. P. Martinez, 'Gender, Shifting Boundaries, and Global Cultures', in D. P. Martinez (ed.), *The Worlds of Japanese Popular Culture: Gender, Shifting Boundaries and Global Cultures* (Cambridge: Cambridge University Press, 1998), p. 10.

15. Davis, 'Reigniting Japanese Tradition within *Hana-Bi*', p. 65.

16. Tim Craig, 'Introduction', in Timothy J. Craig (ed.), *Japan Pop!: Inside the World of Japanese Popular Culture* (New York: M. E. Sharp, 2000), p. 16.

17. Ibid.

18. Ivy, *Discourses of the Vanishing*, p. 241.

19. Harootunian, 'Visible Discourses/Invisible Ideologies', p. 80. For Harootunian, this 'relational social order' becomes increasingly obvious when conceived in relation to the contradictory trajectories of holism and individualism, social constructs prom-inent within the 'Western World' (p. 81).

20. Martinez, 'Gender, Shifting Boundaries, and Global Cultures', p. 3.

21. Even these traditions are not mutually exclusive. For instance, in Komizu Kazuo's exploitation film, *Entrails of a Beautiful Woman* (1986), a young girl is brutally raped and tortured by members of the Yakuza, only to have her psychiatrist exact a gruesome revenge.

22. Harmony Wu, 'Tracking the Horrific', *Spectator: The University of Southern California Journal of Film and Television Criticism*, 22, 2 (Fall 2002), p. 3.

23. See Gregory Barrett, *Archetypes in Japanese Film: The Sociopolitical and Religious Significance of the Principle Heroes and Heroines* (Selinsgrove, PA: Susquehanna University Press, 1989). For a detailed study of hair in Japanese culture, see John Batchelor's *Ainu of Japan: The Religion, Superstitions and General History of the Hair* (Mansfield Centre, CT: Martino Publishing, 2000).

24. Martinez, 'Gender, Shifting Boundaries, and Global Cultures', p. 7.

25. Tateishi, 'The Contemporary Japanese Horror Film Series', p. 4.
26. Susan Napier, *Anime from* Akira *to* Princess Mononoke: *Experiencing Contemporary Japanese Animation* (New York: Palgrave, 2001), p. 80. See also Ann Allison, *Permitted and Prohibited Desires: Mothers, Comics, and Censorship in Japan* (Berkeley, CA: University of California Press, 2000). This is not to suggest that the collapse of the culturally erected partitions separating social spheres traditionally occupied by men or women is imminent. On the contrary, as Martinez reminds us, 'these sharp divisions between the male and female domains in Japan . . . are held to be complementary and necessary for the construction of the social' (p. 7).
27. Mark Jancovich, *Rational Fears: American Horror in the 1950s* (Manchester and New York: Manchester University Press, 1996), p. 2.
28. Philip Brophy, 'Introduction', *Kaboom! Explosive Animation from America and Japan* (Sydney: Museum of Contemporary Art, 1994), p. 9.
29. Joshua La Bare, 'The Future: "Wrapped . . . in that mysterious Japanese way"', *Science Fiction Studies*, 80, Vol. 27, Pt 1 (March 2000), p. 43.
30. Chuck Stephens, 'High and Low Japanese Cinema Now: A User's Guide', *Film Comment* (January/February 2002), p. 36.
31. Eugene Thacker, 'Biohorror/Biotech', *Paradoxa: Studies in World Literary Genres*, 17 (2002), p. 111.
32. Ibid., p. 112.
33. Kelly Hurley, 'Reading like an Alien', in Judith Butler and Ira Livingston (eds), *Posthuman Bodies* (Bloomington and Indianapolis, IN: Indiana University Press, 1995), p. 203.
34. Sharalyn Orbaugh, 'Sex and the Single Cyborg: Japanese Popular Culture Experiments in Subjectivity', *Science Fiction Studies*, 88, Vol. 29, Pt 3 (November 2002), p. 440.
35. Jack Hunter, *Eros in Hell: Blood and Madness in Japanese Cinema* (London: Creation Books, 1999), pp. 159–60.
36. See Stephen Biro, *The Guinea Pig History Page*, at: http://www.guineapigfilms.com/History.html (accessed 25 February 2003).
37. Mikita Brottman, *Offensive Films: Towards an Anthropology of Cinema Vomitif* (Westport, CT: Greenwood, 1997).
38. Thomas Weisser and Yuko Mihara Weisser, *Japanese Cinema Encyclopedia: Horror, Fantasy, Science Fiction* (Miami, FL: Vital Books, 1997), p. 21; emphasis added.
39. Ibid.
40. Philip L. Simpson, *Psycho Paths: Tracking the Serial Killer through Contemporary American Film and Fiction* (Carbondale, IL: Southern Illinois University Press, 2000), p. 2.
41. Gregory Hoblit's 1998 film, *Fallen*, stands out as a notable exception here.

RECOMMENDED FILMS

Audition (Ōdishon, Miike Takashi, 1999)
Battle Royale (Batoru rowaiaru, Fukasaku Kinji, 2000)
Godzilla (Gojira, Honda Ishirō, 1954)
Guinea Pig Series (Za ginipiggu, eight episodes; Satoru Ogura et al., 1988–93)
Kwaidan (Kaidan, Kobayashi Masaki, 1964)
Urotsukidōji: Legend of the Overfiend (Chōjin densetsu Urotsukidōji, Takayama Hideki, 1989)
Onibaba (Shindo Kaneto, 1964)

Ringu (*Ring*, Nakata Hideo, 1998)
Tetsuo: The Iron Man (Tsukamoto Shinya, 1990)
Uzumaki (Higuchinsky, 2000)

RECOMMENDED READINGS

Broderick, Mick (ed.) (1996) *Hibakusha Cinema: Hiroshima, Nagasaki and the Nuclear Image in Japanese Film*. New York: Columbia University Press.

Davis, William (1996) *Picturing Japaneseness: Monumental Style, National Identity, Japanese Film*. New York: Columbia University Press.

Hunter, Jack (1999) *Eros in Hell: Sex, Blood and Madness in Japanese Cinema*. London: Creation Books.

Lu, Alvin (2002) 'Horror: Japanese-Style', *Film Comment*, 38, 1 (January/February), p. 38.

McRoy, Jay (ed.) (2005) *Japanese Horror Cinema*. Edinburgh: Edinburgh University Press.

Napier, Susan (2001) *Anime from* Akira *to* Princess Mononoke: *Experiencing Contemporary Japanese Animation*. New York: Palgrave.

Richie, Donald (2002) *A Hundred Years of Japanese Film*. Tokyo: Kodansha International.

Schilling, Mark (2000) *Contemporary Japanese Film*. New York: Weatherhill Press.

Tateishi, Ramie (2003) 'The Contemporary Japanese Horror Film Series: *Ring* and *Eko Eko Azarak*', in Steven Jay Schneider (ed.), *Fear Without Frontiers: Horror Cinema Across the Globe*. Guildford: Fab Press, pp. 295–304.

Weisser, Thomas and Weisser, Yuko Mihara (1997) *Japanese Cinema Encyclopedia: Horror, Fantasy, Science Fiction*. Miami, FL: Vital Books.

PART VI

AMERICAN AND TRANSNATIONAL TRADITIONS

16. THE 'NEW' AMERICAN CINEMA

Robert Kolker

First, let's assume that American film is an 'art'. It is, after all, the product of the imagination expressed in a specific visual language and made to declare feelings and ideas. However, unlike other arts, it is the product of many hands. It is a collaborative art. Also, it is a *product*, a commodity – and a mass commodity at that. Films are made to make money, from theatrical release, foreign sales, DVDs, cable and, finally, commercial television release. The companies who put up the money to make a film want to see an enormous return on their investment. They are, therefore, very timid about what they will 'green light', instead attempting to create variations on past successes and rarely taking chances on something new or complex. They almost never allow a film to be released that breaks with the traditional forms of cinematic storytelling.

But no art can exist with some kind of renewal, an influx of imaginative energy that, no matter how constrained by commercial necessity, creates important variations on the formal and thematic conventions of the art. American film has gone through a number of such 'renewals', often introduced by individual directors, sometimes by a number of people, not necessarily working together, but responding to something in the culture and in their art itself to create something new.

SOME PRECURSORS

Orson Welles's *Citizen Kane* (1941) was such a film, made by a newcomer to Hollywood, working for a studio that – for a moment – was willing to take risks. *Kane* not only broke with the dominant studio styles of the 1930s –

bright, even lighting, conventional stories told in conventional ways, most with conventional happy endings – and ushered in a new way of cinematic seeing. Welles used dark as much as light: he sculpted his figures into and out of the darkness. He used depth of field, which asked viewers to look at all levels of the composition, from front to rear, to see many actions occurring at once. And he made his main character a mystery, someone no one could figure out and who did not come to a happy end.

Kane emerged from an older tradition in film and the other arts, German expressionism, and it was one of the driving forces of something new in American film that was named '*film noir*' by the French, because American filmmakers and viewers were not consciously aware they were creating something new. This was, as the name implies, a dark cinema, both visually and thematically. Men were victims rather than heroes, women often killers. No one won anything in *film noir* – events almost always came to a bad end. But American film itself won because it was renewed by this new way of telling often grim stories.

The French, who invented the term '*film noir*', actually did not see many of the films until some time after they were made. American cinema was embargoed during the Nazi occupation of France (1940–45). *Citizen Kane* did not premiere in Paris until 1946. But when it did, and hundreds of other American films suddenly became available, the French, and in particular a group of young film enthusiasts, were dumbfounded. They saw these films without understanding English and learned the language of American cinema from the images themselves. They were thrilled with the inventiveness of this cinema, and drew on it when, known as the French New Wave, they made their own films, such as Jean-Luc Godard's *Breathless* (1959) and François Truffaut's *400 Blows* (1959) and *Shoot the Piano Player* (1960).

THE NEW AMERICAN AUTEUR: FRANCIS FORD COPPOLA

These films and others were of enormous importance to a new group of American filmmakers who began emerging in the late 1950s to the 1970. (Even later, Quentin Tarantino took the title of another Godard film, *Bande à part* (*Band of Outsiders*, 1964), as the name of his production company.) Many things were happening in Hollywood during this time that made it possible for something like an American new wave to occur. One of the most important events was the breakdown of the old studio system, those great film factories, like MGM, Paramount, Warner Bros, 20th Century Fox, that owned all the means of production, including actors and directors, held by bullet-proof contracts. These contracts began running out in the late 1940s and early 1950s. A legal decision made it impossible for the studios to own their own movie theatres. The great red scare of the early 1950s turned the studios so cowardly in the face of government hearings that they blacklisted (in other words fired in such a way that they couldn't get jobs elsewhere in the industry) any personnel who might be considered left of centre politically.

At the same time, television allowed an opening for some important new directorial and writing talent during its so-called 'Golden Age' of live drama. The first filmmakers of the new American cinema came from television – writers like Paddy Chayevsky and George Axelrod; directors like John Frankenheimer and, especially, Arthur Penn, who began making astonishing films. Penn's 1965 *Mickey One*, with its oblique, fractured narrative and its main character who is never adequately explained to us or to himself, owes a great deal both to American *film noir* and the French New Wave. It was a difficult film, and it pushed on the conventions of film form and audience response. In 1967, Penn's *Bonnie and Clyde* broke almost completely with Hollywood conventions. Set in the 1930s but very much responsive to the youth culture of the 1960s, it created attractive thieves with whom we identify so completely that we experience their deaths almost viscerally. The film changed the representation of screen violence forever – showing wounds and their resulting pain in ways older filmmakers would never consider. Critics hated this film on first viewing, but in a most unusual step, many came back for a second screening, where they began to discover Penn's extraordinary methods.

Other young filmmakers came from film school, an unknown phenomenon up to the late 1960s. Formerly, directors moved up the ranks within the studios. Doing it this way, they basically copied the methods they saw being carried out everyday during shooting and editing. The new crop came to filmmaking with a scholarly knowledge of film's history, just like their French colleagues. They showed off their knowledge, again like the French, by alluding to other films, other shots, other camera movements in the films they made. But, most importantly, they came to filmmaking expressing themselves by experimenting with the language of their art rather than retelling the old stories in the old ways.

Take, for example, Francis Ford Coppola. He had a brief period in film school and then went on to make films himself. He became acquainted with one of the most important figures in the new American cinema, a director and producer of low-budget horror and biker films (many of them excellent), Roger Corman. Corman provided a low-budget haven for many young filmmakers and actors: Coppola, Martin Scorsese, Jonathan Demme, Peter Fonda, Jack Nicholson, Robert De Niro, among many others. Corman offered, and Coppola (after a brief career doing pornographic movies) made an ultra-cheap horror film, *Dementia 13* (1963), for him. As awful as the film is, it provided him with entry into the mainstream, where he changed the course of American film.

Coppola did a good deal of film work before the first *Godfather* (1972), directing small, new-wave-influenced films, *The Rain People* (1969) and *You're a Big Boy Now* (1966), and a big-ticket musical, *Finnegan's Rainbow*, with Fred Astaire (1968). *The Godfather* began in typical Hollywood fashion as a studio film of a best-selling novel – that is, its studio, Paramount, owned the property and chose Coppola to direct it. Coppola's script and direction, however, were not typical. Like Penn, he turned the gangster genre inside out, dealing not with a couple of violent thieves, but with organised crime – not a new subject, but a new treatment. He gave the Mafia a kind of mythical standing that, curiously, placed it in the pantheon of films that glorified the family. The Corleone family were brutal, but they were protective; they were outlaws, and they had senators in their pockets; and they looked after their own, even if they had to kill horses and men to do so. They were dysfunctional, violent, and they finally, in Michael Corleone, produced a lonely, immoral monster.

But the change in perspective on the gangster genre and all of its conventions was only a part of what went on in the film. Coppola's visual treatment was unlike any other gangster film. Usually 'B' (meaning low budget) films, the gangster genre was shot rawly, often on location and in black and white. In *The Godfather*, the physical design of the film, in colour, by Dean Tavoularis, is a detailed evocation of the domestic and city spaces of 1950s New York. The compositions by cinematographer Gordon Willis are bold and revealing, the lighting subtle, using light and shadow to articulate the emotions and the state of the characters' minds and situations. The use of dark and shadow in a colour film presented the Corleone family as threatening and protective at the same time, an inner sanctum of illusory warmth into which the world slowly intrudes.

The first two *Godfather* films (Part II appeared in 1974) made a fortune for Paramount Pictures and for Coppola. He was so prolific at this point that between the two *Godfathers*, he made a small film, and one of his best. *The Conversation* was, like Penn's *Mickey One*, influenced by the new European cinema. It is a subdued meditation on a man who makes his living listening in on other people and is morally destroyed by his work. Sound, of course, plays an important role in the film; but so does the intensity of its gaze. This is a film about looking and listening – in effect a film about filmmaking (which is, to one degree or another what all the films of these new directors were about) – of small gestures and few words, and of that rarest of all things in films, morality, as opposed to cheap moralising.

A year after *Godfather II* appeared, a director who did not go to film school, but, like many of the new directors before him, worked in television, released *Jaws*. Like the *Godfathers*, it too made a fortune, and Steven Spielberg, along with Coppola, suddenly made it possible for even Hollywood to recognise, however begrudgingly, the director as the guiding force of a film, just as he or she was up to the studio period in the early 1920s when the producer system took over. The 'auteur theory' was developed by those same critics who became the French New Wave as a way to catalogue films according to the coherent visual style and narrative construction of individual directors. For the French, it signalled new ways of looking at the world through cinematic eyes, rethinking genres so that they were responsive to the realities of the world they represented – in short, using the medium of film the way a novelist uses language to express him or herself.

No American director ever has ever had absolute control over his or her films as their counterparts had in Europe. And the 'birth' of the auteur in America was, like all such things, an economic as much as an aesthetic phenomenon. Coppola and Spielberg were, and Spielberg still is, recognised for the quality of their films, which also happened to make a lot of money. Spielberg never really experimented with the form and conventions of American cinema as did some of his colleagues; he merely exploited, profitably, the conventions better than many others. However, by the late 1970s the director's name often appeared above the title.

But Hollywood's love for the director was short-lived. Michael Cimino, after making a great deal of money for his studio with his Vietnam film *The Deer Hunter* (1978), bankrupted United Artists with his big-budget, box-office failure, the left-leaning Western, *Heaven's Gate* (1980). When money is at stake, Hollywood's enthusiasms are great, so great that they will let greed for potentially more money-making films take over, and then be temporarily ruined in the process. In this instance, United Artists, one of the oldest and finest of the studios, founded by D. W. Griffith among others, and dedicated to the distribution of quality films (they distributed Stanley Kubrick's earliest films) never quite recovered.

The rise and fall of Hollywood's love for the 'auteur' may have been rapid, but the fact remained that a change in the system occurred. Throughout the 1970s, new directors were allowed to make films with a stamp of originality. The best of them managed to create long careers. One, Stanley Kubrick, did this by leaving Hollywood and the United States entirely. After beginning his career in the 1950s, and finding that working under the producer system on *Spartacus* (1960) was intolerable, Kubrick made the rest of his films in England. He became an expatriate artist and, working alone and in complete control of his films, performed more like a novelist than a filmmaker. Of course, it helped Kubrick immensely that Warner Bros became his permanent backer and distributor in the late 1960s. Still, Kubrick stands not only as the creator of extraordinary films that resonate deeply visually and emotionally and reveal more and more with each viewing, but also as an American director who worked most like his European counterparts.

Martin Scorsese and Robert Altman

At this point, we need to look more closely at exactly what the 'new American cinema' was beyond the economics of production. In other words, what is it about their films that was 'new'? I want to take two examples among many possibilities. One, Martin Scorsese, came to Hollywood from New York University film school, one of the first in the country. The other, indeed one of the oldest members of the 'new' American directors, Robert Altman, came from the Mid-West, where he made institutional documentaries (promotional films for companies) before turning to television directing and finally to features in the late 1950s, gaining incredible fame and fortune with *MASH*, a film for which he was not the first choice to direct. Both directors had, in their best work, one thing in common: they did not take any of the rules, the conventions, the written or unwritten dos and don'ts of how to make a theatrical feature for granted. They used them to subvert them.

As a film student, film lover and film collector, Scorsese came to filmmaking carrying the knowledge of film's history with him. His work is full of allusions to other films. Allusion is the hallmark of the French New Wave and of the modernist movement in all the arts. A serious artist in any discipline learns from watching or reading a number of films, poems or novels. A young artist comes to understand that there is a 'world' made up of other works that he or she is, in effect, joining. By allusion, the new filmmaker celebrates the work that came before, and by alluding to it, deepens the meanings of her or his own films, creating a kind of echo chamber across the historical spaces of his or her art. Scorsese, for example, will go so far as to imitate shots from other filmmakers. In *GoodFellas* (1990), for example – his best gangster film – he gives at least two nods to very different films. He recreates a famous shot of a famous early film, Edwin S. Porter' *The Great Train Robbery* (1903). Here a character shoots a gun directly at the camera. He also alludes to the first sound gangster film, Mervyn Leroy's *Little Caesar* (1931), where the main character is introduced to the mob by the camera assuming his point of view and circling the table where they greet him. In *GoodFellas*, Henry (Ray Liotta) introduces the viewer to his gang, as in *Little Caesar*, by circling around the bar, each character 'greeting' him as he passes. At the end of the film with Henry now in the witness protection programme, we suddenly see an image of Jimmy (Joe Pesci), shooting his machine gun directly at the camera, as in *The Great Train Robbery*.

But there is another, more subtle kind of allusion, in which an entire film can be 'seen' as lying behind the filmmaker's own work, and this is an important element in Scorsese's films. *Taxi Driver*, for example, is a film the likes of which few had seen before its appearance in 1977. It clearly borrows from the traditions of *film noir*. But it does something else. *Taxi Driver* is a tale of a lunatic, and we see the film almost entirely through his eyes and his deteriorating mind as it journeys through the city of dreadful night. We have sympathy for and fear about Travis Bickle, and we watch his decline with awe. Scorsese is working in a similar manner as Alfred Hitchcock did with our perception of Norman Bates in *Psycho*. The connection to that film is crucial and deep, so deep – and conscious – that Scorsese had Bernard Herrmann, Hitchcock's long-time collaborator, write the score for the *Taxi Driver*, a score that contains chord structures similar to those used by Herrmann in *Psycho* itself.

Taxi Driver is also a film about captivity. The mad hero decides to save a young girl who has become a prostitute to a pimp who dresses something like an Indian. Travis, finally gone mad, gives himself a 'Mohawk' haircut and confronts the violent pimp with more violence than he ever imagined. The whole narrative structure, including the way the characters look and act, is reminiscent of another film, one that is perhaps the greatest influence on the generation of filmmakers we're talking about, John Ford's 1956 *The Searchers*. This film takes the great American captivity myth – the damsel abducted by a villain – and puts it into a revision of the Western genre. The hero of the film, played by the icon of the West, John Wayne, is an outsider, perhaps an outlaw, and a man obsessed with hatred of the Indians. His niece is captured in a raid that wipes out his family, and he becomes as vicious as the Indian he hates. He becomes the Indian's double, as Travis becomes the double of the pimp, Sport in *Taxi Driver*.

This technique of allusion was relatively new to Hollywood, and its importance lies in the fact that it allows for originality through a palpable, visible recognition and rethinking of the old. The 'new' American filmmakers raised American film to a level of importance it had never had; they recognised its importance and celebrated it by building their own films on it. While introducing and revising the language of classic American film, they honoured that language and the stories it told, creating new from old.

Similarly with Robert Altman, the old man of the new cinema. Altman's films completely rethink the visual terms of American films; but they also rethink the genres of American film. Genre, or a 'kind' of film, is marked by variations on typical settings, characters, periods and narrative conventions. A genre, like the Western, tended to look – to create – a West whose history may have had very little with the West that actually existed. John Ford knew this, when he had a character in his 1948 film, *Fort Apache*, say 'when truth becomes legend, print the legend!' When Altman made his first 'Western', *McCabe and Mrs. Miller* (1972), he turned the genre inside out. Instead of the wide open spaces, like Ford's Monument Valley, the setting for *McCabe* was a cold, filthy, claustrophobic place, which he photographed with a telephoto lens. Such lenses make distant objects appear close, but when they are not used for objects far away, they tend to compress space. This compression, especially when used within the wide screen Altman loved to play with, resulted in the internal space of the composition playing against the width of the screen, from which Altman picked out faces with an almost continuing series of zoom shots – creating, finally, a West that was imploding rather than expanding.

Almost every Western must have a stranger riding into town. *McCabe* is no exception, but for the fact that the stranger, John McCabe, is not a gunman, but a small time gambler who comes to town to set up a whorehouse.

However, the townspeople convince themselves that he is a famous gunman, with 'a big rep', and he begins to believe them when the town comes under siege, not by Indians or outlaws but by corporate raiders. Altman's outlaws are the henchmen of the rich who expand into the West in order to own it and stop at nothing to get what they want. McCabe actually does become a hero and kills the corporation's hit men, but only to die himself, piled high with snow, while the townspeople help put out a fire in a church they had up to now never cared about.

It would be easy, if based only on this summary, to dismiss Altman as being merely cynical. In fact, *McCabe and Mrs. Miller* is a lyrical, almost elegiac film. It seems almost to wish that the West of the classic Hollywood Western might have been true. In his other films, that elegiac element is more often than not replaced by downright anger at the way genres have distorted the culture's view of itself and its history. Other filmmakers uprooted the Western in similar ways. Arthur Penn's *Little Big Man* (1970) flipped the conventional poles of the Western, so that Indians were the 'human beings' and the white man the savage. Sam Peckinpah's *The Wild Bunch* (1969) emphasised the violence of the Western in ways the old genre never managed; he also turned the genre into a modern allegory of the US role in Vietnam. The result was another kind of elegy, a particularly bloody one, and these three films, along with the Italian, Sergio Leone's, 'spaghetti Westerns', which turned the genre from horse opera to grand opera, finished it off.

Actually, it was more than the films. Vietnam itself conspired to make the culture – for a moment, at least – unable to accept the old narratives of manifest destiny and the inherent rightness of our taking other people's lands, destroying those who stood in our way. The new Westerns just brought this to visible consciousness. Therefore one of the things the new American filmmakers brought was a greater degree of realism to their work. It has always been Hollywood's claims that their films are 'realistic'. But what they actually, perhaps unconsciously, meant was that each film repeated, with variations, the same formal compositional and editing style as the previous and the following film.

Filmmakers like Altman, Scorsese, Peckinpah, Kubrick, Coppola, John Cassavetes and many others showed that by exploring and pushing the edges of the old style, making movies by exploiting all the cinematic tools at their disposal, they could also use their art to more closely explore the culture and its preconceptions. Their films had an immediacy and a complexity largely unknown in American film before and after.

CONCLUSION: THE CONTEMPORARY AMERICAN 'INDEPENDENT' FILM

The new American film is gone now, gone with the counter-culture of the late 1960s that helped create and support new filmmakers, gone as studios found they could not necessarily make money when, with the possible exception of Spielberg, they rested the film on the director's name, gone as those same studios became increasingly the holdings of large, multinational corporations. The filmmakers themselves are older and while many still experiment and push the limits, others have dropped out, like Coppola, or have moved comfortably into the mainstream, as Scorsese seems to have done. This is not to say that new talent, new experimentation, has stopped entirely. In the 1990s Oliver Stone and David Fincher emerged, each with very different styles, but both exploiting the commonplaces of form and content to create films that inquired, probed, expanded film and invited their viewer to look hard and make connections that were not always obvious.

An 'independent film' also developed, in which units of the big studios, or even stand-alone production houses, back films for small audiences by directors who could not get funding anywhere else (and, interestingly, when they do find funding, some of these filmmakers, like Jim Jarmusch, get it from European television). Many independent films don't look very different from big studio films. Others bring back the sense of intensity and exploration of the previous generation. Todd Haynes, Todd Solondz, Jim Jarmusch, to name only three, continue – even though some of them now have their films distributed by the major studios – to keep film vital. Without an infusion of imaginative energy, it would otherwise wither and die. And one of the many remarkable things about American film is its ability to renew itself.

RECOMMENDED FILMS

2001, A Space Odyssey (Stanley Kubrick, 1968)
Bonnie and Clyde (Arthur Penn, 1967)
Breathless (À bout de souffle, Jean-Luc Godard, 1960)
The Conversation (Francis Ford Coppola, 1974)
Faces (John Cassavetes, 1968)
Four Hundred Blows, The (François Truffaut, 1959)
Mean Streets (Martin Scorsese, 1973)
McCabe and Mrs. Miller (Robert Altman, 1971)
Taxi Driver (Martin Scorsese, 1976)
The Wild Bunch (Sam Peckinpah, 1969)

RECOMMENDED READINGS

Clover, Carol (1992) *Men, Women, and Chainsaws: Gender in the Modern Horror Film*. Princeton, NJ: Princeton University Press.
Hillier, Jim (1993) *The New Hollywood*. London: Studio Vista.
Jacobs, Diane (1977) *Hollywood Renaissance*. South Brunswick, NJ and New York: A. S. Barnes.
Kolker, Robert (2000) *A Cinema of Loneliness: Penn, Stone, Scorsese, Kubrick, Altman*, 2nd edn. New York: Oxford University Press.
Lewis, Jon (ed.) (1998) *The New American Cinema*. Durham, NC and London: Duke University Press.

Monaco, James (1976) *The New Wave*. New York: Oxford University Press.
Schneider, Steven Jay (ed.) (2004) *New Hollywood Violence*. Manchester: Manchester University Press.
Self, Robert T. (2002) *Robert Altman's Subliminal Reality*. Minneapolis, MN: University of Minnesota Press.
Stern, Leslie (1995) *The Scorsese Connection*. Bloomington, IN: University of Indiana Press.
Walker, Alexander (1999) *Stanley Kubrick, Director*. New York and London: W. W. Norton.

17. THE GLOBAL ART OF FOUND FOOTAGE CINEMA

Adrian Danks

Of all the countless varieties of filmic expression, none is as clearly a product of evolution as found footage films, rising naturally and inevitably from the disposable culture like saplings from a landfill.[1]

INTRODUCTION

Found footage, compilation, collage or 'archival'[2] cinema is a broad filmmaking practice encompassing the use of file footage in documentary cinema, stock footage in fictional cinema, home-movie footage in some feminist cinema and the often radical recontextualisation of a vast array of images and sounds in examples of avant-garde cinema. This chapter will touch on the practice of found footage cinema across a number of national 'industries' and forms of cinema (including Soviet montage, the postwar American avant-garde and post-1960s feminist filmmaking), while focusing on specific avant-garde films that use 'found' images and sounds as their key 'raw' materials or sources, often fashioning new and explicitly critical works out of the bric-a-brac of other films. As found footage theorist William C. Wees observes of this type of film: 'Whether they preserve the footage in its original form or present it in new and different ways, they invite us to recognize it *as* found footage, *as* recycled images'.[3]

It is important to recognise that found footage cinema is an inherently hybridised and impure tradition, emerging, as Michael Atkinson suggests in the opening quotation, from the largely disposable nature of contemporary consumer culture. It can be argued that the appearance of found footage films is emblematic of this culture, often reusing ephemera culled from such forms of 'incidental cinema'[4] as travelogues, B-movies, scientific films, government-sponsored public service films and advertising, forms which are partly defined by their limited shelf-life. In keeping with this, the practice of using found footage in cinema has been variously claimed as a 'junk aesthetic'[5] or as an 'aesthetic of ruins',[6] descriptions that recognise its status as an alternative, subcultural, underground, environmentalist and even anti-capitalist mode of artistic expression.

Despite the historical and political significance of found footage and broader collage practice, it is impossible to trace or conceptualise a cohesive, progressive or teleological account of this tradition. It is difficult to accurately apportion the influence of prior forms and traditions on this dispersive field because it is both a distinct entity yet implicated in the very materiality of the cinema. Found footage cinema has its point of origin and departure in a plethora of eclectic sources, such as the formation of early stock-shot libraries and companies, specific ethnographic and scientific documentaries of the 1910s and 1920s, animator Len Lye's *Trade Tattoo* (1937), Soviet montage cinema and the appropriated shots of scorpions that opens Luis Buñuel's *L'age d'or* (1930).

The deployment of found footage in cinema often complicates the easy definition and categorisation of what might otherwise seem a distinct tradition. In his seminal book on found footage, *Recycled Images*, William C. Wees argues for a relatively clear demarcation between the documentary compilation film, the avant-garde found footage or 'collage' film and the appropriation of similar techniques in some music video.[7] Wees opts for a fairly neat distinction between these three forms as embodying, in turn, realist, modernist and postmodernist aesthetic practices. In this regard he sees only the avant-garde cinema as offering a usefully critical and explicitly political perspective on these recontextualised or recycled images, the realist or postmodernist approaches being, in turn, too preoccupied by either the assumed fidelity of the image to its 'real-world' referent or the total loss of this fidelity in the late twentieth-century realm of simulation: 'Collage is critical; appropriation is accommodating. Collage probes, highlights, contrasts; appropriation accepts, levels, homogenizes'.[8] As I will argue throughout this chapter, such clear distinctions go against the 'global' or dispersive spirit of many found footage films, which aim to break down the clear demarcation between forms, incorporating images and sounds from a wide variety of analogue and digital, filmic and televisual, archival and contemporary sources. As Catherine Russell suggests: 'The deep ironies of this mode of filmmaking derive from the overlapping and coextensive aesthetics of realism, modernism and postmodern simulation'.[9]

BELOW THE SURFACE

In contrast to the more global and impure terrain that actually defines and drives found footage practice, a number of writers and filmmakers have singled out both the 1950s and the United States as key sources for these 'found' filmic materials and the discursive frameworks that seemingly corral their meanings. For example, in his article surveying contemporary 'detritus cinema' Scott MacKenzie argues that, 'For the new wave of avant-garde and underground filmmakers who work with image appropriation, the cinematic style of the 1950s industrial and educational films are, in many instances, read as the key to the formation of the North American cultural psyche'.[10] Although the social engineering attempted by many of these source films is significant, it is the wide-spread availability, circulation and discarded nature of these images that are the keys to their large-scale 'reappearance' in the avant-garde cinema of the last forty years, particularly in the US. Thus, the large bulk of found footage films appear from the 1960s onwards, reflecting both the seemingly pervasive circulation of these images – in multiple prints and wildly varied screening contexts – and the increasing domestication and democratisation of broader image-making processes through changing technology, as well as the general rise of alternative culture and like-minded art movements such as pop and conceptual art.

These images and sounds emanating from the 1940s, 1950s and early 1960s, and the frameworks in which they appeared – often as part of instructional documentaries with controlling voice-overs – have held a long-term fascination for the found footage film. Even those films that respond directly to the history of cinema or to a particular film are often drawn back to this period. For example, Austrian director Martin Arnold's *Passage à l'acte* (1993) fixates on a scene from *To Kill a Mockingbird* (1962), while Matthias Müller's *Home Stories* (1990) montages together shots of windows and doorways from 1950s Hollywood melodramas. In so doing, these films continue a practice of sub-textual analysis characteristic of many critical accounts of mainstream Hollywood cinema. For example, it is difficult to imagine Müller's film outside the revisionist framework of Rainer Werner Fassbinder's lurid account of Douglas Sirk's family melodramas of the 1950s.[11] Filmmakers such as Müller, Arnold and self-proclaimed 'media savage'[12] Craig Baldwin see the core function of their films as the revelation of subconscious meanings, behavioural tics, subtexts and dream logics through the manipulation and recontextualisation of found images and sounds.

For example, Arnold's *Alone. Life Wastes Andy Hardy* (1998) 'uncovers' a disturbing Freudian subtext in a seemingly benign Andy Hardy movie by slowing down, obsessively repeating and re-editing several moments from the film. This film's approach is characteristic of the ways in which found footage cinema has become increasingly linked to such broader, 'non-cinematic' aesthetic practices that have 'emerged' in the last twenty-five years as a greater emphasis on the recycling of materials and sources, sampling, turntable scratching, digital vision-mixing and the greater prominence given to the upholding and transgression of copyright provisions. The two key aesthetic characteristics of the found footage film are reflective of these practices: rapid-fire editing that simulates the distracted viewing encouraged by the television remote control or the point-and-click hyperlinking of the Internet, and the radical slowing down and repetition of images which explore the visual subtexts of found scenes and snippets of footage.

However, films incorporated within found footage cinema are seldom exclusively experimental or avant-garde, with many moving over into such realms as ethnography, the essay film, compilation-based documentary or mainstream narrative cinema (e.g. Oliver Stone's talismanic incorporation of the Zapruder footage in *JFK* (1991)). In fact, it is from the compilation-based documentary that found footage cinema seems to take its chief inspiration, specifically the opportunities for the recontextualisation and juxtaposition of images and sounds that it offers but seldom exploits. Thus found footage cinema is defined by an often radical and experimental rethinking of context, the realignment and appropriation of images and sounds taken from the huge databank and refuse of modern culture. It is a form preoccupied with the processes of history and memory, and the 'capabilities' of modern audio-visual media to corrupt, prostheticise and forge particular meanings within these two informing frameworks. In this respect, the key project of found footage cinema involves both unsettling the accepted meaning of particular images and the discursive frameworks they are commonly placed within, as well as the expression of a degree of personal and cultural empowerment through the reappropriation of images and sounds produced by dominant or mainstream culture (for the filmmakers sitting in front of their editing table, TV monitor or computer screen, as well as for the audience).

Thus these films commonly deal with the complex relationship between 'public' representation (home movies, industrial films, stock footage, bits snipped from narrative features and documentaries) and a kind of 'private' imaginary (relating to how one rereads these materials). They also force audiences to question where the act of filmmaking actually lies, once faced with the concept of an expressive, personal film being made largely without the aid of a camera. This is particularly true of those films that barely alter the 'source' material they are using, such as Hollis Frampton's *Works and Days* (1969), a found documentary about gardening that the director just renamed and put his own credit on.

The implications of this practice are extended in such hybridised compilation-based, avant-garde works as Yervant Gianikian and Angela Ricci Lucchi's *From the Pole to the Equator* (*Dal polo all'equatore*, 1987), Vincent Monnikendam's

Mother Dao: The Turtlelike (*Moeder Dao, de schildpadgelijkende*, 1995) and Gustav Deutsch's *Film ist. 7–12* (2002) to incorporate an explicit interrogation of film history, the documentary form and their interlocution in discourses of early twentieth-century colonialism and modernity. These films present a critique of their images' content while also presenting a vehicle to help preserve and celebrate the romantic legacy of these often aesthetically beautiful films. It is also an approach taken up by a range of films – some more formally experimental than others – that interrogate and reclaim domestic images produced by either the filmmaker's family or the broader culture of home movie-making, thereby critiquing the straitjacketing roles formulated by these restrictive image-making processes. Michelle Citron's *Daughter Rite* (1978), Su Friedrich's *Sink or Swim* (1990), Louise Bourque's *Just Words* (1991) and Merilee Bennett's *A Song of Air* (1987) all offer potent examples of this critical, gender-defined and redirective found footage practice.[13]

FINDING ORIGINS

Many accounts of found footage cinema begin with an explanation of its origins from both within cinema and other art forms. It is not surprising that the two most lauded early practitioners of the form – reluctant American Surrealist and found object artist Joseph Cornell and 'sculptor' Bruce Conner – came to cinema from 'outside', furthering many of their prior preoccupations and techniques within the realm of cinema. This common focus on Cornell and Conner helps place found footage cinema within a broader-ranging art history that incorporates Pablo Picasso and Georges Braque's Cubist experiments with collage, assemblage and post-Renaissance vision and perspective, Marcel Duchamp's ready-mades and the radical juxtapositions of imagery and language characteristic of Dada, Surrealism and Russian Constructivism.

It is also not surprising that several commentators have seen a direct link between the Surrealist practice of 'sampling' cinema by the audience/artist moving restlessly from film to film, cinema to cinema, and the collage or montage form favoured by found footage filmmakers. Although these earlier ephemeral practices do link interestingly and productively to that of found footage, this filmic tradition truly has its origins in the very nature of cinema itself. Cinema has always held a complex and somewhat contradictory relationship to modernist aesthetics, emerging at around the time when specific formal 'advances' were being made in painting, sculpture, music and other art forms. In some ways cinema can be seen as an endemically modern form, the radical juxtapositions of time and place characteristic of the condition of late nineteenth- and early twentieth-century modernity already inscribed within the shifts of perspectives and point-of-view that characterise filmic space and time (even within such highly regulated forms as classical narrative cinema).

Also, unlike such forms as painting, cinema 'automatically' puts into question such things as the dominion of individual authorship, the critical preference for the original over its 'copy' (what constitutes an 'original' in the composite terrain of cinema?) and the organic (rather than mechanical) nature of art.

Thus it is not surprising that the practice of compilation cinema – an important precursor to its often more 'radical' found footage counterpart – emerges very soon after the birth of the medium, a form prefigured by the innate powers of filmic editing. It can be argued that part of the distinction between these forms lies in the material awareness produced by the deployment of found footage, essentially of whether and to what extent the footage's recontextualised materiality is recognised or insisted upon. In regard to this, the function of stock or even archival footage in fictional cinema is predominantly economic, the ideal goal of its use being that it won't be noticed by its audience. Similarly, the use of such footage in most conventional, TV-based documentaries is not meant to be disruptive, noticed or critically interrogated; rather it is there to provide a consistent, reiterative and often redundantly illustrative visual field to support the soundtrack. Even such voice-over-free compilation films as Jayne Loader, Kevin and Pierce Rafferty's *The Atomic Cafe* (1982) position their footage less as something to be materially analysed than as the cultural expression or memory of a particular time and place.

This is further illustrated by the conventional use of strategies of continuity editing and crosscutting to develop specific narratives or scenes in this and other similar films. Equivalent moments in such avant-garde films as Conner's childhood reverie *Valse Triste* (1977) or Baldwin's alien invasion conspiracy extravaganza *Tribulation 99: Alien Anomalies Under America* (1991) emphasise the disparity between individual shots, making us question the construction of the film, its arguments and hopefully a broader filmmaking practice. The most famous instance of this more critical approach occurs in Conner's seminal *A Movie* (1958), whereby a shot of a naked woman on a bed intercut with the image of a submerging submarine, the firing of its torpedo and the subsequent nuclear explosion suggest an associative, apocalyptic metaphor for sexual congress or desire.

FINDING FORM

It can be argued that the first films of Cornell and Conner establish the key parameters of found footage cinema. Harking back to both the varied origins of the form and suggesting many of its future directions, their two first films are studies in contrast, mapping out key, often opposing approaches that preoccupy subsequent found footage cinema. Cornell's *Rose Hobart* (1936) exemplifies the obsessive and analytical nature of much found footage filmmaking, focusing its 'gaze' on the aura of a now mostly forgotten Hollywood actress, Rose Hobart. Conner's *A Movie* provides a more expansive and global approach and structure, incorporating a range of footage taken from travel documentaries, newsreels, 1930s Hollywood serials and elements normally masked by the projectionist such as the countdown leader. Both films emerge from a personal experience of the cinema and are inevitable, expressive outcomes of the various practices of producing, promoting, distributing and exhibiting motion pictures.

Although widely seen as an inevitable outcome of modern culture, found footage cinema is also clearly linked to earlier experiments in dialectical montage. A key precedent for the work carried out by Cornell and Conner, and later by Baldwin, Arnold, Ricci Lucchi and Gianikian, are the compilation films made in light of the early montage experiments of Soviet directors Sergei Eisenstein, Vsevolod Pudovkin and Lev Kuleshov. In fact, Kuleshov's experiments in Pavlovian associative montage can be seen as isolating the key formative principle of found footage cinema: to change and unsettle the meaning of individual shots and images through the simple 'act' of montage and associative juxtaposition. While Kuleshov's influence is self-evident, the more analytical and full-scale editing practices of Esfir Shub, and experiments in optical printing and virtual animation by Eisenstein (e.g. the 'rising' stone lions of *The Battleship Potemkin* (*Bronenosets Potyomkin*, 1925)), create a more wide-ranging legacy. Like the later *Why We Fight* series co-produced by Frank Capra in the US during the Second World War, Shub's Soviet-era films appropriate and refashion existing footage, often turning around its 'intended' meanings and proposed ideological functions (for example, Shub's *The Fall of the Romanov Dynasty* (*Padeniye dinastij Romanovykh*, 1927) utilises footage shot by the West and under the Czarist regime). This practice definitively informs compilation-based documentaries, but is closer in spirit to the often iconoclastic and redirective tendencies of its found footage cousin.

Cornell's *Rose Hobart* consists almost exclusively of footage taken from the 1931 B-movie *East of Borneo*, stripping away most of the shots that don't feature Hobart and excluding all of the film's action scenes; the 'action' scenes which *do* appear – of a volcano erupting – are reportedly from another source. Despite Cornell's film often being aligned to a broader Surrealist practice, it is its graphic fixation upon a specific movie and iconographic figure that is its key influence on the found footage cinema to come. It is possible to draw a direct link between *Rose Hobart* and such later, explicitly structuralist found footage films as Malcolm Le Grice's *Berlin Horse* (1970) and Ken Jacobs's *Tom, Tom, the Piper's Son* (1969). Although these films are equally concerned with the form of earlier cinema, their interrogation of its syntax is more clinical than Cornell's. Structuralists like Le Grice and Jacobs are much more concerned with exploring the materialist dimensions of cinema – the limits of the frame, the sprocket-holes and scratches in the emulsion – than Cornell's work, which results in something closer to a nostalgic, obsessive transformation of the original. This tension between the primary beauty of the original footage and an inevitable critical distance is at the core of many of the strongest found footage films of the last forty years.

Sound is an often overlooked component of found footage cinema, its nomenclature alone prioritising the image. Nevertheless, sound is a key element in this tradition, whether it involves the manipulation of existing synchronised sound (as in *Alone. Life Wastes Andy Hardy*), the scoring of images to music or other found sounds, the presence of a voice-over, or the marked 'absence' of a soundtrack in the conventional sense. The found footage soundtrack commonly acts as a means to regulate what might seem to be a largely scattered field of images (as it also does in many essay films, a closely aligned form) or as a counterpoint that can both resonate with and grate against what we are seeing.

For example, *Rose Hobart*'s soundtrack reinforces its slightly somnambulistic, surreal and exotically distanced quality. Like many found footage films it is scored by 'found' music, in this case two samba records repeated three times each. It is important that these records also contain imperfections, the crackles and pops which signify their previous use. Although the music at times adds to the images, it functions equally as counterpoint, creating a mood or sensibility which flows with and operates in contrast to what is unfolding on screen. Thus *Rose Hobart* also suggests nascent possibilities for the use of sound in this form of cinema, linking back to its foundations in the silent era and its later appropriation by music video and advertising.

In contrast to *Rose Hobart*, Conner's *A Movie* takes a much more expansive and inherently 'cinematic' approach to its material, privileging the dynamic relationships created by associational montage and the scoring of images to specific music (Ottorino Respighi's *Pines of Rome*, 1952). Conner's is the more influential of these two seminal films, leading Michael Atkinson to claim that 'it wasn't until 1958, and Bruce Conner's *A Movie*, that the subgenre was authentically born – a form of film made without cameras, culling images instead from the junk drawer of movie past and present'.[14] In Atkinson's statement we can isolate what he considers to be the paradigmatic elements of the found footage film: essentially, a 'movie' made mostly without a camera which reuses footage from across film history and recombines it in imaginative and critical ways. *A Movie* is largely constructed out of footage that Conner bought at a local film exchange in the 1950s, incorporating those elements – such as countdown and black leader – that are normally masked by the film projection process. Conner initially conceived of the film as an expression of his own experience of the cinema, a virtual palimpsest of the endless film programmes he watched as a child.[15] He was also inspired by the widespread use of stock footage in American narrative cinema. As a denizen of the local movie-house he often saw many of the same shots of places and spectacular events reappear from week to week in B-movies and serials. It can be argued that this relatively sedentary and specifically located experience granted Conner a more materially aware view of the cinematic process, and educated him in the myriad stock situations, shots and technical devices that congregate in *A Movie*, and in mainstream cinema more generally.

In so doing, *A Movie* constantly plays with its audience's expectations of both cinematic form and content: opening with 'nudie' footage from which it then teasingly cuts away, and intercutting such title-cards as 'The End' and 'A Film by Bruce Conner', in a fashion that explicitly plays with the conventional boundaries of a film. The film is structured around images of action, death, sexuality and apocalypse, and yet it most evocatively communicates a set of moods and emotional responses, with some images retaining something close to their 'intended' meanings, others being set 'free' through a sea of other associations and poetic possibilities. *A Movie* has also been extremely influential for the ways in which it orders its images through complex patterns of categorisation and association. Although it may at times seem random, expedient to the limited materials that were at hand, it nevertheless groups images – in terms of screen direction, a particular category of content such as 'transport' and a micro-history of mid-twentieth-century disaster, for example – in a manner that leads the viewer through an encyclopaedic tour of twentieth-century image culture, growing ever darker. The film's meanings are seldom explicit, relying instead on an implicit level of communication that is again a dominant characteristic of the avant-garde found footage form. A musical precision of rhythm, motif and tempo emerges in Conner's film that contrasts to the looser, oddly organic structure of Cornell's.

RISING TO THE SURFACE

It can be argued that virtually every key movement or subgenre of avant-garde cinema in the last forty-five years has seen found footage or other connected forms of collage, assemblage and appropriation as offering a key to the possibility of a freer and more critical cinematic practice. In his critical overview of post-Second World War American avant-garde cinema, Paul Arthur argues: 'The widespread post-"60s" appetite for found footage was fed by two interdependent initiatives: the desire to reformulate tropes of historical narrative, and the micro-political critique of historical exclusion or distortion enacted by disenfranchised groups on the terrain of dominant representation'.[16] Thus the practice of found footage has been taken up by a range of often marginalised identity-based groups and subcultures as a means of uncovering and inscribing new meanings into what might otherwise be seen as hegemonic forms and texts.

For example, much of the feminist work done with home movies and other forms of domestic imagery attempts to break down and question the often happy and exclusive imagery that characterises the dominant form. This is achieved through a barrage of techniques, many of which simulate and rhyme with conventional aspects of domestic image-making and consumption: the voice-over which serves to recognise 'ruptures' in the footage rather than provide a soothing continuity; the slowing-down of images to reveal previously hidden or masked expressions and gestures; and the juxtaposition of these 'found' or ceded images with footage which counters what they purport to represent. These techniques offer the possibility for redirection, critical analysis and a limited form of empowerment; new subject positions are created through the appropriation of seemingly old, fixed imagery. Queer filmmaker Mark Rappaport also adopts this approach in his dissection of the 'heterosexual' image of Rock Hudson in *Rock Hudson's Home Movies* (1992), to the point where it becomes difficult to ascertain whether Rappaport is providing a critique of Hollywood's dominant representation, or showing the multiple expressive possibilities available within seemingly monocular texts. The recycling of pornographic materials in Austrian filmmaker Dietmar Brehm's work (e.g. *Blicklust*, 1992) and Naomi Uman's *Removed* (1999) takes this approach to a more 'extreme' level.

However, it is mainly in the last twenty or so years that found footage and the broader practice of appropriation has come to dominate avant-garde cinema, becoming, as Arthur wrote in 1995, 'easily the most ubiquitous practice of the last decade'.[17] This dominance recalls the prominence of such forms and aesthetic practices in early twentieth-century art: 'the current rage for found footage harks back to the great European tradition of politicized collage'.[18] This contemporary practice is often linked to the splintering of experience and subjectivity characteristic of postmodernism or reflective of, as Craig Baldwin suggests, 'the ruins of post-industrial culture'.[19]

The key reason given for its dominance is the exhaustion of the expressive potential of the cinematic avant-garde, with filmmakers either migrating to new media or learning to work with the detritus and overwhelming image-bank ceded by modern industrial or post-industrial culture. However, in these contemporary works, and the artist's statements that support them, there is often a lack of recognition of the long and varied cinematic tradition I have been outlining here. For example, self-proclaimed 'archival film producer and researcher' Sharon Sandusky states that, 'for many of us creating cinema now, when it seems that all novelty has been exploited, a primary escape route out of this quandary is through close examination of kernels of meaning within now old images'.[20] Despite wanting to express the progressive potential of found footage cinema, such claims emphasise and foreground the kind of exhaustion these films are said to redress; somewhat nostalgically retreating to the past in order to uncover hidden meanings within what can now be reconfigured as fixed cultural, political and social moments and histories (largely of the 1940s, 1950s and early 1960s).

Of greater significance are those contemporary films and filmmakers who see the found footage tradition as a key form of counter-history, whether in relation to cinema itself or to broader cultural, political and social movements. Craig Baldwin, somewhat of a spokesperson for this tradition, regards found footage practice as the only way of dealing with the overwhelming volume of media consumed on a day-to-day basis: 'I think it's healthy to work with all the materials cluttering up our brains: *The Flintstones*' tune; the Shell sign; "snap, crackle, pop" '.[21] Keith Sanborn, meanwhile, appears to argue for a combination of these approaches, for films that are attentive to the historicist potential of found footage cinema as well as the overwhelming proliferation of images: 'And the other thing for me, for my generation, was the sense that formal experimentation was at a dead end, that in fact there were too many films already, and that what was needed wasn't new films or formal innovation in that sense, but rather a better understanding of what was already out there'.[22]

The most significant examples of found footage cinema have long attempted to fuse these implicated and critical impulses, empowering both the viewer and filmmaker to intervene in this flow of images and bathe in their wondrous, deadly afterglow. They also enable images and sounds to float within and beyond established national, industrial, cultural and economic boundaries, creating a global practice that moves across cinematic forms while producing both a celebration and a critique of twentieth-century audio-visual culture. Looking at *Rose Hobart* one again, we can see Joseph Cornell as the epitome of this practice, as both the collector and reinterpreter of images and the subject of their paralysing, seductive gaze.

NOTES

1. Michael Atkinson, 'Collective Preconscious', *Film Comment*, 29, 6 (November–December 1993), p. 78.
2. Catherine Russell, 'Archival Apocalypse: Found Footage as Ethnography', in Catherine Russell, *Experimental Ethnography: The Work of Film in the Age of Video* (Durham, NC: Duke University Press, 1999), p. 238.
3. William C. Wees, *Recycled Images: The Art and Politics of Found Footage Films* (New York: Anthology Film Archives, 1993), p. 11.
4. Atkinson, 'Collective Preconscious', p. 78.
5. Michael O'Pray, 'From Dada to Junk: Bruce Conner and the Found-Footage Film', *Monthly Film Bulletin*, 54, 645 (October 1987), p. 316.
6. Russell, 'Archival Apocalypse', p. 238.
7. See Wees, *Recycled Images*, pp. 33–4.
8. Ibid., pp. 46–7.
9. Russell, 'Archival Apocalypse', p. 240. Russell goes on to argue that this combination of somewhat contradictory realms 'might most adequately be subsumed within the theory of allegory' (p. 240).
10. Scott MacKenzie, 'Flowers in the Dustbin: Termite Culture and Detritus Cinema', *CineAction*, 47 (September 1998), p. 27.

11. See Rainer Werner Fassbinder, 'Fassbinder on Sirk', *Film Comment*, 11, 6 (November–December 1975), pp. 22–4.
12. Atkinson, 'Collective Preconscious', p. 83. Atkinson evocatively introduces Baldwin as 'a polemical "media savage" whose films naturally spring from his work as a programmer of alternative media and collector of industrials, typically characterized as offering "a delightful rear entry into a pop cultural limbo of transcendent banality"'. This broader engagement with cultural history and production is an important characteristic of many found footage practitioners.
13. For a further discussion of this practice, see my 'Photographs in Haunted Rooms: The Found Home Experimental Film and Merilee Bennett's *A Song of Air*', *Senses of Cinema*, 23 (November–December 2002), at: http://www.sensesofcinema.com/contents/02/23/haunted.html (accessed 5 December 2003).
14. Atkinson, 'Collective Preconscious', p. 79. Atkinson's revealingly titled article ('Collective Preconscious') attempts to fill in the history and contemporary ubiquity of the found footage form.
15. For a fuller account of Conner's formative film-watching experiences see Bruce Jenkins, 'Explosion in a Film Factory: The Cinema of Bruce Conner', in *2000 BC: The Bruce Conner Story Part II* (Minneapolis, MN: Walker Art Center, 1999), pp. 185–223.
16. Paul Arthur, 'The Status of Found Footage', *Spectator*, 20, 1 (Fall–Winter 1999–2000), p. 60.
17. Paul Arthur, 'Bodies, Language, and the Impeachment of Vision: American Avant-Garde Film at Fifty', *Persistence of Vision*, 11 (1995), p. 14.
18. Ibid., p. 19.
19. Baldwin, quoted in Wees, *Recycled Images*, p. 68.
20. Sharon Sandusky, 'The Archaeology of Redemption: Toward Archival Film', *Millennium Film Journal*, 26 (1992), p. 3.
21. Baldwin, quoted in MacKenzie, 'Flowers in the Dustbin', p. 25.
22. Keith Sanborn, cited by Wees, *Recycled Images*, p. 90.

RECOMMENDED FILMS

Alone. Life Wastes Andy Hardy (Martin Arnold, 1998, Austria)
The Atomic Cafe (Jayne Loader, Kevin and Pierce Rafferty, 1982, USA)
Domweg gelukkig ('Meanwhile Somewhere . . ., 1940–43', Péter Forgács, 1994, Hungary)
From the Pole to the Equator (Yervant Gianikian and Angela Ricci Lucchi, 1986, Italy)
A Movie (Bruce Conner, 1958, USA)
Rose Hobart (Joseph Cornell, 1936, USA)
Society of the Spectacle (Guy Debord, 1973, France)
A Song of Air (Merilee Bennett, 1987, Australia)
Tom, Tom, the Piper's Son (Ken Jacobs, 1969, USA)
Tribulation 99: Alien Anomalies Under America (Craig Baldwin, 1991, USA)

RECOMMENDED READINGS

Arthur, Paul (1999–2000) 'The Status of Found Footage', *Spectator*, 20, 1 (Fall–Winter), pp. 57–69.
Atkinson, Michael (1993) 'Collective Preconscious', *Film Comment*, 29, 6 (November–December), pp. 78–83.
Danks, Adrian (2002) 'Photographs in Haunted Rooms: The Found Home Experimental Film and Merilee Bennett's *A Song of Air*', *Senses of Cinema*,

23 (November–December), at: http://www.sensesofcinema.com/contents/02/23/haunted.html (accessed 3 March 2005).

Jenkins, Bruce (1999) 'Explosion in a Film Factory: The Cinema of Bruce Conner', in *2000 BC: The Bruce Conner Story Part II*. Minneapolis, MN: Walker Art Center, pp. 185–223.

MacKenzie, Scott (1998) 'Flowers in the Dustbin: Termite Culture and Detritus Cinema', *CineAction*, 47 (September), pp. 24–9.

O'Pray, Michael (1987) 'From Dada to Junk: Bruce Conner and the Found-Footage Film', *Monthly Film Bulletin*, 54, 645 (October), pp. 315–16.

Peterson, James (1994) *Dreams of Chaos, Visions of Order: Understanding the American Avant-Garde Cinema*. Detroit, MI: Wayne State University Press, pp. 126–77.

Russell, Catherine (1999) 'Archival Apocalypse: Found Footage as Ethnography', in Catherine Russell, *Experimental Ethnography: The Work of Film in the Age of Video*. Durham, NC: Duke University Press, pp. 238–72.

Tobing Rony, Fatimah (2003) 'The Quick and the Dead: Surrealism and the Found Ethnographic Footage Films of *Bontoc Eulogy* and *Mother Dao: The Turtlelike*', *Camera Obscura 52*, 18, 1, pp. 128–55.

Wees, William C. (1993) *Recycled Images: The Art and Politics of Found Footage Films*. New York: Anthology Film Archives.

INDEX